£10.50

ML

Money, Growth and Stability

Money, Growth and Stability

Frank Hahn

Basil Blackwell

First published 1985
First published in paperback 1987
Basil Blackwell Ltd
108 Cowley Road, Oxford OX4 1JF, UK

Basil Blackwell Inc.
432 Park Avenue South, Suite 1503
New York, NY 10016, USA

British Library Cataloguing in Publication Data

Hahn, F. H.
    Money, growth and stability
    1. Macroeconomics
    I. Title
    339   HB172.5

ISBN 0-631-14354-8

ISBN 0-631-15586-4 Pbk

Typeset by Unicus Graphics Ltd, Horsham
Printed in Great Britain by Bell and Bain Ltd, Glasgow

Contents

Contents

Acknowledgements

The publishers acknowledge with gratitude permission to reproduce the following texts:

'Money and General Equilibrium' from the *Indian Economic Journal*, **23**, 109–22 (Special Number in Monetary Economics, Oct.–Dec. 1975). 'The General Equilibrium Theory of Money: a Comment' from *The Review of Economic Studies* (1952–3), **19**, 179–85. 'The Rate of Interest and General Equilibrium Analysis' from *The Economic Journal* (1955), **65**, 52–66 (Cambridge University Press). 'Equilibrium with Transaction Costs' from *Econometrica* (1971), **39**, 417–39. 'On Transaction Costs, Inessential Sequence Economies and Money' from *The Review of Economic Studies* (1973), **40**, 449–61. 'On Non-Walrasian Equilibria' from *The Review of Economic Studies* (1978), **45**, 1–17. 'Exercises in Conjectural Equilibria' from the *Scandinavian Journal of Economics* (1977), **79**, 210–26. 'On Some Propositions of General Equilibrium Analysis' from *Economica* (1968), **35**, 424–30. 'On the Stability of a Pure Exchange Equilibrium' from the *International Economic Review* (1962), **3**, 206–13. 'A Theorem of Non-tâtonnement Stability' with Takashi Negishi from *Econometrica* (1962), **30**, 463–9. 'Uncertainty and the Cobweb' from *The Review of Economic Studies* (1955–6), **35**, 65–75. 'On Two Sector Growth Models' from *The Review of Economic Studies* (1965), **32**, 339–46. 'Equilibrium Dynamics with Heterogeneous Capital Goods' from *The Quarterly Journal of Economics* (1966), **80**, 633–45. © The President and Fellows of Harvard College. 'On Warranted Growth Paths' from *The Review of Economic Studies* (1968), **35**, 175–84. 'The Stability of Growth Equilibrium' from *The Quarterly Journal of Economics* (1960), **74**, 206–26. © The President and Fellows of Harvard College. 'On the Disequilibrium Behaviour of a Multi-sectoral Growth Model' from *The Quarterly*

Journal of the Royal Economic Society (1963), **73**, 442–57 (Cambridge University Press). 'On Some Equilibrium Paths' from *Models of Economic Growth*, ed. J. A. Mirrlees and N. H. Stern (Proceedings of a Conference held by IEA at Jerusalem), pp. 193–206. 'Savings and Uncertainty' from *The Review of Economic Studies* (1970), **37**, 21–4. 'Excess Capacity and Imperfect Competition' from *Oxford Economic Papers*, new series, volume 7, no. 3, October 1955 (Oxford, Clarendon Press), pp. 229–40. 'On Optimum Taxation' from *The Journal of Economic Theory* (1973), **6**, 96–106. © Academic Press, New York and London. 'On Equilibrium with Market-Dependent Information' from *Quantitative Wirtschaftforschung*, pp. 245–54.

Introduction

The papers which follow are more technical than those of the previous volume, *Equilibrium and Macroeconomics* (Basil Blackwell, Oxford, 1984). But they should be accessible to anyone familiar with a modern text. By way of introduction I have included my Jevons Lecture, 'In Praise of Economic Theory'. In it I discuss what I think we are doing when we theorize and I argue that this is a worthwhile activity.

In the remainder of this introduction I briefly comment on the papers which follow.

I MONEY

My interest in monetary theory derives largely from the difficulty one has in incorporating it into classic theories of the economy which in other respects seem satisfactory. It is, of course, widely known that Arrow–Debreu theory will not allow such incorporation at all. But recent work on models of overlapping generations in which money appears are equally unsuitable as long as it is the only asset, and when it is not it raises all sorts of difficulties. Some of these are quite old in the literature. Sometimes it seems as if the world is coming to the aid of the theorist. Thus, interest-paying current accounts are becoming more widespread and thereby one old puzzle is sidestepped. But this phenomenon also shows that the theoretical puzzle has real substance: there is a tendency for other assets to drive out 'sterile' money. In paper 1 I give an account, of a rather non-technical kind, of the way general equilibrium theorists have tried to incorporate non-interest-bearing, intrinsically worthless, money into their theorizing.

In the 1950s the most notable attempt in this direction was that of Patinkin (2nd edn, 1965). In some of his early papers he failed to model adequately the essential intertemporal aspect of money. In paper 2 I pointed out why that was wrong. Of course, it was only a slip on Patinkin's part, and I reprint it only because it makes the point concerning the central importance of the intertemporal aspect rather simply.

In the 1950s also the battle still raged between 'loanable funds' and 'liquidity preference' theories of the rate of interest. This episode is now, deservedly, almost forgotten. But the bad habits of the debate have persisted in other contexts. In particular, there is the habit of writing that some price is 'determined' in one particular market without giving this claim the precision it needs to be meaningful; examples are 'Inflation is a Monetary Phenomenon' and 'Investment determines Savings'. This means that paper 3 may still be of interest since it is an attempt, in a particular context, to sort out this sort of muddle.

The next two papers represent my most serious attempt to fashion a general equilibrium theory in which money can find a place. The first of these is not easy or pleasant reading because the complications of an economy with transaction technologies are rather large. Foley (1970) had pursued the same line at the same time and independently. However, he did not examine the inter-temporal problems which gave rise to the possibility of inefficient equilibria. This came as a surprise to me, since the inefficiency in question is relative to the transaction technology. Starrett's example (1973) is a beautifully clear one, and readers interested in these matters should read it as a companion piece to paper 5. Kurz (1972) made further clarifications possible, and the whole matter has recently been magisterially discussed by Gale (1982). I do think that this whole episode has improved our understanding of monetary theory. But there are still large gaps. The 'transaction technology' is *ad hoc* and not properly grounded, as it should be, in information theory. Moreover, although Heller and Starr (1976) have relaxed the assumption somewhat, it is still the case that we cannot deal at present with the likely significant non-convexity of transaction technologies. Clearly, one needs to dig more deeply to the level at which the information of exchanging agents can be studied.

II NON-WALRASIAN EQUILIBRIA

Perfectly competitive economies are now understood rather well. I have, however, been puzzled by the many economists who seem to consider that this abstraction is satisfactory both intellectually and for the study of actual economies. To take just one example, it seems that the fraction of UK GNP spent on advertising was for long comparable to that spent on education. Such a dissonance between theory and gross observation would certainly give pause to, say, physicists, but not to many economists, who are apt to mumble something about looking for lost keys under a street light or appealing to the metaphysics of 'as if'. Even if somehow this odd stance could be defended, it would still be highly peculiar not to be interested in the challenge of studying economies in which agents must act strategically. In any case, for the last ten years or so I have been much interested in departures from Walrasian economies, although I cannot claim to have advanced far along this difficult road.

The Belgians led by Drèze (1975) and the French led by Malinvaud (1977) went, as it were, to the other extreme and studied economies with exogenously given prices and consequent rationing. They considered what in paper 6 I called 'orderly equilibria', that is, equilibria where only the 'short side' in any market is rationed. This was the basis of the dynamic process studied by Negishi and myself (see paper 10 below). In the first part of paper 6 I was interested in an existence proof for a Drèze equilibrium. I found it useful to study an associated economy with coupon prices as rationing devices for this purpose. But the aim of that paper was to move beyond exogenously given prices. For that purpose I introduced the term 'conjectures' to describe theories of firms of the reaction of the economy to their own actions. Of course, this was related to Negishi's (1961) perceived demand curve but was rather more general. Paper 7 considers some examples of conjectural equilibria.

In the theory which I develop in paper 6 I introduced the notions of *rational* and of *reasonable* conjectures. The first of these was badly christened since it triggers a wrong reaction in game theorists (see Makowski, 1983). I should have named them *correct* conjectures, and even that terminology needs further elaboration. The idea is this. Agents have theories of what will happen to, say, their profits if they deviate from some given status quo. I considered only small deviations and implicitly supposed that the direct consequences of such a deviation would be spread over many agents. I did not have a duopoly or oligopoly game in mind. I therefore took the consequences of a small deviation by a single agent to be calculable from the equilibrium of the rest of the economy after the deviation and when all other agents keep to *their* conjectures. This becomes clear in the examples of paper 7. I certainly was *not* thinking of dynamics, nor of games in extensive form. No agent is playing against another who reacts to his deviation by calculating the best responses. Rather, any one agent has an anonymous opponent – the rest of the economy – and for my purposes the agents who constitute that economy need not know who has deviated and may indeed regard the new signal as being due to some change in the state of the economy.

I hope it is clear from this that my intention was not to take a shortcut through the intricacies of rationality in an economy-wide game. As far as I know, game theory and general equilibrium theory have met only in circumstances in which a perfect competitive equilibrium is the outcome. Moreover, those studies seem to have all been concentrated on pure exchange. The main exception to this is the book by Marschak and Selten (1979), which proceeds in a manner not markedly dissimilar from the one which I followed. (It preceded my own work, but I only became aware of it later.) In any case, I have to confess that I have some doubts that it will prove possible to bring about a marriage of recent rather beautiful advances in game theory and economy-wide analysis. Certainly when I wrote my papers I knew that it was beyond me. I accordingly opted for what is essentially a Chamberlinian approach (see Hart, 1983). I will not be surprised if it transpires that that was a wrong move.

III STABILITY

I can be brief in my comments on papers 8, 9 and 10. In the first of these I am concerned rather less with stability than with the existence of equilibrium. I showed how, in an economy with the gross substitutability property, one could develop an existence proof by induction (and so without a fixed point theorem). I needed gross substitutes because I needed equilibrium to be unique for every way of forming a certain composite commodity out of two commodities. I now believe that it may be possible to carry out the same proof with only the postulate that the economy is always regular (Debreu, 1970). But I have not tried to do this since there are more interesting things to do instead.

Both the remaining papers concern a price adjustment process for a pure exchange economy in which trading takes place at all dates when it can take place. It turned out that non-tâtonnement was easier to analyse than was tâtonnement and that it yielded stability without special restrictions on the forms of the excess demand functions. This was further studied in a much more general setting by Smale (1975) and extended to include production by Fisher (1983). Even so, we are a long way from understanding the operation of any actual price mechanism. (The currently fashionable procedure of simply postulating prices to be at all times market-clearing can have no attraction to the intellectually fastidious.)

Paper 11 was written a long time ago and probably shows it. But it considers a question which is rarely discussed but which seems important: How is uncertainty related to stability? I study this in the context of a simple cobweb. The idea is that the more uncertain the expectation of future price, the less responsive an agent will be to deviations of current price from its equilibrium value. This in turn has implications for cobweb behaviour. My guess is that there is further worthwhile work to be done on this class of problems in the light of what we have learned in the intervening thirty years.

IV GROWTH

Growth theory is now less fashionable than it was in the 1960s which was its period of boom. None the less, much current work (e.g. the new macroeconomics) relies rather heavily on it. My own interests were two-fold: to study growth in the framework of general equilibrium analysis, and to examine the stability of growth equilibrium.

In paper 12 I use straightforward general equilibrium theory in the attempt to impose some order on the many anecdotal results which were being produced at the time. The main issue was the uniqueness of temporary equilibrium which was required for a straightforward analysis of a sequence of such equilibria. It turned out that this could best be studied by the use of the Weak Axiom of Revealed Preference in a particular formulation.

Papers 13 and 14 show why with certain assumptions the steady state was a saddle-point in a certain subspace. There has been a good deal written on this since (e.g. Shell and Stiglitz, 1967; Kurz, 1968; Cass and Shell, 1976). I took my result to show that warranted paths of the economy as defined by Harrod did not in general seek the steady state. It never occurred to me that anyone would wish to posit perfect foresight over the infinite future. But I was wrong: such a postulate is now commonplace. It still strikes me as dotty. On the technical side, developments since I wrote have shown that with many consumption goods (I assumed only one such good) there would be a cone of paths which approach the steady state. These results make my own non-convergence propositions less dramatic but raise the new problem of the non-uniqueness of perfect foresight paths. The relevance of all of this to the rational expectations literature will be clear.

In papers 15 and 16 I study stability not of equilibrium paths but of actual paths. In the first of these I postulate certain responses to an excess demand for finished goods and for inputs. However, as Sargent (1962) pointed out later, I paid too little attention to who got what when the economy is out of equilibrium. None the less, certain of the insights may be of interest.

In paper 16 I looked at a situation not too different from the 'fix-price' literature of recent years. By postulating a substitution theorem economy I could determine relative steady-state prices as a function of the interest rate and independently of excess demand. I then assumed a price formation process which proceeded independently of excess demand and was governed largely by expectations. I showed that it converged under certain assumptions. On the other hand, excess demands at substitution theorem prices were met out of inventories. The accumulation and decumulation of the latter were governed by a 'flexible accelerator' mechanism. I showed that the steady-state equilibrium was stable in the small under this mechanism. A shortcoming of the paper is certainly that it assumed labour never to be in short supply; but it seems to me that it may none the less be a promising beginning.

In paper 17 I use duality theory to examine the behaviour of equilibrium paths. I then proceed to examine a suggestion of Shell and Stiglitz (1967) that inelastic expectations (i.e. non-rational expectations) are stabilizing. It turns out that this is by no means always the case.

V MISCELLANEOUS

The four papers in this last part are on various topics. Paper 18 was occasioned by one by Levhari and Srinivasan (1969). It deals with the question of whether an increase in the uncertainty of the future productivity of capital would lead to an increase or decrease in the optimal amount of savings. In writing this paper I gained much from conversations with Jim Mirrlees, who had written a celebrated thesis on optimum accumulation under uncertainty.

Paper 19 was inspired by Hicks (1954). It is concerned with excess capacity and entrance deterrence. It, of course, does not have the benefit of recent advances in the application of game theory to these problems. But Hicks made the important point that the story rather depends on the preferences of the people who run firms. This point is not much discussed in current work and it may be important.

Paper 20 was written to clarify (partly to myself) the well-known taxation results of Diamond and Mirrlees (1971). It proceeds slightly more generally than they did. However, I did not pay sufficient attention to the fact that knowledge of the distribution of characteristics of agents on the part of government was all that was required for the Diamond–Mirrlees results.

Paper 21 was also an attempt to understand. Joe Stiglitz had given a preliminary version of the famous Rothshild–Stiglitz (1976) paper at a Cambridge seminar. I could not then put my finger on just what feature of the example was responsible for the non-existence of an equilibrium. Paper 21 was an attempt to do so. This has since been studied more deeply and satisfactorily by Dasgupta, Hammond and Maskin (1979).

ACKNOWLEDGEMENTS

I am very grateful to Mr K. Gatsios of the Faculty of Economics and Politics at the University of Cambridge for proofreading. My intellectual debts will mostly be obvious. But one of these may not be. For twelve years Terence Gorman and I were colleagues. Many of the papers here reprinted I discussed with him. He usually went to the heart of the matter almost before I had time to tell him what I was about. He set an intellectual standard which I could aim at but not achieve.

REFERENCES

Cass, D. and Shell, K. (1976). 'The Structure and Stability of Competitive Dynamical Systems', *Journal of Economic Theory*, **12**, 31-70.

Dasgupta, P., Hammond, P. and Maskin, E. (1979), 'The Implementation of Social Choice Rules: Some General Results in Incentive Compatibility', *Review of Economic Studies*, Symposium on Incentive Compatibility, **46**, 183-215.

Debreu, G. (1970), 'Economies with a Finite Set of Equilibria', *Econometrica*, **38**, 387-92.

Diamond, P. and Mirrlees, J. (1971), 'Optimal Taxation and Public Production', *American Economic Review*, **61**, 8-27 and 261-78.

Drèze, J. (1975), 'Existence of Equilibrium under Price Rigidity and Quantity Rationing', *International Economic Review*, **16**, 301-20.

Fisher, F. (1983), *Disequilibrium Foundations of Equilibrium Economics*, Oxford University Press.

Foley, D. (1970). 'Economic Equilibrium with Costly Marketing', *Journal of Economic Theory*, **2**, 276-91.

Gale, D. (1982), *Money: In Equilibrium*, Cambridge University Press and Nisbet, Cambridge Economic Handbooks.

Gale, D. (1983), *Money: In Disequilibrium*, Cambridge University Press and Nisbet, Cambridge Economic Handbooks.

Hart, O. (1983), 'Monopolistic Competition in the Spirit of Chamberlin' and 'General Model and Special Results', ICERD Discussion Papers no. 82 and 85, London School of Economics.

Heller, W. and Starr, R. (1976), 'Equilibrium with Non-convex Transaction Costs: Monetary and Non-monetary Economics', *Review of Economic Studies*, **43**, 195-215.

Hicks, J. R. (1954), 'The Process of Imperfect Competition', *Oxford Economic Papers*, **6**, 41-54.

Kurz, M. (1968), 'The General Instability of a Class of Competitive Growth Processes', *Review of Economic Studies*, **35**, 155-74.

Kurz, M. (1972), 'Equilibrium in a Finite Sequence of Markets with Transaction Costs', Stanford University, Institute of Mathematical Studies in the Social Sciences, Technical Report no. 51, January, Stanford, California.

Levhari, D. and Srinivasan, T. N. (1969), 'Optimal Savings Under Uncertainty', *Review of Economic Studies*, **36**, 27-38.

Makowski, L. (1983), ' "Rational Conjectures" aren't Rational and "Reasonable Conjectures" aren't Reasonable', SSRC Project on 'Risk, Information and Quantity Signals in Economics', Cambridge University Discussion Paper no. 66.

Malinvaud, E. (1977), *The Theory of Unemployment Reconsidered*, Basil Blackwell, Oxford.

Marshak, T. and Selten, R. (1979), *A General Equilibrium Model with Price-making Firms*, Springer, New York.

Negishi, T. (1961), 'Monopolistic Competition and General Equilibrium', *Review of Economic Studies*, **28**, 196-201.

Patinkin, D. (1965), *Money, Interest and Prices* (2nd edn), Harper and Row, New York.

Rothshild, M. and Stiglitz, J. (1976), 'Equilibrium in Competitive Insurance Markets: An Essay on the Economics of Imperfect Information', *Quarterly Journal of Economics*, **90**, 629-49.

Sargent, (1962), 'The Stability of Growth Equilibrium: Comment', *Quarterly Journal of Economics*, **304**, 494-501.

Shell, K. and Cass, D. (1976), 'The Structure and Stability of Competitive Dynamical Systems', *Journal of Economic Theory*, **12**, 31-70.

Shell, K. and Stiglitz, J. (1967), 'The Allocation of Investment in a Dynamic Economy', *Quarterly Journal of Economics*, **81**, 592-610.

Smale, S. (1975), 'An Approach to the Analysis of Dynamic Processes in Economic Systems', in *Equilibrium and Disequilibrium in Economic Theory*, ed. G. Schwoohauer, Reidel, Boston.

Starrett, D. (1973), 'Inefficiency and the Demand for Money in a Sequence Economy', *Review of Economic Studies*, **40**, 437-48.

In Praise of Economic Theory

I come before you today to blow the trumpet for economic theory largely because it is so often under attack and so often misunderstood. But I have not come to damn other endeavours in economics. This is not entailed by praising theory and would be odd in a Jevons Lecturer. Jevons was both a theorist and an applied economist and on occasions excelled as both. There 'are many mansions . . . ', and in concentrating on one I do not wish to be taken as implying anything about the others.

In thinking what I should say on this occasion it soon became clear that I had chosen a somewhat unsatisfactory title, if for no other reason than that it reminds one of Erasmus and his *In Praise of Folly*. But there is another reason why, if it had not been too late, I would have changed it to 'In Praise of Theorizing in Economics'. For to announce praise for economic theory leaves one open to the question, which of a number of theories one intends to praise. As a matter of fact, I shall want to argue that the variety of competing economic theories is much smaller than popular opinion takes it to be. But I do not want to start with either that question or that argument. For what I am centrally interested in is the enterprise of theorizing in economics. By this I mean the undertaking to gain understanding of the particular by reference to generalizing insights and in the light of certain abstract unifying principles.

I want to emphasize the word 'understanding' and that it is not directly related to positivist prediction. For instance, we understand the cause of earthquakes but cannot at the moment predict them. We can understand *why* two people are seen to exchange without being able to predict that they will do so. Somewhat more sophisticatedly, we may be able to understand an allocation of resources as one of a number of possible equilibrium allocations without being able to predict which equilibrium will be observed in any one case. In the first instance the claim 'I understand' does not logically imply that I also assert that I can predict.

But what does it imply? I am aware that these are deep Wittgensteinian waters, in which however I do not propose to splash or drown. It seems to me that there are at least three necessary conditions that a claim to understand an event or a series of events must satisfy. First, I must have a theory which comprises the event or events; second, the event or events must not contradict the theory; and third, the theory must be in the public domain, by which I mean that it should be communicable to others in a language and grammar that is common. If you have a theory which cannot be communicated to others, then others can give no meaning to your claim that you understand.

I do not, as I have already said, want to argue for this view in any detail. The first desideratum is, I suspect, not controversial. The second is really the possibility of *ex post prediction*: my theory includes the possibility of that event and it would have been in the support of any probability distribution of events allowed by my theory. The third I have already partly justified. It does not mean that 'truth' is a matter of sociology, but rather that uncommunicable truths or modes of understanding concern the inner processes of an individual and not the theory of a subject. In any case, I shall consider theorizing in economics to be an ongoing search for understanding in this sense.

There is one further methodological matter which I can get out of the way now. Understanding does not imply the ability to manipulate events, although understanding may be a necessary precondition. It is not at all the case, for instance, that if one believes that one understands the causes of unemployment one must then also know how to cure it. It is often believed that understanding which does not facilitate manipulation is a useless luxury. This must however be wrong. For understanding can certainly aid us in recognizing futile or misdirected attempts at manipulation. For instance, we cannot change the orbit of the moon by praying to the sun, and we cannot cure poverty by minimum wage legislation. Indeed, one of the great uses of understanding is that it is a line of first defence against madmen and witches. But even if that were not so, I have never seen an argument to show that, while chocolate, lipstick, cars, etc., are intrinsic goods, understanding of the world needs justification in terms of other things. G. E. Moore's chapter on the 'Naturalist Fallacy' can easily be adapted to demonstrate the confusion of such a view.

Coming now to my topic, one recognizes that theorists are not the only economists in the quest for understanding; indeed, one might want to argue that almost all academic economists at least are thus engaged. That is why earlier I added 'by reference to generalizing insights and in the light of certain abstract unifying principles'. It is this more particular mode of proceeding which I want to convince you is worthy of praise.

Let me call 'the abstract unifying principles' axioms and distinguish these from assumptions. A theory will typically have a logical structure derived from axioms. To some economists axiomatic-logico-deductive theory is anathema; for instance, that is the case for Professor Kornai and Lord Kaldor. However, it seems to me that any coherent general propositions are decomposable into this form. For instance, if one starts with observation one requires at the very least an axiom of induction but in general a much richer array. One of my first reasons for praising theory, at least in its modern mode, is that it comes clean on both its axioms and its assumptions. They do not need to be searched for by backward recursion from propositions. In this theorists show not only an engaging modesty but also honesty.

Axioms are not plucked out of thin air, and far from distancing the theorists from what somewhat mysteriously is called the 'real' world, they constitute claims about this world so widely agreed as to make further argument unnecessary. Indeed, often in axiomatizing a theory one is attempting to see whether its propositions are deducible from elementary agreed features of the world. For instance, the von Neumann axiomatization of expected utility includes the 'sure thing principle'. It appeals to our intuition and it appeals to what we know about ourselves.

The best known and most important axiom is, of course, that of the rational agent and I shall now discuss that axiom in some detail.

The nomenclature is somewhat unfortunate because it invites philosophical debate on the meaning of 'rational'. It also arouses hostility among those romantically inclined:

A levelling rancorous rational sort of mind
That never looked out of the eye of a saint
Or out of a drunkard's eye

(Yeats, *Seven Songs*)

as Yeats has it, and I am sure I do not need to quote Ruskin to you. But economists mean something quite precise and far less offensive. The rational agent knows what he wants, and from among the alternatives available to him chooses what he wants.

By 'knowing what he wants' we mean that he has a proper preference ordering over a relevant domain. This domain may be large and complex. It may include beef and mutton and the happiness of one's grandmother. For many purposes, of course, one will be interested only in the projection of this domain on to a smaller one (one with lower dimension). For instance, we will neglect the grandmother's happiness when studying the choice between beef and mutton but not when we consider the choice of homes in different locations. This cutting down of the domain will be the role of assumptions. The description of the domain is important. For instance, our axiom may have more power in a theory of advertising if we consider preferences over characteristics of goods rather than over goods themselves.

There is little doubt that even at this level of generality the axiom yields a rich harvest with few assumptions – for instance, the symmetry of the substitution terms, the excess burden of non-lump-sum taxation, a notion of efficiency in the allocation of goods and an understanding of what it is we do when we make cost of living index numbers. On general domains it is the foundation of Arrow's Impossibility Theorem which stands like a granite tower in the otherwise indistinct and shadowy landscape of political theory. Certainly all of this is achieved with great economy of means and with elegance, so let us at least give it some marks for that.

But I am more ambitious, since I want to argue in favour of the axiom itself. That is, I do not propose to follow the Friedmanite route whose singleminded concern with prediction I have already disclaimed. The 'as if' argument is in any case shaky. It does not allow one, for instance, to distinguish between agents who act on their own preferences and those who are compelled to act on the preferences of a hypnotist. For purposes of 'understanding', the status of the axioms matters a great deal.

In the first instance, then, I want to maintain that the part of the axiom for which agents have preferences is the claim that they are persons. If so, then this is sufficiently agreed to be so as to make it acceptable as an axiom.

Suppose there is someone without any preferences at all. Between any A and B from a rich domain he can either not put them into any preference relation or not understand what is meant when he is asked to do so. This person would have no reasons for his actions whenever they can be the subject of choice. Remember that he is not indifferent between all elements in his domain – rather, he has no views on them at all. There would be no way to describe this someone other than by his physical characteristics. Even if his actions 'revealed' preferences, we could not invoke these to understand the actions. In short, he would be an animal and not a person; for animals can give no reasons for their actions and neither can this someone. In the first instance, then, the axiom says that economic agents are persons.

But, of course, it is stronger than that. For instance, persons may make mistakes in their preferences and they may have no preferences over parts of the domain in which they are not offered choices. It may be the case that a person's preferences are not transitive. There are two things to be said here. First, much of the theory can proceed with a weaker version which does not postulate transitivity. For this I refer you to a famous paper by Sonnenschein (1971). Second, we would expect that a person would re-examine his preferences if their intransitivity were pointed out to him. This would be the case particularly if such intransitivity made it impossible to give reasons for his actions. However, at the end we shall have to agree that the genuine axiom, persons have some preferences, has been idealized and strengthened by theorists beyond the point at which it commands universal consent.

The sharpening and idealization of agreed features of the world is one of the distinctive marks of theorizing. One attempts to understand events in the light of refined descriptions of commonplace regularities and their logical entailments. One understands, in so far as one can give no reason why the sharpening and idealization of the agreed axiom should mislead one.

Take as an example the case of a Giffen good, that is, a good the demand for which varies positively with price. Our axiom has led us to a distinction between substitution and income effects. We understand that a rise in price of the good will cause consumers to seek a substitute while a significant decline in real wealth resulting from the price rise may lead them to consume more of it because it is of a kind that low-wealth people have to consume proportionately more of. When I say we understand I mean two things. First, the observation of a Giffen good case fits into the theory, and the explanation conforms with what we know of ourselves and others. But I mean something else as well: we can explain to someone surprised by the deviation of a Giffen good observation from observations common for other goods how both kinds of observation can be traced back to a common account of choice. This we can do only by making the axiom sufficiently precise. But we can also argue that there seems no argument which would, by, say, considering mistaken preferences, make our explanation invalid. For we understand everything we do think we understand by just such an abstraction. No two chestnuts are alike in every particular but we speak of the property of chestnuts, and no couples love in the same way and yet we claim to understand something about love. We may often think that we have understood when we have not, but we shall never understand anything if we neither generalize nor idealize.

But perhaps I protest too much. I shall admit that and turn it to my advantage.

Simon (1955) has drawn attention to the fact that the theory of the rational agent is seriously incomplete in failing to distinguish between what this agent knows and what in principle he could know. In addition, if we forswear Friedman, the theory often makes quite implausibly large demands on an agent's computational ability. Knowledge and computation are themselves objects of choice, and that seems to leave the theory dangling by its bootstraps.

Who can deny that Simon has a good point? But who also can deny that 'satisficing' does nothing much to meet it? The only economist who to my knowledge has given this notion a serious run for money is Radner (1980). The work shows that periods of routine will be punctuated by periods of search when aspiration levels are breached. It is quite easy to translate this into a somewhat richer model of rational choice than the one of the textbook. But paradoxically, what Simon has done is to appeal to our intuition of what constitutes rational choice and in particular what is an appropriate domain of preferences. It is not reasonable to suppose that time and effort spent in discovering the set of possible choices is not itself an element of this domain. The same goes for the trouble, etc., of self-scrutiny involved in having complete and consistent preferences. Simon's argument gains what force it has by the existence of the pure theory which he finds wanting.

Above all, however, I want to praise economic theory for providing the language in which proposals like those of Simon can be discussed. I recall arguing with Sraffa when he claimed that consumer behaviour was entirely a matter of habit; I asked whether that meant that they always consumed the same things independently of prices or income. He was not willing to agree to that. After some time it seemed that we could agree that consumers had a habitual response to income and prices, at which point I could not forbear to translate this into: Consumers have rather stable preferences. In exactly the same way can Simon's critique be used to deepen understanding of what we already have. A consumer buys a good at a price higher than prevails for an identical good elsewhere. How do we understand that, and why is there something here which we need to understand? We have a prima facie puzzle because the pure theory does not account for the event. Simon really comes to its aid by proposing that the consumer may not know of the cheaper good and that he would have to expend effort to find out. He will spend that effort if his aspirations not to be taken for a ride are seriously impaired, i.e. when he believes the gain from search large enough.

I do not, of course, wish to argue that all roads lead back to the textbook theory. What I do want to maintain is that it has made possible an orderly and coherent deepening of understanding. I need only remind you of the recent flowering of the economics of information to make this point. The initial theory, once digested, threw a kind of searchlight on the unexplained: Why can similar goods sell at different prices? How are potential exchange possibilities made known, and is it possible that unsatisfactory states where they are not all known can persist? How is the market for loans affected by moral hazard, and how is that connected with some rationing of credit? One can go on and on to demonstrate how theory generates the question and provides the language for attempted answers. Without that abstract theory we would know neither when to ask 'why' nor how to proceed when we do ask.

I have spent a long time on this most contentious aspect of theorizing, the rational agent. There are other directions to explore. However, before I do that two other aspects deserve some comment.

The first of these is easily and quickly discussed. Opponents of theory often argue that it is tautologous because it consists of logical deductions from axioms and assumptions. If one is kind to such critics one interprets them as signalling that they do not care for these axioms and these assumptions. In any case, all theory in all subjects proceeds in this manner. In the present context one sometimes hears it maintained that the theory of choice simply says that a person will do what he prefers and that there is no way of falsifying *that*. But that is to misunderstand the theory. An agent whose preferences are continuously in flux is like an agent without any preferences at all. The theory thus postulates that this is not the case, and so the charge that our understanding is not tested by observation is false. Connected with this is the endless refrain of some that most of our preferences are socially determined. If I understand that correctly, then I can only answer: Of course they are. It is however a puzzle why this observation should, for instance, affect my analysis of Giffen goods unless once again it is proposed that social forces are continuously leading to a change of preferences.

The second matter is more complex and I can only touch on it. This is the observation that the rational agent and the theory he supports is a powerful tool in the discussion of many policy issues. One does not need to be a utilitarian to agree that the preferences and welfare of individuals are relevant to policy debates. They need not of course be decisive. The theory constructed by economists provides a subtle and elegant language in which this aspect of policy can be discussed. Any economist who has been on committees with non-economists will be conscious of the advantage which he has in discussion even of such imponderables as the allocation of research money between astronomy and dentistry. The theory allows him to organize his thoughts and to recognize what is relevant. Nor is it true, as economists gone sour with public responsibility sometimes argue, that only the most elementary and obvious ideas such as opportunity cost are involved. Questions of the appropriateness of market prices and interest rates in calculations of such costs arise, and I would not trust anyone unfamiliar with quite sophisticated theory to get it right. I would agree that theorists sometimes write as if all of moral philosophy were embodied in a Benthamite calculus. They also often forget the importance of the lack of markets for future goods and the relative paucity of insurance markets. But then the proper theory *is* available and a certain diffidence in questions of the 'good' can be instilled in some. However there can be no doubt that, without the economic theory which we have, very many matters of policy would literally not be discussable, which means that they could not be subjected to any coherent thought. I think that this is a matter for praise.

These last remarks suggest that economic theory not only seeks understanding, which is its own reward, but is also on occasions useful. Yet just now in Britain it also seems dangerous. Indeed, only the other day a politician warned against it at the Conservative conference. Certainly if what Mr Lawson asserts is taken to be economic theory, then the case is proved. But this is all wrong, not just in a rather obvious way but also in an interesting way.

I have suggested earlier that we need to distinguish between axioms and assumptions. That people have preferences and try to satisfy them we treat as an axiom, while universal perfect competition, for instance, must count as an assumption. By this I mean that neither introspection nor observation makes it self-evident up to an acceptable margin of error that agents are price-takers in all markets. But assumptions are no more capriciously imposed than are axioms. They serve to simplify – that is, to make argument possible – and they also often attempt to encapsulate a sort of casual empiricism. That managers have preferences is an axiom; that they take a particular form – for instance that they are linear in expected profit – is an assumption which both simplifies and seems not implausible in the light of experience. Whatever it is, a theory suggests that we understand, that understanding is contingent on both the axioms and assumptions. It certainly is also contingent on the logical entailment of the propositions of the theory by the assumptions and axioms.

Consider a fashionable example. The proposal that we should take it that an agent whose forecasts of future events are systematically disappointed will change his forecast seems to me axiomatic. It is difficult in the light of introspection and experience to deny it, although I have no doubt that one can find exceptions. But that an agent will normally have learned to make forecasts which are not systematically disappointed is hardly a self-evident truth. More seriously, there are great difficulties in understanding how the agent could reach this satisfactory state; for the learning of agents affects what there is to be learned. Sterling pioneering work on this matter by such economists as Margaret Bray (1982) illustrates this. Hence the proposition that agents have rational expectations is an assumption. Certain not very careful people have thought that this assumption is implied by what I have granted as an axiom: viz., that people will not persist in an erroneous belief. Such a step is just wrong. It is not made right by rational expectations econometrics with good fits. That is so because we cannot understand why it should fit well. As I have argued elsewhere, the evidence for miracles at Lourdes is stronger than is this econometrics. Yet without understanding it does not persuade.

What a rational expectations theory provides is an understanding of an imagined economy which satisfies the assumption. As such it may be of great use. For instance, it allows us to study pathologies which cannot be traced to expectational mistakes. Or, again, it leads to an understanding of how market variables, by revealing information to the uninformed, reduce (or negate) the benefits of special information. Or, yet again, it allows us to grasp the informational disturbances introduced by an unknown monetary policy. It is a vulgar misunderstanding of theory and its aims to dismiss rational expectations theorizing because of its assumptions. I repeat again that I do not hold this view on 'as if' grounds.

But it ought to be emphasized that, from a theoretical point of view, the rational expectations story, even when taken as a useful 'Gedanken experiment', is pretty shaky. For instance, there is in general a continuum of rational expectations equilibria over finite time. To get rid of this one needs to suppose that people have rational expectations over the infinite future. Even that extravagance often does not suffice, and one must cook the story to yield a long-run stationary state which is also a saddle point. We have robust examples of an infinity of rational expectations equilibrium cycles. I am not here concerned to dot the i's of this argument. My concern is to document what I claimed earlier: that theory is powerful in saving us from cranks and witches only if it is taken seriously. For who can understand the precisely formulated theory of rational expectations equilibrium and claim that he understands it as description? At the very best, the new macroeconometricians are like someone who noticed that beans grew better when kitchen waste was dug into their soil. That is an observation and not a theory. I want to emphasize here 'at best'.

Exactly the same problems arise with equilibrium theory in general. It takes a little sophistication to see why the study of economics in equilibrium is an important step in understanding actual economies. For instance, even if we know nothing of detailed dynamics, disequilibrium is an occasion for change and so an explanation of change. But it seems to take much more sophistication to understand what one is about in equilibrium theorizing.

I want here to praise the giants of equilibrium theory, Arrow and Debreu. In the first place they deserve praise for writing down precisely, and beyond the power of misunderstanding of a normal person, what state of the economy was to be designated as an equilibrium. In particular, this left many possible states which were not equilibrium states and one needed to prove that there are some which were. In doing this it became clear that without certain assumptions it would always be possible to describe an economy of the kind which they considered for which no equilibrium existed. No ambiguity of what it is that is being done is possible. We are concerned with the existence of a particular state of the economy in which the best choices of individuals are mutually compatible when these choices are entirely determined by preferences, technology, endowments and market prices. There is nothing here to tell us that any given economy will be in that state or that it tends to that state. The theory is what it is and not something else.

In giving us this precise formulation and these existence proofs, Arrow and Debreu vastly increased our understanding of what had gone before and laid the foundations for a great deal more. As I have argued elsewhere, they provided the first essential step in any serious discussion of the Invisible Hand 'with its task accomplished'. The elegant definition of a good made it clear to the naked eye that the market structure would have to be much richer than in fact it is if an actual economy in equilibrium should correspond to theirs. The fundamental theorem of welfare economics then underlines the message that, even if actual economies are in equilibrium, they may be inefficient. It became clear that economies with money would have to be modelled in a special way and that that special way was connected with having too few markets. It also became possible to connect equilibrium concepts of game theory with market equilibrium and thus to bring about a much deeper understanding of the postulate of perfect competition. Who can read the Core theorem without even a flicker of pleasure in the beautiful and not obvious role of the Arrow–Debreu equilibrium? Who can read them without finding their understanding of market power and the role of markets deepened?

The Arrow–Debreu theory has been widely misunderstood and misused. One of the coarsest criticisms is to say that if used in a comparative statics way it has generally very low, or no, predictive power: 'anything', it is said, 'can happen'. Exactly so. The theory is crystal clear as to its foundations – the fundamental axioms which I have already discussed. If you want more out you have to put more in, that is, you must supplement those axioms with assumptions, e.g., that production functions are Cobb-Douglas. What the theory provides is a coherent manner of studying the implications of these assumptions for equilibrium. Most other criticisms have turned on its lack of realism, but the aim is not realism but aid to understanding. Think of externalities, of imperfect competition, of increasing returns and many other 'realistic' phenomena, and ask how we would fit them into our comprehension without the ideal reference point provided by Arrow–Debreu. We understand a basic problem with public goods because of our understanding of the private goods case. We can for the same reason give some precise meaning to significant and insignificant increasing returns. The work which has gone before pinpoints precisely where there will be difficulties with equilibrium of an imperfectly competitive economy. Is our understanding of Keynesian claims not deepened and modified by making the connection to missing markets? If we did not have the Arrow–Debreu theory it would be priority number one to construct it; for, while it does not describe the world, it is a solid starting point for the quest for understanding it.

But of course there are influential economists who take a version of the theory as descriptive. For instance, they hold the view that the British labour market in 1984 can be understood as a Walrasian market in equilibrium.

Let us notice straight away that there is no axiom to the effect that an economy is in equilibrium at all times. If there were, then Arrow and Debreu certainly wasted their time. For it would be exceedingly odd to accept this axiom and prove at the same time that equilibrium exists. It also, of course, does not further understanding to answer Adam Smith's fundamental question, Can a decentralized economy with self-interested agents have a coherent allocation of resources?, with the affirmative answers in the form of an axiom. By adopting the axiom these economists remove a major part of any problem from the possibility of understanding. This of course is still true if the 'as if' interpretation were put on the axiom.

In fact, there have been attempts to justify this procedure by an appeal to the fundamental axiom of rationality. First, it is said that a rational agent will always act to his best advantage given the opportunities which he faces. Thus all actions are equilibrium actions. This indeed is part of the requirement of Arrow–Debreu equilibrium and it is also a proper use of the fundamental axiom. But what of the other requirement of equilibrium that the individual actions of agents should be compatible economy-wide? The answer given is this. If they were not compatible there would be Pareto-improving moves which have not been exploited. But that is not rational. Hence the equilibrium actions must be compatible. That this syllogism does violence to the foundations of a theory of decentralized choices seems to me so obvious as not to require discussion. I refer you to the Prisoner's Dilemma as a vivid example of this observation. The justification of an axiom of perpetual equilibrium can be dismissed.

But that is just as well; for if we accepted it in this form, a vast range of economic phenomena, as I have already said, would at once be removed from enquiry and so from the realm of understanding. One would have a theory which closes rather than opens doors. I want to emphasize that this does not apply to a proper version of the axiom that all actions are equilibrium actions – that, after all, is just the axiom of rationality which I have defended. By a 'proper version' I mean one which properly states the information and expectations of the agent in the light of which the equilibrium action is undertaken. This leads us back to rational expectations which I have already discussed.

But I have come to praise theory, and here I seem to be found attacking it. Not so. To make this clear I have once again to return to the beginning.

The economists I have been discussing might be taken to be engaged in the following programme: to enquire how far observed events are consistent with an economy which is in continuous Walrasian equilibrium. Such a programme would be of considerable value. For we might find that events which we had explained as being due to disequilibrium or, indeed, to trade unions and monopolists could be accounted for without these. That surely would be valuable for understanding; but it would not be true that we understood the events. For we would not understand how continuous equilibrium is possible in a decentralized economy, and we do not understand why a world with trade unions and monopolies behaves like a perfectly competitive one. Theorizing in economies, I have argued, is an attempt at understanding, and I now add that bad theorizing is a premature claim to understand.

What has happened in this instance is that 'as if' prediction methodology has taken over. Recall Friedman's example: leaves on a plant orientate themselves as if the plant were maximizing the surface area of leaves exposed to the sun. This may well predict the orientation of leaves, but it is not an account which we understand, precisely because we know that plants are not, as Friedman notes, capable of any calculations. So we do not leave matters there. We investigate chemical feedback mechanisms which account for the observation and which we understand. They fit into what we know generally about chemical substances in quite different contexts and into what we quite generally stipulate about causal processes. All the economists I have been discussing are much more concerned with 'as if' than with understanding, as their numerous econometric exercises testify. There is nothing wrong with this predictive programme. But all theory could claim is that this and this is not inconsistent with an economy in perpetual Walrasian equilibrium, and not that this and this is explained by such an equilibrium. They would have to be that modest because of the many things left unexplained.

I now leave these central but somewhat abstract arguments to call Jevons to my aid, although, as will be seen, not exactly in a straightforward manner.

In a review of the sixth volume of Jevons' papers and correspondence edited by Collison-Black, Stigler (1983) pokes fun at Jevons' sunspot theory. He reports that recent American investigation into that theory had to conclude that Granger causality analysis showed the American economy as having a significant impact on sunspots and not the other way round. Stigler also says: 'All his life Jevons played with numbers' and that he was 'not by instinct a formal theorist'.

The Granger causality result makes us smile because, coming back to my old refrain, there is no way in which we can understand it. That, of course, does not establish that it is wrong. For that, other theoretical arguments are required which show that there could be no influence on the sun from American economic activity, with which, we may note, economic activity all over the world is probably correlated. Far less does the Granger causality test establish that sunspots exert no influence on economic activity. The trouble with Jevons' sunspots was not that he could never clinch it with numbers, but that he would never clinch it with theory; that is, he could never bring it into consonance with the existing understanding of the working of an economy. In fact, unlike some current macroeconometricians, I cannot see how any economic argument which we do not understand can be clinched without misunderstanding.

Jevons was a practitioner of what Keynes called 'the black inductive art', but he also provided the first English axiomatic formulation of economic theory. In the matter of sunspots the black art was at the forefront, although he did attempt to provide an understanding of what he claimed to be the case by an appeal to Indian harvest fluctuations. But it is clear that this was what one might call 'casual theorizing'. Certainly no precise or detailed picture of international economic relations is to be found in this work of Jevons. No connection was made, as Keynes notes, with his own earlier analysis of the role of durable goods in the understanding of fluctuations. Above all, Jevons seems to have believed that his simple explanation could be tested by simple means, a sure sign that he did not fully grasp the difference between plausible hypothesis and serious theory.

I therefore want to way that it is a misuse of language to say that Jevons had a sunspot theory of economic fluctuations. What he had was a hypothesis which he tried to confirm from data. A hypothesis is not a theory, although in common parlance these two are often used indifferently. I do not 'understand' economic fluctuations by being told that they are correlated with sunspots. I do not understand the formation of prices by being told that the price level and some measure of money are correlated. At best, such observations and such hypotheses may cause one to re-examine matters already filed away as understood.

But Jevons' sunspots are back in the theoretical literature, and this time, although they are only named so metaphorically, we do have a theory of how they might be related to fluctuations. I refer here to the work by Azariades (1981), Cass and Shell (1983), Woodford (1984) and others on overlapping generations models of the economy. The theory is simple, although there is some complexity in its full development. It is that, if agents condition their expectations of economic variables on sunspots or indeed any other state of nature whatever, then these sunspots will have an influence on the evolution of the economy. Conditioning expectations on an intrinsically cyclic state helps in generating cycles. But theory and understanding do not stop here; for it is shown that each agent in the economy acts rationally and estimates future events rationally. In particular, the fluctuating economy is at all times in rational expectations equilibrium. If asked, 'Why do you take notice of sunspots in forming your expectations?' my rational answer is, 'because others do'. I ought to add that Grandmont (1985) has shown that rational expectations equilibrium cycles are also possible in a deterministic world.

I hope that this example will convince those who need convincing of the usefulness of theorizing. The work which I have just reported does not depart from the fundamental rationality axioms, or indeed from any of our traditional models of understanding, and so accounts for something hitherto unconsidered in a language we already understand. It is not tied to actual sunspots. The same account will do if the *deus ex machina* is the pronouncement of a guru *or*, I am tempted to add, the numbers for M3. And notice why it is important that the theory has the form it has: we do not have to invoke individual irrationality verging on madness to explain what we want to explain. That means that we do not need to invoke something we know nothing about to understand what is involved. It is a gain in understanding to know that irrationality need not be involved and all will see that this is not the same thing as claiming that people everywhere and always are rational. Lastly, of course, it *is* now a matter for empirical research to see whether, in forming their expectations, people are influenced by events to which we can assign no direct economic role or significance.

I now want to conclude with much simpler matters. These turn on some of the most frequent criticisms one hears of current modes of theorizing.

The mathematical form of much of modern theorizing is frequently under attack. Slack and intellectually lazy *obiter dicta* of Marshall and Keynes are often invoked. Walras noted how some people found it offensive to their view of humanity to see it studied in symbols. It is very difficult to consider a criticism appealing so much to sensibility and so little to reason. For instance, consider the pronouncement of Marshall (I believe) that one must always translate mathematical propositions into words to make sure that they make sense. It seems to view mathematical reasoning like automatic writing, not guided by volition. In any case how, to take an example, do you translate into English that certain economic processes can be represented by equations with complex roots which give rise to cyclical behaviour? Even if somehow translated, what is gained? Or there is the view that mathematical reasoning *ipso facto* makes theory unrealistic and irrelevant – a view surely not worth discussing.

As far as I can see, there are only two possible coherent arguments. One is that the use of mathematics makes a theorist ignore matters which cannot be thus captured. The other is that the search for rigour inhibits creative thinking which in its first stages may be far from rigorous. I believe that there is something to both objections and perhaps especially to the second one. Certainly, a mathematical formulation is not a necessary feature of acceptable theorizing. But when I consider how much our understanding owes to mathematically minded theorists, how they have liberated us from arguments by arithmetical example as for instance in Böhm-Bawerk, Marx and Ricardo, how they have produced definiteness and comprehension where there was flabby hand-waving, and how they have forced us to specify rather exactly the basis of any pronouncement, these objections become insignificant. Indeed, let us praise mathematical economics for these achievements. Let us also forswear the sentence, 'this is mathematics and not economics', unless we can say what it means. For instance, the study of sufficient conditions which will ensure that aggregate demand functions are differentiable is largely mathematical in nature; but why is it not economics? That is, why is it not relevant to things we wish to say about the economy?

The other grand objection to theorizing I have been really discussing throughout. That is of course that it is unrealistic, like a chess game in fact, and of no use to anyone. I have never been able to understand this objection. What exactly is realistic economics? I think what is frequently meant is that someone through practical experience and knowledge claims to have direct knowledge of how an economy works but appeals to 'his judgement' for authority. But in any case ask, Why is theory often such an imperfect mirror of the world? The answer is not love of obfuscation or of abstraction but the limits on what we are capable of understanding. I recall here my earlier requirement that understanding must be publicly accessible. Of course, theorizing leaves out much of interest and importance and there are many phenomena it cannot account for adequately, but that is not so by devilish design but by the limitations of our capacity to form a unified and coherent account of the whole economic world. For the recognition of this limitation we should praise rather than condemn theorists.

Of course, there are silly theories and there are also silly questions on which sometimes too much effort is expounded. But listening and reading the 'practical' economists does not suggest that living in the world is a guarantee of sense.

Indeed, it is one of the great virtues of theorizing in economics that it leaves the practitioner with a suspicion that, what I suppose was once a programme for economics, may be impossible to carry out. It goes of course without saying that economics is not like physics. But I rather think it may not be much like meteorology, either. The law of large numbers does not self-evidently operate in the social world in which customs and views of some contaminate those of others. It is not just that there are many variables and complex interactions: it is that the constraints on what is possible seem much weaker than is the case with physical processes studied in meteorology. A theorist then will be surprised if there are 'laws of economies', in the sense of propositions holding universally, to be discovered. He will be surprised if deep knowledge of 'affairs' were to reveal some fundamental or invariant structure of an economy. He will know better than many who profess the modern version of 'political economy' the incompleteness and partial nature of what we have and what it seems we may ever have. Of course, he hopes to illuminate the darkness, but few, unlike so many practical men, would claim to have turned it into daylight, and some, myself included, may have the view that shadowy mists may be the best we can ever hope for.

Lastly, I turn to the matter of there being many contradictory economic theories. This, of course, is a cause for merriment and contempt to journalists and men of judgement. We have only ourselves to blame. The display of certainty by many economists in discussing matters of economic policy is not only lacking in honesty but extremely harmful to the subject. In any case, I hold the view that it is not the case that there are many rival and contradictory economic theories. And I mean theories, and not the beliefs of, say, Mr Lawson or Mr Benn.

Take monetarism in any of its forms as an example. In the 'language of theory', as Debreu puts it, it is quite clear that certain of the new macroeconomists' propositions concerning rational expectations Walrasian equilibria can be correct. Certainly in deriving these they and, say, I follow the same steps and the same theory. Where we part company is that they take the construction as descriptive and as immediately applicable while I do not. One of the reasons why I do not is because I can use the same theory to deduce valid propositions quite contrary to theirs. The difference is not one of theory but rather in the evaluation of what theory is about and what it can deliver. Another difference is, of course, the mysterious belief so many monetarists have in the confirmatory power of their econometric exercises. But I want to emphasize that one is not here concerned with rival theories at all in the sense in which I have used the term.

I would, if there were time, argue that even Marxian economics and neoclassical economics are not rival theories where they study the same problem and where no logical mistakes are made. Let me only note that it is neoclassical economics which made some sense of the labour theory of value and it was Marx who built one of the first miniature general equilibrium models. On 'the laws of history', whatever that means, there is no dispute since neoclassical economists have not proposed any.

What I am arguing, then, is that it is hard to find rival theories but easy to find contradictory opinions. The contrary impression stems from a misunderstanding of theorizing and of course from the wilful obfuscation of those who seek power and influence or who are driven by millennial dreams.

At the end of it all, I want to praise theorizing in economics because it is one of the highways to understanding and because it has already provided a good deal of it. I want to praise it for its modesty and honesty and also for the occasional excitement and beauty which it provides. Above all, I want to praise it for this: no one who has seriously theorized can be enslaved by the slogans and shibboleths of practical men and women who have not. No one accustomed to the discipline of coherence and proof will fall a victim to such pepole. If we were all theorists, it just might be a better world.

REFERENCES

Azariades, C. (1981), 'Self-fulfilling Prophecies', *Journal of Economic Theory*, 25.

Bray, M. (1982), 'Learning Estimation and the Stability of Rational Expectations', *Journal of Economic Theory*, 26.

Cass, D. and Shell, K. (1983), 'Do Sunspots Matter?', *Journal of Political Economy*, 91.

Grandmont, J. M. (1985), Forthcoming article in *Econometrica*.

Radner, R. (1980), 'Collusive Behaviour in Non-cooperative Epsilon-Equilibria of Oligopolies with Long But Finite Lives', *Journal of Economic Theory*, 22.

Simon, H. (1955), 'A Behavioural Model of Rational Choice', Cowles Commission Papers, New Series, no. 98, Chicago.

Sonnenschein, H. (1971), 'Demand Theory without Transitive Preferences with Applications to the Theory of Competitive Equilibrium', in Chipman, J., Hurwicz, L., Richter, M. and Sonnenschein, H. (eds) *Preferences, Utility and Demand*, Harcourt Brace Jovanovich, New York.

Stigler, D. (1983), 'Review of Black (R. D. Collison) (ed.) *Papers and Correspondence of William Stanley Jevons*, Vol. VII, *Papers on Political Economy*', *Economic Journal*, 9, 3.

Woodford, M. (1984), 'Indeterminacy of Equilibrium in the Overlapping Generations Model: a Survey', mimeo, Columbia University.

Part I

Money

1

Money and General Equilibrium

The Arrow–Debreu model describes a world in which none of the problems which interested Keynes can occur. Nor is it the case that this model can accommodate money in any interesting or essential way. Many theorists now working on monetary and related problems have therefore found that they are really engaged in a reconstruction of the only fully understood foundation of our subject. Not unnaturally, they are much at sea. This present paper discusses some of this work but also contains some new material. Before I start there are several preliminary remarks I should like to make.

What follows is in no way meant to be a comprehensive survey of recent monetary theory; indeed, I shall be only partly concerned with the work of others. I have picked out for discussion matters which interest me and which are relevant to my topic. It is not an implication therefore that studies which are not discussed are regarded as unimportant or as inferior.

In particular, I shall only make occasional references to 'monetarists' or what *The Times* called 'modern monetary theory'. This is due partly to the difficulties I have had in discovering a precise statement of this theory and partly to the fact that many monetarists seem to base themselves on empirical induction rather than on theoretical propositions which are my prime concern here. But Professor Pearce recently announced in a letter to *The Times* that 'an increase in the quantity of money is a necessary and sufficient condition for a rising price level.' So there seem to be theorems, and when their proofs become available they will have to be taken seriously.

The second preliminary remark is motivated by the fear that, as on a previous occasion, I may inadvertently give comfort to those who are the enemies of modern mathematical economics. When, as I shall do, I criticize this or that construction or point to great areas of ignorance, I do not want to be taken to mean that there is some alternative available which either does better or which commands respect. Indeed, I am daily more convinced that the only serious battle now being waged against our considerable ignorance is by those who are familiar also with the theoretical achievements of the last generation. They at least are constructing a raft of sorts; the man of judgement and the pundits are prepared to walk on the waters. I have nothing to say which they would find of interest, and I much hope that they will find nothing to comfort them.

II   THE QUESTIONS

The questions one asks are of course more than half the battle and so I start with them.

Certainly the Arrow–Debreu economy has no medium of exchange and has great difficulties in accommodating one; but it is not a barter economy either. That is because neither the process nor the technology of exchange is described and because it makes no sense to ask in this connection what does A exchange against what with whom in order to reach his allocation. As everyone knows, the description of this economy, for instance the pure exchange case, is complete when one is given the commodity space R^l_+, the number of households (H), their consumption sets X_h, their ordering $(\underset{h}{\succsim})$ on X_h and their endowments $\bar{x}_h \in R^l_+$. It is then taken for granted that there are known terms of exchange in prices, one price for each good and the same price for each agent, and that any action which satisfies the budget constraint at these prices is feasible for an agent.

But certainly an old question is, Why is there a medium of exchange? And an old way of answering it is to consider an economy which does not have one. Although the question and answers are old, it has only recently been possible to make them precise. I am thinking here of the work of Niehans and Starr and of Ostroy and Starr as well as the various models of exchange processes such as those of Uzawa, Negishi, Hahn, Hurwicz, Radner and Reiter. I return to this later and write down.

Question 1 (a) How do we supplement the traditional description of the economy in order to compare an economy with a medium of exchange to one without one? (b) What do we learn when we have done that?

To this we can straight away add a further question, which as yet has not been answered and which seems important. One of the traditional advantages claimed for a monetary over a barter economy is that the former permits a far greater division of labour than does the latter. But this raises two related difficulties. If we want to make sense of this proposition with classical convex production sets, then a barter equilibrium will have to be Pareto-inefficient and the terms at which goods exchange will have to differ between agents or some other important feature in the description of an equilibrium must be missing. Alternatively, if, as I believe, the advantages of the division of labour are to be understood as stemming from important increasing returns to scale to specialization, then we face well known problems. In particular, it is not clear that Starr-like approximation methods of dealing with them will not throw out the baby with the bath water. In any case, I write

Question 2 How do we study the connection claimed to exist between the method of exchange and the division of labour?

It is possible to bypass the questions posed so far and to start with an economy which already has a medium of exchange. But even so practically oriented an economist as Keynes felt bound to ask why we have the particular medium we do have. Indeed, as I shall argue later, this is an eminently practical question. His answer, given in a largely incomprehensible chapter, turned on the relative stability of wages in terms of different potential media. As far as I know, no one has succeeded in making this into a theory. Nor do I know of any satisfactory modern discussion of the question. In any case, I pose it.

Question 3 What essential features of an economy must be captured by a model if it is to account for the use, or exclusive use, of a particular medium of exchange?

This question too has often been bypassed and the analysis started at the point where the medium of exchange is an intrinsically worthless one, i.e. fiat money. To do this, Patinkin, for instance, and latterly Clower and his many followers have simply stipulated that 'only money buys goods.' This becomes an axiom of the model and it is not a harmless one. In particular, it should be rather sharply distinguished from the related but basically quite different axiom that the ability to acquire goods is conditional on the ability to dispose of goods. It is not the case that the distinction between effective and notional demand depends logically on a particular, or indeed on any, medium of exchange.

By accepting the procedure of axiomatizing the use of fiat money, this must still be made consistent with a theory of the economy and this theory cannot be Arrow–Debreu. For unless we have a theory in which exchange takes place at each date, it will be difficult to account for the holding of the worthless medium of exchange at each date. Nowadays we say that we must study a sequence economy.

There are still many unsolved conceptual and technical problems to be solved in the formulation of such an economy. Foley, Hahn, Kurz, Heller, Starrett and others have studied the sequential structure as arising from transaction costs, while Radner has given the more fundamental interpretation in terms of the differential information available to agents. Not a great deal of progress has so far been made with allowing for the intrinsic non-convexities of transaction costs or for the intrinsic public good aspect of at least some information. But these matters, while importantly related, are not at the centre of the monetary stage, and once again they can be, at least partly, bypassed by simply postulating a sequential structure, i.e. by *a priori* enumerating the markets on which trade can take place. But I return to some of these matters when I discuss the ideas of liquidity.

As far as I know, sequence economies were first studied by the Swedish economists in the 1930s and then given a general equilibrium formulation by Hicks. At a certain level we know what we are about when we model them, while at another we still seem much at sea. I pose some of the most important questions here and leave certain other, more technical, ones until later.

The moment we study sequence economies we must supplement the description of agents given so far by their expectations. Of course, in the Arrow–Debreu description of commodities, expectations in the sense of probability distribution over states of nature are included in the notion of preferences. So the novelty, as far as that model is concerned, is that we must adjoin at least expectations concerning future terms at which trade can take place. These will be conditional expectations. One very non-

Keynesian proposal is to take the expected price to be conditioned by the state of nature and so independent of observed prices. Sonderman, Green, Grandmont and others have studied models where the expectations are a map from observed prices into a suitable space of probability distributions of prices. In any case, a more or less uncertain future casts a shadow over the present, and not only are we closer to Keynes but, more importantly, to reality.

The precise formulation of this class of models has revealed technical problems which are more than technical. For instance, to name just two, there is a difficulty arising from the possibility of unbounded actions, e.g. borrowing and lending, as well as difficulties with bankruptcy. One says: no one can borrow more than a certain amount at any price as a matter of common sense, but is left with the task of modelling this as a matter of rational choice. There is also the question of what managers of firms whose shares may be held by agents with diverse expectations exactly are supposed to do. Although recent work by Diamond, Stiglitz, Dreze, Wilson, Radner and Leland has cast some light, much is still in darkness. But there are heroic assumptions, some of the most heroic, I fear, in Arrow–Hahn, which at least allow one to proceed.

Once a sequence formulation of the Walrasian economy has been achieved, new equilibrium concepts become available. In particular, one would wish to distinguish between the equilibrium of an economy at a moment in time-temporary equilibrium and equilibrium through time. The definition of the latter is not now obvious since the underlying randomness, say, of the states of nature, combined with spot trading at each date, will at best generate a price distribution. Radner has done some pioneering work here, but other sources of randomness, e.g. of tastes of endowments and an associated equilibrium concept, have been studied by Hildenbrandt, Malinvaud and others. For my present purposes I shall however concentrate largely on the short period and so only write

Question 4 Has it been possible to construct a logically consistent model of short-period Walrasian equilibrium; i.e., does such an equilibrium exist? How palatable are the assumptions?

But we want more. In particular, we wish to accommodate money in this construction and so want to ensure that, in any short-period equilibrium there might be, money has a positive exchange value. Here there seem to be continued difficulties. For instance, sometimes it is assumed that money is the only storeable good (Grandmont), which makes it both rather uninteresting and certainly not promising for Keynesian speculation. (I might note here in parenthesis that the sequence structure ensures that one can use a Bellman dynamic programming function which has the money stock as an argument, that this function in general behaves like a utility function, and that one need not have money as an argument of the latter.) Sometimes brute force is used, as when it is assumed that only money buys goods *and* that the current receipts of money from sales cannot all be used for current purchases (Grandmont). Sometimes a bond is introduced, as well as money, but we find that while the agent can issue bonds he cannot buy them (Grandmont and Laroque). Finally, the speculative motive, together with an expectational hypothesis called uniform tightness, which I discuss later, is invoked to ensure the desired result (Younes). This leaves the question open of whether the functioning of a monetary economy depends on uncertainty. In any case we certainly have

Question 5 Can one ensure a positive exchange value of money in every short-period equilibrium without making money uninteresting or making rather odd assumptions? Can this task be performed for an economy which has either single-valued expectations or risk-neutral agents?

Suppose these two last equations are answered satisfactorily. One would notice one important Keynesian feature: not only would the equilibrium hang on the bootstraps of a conjectured future; it would also feel the dead weight of the past since it is the latter which alone conditions expectations. If one then agrees with Keynes that fastidious and unpretentious people do not concern themselves with the long run, one will say that a large part of an explanation of what we observe today is to be found in what happened yesterday so that economic theory is given a historical context.

Just trying to accommodate money in our model has thus profound implications for the model we construct and the conclusions we can draw. For instance, well-known efficiency propositions seem to die a natural death in this enterprise. On the other hand, this is all the Keynesian juice which we can extract. Equilibrium is equilibrium, and so it would appear that, for instance, at a positive equilibrium wage labour markets clear. There is no involuntary unemployment, and while money has forced us back into an older sequential framework, it is not as such of any far-reaching significance.

It is at this point that it is easy to lose one's nerve and that nerves have been lost. One line of argument – I believe it is to be found in Los Angeles – is simply to say that, yes indeed, there is no involuntary unemployment. If it is supposed that heterogeneous labour does not fully know the current wage structure and the places where particular wages are offered, then some of the labour will be searching rather than working. But there is a voluntary and an inevitable feature of any equilibrium in which information imperfections have been modelled. I do not wish to deny the interest and importance of the search phenomenon. Mortenson, for instance, has shown how it might be handled properly in a general equilibrium framework, but I do not think that it remotely catches the real problems of unemployment.

The reason is really rather straightforward. Suppose it to be the case that there is always some wage and some job a man could have. If he does not accept it, then he is not voluntarily unemployed but voluntarily unemployed in *that* job and at *that* wage. He is unemployed involuntarily at the kind of job and wage which the past has led him to expect as available after customary search. One still wants models which are rich enough to enable us to study the obvious fact that there are times when many more are unemployed in that sense than there are at other times.

There is another line of argument – it used to be a favourite one after the war – for instance, Klein was to interpret Keynes as saying that a short-run Walrasian equilibrium may not exist because of a low interest elasticity of demand for investment or a very high interest elasticity of demand for money. Unfortunately, in the context of the models put foward by these authors, it is easy to show that the argument is false.

It certainly would then appear that one will have to argue that all the well-known phenomena which we think of as Keynesian are features of disequilibrium and/or that a Walrasian equilibrium has abstracted crucially from some important real features. Both these approaches are much studied just now especially, since Clower and Leijonhufvud have looked seriously again at the General Theory rather than at 'Mr Keynes and the Classics'. So let us, for a moment, return to the beginning.

In the Walrasian world all agents are price-takers and the only signals relevant to their actions are prices, and their expectations concern only prices and states of nature. But when we think of Keynesian theory – and this not only because it is a macro-theory – we take agents' actions as also conditioned by quantities. The consumption function seems an obvious example as does the accelerator. Now formally price-taking may be thought of as consisting of two separate, and, to some extent at least, independent, parts: (a) the agent believes that all his transactions must be on terms which have been given to him, and (b) the agent believes that all his intended transactions at these terms can be carried out. Certainly (a) does not logically entail (b). If the latter is removed from our specification of what we mean by price-taking, then it is plain that agents will now have to form expectations not only as to prices but as to the transactions they will in fact achieve, and these expectations in turn will not only depend on observed past prices but also on observed past transactions.

This modification – much less drastic than others that have been proposed – requires a new model, and I know of no formal one in the literature. But it also requires a modification in the notion of short-period equilibrium. For if I, for instance, expect to sell my labour at the going wage only with a certain probability, then not actually selling it in a given short-period realization is not self-evidently inconsistent with a notion of equilibrium. Of course, the not selling must be made consistent with any actual buying, and so one must be careful to get the Cloweresque budget constraint right. The importance for monetary matters of this approach is two-fold: (a) the risk of not being able to sell is, as Foley and Hellwig recently showed, a good explanation for holding money, and (b) the money stocks available to agents as well as the price of loans is an important determinant of what can be bought when one has not sold. In any case, we have

Question 6 What is the appropriate short-period equilibrium notion for an economy which is price-taking only in the sense of (a)? Is a logically consistent model possible, and will it under plausible assumptions allow a positive equilibrium price of money and involuntary unemployment in the sense that more labour would have been sold at the going price if it had been in demand?

Although, as I have said, I know of no formal answers to this particular question, a related one has recently been studied. Suppose that, in the now usual, short-period Walrasian model, we impose the conditions that the money wage shall not be lower than some pre-assigned positive number. Then, as the classics and neoclassics knew, we cannot be sure that we have sufficient flexibility in the remaining prices to ensure the existence of a market-clearing equilibrium. In the footsteps of Dreze, Grandmont and Laroque modify both the theory of the agents' actions and the notion of an equilibrium. The agent is now constrained by the ration of work – which may be less than he desires at the going wage which he receives. His expectations are taken as independent of this information but need not be so taken, as Benassy has shown. With a number of assumptions, some of which I take up again, an equilibrium with rationing is shown to exist. What does this equilibrium amount to? No more than the proposition that all non-rationed markets can be cleared when consumers' actions are consistent with their being rationed.

But really, as Grandmont and Laroque argue, this is not much use to anything Keynesian. The idea that the Keynesian revolution consisted in showing the possibility of unemployment pseudo-equilibrium when money wages are fixed or cannot fall below a certain level one alas encounters in textbooks, but it is nonsense. Quite properly, Grandmont and Laroque notice that their model, given the expectation assumption still to be discussed, always has a nice full employment equilibrium when the money wage is bounded below by zero. They say that this shows that reduction in money wages can cure unemployment in this construction, but of course they don't mean that and they are only asserting the existence of a money wage at which the pleasant consequences are possible. So this way out of the Walrasian tunnel to Keynes is not promising.

It is worth noticing that the fixing of the minimum wage in terms of money is quite inessential – similar results are obtainable if it were fixed in terms of peanuts. Indeed, money has no peculiar role in all of this other than being the only connecting link between the present and the future. Moreover, it would not matter if money could be eaten and if it gave satisfaction. In fact, there is no particular connection between money and anything in particular.

In any case, the next step which has been taken seems to me to be in the right direction but not free from muddle. Certainly the suspicion that equilibrium analysis only yields equilibrium seems as well founded as the view that perhaps the peculiar role of money and phenomena like involuntary unemployment are perhaps best studied in the context of disequilibria. A more drastic departure from Arrow–Debreu seems called for. But it is easy to overdo the novelty of what one is about and easy to believe that one has uncovered as essential some feature which in fact is only incidental.

A number of recent authors from Leijonhufvud to Iwai and the French have picked on market-clearing prices as the culprits. Grandmont and Laroque go so far as to claim that neoclassical economics assumes that prices adjust instantaneously to clear markets. They don't like this assumption, although I have never myself encountered it anywhere. Certainly they, as well as Iwai and Debassy, want to do without the auctioneer and allow prices to be set by agents whose actions are part of the economy. As Arrow noted, the assumption of perfect competition makes this programme hard, almost certainly not possible. The reasons are obvious and do not require repetition. Some form of monopolistic competition may therefore have to be modelled if we believe that some of the most important phenomena are only to be understood by viewing the economy along some actual trajectory and by studying the actual process of price determination. In any event, the view has gained ground that a Keynesian economy essentially requires the postulate of non-perfect competition. A happy conjuncture is thus achieved between the two major theoretical innovations of the 1930s. I am happy to see it although, unlike some of the authors mentioned, I do not think, as indeed Keynes did not think, that there is here a matter of logical entailment. Certainly we could study a world in which producers believed that their actions could not affect the terms at which they can trade but who do not exactly know what these terms are. They set a price experimentally, as it were. Adjustments can then be studied without the auctioneer. But let me write

Question 7 Can Keynesian phenomena be understood in a model of perfect competition?

The remaining steps are now rather clear, although some technical ingenuity is required. We want to take a snapshot of the economy during a non-tâtonnement adjustment path, and we want no truck with auctioneers. We are concerned with real and not with model time. Since adjustments are not instantaneous, the prices in our snapshot period may be taken as determined by the expectations and happenings of an earlier moment. Quantities available may or may not be fully determined as well and certainly may have to be rationed. But also in the snapshot period actions will depend on expectations concerned with the future – e.g. investment or the hiring of labour – and these expectations will in turn depend on current events. One needs a consistent model of how the economy emerges at the end of the snapshot. This consistent model is called by Grandmont–Laroque an equilibrium with rationing, but sometimes they and their predecessor Debassy call it a Keynesian equilibrium for short. Work in the same spirit but in macro-terms has been done by Solow and Stiglitz and by Grossman; but they do not call it equilibrium, and I rather think they are right not to do so. In a pure exchange context similar rationing models were studied by Hahn–Negishi and by Arrow–Hahn. The most striking resemblance of this new approach is however to Robertson and his Swedish predecessors. They did not ration anything except available work but postulated sufficient inventories to fill excess demand flows. The actions of agents depended on expectations, including quantity expectations, and in the snapshot period households could only spend – or attempt to spend – what they had earned and accumulated before the period started. I hope that I may be forgiven the piety of suggesting that Robertson is eminently worth reading.

It is as plain as a pikestaff that in any given snapshot period agents may be willing to sell more labour than they can sell. Exactly the same is true in a perfect competition non-tâtonnement world with an auctioneer. Marshall and Pigou would have had no difficulties in agreeing that such markets can be observed. So what makes this picture Keynesian? What has money got to do with it? Certainly it is my understanding of the General Theory that Keynes would have regarded such moments on an adjustment path as uninteresting in a world which could get along without money.

Now one can ask what would this momentary picture look like if it had started with lower money wages. Grandmont and Laroque notice that, since the present demand for labour must depend on further prospects imagined by non-competitive producers, it may happen that lower money wages do not go with a greater demand for labour. Correct. But the same argument applies if wages were quoted in terms of butter, and that leaves one of the most famous Keynesian contentions unaccounted for. This, as you recall, was that his predecessors were mistaken when they did not consider the consequences of wages being quoted in money terms. Since the model I am now discussing has no durable physical assets, that other Keynesian enemy of neoclassical economics, liquidity preference, is also given no role. So most of the meat is in the monopolistic competition postulate which makes agents act on quantity as well as on price expectations. Of course, it may be that this is all the meat there is to be found and that Keynes was mistaken in giving such a central role to monetary matters. We have

Question 8 Is money peripheral in a theory of involuntary unemployment?

I have now reached the end of a particular line. Patinkin was the first to see that there were problems in the integration of money into traditional neoclassical value theory. He was not concerned with 'existence' and left some gaps. His expectation hypotheses were not elaborate. But he set the stage and also gave another boost to neoclassical, or what my colleague Professor Robinson more robustly calls 'bastard', Keynesianism. The real balance effect came of age and echoes still in the works I have been considering. The question was, Do there exist prices, including a positive price of money, at which neoclassical short-period equilibrium can be shown to exist? The false answer was 'yes'. It was false because insufficient attention had been paid to problems connected with price expectations and because debt inherited from the past and denominated in money had been ignored. Arrow and Debreu had to be thoroughly digested before we understood what the real questions were. Many of these are conceptual and have to do with what kind of equilibrium, or indeed whether equilibrium of any kind, is useful to utilize and how to model decisions, actions and allocations in a world in which money can find a home. Existence questions continue to occupy us, but they are not at the centre of the stage. I doubt whether one can follow some authors who, having demonstrated the requirement of some assumption for an existence proof, draw the ominous conclusion that if it were not met capitalism could not function. None the less, such proofs remain an essential intellectual discipline at present. Although I have been critical, I believe that at present there are more noses pointing in the right direction than for some time past.

Before I turn to somewhat more technical matters there are two further topics which I take up briefly.

The first concerns the connection between macroeconomic models which are the traditional tool of monetary theorists and general equilibrium analysis. We will surely agree that it is a singular circumstance that at most universities there are courses labelled macroeconomics and courses labelled microeconomics, and that what one is taught in one is quite different from what is provided in the other. There is some progress in getting to grips with this anomaly to report. Recently Hildenbrandt and Grandmont have shown how, in a model in which there is a distribution of agents by type, one may legitimately speak of an abstract, or representative, agent. The line of research which has led to quantity signals being of significance also promises a line to the otherwise puzzling appearance of quantities as arguments of macro-functions. But whether there are important macroeconomic phenomena which cannot be captured by microtheory, as is the case in physics, remains an open question. None the less, we seem to be in better shape to build the required bridge than we have been in the past.

The second topic concerns the long run. The economy staggers from one 'short period' to another and we certainly want to study this path. The first step has been to start with the abstraction of a long-run equilibrium. However, this should now be a different animal from the one so much studied in the 1960s because informational deficiencies, lacking markets and uncertainty seem intrinsic to the enterprise when we want to study money. My own view is that without these features not very much can be learned that one can have confidence in. Thus, in the well-known work of Tobin and of Cass and Yeari, it is a common feature that money has no intrinsic role in the economy. For Tobin 'money matters' in long-run equilibrium only because each new generation is given a gift of wealth (here, money). For Cass and Yeari, 'money matters' because it is an asset not directly used in production. In neither model does money have any intrinsic significance.

Indeed, the question, Does money matter? – a very old one in economics – is not well posed if we compare two economies exactly alike in their exchange and production opportunities except that one also has money. To anyone who has ever tried barter, the question thus posed must surely seem absurd. It is clearly desirable to study economies which have been modelled in a way in which the phenomena which account for the use of money are intrinsic. One can then ask how alternative institutional arrangements might operate or indeed how monetary policy would manifest itself.

That this is not only theoretically correct but also very promising has recently been demonstrated in a brilliant paper by Lucas. His is the only attempt known to me to study the consequences of the informational confusion which may be caused by varieties in the monetary supply. This is done in the context of a stochastic model. His equilibrium notion is close to Radner's statistical equilibrium, and he shows how the equilibrium distribution of prices may be dependent on the behaviour of the money supply. In the process he also shows how the Phillips curve may, when statistically well confirmed, not imply what it has been taken to imply. Certainly, Lucas has shown how much has been missed when one grafts money into deterministic growth models.

It cannot be said, however, that the long-run story is in a satisfactory state as yet. There are for instance technical problems connected with both a finitely and an infinitely long-run model. In the former, Starr, Heller and Hahn have had to introduce unsatisfactory terminal conditions, while the infinite model is available only in a deterministic simple life-cycle form. But there are also many serious conceptual problems.

On the other hand, one can hardly study inflation in the context of monetary equilibrium. It is perhaps not surprising therefore that theorists at least are so much at sea on this matter. For instance, in a deterministic old-fashioned long-run model one finds that 'fully anticipated inflation does not matter.' What inflation has been more fully anticipated than the present one? And it certainly seems to matter. When uncertainty is taken into account that makes good sense, but a good formalism is not available.

REFERENCES

Foley, D. K. (1970), 'Economic Equilibrium with Costly Marketing', *Journal of Economic Theory*, 2.

Grandmont, G. M. (1980), 'On the Temporary Competitive Equilibrium', unpublished paper, University of California, Berkeley.

Grandmont, G. M. and Younes, Y. (1973), 'On the Efficiency of Monetary Equilibrium', *Review of Economic Studies*, **40**.

Green, J. R. (1973), 'Temporary General Equilibrium in a Sequential Trading Model with Spot and Future Transactions', *Econometrica*, **41**.

Hahn, F. H. (1962), 'On the Stability of Pure Exchange Equilibrium', *International Economic Review*, 3.

Hahn, F. H. (1971), 'Equilibrium with Transaction Costs', *Econometrica*, **39**.

Hahn, F. H. (1973), 'On Transaction Costs, Inessential Sequence Economies and Money', *Review of Economic Studies*, **40**.

Heller, W. H. (1972), 'The Holding of Idle Money Balances in General Equilibrium', unpublished paper.

Klein, L. (1966), *The Keynesian Revolution*, 2nd edn, Macmillan, New York.

Kurz, M. (1974), 'Equilibrium with Transaction Cost and Money in a Single Market Exchange Economy', *Journal of Economic Theory*, 7.

Negishi, T. (1961), 'On the Formation of Prices', *International Economic Review*, 2.

Niehans, J. (1969), 'Money in a Static Theory of Optimal Payment Arrangements', *Journal of Money, Credit and Banking*, 1.

Ostroy, J. and Starr, Ross M. (1977), 'Money and Decentralisation of Exchange', *Econometrica*, 41.

Radner, R. (1970), 'Existence of Equilibrium of Prices and Price Expectations in a Sequence of Markets', unpublished paper, University of California.

Radner, R. (1971), 'General Equilibrium with Uncertainty', *Econometrica*, 39.

Starr, R. M. (1972), 'The Structure of Exchange in Barter and Monetary Economics', *Quarterly Journal of Economics*, 86.

Starrett, D. (1973), 'Inefficiency and the Demand for "Money" in a Sequence Economy', *Review of Economic Studies*, 40.

Uzawa, H. (1962), 'On the Stability of Edgeworth's Barter Prices', *International Economics Review*, 3.

2

The General Equilibrium Theory of Money: A Comment

Recent discussions on the relationship between classical and Keynesian monetary theory have done much to clarify what has for some time been an obscure subject.[1,2] For some considerable time now it had been customary to argue that the Keynesian system differed from that of the classical only with respect to certain empirical assumptions, for instance, rigid money wages and/or rigid interest rates and/or interest inelasticity of the investment and savings schedules (see, e.g., Hicks, 1937; Modigliani, 1944). It is the great contribution of Professor Patinkin and others to have shown that the classical system is also inconsistent or indeterminate. A strict classical system which is also consistent is a system in which money acts only as a unit of account, and is thus incapable of providing a monetary theory, while a classical system in which money also acts as a medium of exchange is indeterminate (and possibly inconsistent). Once these shortcomings are rectified, it is possible to see what sort of empirical assumptions must be made in order to lead to such Keynesian conclusions as (say) the possibility of permanent unemployment.

In a recent paper Professor Patinkin (1949–50; henceforth referred to as 'Patinkin') has used such a 'corrected' classical system to re-examine certain propositions in the theory of money. In particular, he has attempted to show that in certain circum-

---

[1] I am greatly indebted to Mr W. M. Gorman for a very helpful discussion of this paper and for weeding out certain errors from a first draft. I have also had very useful advice from Mr C. Kennedy and Mr Jan Graaf. I am, of course, solely responsible for such mistakes as remain.

[2] See Patinkin (1948, 1949, 1951). Other participants in the discussion have been Hickman (1950), Leontief (1950), Phipps (1950) and Brunner (1951); also Marschak (1950).

stances the classical propositions concerning the independence of the rate of interest of the quantity of (nominal) money and (real) liquidity preference are correct, and he has thus 'rehabilitated' parts of classical monetary theory.

It is the purpose of this paper to show that:

1   Patinkin's system is over-determinate in the special case where 'distributional effects' of bond holdings can be ignored;
2   this is due to the exclusion of bond earnings from the consumer's utility function;
3   Patinkin's model is unsuitable for a discussion of the rate of interest, and certain 'dynamic' elements must be introduced;
4   little meaning can be attached to 'shifts in liquidity preference' in Patinkin's model;
5   it is not correct to argue that an equiproportionate fall (rise) in all goods prices will necessarily lead to a substitution of goods (bonds and money) for bonds and money (goods).

I

Patinkin's 'corrected' classical model can be summed up as follows: given that a monetary theory is one which can explain (a) the absolute level of prices and (b) the existence of positive stocks of money (see Marschak, 1950, pp. 1–2), it follows, because of (b), that in any model of the economy capable of providing a monetary theory, the demand and supply of at least one good (or service) must be a function not only of relative but also of absolute prices. For in such a model a given change in the price level will make at least some individuals (holders of positive money stocks) better or worse off and, therefore, will affect their purchase and sales plans.[3] In a perfectly general model of this kind, therefore, we can include a term involving the absolute level of prices, as well as relative prices, in all demand and supply equations. If we also assume that individuals are only concerned with the real value of their assets,[4] then this term will be the real value of assets held at the beginning of the period. If now all goods prices were, say, to rise in a certain proportion, then the real value of stocks of goods held at the beginning of the period remains the same, since the price of any individual good held increases in the

[3] Except in the trivial case where income effects are zero.
[4] Patinkin calls this 'the absence of "money illusion"' (Patinkin, p. 43).

same proportion as the price level. This, however, is not true for stocks of money and bonds, for their prices are assumed constant, and their real value will, therefore, fall. Hence all demand and supply equations will be affected by an equiproportionate change in all goods prices. If, however, the stock of money and bonds (at constant bond prices) had increased in the same proportion as prices of goods, then the real value of assets would have remained unchanged and all demand and supply equations would have remained unaffected.

Let us now see what happens when the quantity of money increases. Let us first assume that there are no bonds (i.e. also no interest). Then if the increase in the quantity of money is accompanied by a rise in all goods prices in the same proportion as the quantity of money has increased, the real value of assets will remain the same. We now make Patinkin's assumption of the absence of a money illusion. Individuals are concerned only with the real value of their assets; hence any change in the parameters of the system which leaves the real value of assets unchanged will leave all purchase and sale plans unchanged.[5] This assumption ensures that the stipulated rise in goods prices (following an increase in the stock of money) will leave the real situation, and hence equilibrium, unaffected.

This system, without bonds, is fully determinate. For there will be $(n - 1)$ excess demand equations for goods, all expressed as a function of the $(n - 1)$ price ratios, and of the real value of assets (defined as the money value of assets divided by an index of prices), and there will be one equation defining the price level. The excess demand equation for money will, by Walras' Law, follow from the $(n - 1)$ excess demand equations for goods. Thus we have n equations to determine $(n - 1)$ relative prices and the price index, i.e. n unknowns.

Let us now introduce bonds. Patinkin makes the following assumptions: (a) the net value of bonds for the community as a whole is zero,[6] and (b) the distributional effects consequent upon a change in the real value of bonds can be ignored. Put differently, the actions of debtors and creditors consequent upon an equiproportional change in goods prices will cancel out. Since, as we

---

[5] That is, these equations are homogeneous of degree zero in the prices of goods and the initial stocks of money and bonds.

[6] That is, in the notation of the text, $\bar{Z}_{n-1} = \Sigma_a^m \bar{Z}_{n-1a}$ (where m is the number of individuals). 'That is every debt is owed by one member of the community to another' (Patinkin, p. 48). (It should be remembered that $\bar{Z}_{n-1a} \gtrless 0$.)

shall see presently, future goods and bond earnings are not included by Patinkin in the utility function of the individual, this means that income effects of a change in the real value of bonds, for the community as a whole, are assumed to cancel out; i.e., the aggregate income effect is zero.

We will now show that Patinkin's system is over-determined. Let us write the budget constraint for the ath individual:[7]

$$\sum_i^{n-2} \frac{P_i}{P}(Z_{ia} - \bar{Z}_{ia}) + \frac{Z_{n-1a} - \bar{Z}_{n-1a}}{P_r} + \frac{Z_{na} - \bar{Z}_{na}}{P} - \frac{\bar{Z}_{n-1a}}{P} = 0 \quad (2.1)$$

where P_i $(i = 1, \ldots, n-2)$ are the $(n-2)$ prices, P is the (defined) price index of goods, Z_{ia} $(i = 1, \ldots, n-2)$ are the desired and $\bar{Z}_{ia}$ $(i = 1, \ldots, n-2)$ the actual stock of goods, and $Z_{n-1a}, \bar{Z}_{n-1a}, Z_{na}$ and $\bar{Z}_{na}$ are the desired and actual stocks of bonds and money respectively, all for the ath individual; r is the rate of interest equal to the inverse of the price or bonds. Equation (2.1), therefore, says that the real planned holdings of goods, bonds and money, minus the initial real stocks of these, minus the real income from bonds during that period must be zero. Utility is assumed a function of the Z_{ia}, Z_{n-1a}/rP and Z_{na}/P, i.e. of the planned real stocks of goods, bonds and money. Maximizing as usual, we obtain equations of the form:

$$\frac{U_i}{U_t} = \frac{P_i}{P} \qquad \begin{array}{l} (i = 1, \ldots, n-2) \\ (t = n-1, n) \end{array} \qquad (2.2)$$

where U_i and U_t denote differentiation with respect to the ith and tth argument.

Let the dependent variables of the system be $(n-2)$ desired stocks of goods $Z_{ia}, Z_{n-1a}/rP$ and Z_{na}/P. Then the solution of (2.1) and (2.2) will show these as functions of P_i/P $(i = 1, \ldots, n-2)$, and of total real initial assets. It is seen that r nowhere occurs separately.[8] We can, therefore, write the $(n-1)$ excess demand equations of the individual as:

$$X_{ia} = Z_{ia}\left(\frac{P_1}{P} \ldots \frac{P_{n-2}}{P}, \sum_i^{n-2} \frac{P_i}{P} \bar{Z}_{ia} + \frac{\bar{Z}_{n-1a}}{rP} + \frac{\bar{Z}_{na}}{P} + \frac{\bar{Z}_{n-1a}}{P}\right) - \bar{Z}_{ia}$$

$$(i = 1, \ldots, n-2) \quad (2.3)$$

---

[7] This and equation (2.2) are exactly the same as in Patinkin, pp. 48–9, and therefore need not be discussed in detail.

[8] It is here that we diverge from Patinkin. Patinkin makes r occur twice in the demand function, once alone and once in the denominator of the 'real value of bonds' term.

$$X_{n-1a} = P_r Z_{n-1a} \left(\frac{P_i}{P} \cdots \frac{P_{n-2}}{P}, \sum_i^{n-2} \frac{P_i}{P} Z_{ia} + \frac{\bar{Z}_{n-1a}}{_r P} + \frac{\bar{Z}_{na}}{P} + \frac{\bar{Z}_{n-1a}}{P} \right)$$

$$- \bar{Z}_{n-1a} \tag{2.4}$$

The Walras identity. (2.5)

These equations now imply that (a) the demand for any good, or for bonds, is a function of the $(n-2)$ relative goods prices and the real initial holdings of goods, bonds, and money plus the real income from bonds, all taken together; (b) inspection of any one of these equations reveals that a doubling of all prices will not leave the demand for the good (or bonds) unaffected, simply because the real initial asset holdings of money and goods are diminished. The equations are, therefore, homogeneous of degree zero not in the prices but in the prices and $\bar{Z}_{n-1a}$ and $\bar{Z}_{na}$. The system (2.3)–(2.5) is, therefore, not a classical system.

Now aggregating for the system, and making Patinkin's assumptions concerning the absence of distributional effects of bonds, the term $\bar{Z}_{n-1a}/_r P$ disappears from all the demand equations. We must also remember that, if the net holdings of bonds is zero,[9] the aggregated excess demand equations for bonds will not have an initial stock term. Letting X_i stand for the excess demand for the ith good, our aggregated equilibrium system becomes:

$$X_i = Z_i \left(\frac{P_1}{P} \cdots \frac{P_{n-2}}{P}, \sum_i^{n-2} \frac{P_i}{P} Z_i + \frac{\bar{Z}_n}{P} \right) - \bar{Z}_i = 0$$

$$(i = 1, \ldots, n-2) \quad (2.3a)$$

$$X_{n-1} = Z_{n-1} \left(\frac{P_1}{P} \cdots \frac{P_{n-2}}{P}, \sum_i^{n-2} \frac{P_i}{P} Z_i + \frac{\bar{Z}_n}{P} \right) = 0 \tag{2.4a}$$

The Walras identity. (2.5)

(Notice that in (2.4a) we were able to divide across by P_r and thus remove the term from our system.)

We now have $(n-1)$ excess demand equations (we can always ignore the Walras identity) plus one equation defining the price index, all in all n equations to determine $(n-2)$ price ratios and the price level. The system is thus over-determined.

---

[9] For by assumption $\Sigma_a^m \bar{Z}_{n-1a} = 0$ where $\bar{Z}_{n-1a} \gtrless 0$ and we can thus divide through by P_r.

Let us translate this into economics. In Patinkin's model only Z_{n-1a}/rP enters the utility function and not Z_{n-1a}/P. Hence individuals are concerned only with the real value of bond stocks. If now the rate of interest changes, the real value of bonds will change. But since it is assumed that, if one group substitutes bonds for money and goods, another group substitutes goods and money for bonds in such a way that the actions of the two groups cancel out, a change in the rate of interest can have no effect on the system. Moreover, if some people, who previously held no bonds at all, now wish to hold some, there must be another group who wish to borrow more (since there is zero net indebtedness for the whole system), and their respective effects on the excess demand for money and goods will again cancel out by assumption. Hence the rate of interest can be anything at all, and even if Patinkin's system were consistent it would be indeterminate in the rate of interest.

An alternative intuitive way of looking at the problem is the following.[10] Since the aggregate income effect of changes in bond values is assumed zero, this is equivalent (in analytical terms) to assuming that no one holds any bonds at the beginning of the period, but may plan to hold some at the end of the period. This means that all barred bond terms drop out of the budget constraint (2.1). Hence the demand for goods and the demand for bonds cannot be a function of initial bond holdings. Thus a change in the rate of interest cannot affect the demand for goods. It also cannot affect the real demand for bonds, for the latter is a function of relative goods prices and initial real stocks of money and goods only. A change in the rate of interest will therefore lead to a change in the number of bonds until their real value is the same as it was before the change in the rate. Thus, since the real situation is unaffected by changes in the rate of interest, the latter can be anything at all.

Now it would appear that this result is due to two assumptions made by Patinkin:

1   absence of distributional effect;
2   absence of a bond-earning term (Z_{n-1a}/P) in the utility function.

If assumption 1 were not made, then, as Patinkin well realizes, the quantity of money would affect the rate of interest, so we need not concern ourselves with it here.

---

[10] This was suggested to me by Mr Jan Graaf.

If Z_{n-1a}/P is included in the utility function, then the rate of interest will again reappear in the excess demand equations.[11] But the difficulty now arises of how to interpret this new system. The difficulty really is that Patinkin's model is highly, if not completely, unsuitable for a discussion of interest rates. This is so for the following reasons.

1 In a static world without price uncertainty and in which prices are assumed constant over the future, in which there should be complete indifference between asset holdings, Patinkin's model implies that some sort of special (unexplained) utility is attached to assets. In particular, it is difficult to see why, if earnings from bonds are excluded from the utility function, anyone should ever wish to hold bonds. Either earnings are included in the utility function, or we must include planned stocks of goods, bonds and money over future periods.

2 In particular, in a pure exchange model together with Patinkin's assumptions, the rate of interest only makes sense in so far as it determines the combination of future and present goods. For a change in the rate of interest (a) changes the capital value of bonds, the effect of which on the system is assumed to be zero, and (b) affects the distribution of assets over time. Therefore, the budget constraint of the individual must include the present real discounted value of all assets expected to be held over the economic horizon.

3 Individuals borrow only if they expect their future income to be rising. In a pure exchange economy this is tantamount to assuming that some individuals expect prices (or certain stocks they hold) to rise, while others may expect them to be constant, or not to rise by as much, or to fall (i.e. lenders). Expectations must, therefore, be introduced into the analysis. Since in the

---

[11] The possibility that r would reappear in the excess demand equation was first suggested to me by Mr Gorman. That it will, in fact, do so can easily be seen. We have:

$$U = U\left(Z_{1a} \ldots Z_{n-2a}, \frac{Z_{n-1a}}{P}, \frac{Z_n}{P}\right) \tag{1}$$

to be maximized subject to the budget constraint (2.1) (multiplied by P) in text. This will yield for the $(n-1)$th argument:

$$U_{n-1} = \lambda \frac{P}{r} \tag{2}$$

where λ is a Lagrange multiplier. Hence $U_{a-1}/U_n = r$ and this term (r) will appear separately in the excess demand equations.

nature of the problem it is possible that expectations will be inconsistent, and yet that in any one period there is zero excess demand everywhere, it is impossible to deduce 'comparative statics' or 'long-run equilibrium' solutions from an inspection of excess demand equations at one moment of time.

4   If, then, Patinkin's model were adjusted (a) to include earnings from bonds in the utility function, (b) to include future expected assets in both the utility function and the budget constraint, and (c) to make suitable allowances for expectations, then by further suitable assumptions it may be possible to deduce invariance of the interest rate with respect to changes in the quantity of money. It should, however, be noted that these assumptions will turn on the nature of the expectations and elasticities of expectations postulated, and that these assumptions will be of as great importance as the 'distributional' assumption of Patinkin.

5   Lastly, we must note that we are not maintaining that there could be *no* rate of interest in a stationary state in which production is carried on. Our strictures apply only to a stationary economy which is also a pure exchange economy.

We conclude that Patinkin's model as it stands is overdetermined, and, therefore, cannot explain the rate of interest, and that, if Patinkin's model is adjusted as suggested under reason 4 above, the nature of the analysis will be greatly changed. This is not surprising when we remember that an interest theory has been fostered on to the classicals, an interest theory which is derived from a model in which productivity and thrift, in the time-sense understood by those writers, find no place.

Patinkin's discussion of changes in liquidity preference is also difficult to understand. He argues that, if we only concentrate on such shifts in liquidity preference which leave the marginal rate of substitution of bonds for money at the old quantities of these held constant, that then such a shift will not lead to a change in the rate of interest. Thus a shift in liquidity preference entails an attempt not to substitute money for bonds, but on the contrary to substitute money and bonds for goods.

Since, as already noted, Patinkin nowhere explains why anyone holds the particular assets he, in fact, does hold, it is not easy to interpret 'liquidity preference',[12] let alone shifts in the latter.

---

[12] It should be noted that in the absence of 'price uncertainty' and transaction costs, *any* commodity could be held for precautionary motives. I, therefore, do not understand why, in Patinkin's model, there should be liquidity preference in the normal Keynesian sense.

Does not an increased desire to hold money (and bonds) entail the expectation that goods prices are going to fall (or fall more than previously expected)? If so, will not a fall in prices, when no further fall (or increased fall) is expected, lead to a reversal of the tendency to substitute money and bonds for goods? Or is it assumed that individuals suddenly develop a great desire to fondle their money and bonds and a distaste for having real assets? If the latter assumption, together with Patinkin's 'satisfaction equivalence of bonds and money', is made, then no doubt the rate of interest may remain constant. But such assumptions are hardly useful even in a 'model' world.

II

We now turn to a minor, but nevertheless important, point. Patinkin (1949–50) maintains that 'A proportionate change in all (goods) prices will not cause substitution among commodities, but only between commodities as a whole and money' (p. 52). This would lead us to expect a fall in the rate of interest when prices rise, and a rise in the rate of interest when prices fall, and this is rather curious. The following objections can be raised to Professor Patinkin's quoted conclusion.

1   The well-known theorem first put forward by Professor Hicks (1946, pp. 312–13) stating that goods, the prices of which always change in the same proportion, can be treated as a single good, does not imply that there will be no substitution between these goods. All it says is that the total amount spent on these goods will vary in a given manner.

2   Since only real assets, including real money and bond holdings, enter into the consumer's consumption function, an equiproportionate change in goods prices will leave the relative prices of goods, real cash balances and real bond balances unaffected. Hence there will be no substitution effect but only an income effect. As is well known, nothing can be predicted from income effects alone (except, of course, that less of something will be consumed).

3   Thus, even if the rise in prices were to lead to a fall in the demand for goods,[13] we could still not say that it would lead to an increased demand for bonds and money taken together. Professor

---

[13] Patinkin assumes positive income effects.

Patinkin's conclusion, therefore, does not follow from his assumption.

Professor Lange (1944) gets over this difficulty by (a) assuming that the excess demand for real cash balances is constant and (b) including the (real) income from bonds in the utility function. This ensures substitution of either money for goods or money for bonds, and hence the familiar conclusions that an equiproportionate rise in all goods prices (nominal cash balances remaining constant) will tend to raise the rate of interest. Of course, if expectations are introduced this result may be modified.

REFERENCES

Brunner, K. (1951), 'Inconsistency and Indeterminancy in Classical Economics', *Econometrica*, **19**.

Hickman, B. (1950), 'The Determinacy of Absolute Prices in Classical Economic Theory', *Econometrica*, **18**.

Hicks, J. R. (1937), 'Mr Keynes and the Classics', *Econometrica*, **5**.

Hicks, J. R. (1946), *Value and Capital* (2nd edn), Clarendon Press, Oxford.

Lange, O. (1944), *Price Flexibility and Employment*, Cowles Commission for Research in Economics, Monograph no. 8, Principia Press, Bloomington, Indiana.

Leontief, W. (1950), 'The Consistency of the Classical Theory of Money and Prices', *Econometrica*, **18**.

Marschak, J. (1950), 'The Rationale of the Demand for Money and of the "Money Illusion"', *Metroeconomica*, **2**.

Modigliani, F. (1944), 'Liquidity Preference and the Theory of Interest and Money', *Econometrica*, **12**.

Patinkin, Don (1948), 'Relative Prices, Say's Law and the Demand for Money', *Econometrica*, **16**.

Patinkin, Don (1949), 'The Indeterminacy of Absolute Prices in Classical Economic Theory', *Econometrica*, **17**.

Patinkin, Don (1949-50), 'A Reconsideration of the Equilibrium Theory of Money', *Review of Economic Studies*, **45**.

Patinkin, Don (1951), 'The Invalidity of Classical Monetary Theory', *Econometrica*, **19**.

Phipps, C. G. (1950), 'A Note on Patinkin's "Relative Prices"', *Econometrica*, **18**.

3

The Rate of Interest and General Equilibrium Analysis

In spite of the fact that the theory of interest has been exhaustively discussed in the last 20 years, no general agreement seems to have been reached.[1] On the contrary, the area of disagreement seems to have widened in recent times. The dispute between Loanable Funds and Liquidity Preference theorists has flared up again,[2] a number of economists led by Mr Modigliani have sought to re-establish the older classical propositions,[3] while Mr Patinkin has drawn attention to the very special character of some of the Keynesian assumptions.[4] Most of the disputants have this in common: they seek to find one particular supply-and-demand relation (excess demand equation), out of all the supply-and-demand relations which go to make up a general equilibrium system, which can be said to 'determine' the rate of interest. The dispute turns on which out of a number of such relations to choose.

The purpose of this paper is two-fold. First, we shall show that Mr Modigliani's classical revival comes up against certain logical objections to which Mr Patinkin has drawn attention, and must therefore be rejected. The excuse for doing so is partly that Mr Modigliani's model, in spite of Patinkin's criticisms, seems to enjoy

[1] I have had valuable comments on a first draft by Mr R. F. Harrod, Mrs Joan Robinson and Mr H. G. Johnson. I have also benefited from correspondence with Mr D. Patinkin, although we have been unable to reach agreement on a number of points. All errors, of course, are my own.

[2] E.g., Fellner and Somers (1941, pp. 43–8; 1949); Klein (1950, pp. 236–41); Brunner (1950, pp. 247–51); Fellner and Somers (1950, pp. 242–5, 252). See also Johnson (1951–2, pp. 90–105) and Robertson (1951–2, pp. 105–11).

[3] Modigliani (1944, pp. 45–88). (This has been reprinted in *Readings in Monetary Theory* (1952), and subsequent page references will refer to this book.)

[4] See Patinkin's three articles on classical equilibrium systems (1948, 1949, 1951); also Patinkin (1949–50, 1952–3).

a considerable following, and partly because we shall criticize the model in a slightly different way from that followed by Patinkin. Second, we shall draw attention to the divergence which exists between Keynes' definition of liquidity preference (LP) and the present custom of identifying the excess-demand equation for money as representing the forces of liquidity preference. We shall choose a different way of stating the LP theory which seems more in accord with Keynes' definition. Having done so, we shall show that the dispute between LP and loanable funds (LF) turns only on the period which is chosen for consideration.

Before embarking on this task, a few words on methodology may not be out of place. In the main we shall conduct our analysis on the basis of static Walrasian Equilibrium systems. These are unsatisfactory in many respects, and in particular are fairly unrealistic as a description of an expanding capitalist economy. But for the most part all recent discussions in our field, not excluding the General Theory, are conducted in this framework. In particular, it must be emphasized that the 'Keynesian Revolution' was a revolution because it purported to demonstrate certain propositions concerning comparative statics systems which it had been thought could not be demonstrated. (Probably even those most deeply steeped in classicism would have admitted the possibility of 'dynamic' unemployment.) For all these reasons a comparative statics analysis in this paper is the appropriate one.

We begin the paper by a general discussion of what is implied by the statement that one particular supply-and-demand relation 'determines' one particular price.

I

From the theory of consumer's behaviour, we know that the demand for any commodity or service he consumes or supplies will depend not only on the price of that commodity, but also on the prices of all other commodities he consumes and supplies. It will also depend on his wealth, that is on the assets he holds. If all consumers consume and supply something of every good and service and hold certain amounts of all assets, then the aggregate demand for any good will depend on all prices and on the quantity of all assets. If, then, we define the equilibrium price of a commodity as the price at which the excess demand (demand minus supply) for that commodity is zero, we can 'determine' that price from the demand and supply equations for the commodity only if we know the prices of all other commodities and the total quantity of various assets. This is, of course, a well-known Marshallian procedure. If, however, the prices of other goods and services and the quantity of assets held are not known, we need in general at least as many further demand-and-supply relations (excess demand equations) as there are other prices and assets affecting the demand for that particular good. In a general equilibrium analysis, therefore, all prices are 'determined' by all supply-and-demand relations simultaneously, in the sense that we need all of these to find the equilibrium price.

Now it may happen that certain groups of individuals consume only a limited set of goods and that no other group consumes these goods at all. In that case the general equilibrium system could be decomposed into a number of quite independent sub-systems, since by assumption the demand for a certain group of goods is quite independent of the prices of goods falling outside that group. Again, decomposition could arise if we decide, on empirical grounds, that certain prices can be assumed fairly constant, or to have a negligible effect on the demand for the commodities we are considering. These are all possible ways of cutting down the number of demand–supply relations we need in solving for any particular equilibrium price. In the discussions of interest rate theory, for instance, the frequently met assumption that savings and investment are highly interest-inelastic is an obvious way of decomposing the system.

In making such assumptions, however, one very important point must be borne in mind: the price of any one good or service must generally affect at least the demand for one other good or service (see, e.g., Mosak, 1944, p. 25). For we know that a change in the price of any one good will be associated with a substitution effect. This clearly involves a change in the demand for at least one other good, unless we assume that the income effect of the change in price is equal and opposite in sign to the substitution effect, and this would be a very heroic assumption indeed. For similar reasons, the quantity of any asset held must influence the demand for some other good and service unless we assume all income effects to be zero. Thus, unless some very special assumptions, not usually found in the literature, are made, we shall normally require at least two excess-demand equations to determine any one price, or the equilibrium quantity of any asset. If this is correct, it will be impossible for us to find one particular market relation (excess-demand equation) which will be sufficient to determine the equilibrium rate of interest. It is the attempt to do this, none the less, which may be responsible for the continued controversy in this field, especially the LP versus LF dispute. By seeing in advance that such an attempt is usually doomed to failure, we may save ourselves a lot of trouble.

Up to now we have interpreted the phrase 'the price of a good (say i) is determined by the demand and supply for i' as meaning that we can find this price from one supply–demand relation (excess-demand equation) only. There is, however, an alternative interpretation. We could mean the phrase to imply that the price of i changes only if the excess demand for the ith good is different from zero. This interpretation we shall call the Klein interpretation (see Klein, 1950). The meaning of the phrase quoted is now made far more general. For, while the assertion that one excess-demand equation is sufficient to determine the equilibrium price implies the Klein interpretation, the latter does not imply the former. Indeed, no assumptions leading to a decomposition of a general equilibrium system need be made in order to allow us to use the Klein interpretation of the phrase. This is of considerable advantage, especially since, using this interpretation, the assertion of the phrase can be subjected more easily to empirical tests. If then we employ the Klein interpretation in analysing the two statements 'the rate of interest is determined by liquidity preference' and 'the rate of interest is determined by the demand and supply of loanable funds', our main task will be to see whether these two statements imply different behaviour of the rate of interest when there is disequilibrium. If they do, then they are two distinct theories, and the choice between them must be made on empirical and not on theoretical grounds.

So much by way of general introduction. We will now turn to an examination of the classical revival led by Mr Modigliani, which is based on a particular kind of decomposition of a general equilibrium system.

II

Mr Modigliani's model, henceforth referred to as the M-model, is set out below. The notation is as follows: X = total real output, N = amount of labour employed, W/P = the real wage of labour and W its money wage, S = real savings and I = real investment, i is the rate of interest and M the (nominal) quantity of cash.

The model consists of the following seven equations:

$$X = F(N) \tag{M1}$$

$$W/P = F'(N) \tag{M2}$$

$$N = N(W/P) \tag{M3}$$

$$S = S(i, W/P, X) \tag{M4}$$

$$I = I(i, W/P, X) \tag{M5}$$

$$S = I \tag{M6}$$

$$M = L(i, W, P/W, X). \tag{M7}$$

Since the model is well known, we give only a brief statement of the meaning of the equations. (M1) is the production function on the assumption of a constant stock of capital; (M2) states that the real wage of labour is equal to labour's marginal (physical) product; (M3) is the supply function of labour, which is homogeneous of zero degree in money wages and prices; (M4) is the savings function and I the investment function; and (M6) is self-explanatory; (M7) is the equation of the demand for cash as a function of the interest rate, absolute prices and real income. Equations (M1), (M2) and (M3) determine X, N and W/P, equations (M4), (M5) and (M6) determine S, I and i, and equation (M7) determines P.

It is on the basis of this model that Modigliani derives the following two 'classical' propositions.

If the supply function of labour is homogeneous of zero degree in all prices (including money wages), then

1   the rate of interest is determined by investment and savings; and
2   liquidity preference determines the level of prices and *not* the rate of interest.

Both the M-model and its conclusions have been criticized by Patinkin. His criticism, however, has apparently not convinced Mr Modigliani and others.[5] We shall therefore devote this section to showing that both the M-model and its conclusions are incorrect.

That this is so can be shown quite simply. It will be seen that equations (M1)–(M6) determine relative prices, the rate of interest and the output of all goods without involving the absolute level of

[5] That it has not convinced Mr Modigliani must be deduced from the reprinting of his article in *Readings in Monetary Theory* without either alteration or comment. That it has not convinced others can be deduced from Mr Johnson's article (1951–2, p. 104).

prices. The latter is determined by (M7). Money, therefore, in Mr Modigliani's phrase, is 'neutral'. Now, neglecting bonds (as does Mr Modigliani), we know from Walras' Law that the total demand for goods and money taken together must be identically equal to the total supply of goods and money taken together. It is therefore of considerable importance to the M-model to make certain that it is not also true that the total demand for everything excluding money is identically equal to the total supply of everything excluding money. For if this (Say's Law) were also implied, the demand for money would be identically equal to the supply of money, and we would have no equation (as distinct from an identity) to determine the absolute level of prices. It will therefore be sufficient for our purposes if we show that the following statement of Modigliani's is incorrect: 'Under "static" assumptions money is neutral even without assuming Say's Law, if only people are assumed to behave "rationally"; this is all the classical theory assumes or needs to assume' (p. 217).

Let us assume that relative prices and the interest rate are such that the total demand for goods and services exceeds their total supply – a situation perfectly possible as long as we do not assume Say's law. If Mr Modigliani is right, we can now find some level of absolute prices which will make the demand for money equal to its supply. Choosing such an absolute price has, by assumption, no effect on the total demand or supply of goods and services. But we have now arrived at a position where the total demand for goods and services exceeds their supply but the demand for money is equal to the stock of money, and this clearly contradicts Walras' identity described in the previous paragraph. In any case, on Modigliani's assumption, any change in the level of prices must change the demand and supply for money in the same proportion, since the demand for, and supply of, goods is unaffected by such a change in prices. The level of prices therefore cannot equate the demand and supply of money, and the only way of ensuring this equality is to assume Say's Law. Hence the M-model must leave the level of absolute prices indeterminate and Mr Modigliani's conclusion 2 must be rejected.[6]

[6] It may be helpful to restate the argument in symbols. Let X_g and X_m be the excess demand for goods and money respectively. Let P be the absolute price level of goods. By Walras' Law, $PX_g + X_m \equiv 0$. Choose relative prices such that $X_g \neq 0$. We can now find a level of absolute prices P^* such that $X_m = 0$. But whatever the value of P, X_g remains unaffected by assumption. We have now come to the contradiction mentioned in the text, since at $P = P^*$ Walras' Law does not hold. But Walras' Law is an identity and must hold for any value of P. This contradiction can be resolved only by assuming Say's Law: $X_g \equiv 0$.

The intuitive reasons for rejecting the M-model are fairly obvious, and have been extensively discussed by Patinkin in another context. Rational behaviour presumably also refers to the holding of cash. If cash, then, is allowed into the utility function, we easily see that the demand for at least one good must depend on absolute prices if the demand for money depends on absolute prices. For, as was pointed out in Section I, we cannot hope to decompose a system into two parts from restrictions on the utility functions without running into difficulties. Thus, money must be a substitute for all other goods entering into the utility function taken together. If, then, a change in the price level leaves all demands for goods and services unaffected, it must mean that the amount of money people hold is always the equilibrium amount, whatever the price level; and hence the money equation cannot be used to determine the price level.

We have seen that conclusion 2 of Mr Modigliani's is incorrect. What about conclusion 1? One way of avoiding Say's Law in the M-model would be to allow absolute prices to enter into the equations relating to savings and investment. In that case we would need both (M6) and (M7) to be able to solve for the equilibrium rate of interest. In any case, we will need at least two equations, and on Mr Modigliani's interpretation of the word 'determine', conclusion 1 must also be rejected.

But suppose we used the Klein interpretation in our understanding of conclusion 1: could we then not, on the basis of a corrected M-model, say that the rate of interest is determined by savings and investment? To answer this question we must take note of the special interpretation Mr Modigliani places on (M4)–(M6). He warns us that (M4) and (M5) 'should in no way be confused with the schedules of supply of and demand for savings (or supply of and demand for securities)'. In particular, (M4) tells us 'what part of their income people wish to devote to increasing their assets rather than to consumption at different levels of the rate of interest', while (M5) is the 'marginal-efficiency-of-investment function'. Since securities, that is lending and borrowing, do not enter into the model, it is clear that the rate of interest is not determined by any market mechanism. Indeed, only those who save invest, and never more than they save. This not only suggests that the model is rather unrealistic, but also that the Klein interpretation of the word 'determine' is inappropriate. For the latter hinges on the possibility of *ex ante* excess demand, which is clearly impossible here on Mr Modigliani's interpretation of (M4) and (M5). If we then wish to say that the rate of interest is determined (in the Klein sense) by savings and investment, we will not be able to do so on the basis of the M-model.

Before leaving this whole topic, and the only excuse for dwelling on it at some length is the influence the M-model appears to have gained, I would like to draw attention to the interpretation Mr Modigliani places on (M6) (the equality of savings and investment). After saying that (M1)–(M3) determine the level of real income he writes: 'The saving schedule, equation (3.3), tells us what part of this income the community desires to save. The technical conditions (inventions, quantity of capital already in existence, etc.) expressed by the marginal-efficiency-of-investment function (3.2), determine the marginal efficiency of the amount of investment that the giving up of consumption permits undertaking: this is the equilibrium rate of interest' (p. 219). This suggests two things: (1) it appears that savings, in spite of the earlier quotation, are to be taken as independent of the rate of interest, and (2) savings are always *identically* equal to investment. This makes it quite clear that the Klein interpretation cannot be applied to Mr Modigliani's conclusion 1, and hence that the latter must be rejected on both interpretations of the word 'determine' in that conclusion.

III

We have seen that the classical revival, at least as exemplified by Mr Modigliani, suffers from serious logical defects. Indeed, Mr Patinkin has shown that all models based on the assumption of 'neutral' money are open to similar objections. Quite apart from this, however, a realistic theory of interest, in which the latter varies whenever investment is not equal to saving, must allow for lending and borrowing. This, of course, leads us straight into problems connected with liquidity preference and loanable funds. It is the intention of this section to compare the three theories, LP, LF and IS, of the rate of interest, in the setting of a Keynesian model.

We shall assume that there are only three kinds of assets: a capital (or producers') good (K), irredeemable bonds (B), and money (M). The stock of money is assumed constant. A debtor is regarded as holding negative bonds. All other goods are consumption goods and are perishable, so that no stocks of these can be held.

A plan to invest is a plan to increase the holding of K. In so far as investors plan to add to K the same amount as they plan to save out of current income, no market transaction is involved, and no *ex ante* gap between savings and investment can arise. Since this sort of situation is clearly of no interest to us, we shall now assume that investors plan to save nothing. (This is simpler than the assumption that they plan to save less than they invest, and does not affect my argument.) A plan to invest must now be accompanied by a plan to change the holdings of the remaining assets money and bonds. (Investors will plan to supply bonds and/or money.) On the other hand, the plan to save is a plan to add to the holdings of bonds and/or money on the part of savers. Hence if investment and saving plans are fulfilled, the increase in the physical assets (K) of the community is equal to the increase in the stock of money and bonds held by savers. Hence if we write D_a for the demand for more assets and S_a the supply of more assets, and S and I for saving and investment (*ex ante*), respectively, we have

$$(D_a - S_a) = X_a = (S - I) \tag{3.1}$$

and we can refer to this difference as the excess demand for assets (X_a).

We now state the IS theory of the rate of interest: the rate of interest will change if, and only if, the excess demand for assets is different from zero. X_a is made up of the excess demand for bonds (X_b) and the excess demand for money (X_m). The LF theory of the rate of interest now is: the rate of interest will change if, and only if, the excess demand for one asset, bonds, is different from zero. Before stating the LP theory, let us recall what Keynes meant by a decision due to liquidity preference. He writes:

> The psychological time-preferences of an individual require two distinct sets of decisions to carry them out completely. The first is concerned with that aspect of time-preference which I have called the *propensity to consume*, which, operating under the influence of the various motives set forth in Book III, determines for each individual how much of his income he will consume and how much he will reserve in *some* form of command over future consumption. ... But this decision having been made, there is a further decision which awaits him, namely, in *what form* he will hold the

command over future consumption which he has reserved, whether out of his current income or from previous savings. ... In other words, what is the degree of his *liquidity-prefer-ence* – where an individual's liquidity-preference is given by a schedule of the amounts of his resources, valued in terms of money or of wage-units, which he will wish to retain in the form of money in different sets of circumstances? (Keynes, 1936, p. 166)

On the basis of this extract we could phrase the LP theory as follows: the rate of interest will change if, and only if, there is an attempt to substitute money for some other *asset*. I would like to draw particular attention to the word in italics in this quotation. LP is *not* intended to explain why people hold money rather than consumers' goods, but rather why they hold money instead of some other asset. If this is granted, then we are in some difficulty in identifying one particular excess demand as representing LP, as we identified X_a and X_b as representing IS and LF. Let us rewrite (3.1) as

$$X_a = X_m + X_b = (S - I). \tag{3.1a}$$

Suppose we restate the LP theory as: the rate of interest will change if and only if $X_m \neq 0$. Then it is clear that the rate of interest would change if $X_b = 0$ and

$$X_m = (S - I) = X_a \neq 0. \tag{3.2}$$

But now the excess demand for money does not represent an attempt to substitute money for other assets or vice versa, but money for consumption goods or vice versa. Thus, for instance, in the case of $(S - I) > 0$, we would have to say that people as a whole are attempting to become more liquid by supplying more goods and services than they are demanding. But this is not, as the quotation shows, what Keynes understood by the forces of liquidity preference.

Yet in spite of this, the custom of identifying X_m with the liquidity preference equation is well established. The reason for this is not far to seek. The Keynesian model of the General Theory has the following characteristics: (1) money wages are fixed and given from outside: (2) there are constant returns to scale (un-employed resources), so that all prices are wage-determined; (3) there are no lags of any sort. Since all prices are already determined, the only unknowns are income (Y) and the rate of interest. (P_b = the price of bonds = inverse of the rate of interest.) Since (3.1a) is an identity, we can always deduce one of the excess demands (X_a, X_m, X_b) from the remaining two. We thus have two (excess-demand) equations to determine our two unknowns. Now, according to Keynes, incomes change if, and only if, $X_a \neq 0$. In the General Theory and later in controversies with Professor Robertson, he seemed to envisage the following sequence. Suppose $X_a < 0$; then incomes change instantaneously to make $X_a = 0$. When that has happened $X_m \equiv -X_b$. If $X_m \neq 0$ the rate of interest changes to make $X_m = 0$. This may again lead to $X_a \neq 0$, which causes a further change in income, which in turn affects X_m and the rate of interest. The point about this sequence of events is that the excess demand for money is always identically equal to the excess supply of bonds, so that there is never an attempt to substitute money for consumption goods or services. In effect, this kind of sequence is equivalent to conducting a partial analysis, by first fixing interest and finding the equilibrium level of income, and then holding the latter as given and determining the equilibrium rate of interest and so on.

Since, however, there is no reason to expect this sequence of events, and since most of the controversies are due to an attempt to fit interest rate theory into a general rather than a partial analysis, we must, when restating the LP theory in a general model, be careful not to incorporate into it elements which derive from the special procedure of Keynes. In particular, liquidity preference must be taken as determining the *ratio* ('form') in which assets are demanded, and *not* the total quantity of assets demanded or supplied. Once the sequence procedure is dropped, a zero excess demand for money no longer implies that people are holding assets in the 'form' in which they desire and that liquidity preference is satisfied; nor does an excess demand for money different from zero imply that people are attempting to change the 'form' in which they hold assets and that liquidity preference is not satisifed. Since this is a point of some importance to our argument, we will restate it in slightly different terms.

From the quotation of the General Theory given above, it is clear, I think, that if Keynes had written out a utility function he would have included in the latter a term (A) for total assets held and some terms to describe the composition of those assets. Suppose there are only two such assets, a_1 and a_2. Let x stand for all other goods and services consumed or supplied. Then if we wrote the utility function as

$$U = U\left(x, A, \frac{a_1}{a_2}\right) \tag{3.3}$$

the two decisions (the decision to save and the decision concerning the form in which to hold assets) are clearly brought out. This is not the case if we write

$$U = U(x, a_1, a_2). \tag{3.4}$$

Formally, of course, these two ways of writing the utility function should make no difference to the analysis. There is, however, a difference in interpretation. For if a_1 represents money, then on the basis of (3.3) we would say that LP is satisfied when the individual holds assets in the desired ratio a_1/a_2, while on the basis of (3.4) we would say that LP is satisfied when the individual holds all of a_1 he desires. It is the latter interpretation which is customary. But liquidity preference, as the phrase vividly denotes, describes the *preference* of money over other assets. This preference cannot be described by the total demand for money, but only by the demand for money relative to the demand for other assets.

If this interpretation of LP is accepted, we could state the LP theory of interest as follows: the rate of interest changes if, and only if, the ratio in which assets are demanded is different from the ratio in which they are supplied.[7] Let us now see to what sort of model this proposition leads us.

It will be remembered that we assumed there to be three kinds of assets: a capital good (K), money, and bonds. Investors decide to substitute more of the capital good for money and bonds. They therefore supply money and bonds in a certain ratio and demand more of the capital good from the producers of that good. If there are no production lags, their demand for more K will always be satisfied. Savers, on the other hand, decide to increase their total assets held, by demanding more bonds and money in a certain ratio. Let us now also assume a Robertsonian consumption lag so that they total demand for goods and services plus the total

---

[7] There is no difficulty of fitting the 'transaction' demand for money into this formulation. 'Planned', or if we like *ex ante*, LP refers to the form in which people plan to hold assets at the *end* of the period. This, using the Robertsonian consumption lag, then includes provision for transaction purposes in the subsequent period.

demand for money and bonds is identically equal to the income of the previous period plus the stock of money, K and bonds available at the beginning of the period. Since there are no production lags, the total supply of goods and services will always be equal to the total of these demanded. We therefore obtain the following identity:

$$X_a \equiv Y^0 - Y^1 \tag{3.5}$$

where Y^0 is the income of the previous period and Y^1 is the income of the current period.

The first condition of equilibrium is that

$$X_a \equiv Y^0 - Y^1 = 0. \tag{3.6}$$

Now X_a depends on the rate of interest (i), Y^0 and the total volume of assets held (A). It also depends, of course, on prices, but since these are assumed fixed we can ignore them. Following Keynes, we can assume that in the short period the total volume of assets is fixed, i.e., that the addition made to assets by investment is negligible in the short period. We thus have two unknowns, i and Y^0, and at the moment only one equation. Let us now, instead of using either the excess demand for money or for bonds for the missing equation, use the condition that LP must be satisfied; that is, the ratio of money to bonds available should equal the ratio in which they are demanded. Call the difference in these two ratios X_r, so that our condition becomes:

$$X_r = 0. \tag{3.7}$$

X_r will depend on the same variables as X_a. It should also be noted that if both (3.6) and (3.7) hold, X_m and X_b will both be zero.

We have now a formal model incorporating our interpretations of the LP theory of interest: the rate of interest changes only if $X_r \neq 0$. However, models of this sort are of little interest unless they help us to explain the process by which equilibrium is achieved. The simplest way of doing this is to compare LP and LF on the basis of this model.

It will be remembered that our interpretation of the LF theory is: the rate of interest will change only if $X_b \neq 0$. It will easily be seen that if in our model $X_a = 0$, then $X_b \neq 0$ necessarily implies $X_r \neq 0$. Thus in our construction, just as in the usual ones, LP and

LF come to the same thing if *ex ante* saving is equal to *ex ante* investment. Our main interest therefore centres on the case where the latter equality does not hold.

Let us then assume that $X_a < 0$ (*ex ante* saving $<$ *ex ante* investment) that $X_b > 0$ and $X_r = 0$. In this case it would appear that LF predicts a change (rise) in the rate of interest, while LP predicts that the rate of interest will remain constant. We must now, however, take note of a point of considerable importance. All excess-demand equations are interpreted as holding *ex ante*. Plans are thus regarded as being formulated for a certain (finite) period of time, during which they undergo no voluntary change. Following Robertson, we assume savings plans to be formulated for one income period. In our model we have assumed (again following Robertson) that investment plans are fulfilled. But that implies, as Professor Robertson has pointed out in his well-known controversy with Keynes, that investors have secured the necessary 'finance' (Robertson, 1938, pp. 314–18; Keynes, 1938, pp. 318–22). It thus seems that there are *two* transactions involved in a given income period: a sale of bonds for money and a purchase of investment goods. This in turn implies – and to my mind quite realistically – that the planning period for the composition of assets is shorter than the planning period for savings (addition to assets). In our model, however, both X_a and X_r are interpreted as resulting from plans formulated for one income period. It is this discrepancy which will explain why LP and LF seem to give different predictions.

When we say that X_r is defined for one income period in our model, we mean that the plans concerning the composition of money and bonds refer to the composition people desire to hold at the end of the income period. But in the first part of the income period the ratio in which money and bonds are demanded reflects the fact that investors are attempting to become more liquid in order to purchase investment goods in the second part of the income period. Investors are only planning to hold this higher ratio temporarily, and this temporary demand is *not* reflected in X_r in our model.

With this in mind, let us trace out the process under our present assumptions. The rate of interest is such that the ratio in which people plan to hold money and bonds at the end of the income period is equal to the ratio in which they will be available. At the beginning of the period, however, the ratio in which money and bonds are demanded is greater than this, because investors are demanding money with which to purchase investment goods. Hence the rate of interest will rise. Since people planning to invest are offering bonds at the outset of the period, the only way investors can obtain their finance is by inducing some people to increase the ratio of bonds to money in their existing assets. The rate of interest will thus rise to the point at which it is just not worthwhile for investors to offer further inducements to holders of money to substitute bonds for the latter. At that rate of interest the demand for bonds will equal their supply. Once this transaction is complete, investors buy investment goods. In other words, they now reduce their ratio of money to bonds. But that means that the ratio of money to bonds held by other people increases. This leads to a substitution of money for bonds and a fall in the rate of interest. The rate of interest will fall as long as the actual ratio of money to bonds is higher than that desired for the end of the income period. Thus, the rate of interest will again assume the value it had at the beginning of the income period. At the end of the income period, therefore, everyone holds assets in the form they had planned to hold them, the rate of interest is the same as at the beginning of the period, total assets held are higher than planned, and incomes have increased. The unforeseen changes will then lead to a change in the ratio of money and bonds desired for the end of the subsequent period.

If this analysis is correct, then the main difference between LP and IF lies in the period chosen for consideration. The LP theory ignores the intermediate transactions which occur when people are attempting to substitute bonds for capital goods. Professor Robertson, in my opinion rightly, insisted that this obscures the important point that bonds must always first be sold for money, so that the plan to substitute bonds for capital goods involves three groups: the investors, the producers of investment goods, and holders of cash. (Of course, these groups will overlap.) As we have seen, however, the logic of a Walrasian equilibrium system makes it quite possible for the *ex ante* excess demand for money to be zero, while the excess supply of bonds is equal to the excess of planned investment over planned savings. But plans in people's minds affect only market variables, as they are executed and in the manner in which they are executed. Since the bonds are never offered directly to producers in return for capital goods, it is important that the 'sub-transactions' should be taken into account, if we wish to see how and why interest rates (or indeed any other variable) should change when plans are inconsistent. The Walrasian model, by taking one whole income period as its basis, hides these 'sub-transactions'.

If we then assume that plans concerning the composition of assets are continuously variable (as we have done in our example) we can state the two theories as follows:

LP: The rate of interest ruling at the end of one income period will be different from that ruling at the beginning only if people plan to hold money and bonds at the end of the period in a different ratio from that which will be available.

LF: The rate of interest at the end of one sub-transaction period will be different from that ruling at the beginning only if people plan to demand more bonds than they supply for that period. This can be restated in the equivalent form: the rate of interest at the end of a sub-transaction period will differ from the value it had at the beginning of the period only if the ratio in which money and bonds are demanded for the end of that period is different from the ratio in which it will be available.

The predictions of the two theories differ because they concern the value the rate of interest will have at different times.

We must now note two difficulties. First, it must be admitted that the period analysis is highly artificial, since, while people may take decisions discontinuously, not all people take decisions at the same time. This probably means that LF as here formulated is more useful than LP, since we will never be able to find a time when the rate of interest is independent of the demand for 'finance'.

Second, we have allowed only three assets: money, bonds and capital goods. Increasing the number of monetary assets, i.e., having different kinds of claims to debt, will not greatly affect our analysis, since we get as many new equations as unknowns. That is, for each interest rate we have the condition that the ratio in which money and that particular claim are planned to be supplied is equal to the ratio in which they are planned to be held. If we introduce further non-monetary assets, in particular what Mr Kaldor has called 'Verbrauch's Güter' (1939–40, p. 3), then the analysis becomes far more complicated. We would now have to introduce *expected* prices as unknowns, and would almost certainly have to abandon the assumption that all current prices are fixed and given. A complicated stock *and* flow model would result. I have constructed a number of such models, but do not feel that they are at a stage where I can say anything that is useful.

To sum up, LP refers to the composition of assets people desire to hold. In a monetary economy, however, there is a difference between the composition of assets people desire in the course of the income period and that which they desire to hold at the end. Liquidity preference refers to the composition of assets people desire to hold when all market transactions necessary for achieving that composition are completed. Loanable funds, on the other hand, are concerned with the flow of assets on to the market during the income period. It therefore takes account of the intermediate composition of assets people desire when they are still in the process of completing their transactions. Thus investors, desiring to hold at the end of the income period a higher ratio of capital goods to money and bonds, first desire an increased ratio of money to bonds in order to be able to make the desired substitution for capital goods. This desire is not neglected in the LF theory. The predictions of the two theories, however, are not mutually exclusive, for the simple reason that the predictions refer to different time periods. When Professor Robertson refers to the excess demand for bonds it must be understood as holding for any one moment of time; in the LP theory the excess demand for bonds must be interpreted as the excess demand (the incompatibility of plans remaining) after all intermediate transactions have been completed.

Let us now examine the claims of the IS theory. We first note an interesting, formal property of our model. The IS theory states that the rate of interest will change only if $X_a \neq 0$. Suppose, then, that $X_a = 0$ but $X_r \neq 0$. Since by definition incomes change only if $X_a \neq 0$, it follows that neither interest rates nor incomes will change. But, then, there is no means by which plans to hold money and bonds can be made consistent; i.e., there is no mechanism for bringing about an equilibrium in asset holdings. It would therefore appear that on purely formal grounds the IS theory would have to be rejected, although this, of course, does *not* mean that savings and investment decisions have no influence on the rate of interest.

We can now put the reasons for rejecting the IS theory less formally. A discrepancy in plans can affect market variables only in so far as this discrepancy is in some way manifested in the market by the things people actually do or *actively* attempt to do. From our present (Keynesian) assumptions, we know that whatever volume of investment goods investors actually demand will be supplied at constant price. As far as the price of investment goods is concerned, a discrepancy in the plans to save and invest can have no importance. The same is true of the price of consumption goods. We know, however, that a discrepancy in the plans to invest and save will be reflected in discrepancies in the plans to supply and demand money and/or bonds.

To say then that the rate of interest varies only if planned investment and savings differ is the same as to say that it varies only if the sum of the excess demands of money *and* bonds is different from zero. But this in turn implies that, when planned investment equals planned saving, the rate of interest will not change even though there is an excess demand for money and a corresponding excess supply of bonds. That is, the rate of interest will not vary even when there is an attempt to substitute money for bonds or vice versa and when both the 'markets' for money and bonds are out of equilibrium. But then we are left with no market variable, a change of which could bring the two markets into equilibrium.

If these interpretations of LP, LF and IS in a Keynesian model are accepted, then we can sum up our conclusions as follows. People take two decisions: what volume of assets and what composition of those assets to hold at the end of the income period. If plans are incompatible, certain of those plans will not materialize. But the planning period for the composition of assets, in particular the ratio of money to bonds, is much shorter than that for the volume of assets. It is therefore assumed that at the end of the income period the rate of interest is such that, on the basis of the previous period's income, people are willing to hold assets in the form in which they are available. On the other hand, it is not possible for consumption, investment and volume of assets plans to be fulfilled simultaneously. The Keynesian assumption is that it is undesired accretions or depletions in the total volume of assets which reflect the incompatibility of plans. Thus the rate of interest varies during the period to make plans concerning the composition of assets compatible, but it does not affect the plans concerning the volume of assets people desire during the income period. The rate of interest therefore is affected only after undesired changes in the volume of assets (changes in income) have affected the composition of assets people desire. The loanable funds theory, as we have interpreted it, differs from this only in so far as it is concerned with the value of the rate of interest at any one moment of time during the income period.

D

REFERENCES

Brunner, Karl (1950), 'Stock and Flow Analysis: Discussion', *Econometrica*, **18**.

Fellner, W. and Somers, H. M. (1941), 'Alternative Monetary Approaches to Interest Theory', *Review of Economic Statistics*, **23**.

Fellner, W. and Somers, H. M. (1949), 'Notes on "Stocks" and "Flows" in Monetary Interest Theory', *Review of Economics and Statistics*, **31**.

Fellner, W. and Somers, H. M. (1950), 'Stock and Flow Analysis: A Comment', *Econometrica*, **18**.

Johnson, H. G. (1951-2), 'Some Cambridge Controversies in Monetary Theory', *Review of Economic Studies*, **19**.

Kaldor, N. (1939-40), 'Speculation and Economic Stability', *Review of Economic Studies*, **7**.

Keynes, J. M. (1936), *The General Theory of Employment, Interest and Money*, Macmillan, London.

Keynes, J. M. (1938), 'Comment' on 'Mr Keynes and "Finance" ', *Economic Journal*, **48**.

Klein, L. R. (1950), 'Stock and Flow Analysis in Economics', *Econometrica*, **18**.

Modigliani, F. (1944), 'Liquidity Preference and the Theory of Interest and Money', *Econometrica*, **12**. Reprinted in *Readings in Monetary Theory* (1952), The American Economic Association Series, Allen and Unwin, London.

Mosak, J. L. (1944), *General Equilibrium Theory in International Trade*, Principia Press, Bloomington, Indiana.

Patinkin, Don (1948), 'Relative Prices, Say's Law and the Demand for Money', *Econometrica*, **16**.

Patinkin, Don (1949), 'The Indeterminacy of Absolute Prices in Classical Economic Theory', *Econometrica*, **17**.

Patinkin, Don (1949-50), 'A Reconsideration of the Equilibrium Theory of Money', *Review of Economic Studies*, **45**.

Patinkin, Don (1951), 'The Invalidity of Classical Monetary Theory', *Econometrica*, **19**.

Patinkin, Don (1952-3), 'Further Considerations of the General Equilibrium Theory of Money', *Review of Economic Studies*, **50**.

Robertson, D. H. (1938), 'Mr Keynes and "Finance": A Note', *Economic Journal*, **48**.

Robertson, D. H. (1951-2), 'Comments on Mr Johnson's Note', *Review of Economic Studies*, **19**.

4

Equilibrium with Transaction Costs

I INTRODUCTION

It is usual to describe an Arrow–Debreu economy as one in which all markets, including all contingent futures markets, exist.[1] This is rather ambiguous since a market may be feasible but inactive. It is more useful to say that an economy is Arrow–Debreu (A–D) if we may interpret it in equilibrium as one where all transactions are carried out at a single date. In such an economy money can play no essential role.

In the economies we know, there are transactions at every date. It is also not the case that at any date and for every good agents have a choice of transacting forward or spot on terms which leave them indifferent as to which they do. This suggests that one wants to study markets as activities in order to have a theory to account for the presence of active spot markets at every date. This allows one to treat as an unknown in the analysis the markets which are active in an equilibrium. Such a study leads one to an equilibrium of a sequence of markets. It is pretty plain from general considerations that such a construct is required as a preliminary to a satisfactory monetary theory.

This paper is concerned with this preliminary undertaking and it goes only part of the way. By far the larger part of the study is concerned with economies in which all prices are announced and there is certainty. Only in the last section do I offer some remarks on some of the problems encountered in a less restrictive frame-

[1] This paper was originally presented in New York as the Walras Lecture, December, 1969. Mr Duncan Foley has also studied the problem of transactions in general equilibrium. However, he seems to be concerned with single-period models. I should like to acknowledge the debt I owe to the writings of Roy Radner on sequence economies and to discussions which I have had with him. He has also kindly and usefully commented on this paper.

work. For the most part also I am concerned with a pure exchange economy and I need some fairly restrictive technical assumptions. The paper must be regarded as a first step.

Even so, the result is not perhaps easy or pleasant reading, and I take this opportunity to note some of the more important conclusions.

If one regards transactions as using resources of goods available at the transaction date, then one has an immediate reason for the fact that there are normally spot markets at every date. Suppose, for instance, that labour is a required input into a market activity. It would then be odd for an economy to choose, provided it were feasible, to supply labour in the initial period only and none at all thereafter. This in itself is sufficiently strong ground for expecting spot markets at every date.

In formalizing the notion of markets as activities, I distinguish between *named* and *anonymous* goods. This serves to distinguish a given physical good at a particular time and place owned by an agent from the same good when it is being bought by another agent. It has of course the consequence that the buying and selling price of the same physical good at the same time and place may differ.

The single most important consequence of this is that, in general, households face a sequence of budget constraints and there may be no unique set of discount rates applicable to all households which allows one to 'amalgamate' all those constraints into a single present-value budget constraint. The intertemporal transfers open to a household depend on whether at each of the two dates it is a seller or buyer of the good in terms of which such a transfer is most advantageous. Not only will the borrowing and lending rates differ, in general, but each of these rates may be different for different households.

The fact that one has to deal with a sequence of constraints poses certain technical difficulties. But this is not the important point. More interesting is the fact that equilibria need not be efficient. Care must of course be taken with the definition of efficiency. For the set of feasible allocations, unlike that of the usual theory, must for sense be taken relative to a given *distribution* of endowment. In particular, the question whether every efficient allocation may be decentralized may make no sense if endowment reallocations require resources.

But of course the most important consequence of the whole approach is that, since it leads to a sequence of spot markets, one cannot in practice take the prices at future dates as known to the agents at an earlier date. I shall discuss some of these issues, albeit very briefly. In an Arrow–Debreu world all the future is collapsible into the present – in this sort of world the future unfolds. This of course has important consequences to one's views on the allocative efficiency of a perfectly competitive world.

I shall also offer some reflections, as they are best called, on money in the kind of model I have been discussing. The attempt to arrive at a model of the economy as satisfying as Debreu's, but which can accommodate money, is the motivation of this whole enquiry. In execution, the preparatory work has taken most of my time and intellectual energy, and I hope to pursue this problem further at another occasion. But I shall argue here that at least the pure transaction theory of money seems to require in an essential way that the set of marketing activities exhibits a certain kind of increasing returns. I have not been able to formulate this to my full satisfaction. But if the argument is correct, difficulties present themselves in the study of equilibrium. More importantly still, we should not be surprised to find a monetary equilibrium inefficient in a certain sense quite different from Friedman's. It is just possible that, abstract as this research is, it might in due course lead one to formulate public policies to create markets or to abolish some. Adam Smith started on a study of markets and their relation to the division of labour – formal economics has not gotten much further since and indeed has ignored the Smithian analysis.

A note on notation   In what follows, if a and b are two vectors, $a \gg b$ means $a_i > b_i$ for all i, $a > b$ means $a_i \geq b_i$, $a_i > b_i$ for some i. Also, a^+ is the vector with components $\max(0, a_i)$; a^- is the vector with components $\min(0, a_i)$.

II   GOODS AND PRICES

One of the aims of this paper is to make the existence or non-existence of markets an economic question. The natural procedure is to regard a market as an activity which uses resources. To make this precise I shall enlarge the usual commodity space.

Let only one state of the economy be possible and say that a good is of type (i, t) if, when time is measured in discrete intervals, it has the locational and physical characteristics i and is available at t. I let $i = 0, \ldots, n - 1$, $t = 1, \ldots, T$ and call the non-negative orthant, Ω^{nT}, the space of anonymous goods. This nomenclature is designed to underline that these goods can be specified without using the name of any agent.

Let there be H households. I shall call a good of type (i, t) owned by household h, a *named* good (i, h, t). There can be HnT named goods. But in most of what follows, while I shall take it to be of economic significance whether a good of a given type has a name or not, I shall suppose it to be of no significance what the name is. In that case I refer to a named good of type (i, t) as (i, H, t) and the dimension of the commodity space is $2nT$.

At a later stage I shall wish to single out special goods of type (n, t), $t = 1, \ldots, T$, which have the characteristic that they are not subject to the ordering of households or the distinction between named and anonymous. These goods will be called money (of different dates) and when they are included in the analysis the commodity space is $\Omega^{(2n+1)T}$.

A market (i, t) will be regarded as an activity which transforms (i, H, t) into (i, t). It is described in section IV.

The commodity space, however, will have to be further enlarged. To understand this, a matter of considerable significance, it is best first to consider the prices of the goods so far specified.

Let $p, q \in \Omega^{2nT}$ represent the price vectors of anonymous and named goods. Note that (p, q) is 'a price system at an unspecified location at an unspecified instant' (Debreu, 1959). If $q_{rt} > 0$, say, then $(p^t, q^t) = (1/q_{rt})(p, q)$ is the price system viewed from t in terms of the numeraire (r, H, t). If $t' > t$, let us interpret $p^t_{it'}$ as the forward price at t of (i, t'). If $t' = t$ interpret it as the spot price (at t') of (i, t').

With this interpretation, where the ratios are defined, the relative spot prices of a named and anonymous good of any type are the same as the relative forward prices. That is.

$$\frac{p^{t'}_{it'}}{q^{t'}_{it'}} = \frac{p^t_{it'}}{q^t_{it'}}.$$

This at once suggests that our construction is not yet rich enough in goods to allow us to study an economy where markets are activities using resources. For at present, the transaction date is inessential and the interpretation of $p^t_{it'}$ as spot or forward is a purely formal one. For instance, the analysis could proceed just as well if $t > 1$, $t' < t$, so that we would be dealing with 'backwards' prices and markets. When, however, one is concerned with actual market activities, one cannot suppose in advance that a particular relation exists between the anonymous and named price of a good of a given type at any date. Nor is it possible to neglect the direction of time.

This point is of considerable significance since it shows that a study of transactions will involve more than a trivial modification of the familiar model. Indeed, it will lead us to study sequence economies. The next section will serve to clarify this matter further.

If one then further distinguishes goods by the date of their trading but does not allow any good of type (i, t) to be traded at $t' > t$, then the number of possible goods will be $N = 2nT(T + 1/2)$. The number of possible prices will be larger than that. If we take our viewpoint at $t = 1$, then prices of goods traded at $t' > t$ will in practice be the subject of the expectations of households and these of course may be different. For the first part of this study, however, I shall take all prices as announced, so that there are also N prices.

III   HOUSEHOLDS

I shall employ the following notation. A household's activities are indexed $h = 1, \ldots, H$. I write $C^h \subset \Omega^{nT}$ as the set of possible consumptions of h with typical element $\tilde{c}^h$. The vectors c^{hh} and c^h have as components named and anonymous goods respectively and $\tilde{c}^h = c^{hh} + c^h$. The subvectors $\tilde{c}^h(t)$, $c^{hh}(t)$ and $c^h(t)$ have as components goods of type (i, t), $i = 0, \ldots, n - 1$. Note that with this definition C^h is the usual Debreu set of possible consumptions, which also includes leisure of various dates. The vector $\bar{c}^{hh} \in \Omega^{nT}$ is the vector of named goods representing the endowment of h. Also, $\bar{c}^{hh}(t)$ is the subvector whose components are named goods available at t, i.e., of type (i, t), $i = 0, \ldots, n - 1$.

Let $N^* = nT(T - 1)/2$ and let x^{hh} be a vector with $-x^{hh} \in \Omega^{N*}$. Then x^{hh} is household's h vector of forward sales, all components of which are named. The vector $x^h \in \Omega^{N*}$ is household's h vector of forward purchases with only anonymous components. Let $x^h \subset \Omega^{N*}$ be the set of all possible forward net commitments of h, with typical element $\bar{x}^h$. One defines $\bar{x}^h = x^{hh} + x^h$. The vectors $\bar{x}^h(t)$, $x^{hh}(t)$, $x^h(t)$ have as components goods of type (i, t') with $t' > t$, for which the transaction date is t. Thus $x_{it}^{hh}(t)$, a member of

$x^{hh}(t)$, represents the sale made by h at t of named good of type (i, t'), and $\tilde{x}^h_{it'}(t)$ represents the net commitment (positive or negative) made by h at t with respect to good of type (i, t'). The vector $\bar{x}^h(t)$ is the vector of net commitments of h at t from past contracts. If $\bar{x}^h_i(t)$ is the ith component, then

$$\bar{x}^h_i(t) = \sum_{t' < t} \tilde{x}^h_{it}(t').$$

One defines S^h as the set of storage activities available to h. A typical element $\bar{s}^h$ of S^h has as positive components storage outputs and as negative components storage inputs. I write $\bar{s}^{h+}(t)$ as the vector of storage outputs of named goods type (i, t), $i = 0$, $\dots, n - 1$, and $\bar{s}^{h-}(t)$ as the vector of storage inputs of goods of this type. Also

$$\bar{s}^{h-}(t) = s^{hh-}(t) + s^{h-}(t)$$

where all components of $s^{hh-}(t)$ are named and all those of $s^{h-}(t)$ are anonymous.

The vector $w^h(t)$ is defined by

$$w^h(t) = \bar{c}^{hh}(t) + \bar{s}^{h+}(t) + \bar{x}^h(t).$$

A typical component $w^h_i(t)$ is the sum of the endowment of named good (i, t), the amount of that good coming out of storage, and the net commitment to receive or deliver (i, t). Clearly, $w^h_i(t) < 0$ is possible, in which case I shall say that the household has a net endowment of anonymous good type (i, t). If $w^h_i(t) \geq 0$ the household is said to have a net endowment of named good of type (i, t). The vector $w^{h+}(t)$ is the net endowment vector of named goods available at t and the vector $w^{h-}(t)$ is the net endowment vector of anonymous goods available at t.

I write $p \in \Omega^N$ and $q \in \Omega^N$ as the price vectors of anonymous and named goods; p^t and q^t are subvectors of prices of goods traded at t. I write $p^t = [p^t(t), p^t(t'), \dots]$, $q^t = [q^t(t), q^t(t'), \dots]$ where $t' > t$, etc., and $p^t(t')$, for instance, is the vector of prices of anonymous goods type (i, t') traded at t.

Lastly, the household receives profits in unit of account from its shares in marketing activities. I write $\pi^h(t)$ as the profits received at t and π^h as the vector of these profits. Because of the assumptions of the next section we may take $\pi^h(t) \geq 0$.

I shall make the following assumptions concerning households.

Assumption (H1)   (i) C^h is closed and convex; (ii) the ordering of the household can be represented by a continuous, quasi-concave utility function $u^h(\bar{c}^h)$ from C^h; and (iii) there is no $\bar{c}^{*h} \in C^h$ such that $u^h(\bar{c}^{*h}) > u^h(\bar{c}^h)$ for all $\bar{c}^h \in C^h$.

These assumptions are sufficiently familiar. It is worth re-emphasizing that the household's ordering is on C^h so that it is concerned only with the type of a good and not with its name or trading date. This seems sensible.

Assumption (H2)   (i) S^h is convex and compact with $0 \in S^h$; (ii) $\bar{s}^h > 0$ implies $\bar{s}^h \notin S^h$; and (iii) the components of $\bar{s}^{h-}(t)$ are goods of type $(i, t), i = 0, \ldots, n - 1$.

Once again, there is nothing special about assumption (H2). I am stipulating decreasing returns to storage. Also, the inputs at t are all goods available at t.
    A plan of a household is the triple $(\bar{c}^h, \bar{s}^h, \bar{x}^h)$ with $\bar{c}^h \in C^h$, $\bar{s}^h \in S^h$, $\bar{x}^h \in X^h$. It is said to be *feasible* if it also satisfies the following constraints.

Constraint (C1)   The household cannot buy named goods of type (i, t) at t:

$$c^{hh}(t) - s^{hh-}(t) \leqslant \bar{c}^{hh}(t) + \bar{s}^{h+}(t) + \bar{\bar{x}}^{h+}(t).$$

Constraint (C2)   The household's assets at T must be non-negative:

$$q^T w^{h+}(T) + p^T w^{h-}(T) + \pi^h(T) \geqslant 0; \quad x^h(T) = x^{hh}(T) = 0.$$

Constraint (C3)   The household must satisfy the budget constraints

$$p^t[c^h(t) - s^{h-}(t), x^h(t)] + q^t[c^{hh}(t) - s^{hh-}(t), x^{hh}(t)]$$
$$\leqslant p^t(t) w^{h-}(t) + q^t(t) w^{h+}(t) + \pi^h(t). \quad (t = 1, \ldots, T).$$

Constraint (C1) formalizes the notion of named goods. A household cannot use more of a good of a given type than it has without acquiring anonymous goods of that type. On the other hand, when a household buys a good forward it is ensuring that it will have quantities of that good bearing its name. The constraint

(C2) is one of 'financial probity', which prevents a household from making arbitrarily large forward sales. In its present form it is somewhat unnatural in giving all households the horizon T.

It may be worthwhile to spell out constraint (C3) for a given t. The first term on the left of the inequality represents the value of all purchases at t, spot and forward. The second term is the sum of spot purchases at t the household makes from itself ($q^t(t)[c^{hh}(t) - s^{hh-}(t)]$), and the value of all forward sales at t. The first term on the right represents the value of the net obligation to buy anonymous goods at t undertaken prior to t. The second term is the value of the household's net endowment of named goods. The last term is the value of profits at t.

Consider (C1) again. It certainly allows h to consume a named good of type (i, t) even though its net endowment of this good is negative. If it indeed does this, it will have to buy that much more anonymous good of that type to meet its forward commitment. Since its utility depends on $c^{hh}_{it} + c^h_{it}$, it clearly would have been just as well off if it had consumed more of the anonymous good (i, t) and less of the named. Accordingly, we may modify the constraint (C1) to read as follows.

*Constraint (C*1)* $c^{hh}(t) - s^{hh-}(t) \leqslant w^{h+}(t)$.

The set of choices open to the household is thereby modified but the utility attainable is not.

It is clear that, for some $(p, q, \bar{c}^{hh}) > 0$, no feasible plan may exist; then I shall say that h is *bankrupt*. This can only be the case if at $t < 1$ the household undertook commitments for $t \geqslant 1$. However, at the moment when all expectational matters are excluded, bankruptcy is unnatural and I stipulate the next assumption.

Assumption (H3) $\bar{x}^h(t) = 0$ for $t < 1$.

One may interpret assumption (H3) to mean that the household did not exist before $t = 1$. When I come to consider expectational matters this assumption will turn out not to save one from embarrassment.

Next I shall use the following defintion.

Definition (D1)   A feasible plan $(\bar{c}^h, \bar{x}^h, \bar{s}^h)$ is *weakly efficient* at $(p, q, \pi^h, \bar{c}^{hh})$ if any other plan $(\bar{c}^h, \bar{x}^{h'}, \bar{s}^{h'})$ with $\bar{c}^{h'} \gg \bar{c}^h$ is not feasible at $(p, q, \bar{c}^{hh})$.

It is clear that a weakly efficient plan may not exist. Thus $(p, q) > 0$ is consistent with $p^1 = q^1 = 0$, in which case it is easily verified that plans with the desired property do not exist. (The household plans are in fact undefined.) Or again, (p, q) might be such that the implied borrowing rates of interest, in unit of account, are below the lending rates, in which case again there may be no weakly efficient plans. I wish to exclude these cases.

This leads me to the definition of an admissible price set $\mathscr{P}$. In formulating this set one writes $(\bar{p}^t, \bar{q}^t)$ as the set of forward prices at t and also e as the unit row vector which is always conformable with the column vector which it premultiplies. Also, $\epsilon > 0$ is a small, and $B > 0$ a large, scalar.

Definition (D2) The prices $(p, q) \in \mathscr{P}$ if (i) $(p, q) > 0$, $e(p, q) = 1$; (ii) $p \geqslant q$; (iii) there exist numbers $\alpha(t), \beta(t), \alpha(t) \geqslant \epsilon, 0 \leqslant \beta(t) \leqslant B$, such that $\bar{p}^t \geqslant \alpha(t + 1) p^{t+1}$, $q^t \leqslant \beta(t + 1) q^{t+1}$, $t = 1, \ldots, T - 1$, and (iv) letting $\alpha(p^t, p^{t+1}) \leqslant + \infty$ be the largest $\alpha(t + 1)$ satisfying (iii) for $(\bar{p}^t, p^{t+1})$ and letting $\beta(\bar{q}^t, q^{t+1})$ be the smallest $\beta(t + 1)$ satisfying (iii) for $(\bar{q}^t, q^{t+1})$, then

$$\alpha(\bar{p}^t, p^{t+1}) \geqslant \beta(\bar{q}^t, q^{t+1}) \qquad (t = 1, \ldots, T - 1).$$

The economics of (D2) will be discussed presently. First I prove the following lemma.

Lemma 1 (i) For all $(p, q) \in \mathscr{P}$, $(p^1, q^1) > 0$; and (ii) $\mathscr{P}$ is convex and compact.

Proof (i) If not, then in view of (D2(i)) and (D2(ii)) there must be some t' and (i, t) with $t \geqslant t' + 1$, such that $p_{it}^{t'+1} > 0$. Then by (D2(iii)), $p_{it}^{t'} > 0$ and by (D2(iii)) again, $p_{it}^{t'-1} > 0$. Proceeding, one finds $p_{it}^1 > 0$ contrary to assumption.

(ii) It is immediate that $\mathscr{P}$ is convex and bounded. Let (p^v, q^v) be a sequence in $\mathscr{P}$ approaching (p^0, q^0). One shows in the familiar way that (p^0, q^0) satisfies (D2(i)) and (D2(ii)). If it does not satisfy (D2(iii)), then for some t' and $t \geqslant t'$, either $\bar{p}_{it}^{0t'} = 0$, $p_{it}^{0(t'+1)} > 0$ for some i, or $\bar{q}_{jt}^{0t'} > 0$, $q_{jt}^{0(t'+1)} = 0$. Then for v large enough, $\bar{p}^{vt'}(t) > 0$, $p^{v(t'+1)}(t) > 0$, and

$$\alpha^v(t' + 1) \leqslant \frac{\bar{p}_{it}^{vt'}}{p_{it}^{vt'+1}} < \epsilon,$$

and, by a similar argument,

$$\beta^v(t' + 1) \geqslant \frac{\bar{q}_{jt}^{vt'}}{q_{jt}^{vt'+1}} > B.$$

In either case, for v large enough, $(p^v, q^v) \notin \mathscr{P}$.

From their definitions, $\alpha(\bar{p}^t, p^{t+1})$, $\beta(\bar{q}^t, q^{t+1})$ are continuous in their arguments so that (p^0, q^0) satisfies (D2(iv)).

Lemma 2 For all $(p, q) \in \mathscr{P}$, a weakly efficient plan exists when $\pi^h(t)$ and $\bar{c}^{hh}(t)$ are finite, all t.
 Proof (i) Suppose $q^1 = 0$. Then by lemma 1, $p^1 > 0$ and the proposition follows from (C3) with $t = 1$. So from now on take $q^1 \neq 0$.
 (ii) Let

$$z^h(t) = c^h(t) - s^{h-}(t) - w^{h-}(t), \quad z^{hh}(t) = c^{hh}(t) - s^{hh-}(t) - w^{h+}(t).$$

By (C1) the consumption of named goods at $t = 1$ is certainly bounded. If the lemma is false with (C1) it must be false with (C*1). Hence I use the latter constraint so that

$$z^{hh}(t) \leqslant 0 \qquad \text{for all } t. \tag{4.1}$$

 (iii) Let the vectors $\bar{x}^h(t)$ and $\bar{x}^{hh}(t)$ have the components

$$\bar{x}_{it}^h(t) = \sum_{t' < t} x_{it}^h(t'), \qquad \bar{x}_{it}^{hh} = \sum_{t' < t} x_{it}^{hh}(t')$$

so that $\bar{x}^h(t) + \bar{x}^{hh}(t) - \tilde{x}^h(t) = 0$, $t > 1$. Also, let $\alpha^*(t) = \alpha(\bar{p}^t, p^{t+1})$, $\beta^*(t) = \beta(\bar{q}^t, q^{t+1})$, $\hat{\alpha}(t) = \alpha^*(1) \dots \alpha^*(t)$, $\hat{\beta}(t) = \beta^*(1) \dots \beta^*(t)$, with $\hat{\alpha}(1) = \hat{\beta}(1) = 1$. Also write $\bar{q}^1(t)$, $\bar{p}^1(t)$ for the price vectors in period 1 for goods dated $t' > t$. From (D2), one has, for $t > 1$,

$$\hat{\alpha}(t) \, p^t \geqslant \hat{\alpha}(t) \, q^t \geqslant \hat{\beta}(t) \, q^t \geqslant [q^1(t), \bar{q}^1(t)],$$

$$\hat{\alpha}(t) \, q^t \leqslant \hat{\alpha}(t) \, p^t \leqslant [p^1(t), \bar{p}^1(t)].$$

(iv) Multiplying the budget constraint for t by $\hat{\alpha}(t)$ and adding gives

$$G = \sum_{t=1} \hat{\alpha}(t)\, p^t[z^h(t), x^h(t)] + \sum_{t=1} \hat{\alpha}(t)\, q^t[z^{hh}(t), x^{hh}(t)]$$

$$\leqslant \sum_{t=1} \hat{\alpha}(t)\, \pi^h(t).$$

By (4.1) and the inequalities in (iii), one has, using (C2), i.e., $x^h(T) = x^{hh}(T) = 0$,

$$G \geqslant \sum_{t=1} q^1(t)\, z^h(t) + \sum_{t=1} p^1(t)\, z^{hh}(t) + \sum_{t=1} \bar{q}^1(t)\, \bar{x}^h(t)$$

$$+ \sum_{t=1} \bar{p}^1(t)\, \bar{x}^{hh}(t). \tag{4.2}$$

By (D2(i)) and the definitions, one verifies that

$$q^1(t)[\bar{x}^h(t) - w^{h-}(t)] + p^1()[\bar{x}^{hh} - w^{h+}(t)]$$

$$\leqslant q^1(t)[\bar{x}^h(t) + \bar{x}^{hh}(t) - \bar{x}^h(t)] - q^1(t)[\bar{c}^{hh}(t) - \bar{s}^{h+}(t)]$$

$$= -q^1(t)[\bar{c}^{hh}(t) + \bar{s}^{h+}(t)].$$

From the definitions of $z^h(t)$ and $z^{hh}(t)$, therefore,

$$G \geqslant q^1 c^h + p^1 c^{hh} - q^1 \bar{c}^{hh} - q^1 s^{h-} - p^1 s^{hh-} - q^1 \bar{s}^h.$$

But $q^1 s^{h-} + p^1 s^{hh-} + q^1 \bar{s}^{h+} \leqslant q^1 \bar{s}^h$, whence

$$q^1 c^h + p^1 c^{hh} \leqslant q^1 \bar{c}^{hh} + q^1 \bar{s}^h + \sum \hat{\alpha}(t)\, \pi^h(t). \tag{4.3}$$

Since, by (H2), $q^1 \bar{s}^h$ is bounded, and since $q^1 > 0$ and $p^1 > 0$, this inequality establishes the lemma.

Let me now discuss (D2). There is nothing new in (D2(i)) and I pass it by. Definition (D2(ii)) will, in the next section, be justified with reference to the market technology. This, because it uses resources, will ensure that in searching for an equilibrium one need not consider price situations where the price of a named good exceeds that of an anonymous one. The conditions (D2(iii)) and (D2(iv)) are more interesting.

Suppose a household wishes to lend a unit of account at t for repayment at $t + 1$. Then the gain from this operation depends on the good which it buys forward at t, and on whether in its plan it is a buyer or seller of this good at $t + 1$. Thus suppose it buys $(1/p_{it+1}^t)$ units of good $(i, t + 1)$. If, in its plan, it was a purchaser of $(i, t + 1)$ at $t + 1$, it will now save $(p_{it+1}^{t+1}/p_{it+1}^t)$ units of account at $t + 1$. If it was a seller of the good it will sell more of it and receive $(q_{it+1}^{t+1}/q_{it+1}^t)$ units of account. (If it was neither seller nor buyer, the gain is between the sums calculated on the above basis.) Naturally we may define the lending rate of interest, $r_L^h(t, t + 1)$ as the largest one of all the possible rates obtainable by forward purchases. If that involves trading in good $(r, t + 1)$, one has, from what has just been said,

$$r_L^h(t, t + 1)\, p_{rt+1}^t \geqslant p_{rt+1}^{t+1} - p_{rt+1}^t,$$

and from (D2(iii)) and (D2(iv)),

$$\frac{1 - \alpha^*(t)}{\alpha^*(t)}\, p_{rt+1}^t \geqslant p_{rt+1}^{t+1} - p_{rt+1}^t,$$

whence

$$r_L^h(t, t + 1) \leqslant \frac{1 - \alpha^*(t)}{\alpha^*(t)}.$$

By an exactly similar argument, if $b^h(t, t + 1)$ is the household's borrowing rate attained by selling forward at t and either buying spot at $t + 1$ or selling less spot at $t + 1$, one has

$$r_B^h(t, t + 1)\, q_{st+1}^t \geqslant q_{st+1}^{t+1} - q_{st+1}^t$$

and from (D2(iii)) and (D2(iv)),

$$\frac{1 - \beta^*(t)}{\beta^*(t)}\, q_{st+1}^t \leqslant q_{st+1}^{t+1} - q_{st+1}^t,$$

whence

$$r_B^h(t, t + 1) \geqslant \frac{1 - \beta^*(t)}{\beta^*(t)}.$$

So by (D2(iv)),

$$r_B^h(t, t+1) \geqslant \frac{1 - \beta^*(t)}{\beta^*(t)} \geqslant \frac{1 - \alpha^*(t)}{\alpha^*(t)} \geqslant r_L^h(t, t+1).$$

The borrowing rate implied by any $(p, q) \in \mathscr{P}$ is therefore not less than the implied lending rate. Although I have shown this for adjacent intervals only, the reader can easily verify this relationship for any length of interval (by using $\hat{\alpha}(t)$ and $\hat{\beta}(t)$).

It is now of some importance to understand that $\alpha^*(t)$ and $\beta^*(t)$ need not be the discount factor appropriate to any one household. In particular, the rate appropriate for h for any time interval depends on that household's plans. It is important not only whether that household borrows or lends, but also whether the most favourable terms open to it involve a purchase (or a reduction in planned purchase), or a sale (or a reduction in planned sale), at the delivery date. It is because of this that we must deal with sequences of budget constraints (and the richer commodity space), and this is one of the more interesting consequences of paying explicit attention to transactions.

Indeed, let us say that (p, q) has the Debreu property if there are numbers $\lambda(t, t') > 0$ such that, for $t' > t$,

$$p^{t'} = \lambda(t, t')\bar{p}^t, \qquad q^{t'} = \lambda(t, t')\bar{q}^t$$

(where of course $\bar{p}^t$ and $\bar{q}^t$ contain prices of only those goods that are in $p^{t'}$ and $q^{t'}$). Then one can prove the first theorem.

Theorem 1 For every $\bar{c}^{hh} > 0$ and $u^h(\bar{c}^h)$ satisfying (H1) a household will be indifferent between making all transactions at $t = 1$ or engaging in a sequence of transactions, if and only if (p, q) has the Debreu property.

Proof Multiplying the budget constraint for t' by $\mu(1, t') = 1/\lambda(1, t')$ and adding, one obtains, if (p, q) has the Debreu property,

$$p^1 c^h + q^1 c^{hh} \leqslant q^1 \bar{c}^{hh} + \sum \mu(1, t') \pi^h(t') + o^h \qquad (4.4)$$

where o^h is the net profit (positive or negative) from storage calculated at (p^1, q^1). But then the set of $\bar{c}^h$ satisfying (4.4) is exactly the same as the set of $\bar{c}^h$ satisfying the sequence of budget constraints. Hence the sufficiency part of the proposition follows.

If (p, q) does not have the Debreu property, then for some t', $r_B^h(1, t') \neq r_L^h(1, t')$. But then (4.4) cannot be obtained by adding suitably multiplied budget constraints. There will be $\bar{c}^h$ feasible under the sequence that are not feasible under (4.4). An appropriate choice of $\bar{c}^{hh}$ and $u^h(\bar{c}^h)$ then establishes necessity.

Since (p, q), which satisfies the Debreu property, is a subset of $\mathscr{P}$, our formulation is capable, in principle, of exhibiting a Debreu equilibrium. I return to this below.

I shall now suppose that, among feasible plans, h picks the one that maximizes $u^h(\bar{c}^h)$. In doing this I shall take the familiar step of confining the household's choices to $\bar{C}^h \subset C^h$, a closed, convex and bounded subset. I do not change the notation for plans for this artificial problem since one suspects in advance that these fictitious constraints, suitably chosen, will in any equilibrium be inoperative.

Let $a^h = (c^h, x^h, c^{hh}, x^{hh}, \bar{s}^h)$, a $2N$ vector, be a plan or activity of household h. Then I define $F^h(p, q, \bar{c}^{hh})$ by

$$F^h(p, q, \bar{c}^{hh}) = \{a^h \mid c^h + c^{hh} \in \bar{C}^h, \bar{s}^h \in S^h \text{ and (C1) to (C3) hold}\}.$$

Hence $F^h(p, q, \bar{c}^{hh})$ is the set of feasible activities for household h. I now prove the following lemma.

Lemma 3 The set of feasible activities $F^h(p, q, \bar{c}^{hh})$ is convex for $(p, q) \in \mathscr{P}$.

Proof Let $w^h(a^h, t)$ be the net endowment vector of h at t under the plan a^h. If a^h and $a^{h'}$ are two plans, write $a^h(\alpha) = \alpha a^h + (1 - \alpha) a^h$, $\alpha \in (0, 1)$. Certainly also:

$$w^{h-}[a^h(\alpha), t] \geq \alpha w^{h-}(a^h, t) + (1 - \alpha) w^{h-}(a^{h'}, t). \tag{4.5}$$

Write (C3) as

$$p^t[c^h(t) - s^{h-}(t), x^h(t)] + q^t[c^{hh}(t) - s^{hh-}(t), x^{hh}(t)]$$
$$\leq q^t(t) w^h(a^h, t) + [p^t(t) - q^t(t)] w^{h-}[a^h(t), t] + \pi^h(t). \tag{4.6}$$

Then if a^h and $a^{h'}$ satisfy these constraints, since $w^h[a^h(\alpha), t] = \alpha w^h(a^h, t) + (1 - \alpha) w^h(a^{h'}, t)$, it follows from (4.5) and (H2) that $a^h(\alpha)$ will also satisfy the constraints since by (D2(ii)) $[p^t(t) - q^t(t)] \geq 0$. By the same argument $a^h(\alpha)$ satisfies (C2) and it is obvious that it satisfies (C1). Lastly, $\bar{C}^h$ is convex.

It would be useful if F^h always had a non-empty interior. The rather strong postulate $\bar{c}^{hh} \gg 0$ is not enough for this, since there is $(p, q) \in \mathscr{P}$ with $q = 0$. This is a mildly interesting by-product of this analysis, to which I return below. For the moment I sidestep this difficulty by making the following assumption.

Assumption (H4) (i) for each h, $\bar{c}^{hh} \gg 0$; (ii) for each h, $\pi^h(t) > 0$ if $\pi(t) > 0$ $[\pi(t) = \Sigma_h \pi^h(t)]$.

Both assumptions are of course silly. Assumption (H4(ii)), in fact, postulates that each household owns a strictly positive share in every marketing activity.

To establish the next theorem, I need to prove a preliminary result. Let $y^h = [c^h(1), x^h(1), c^{hh}(1), x^{hh}(1)]$ and $W^h = q^1 \bar{c}^{hh} + \pi^h(1)$.

Lemma 4 (i) For every y^h such that $(p^1, q^1) y^h \leqslant W^h > 0$ there is a plan $a^h \in F^h(p, q, \bar{c}^{hh})$; (ii) if $a^h \in F^h(p, q, \bar{c}^{hh})$ and $W^h(p, q) > 0$, then there exists y^h such that $(p^1, q^1) y^h \leqslant W^h(p, q)$ and $c^{hh}(1)$, $c^h(1) \geqslant 0$.

Proof (i) Set $\tilde{s}^h = 0$ and also $\tilde{x}^h(t)$, $c^h(t) = 0$ for $t > 1$. Let $c^{hh}(t) = \max[0, \bar{c}^{hh}(t) + \tilde{x}^h(t)]$, $t > 1$. Then a^h with these components and y^h is a member of F^h.

(ii) If $a^h \in F^h(p, q, \bar{c}^{hh})$ then from (C3) there is some y^h such that $W^h \geqslant (p^1, q^1) y^h - p^1(1) s^{h-}(1) - q^1(1) s^{hh-}(1) \geqslant (p^1, q^1) y^h$.

One can now prove the next theorem.

Theorem 4 The correspondence $F^h(p, q, \bar{c}^{hh})$ is continuous at $(p^0, q^0) \in \mathscr{P}$, when $W^h(p, q) > 0$, all (p, q).

Proof (i) The set (p, q, a^h) satisfying (C1)–(C3), $\tilde{c}^h \in \bar{C}^h$, $\tilde{s}^h \in S^h$, is closed; hence F^h is upper semi-continuous at (p^0, q^0).

(ii) Let $(p^v, q^v) \in \mathscr{P}$ be a sequence approaching (p^0, q^0) and let $a^{h0} \in F^h(p^0, q^0, \bar{c}^{hh})$. By lemma 4(ii) there then exists y^{h0} such that $(p^{10}, q^{10}) y^{h0} \leqslant W^h(p^0, q^0)$. But we may choose a sequence y^{hv} such that $(p^{1v}, q^{1v}) y^{hv} \leqslant W^h(p^v, q^v)$, $y^{hv} \to y^{h0}$, by the well-known method of Debreu (1959), since there is y^{h*} such that $(p^{10}, q^{10}) y* < W^h(p^0, q^0)$. By lemma 4(i) to every y^{hv} in this sequence there is $a^{hv} \in F^h(p^v, q^v, \bar{c}^{hh})$. Hence there exists a sequence $a^{hv} \in F^h(p^v, q^v, \bar{c}^{hh})$ which converges on a^{h0} and so F^h is lower semi-continuous.

Now let $a^h(p, q, \bar{c}^{hh})$ be the set a^h in $F^h(p, q, \bar{c}^{hh})$ which maximizes $u^h(\tilde{c}^h)$. I state without proof (since it is familiar territory) the following theorem.

Theorem 3 $a^h(p, q, \bar{c}^{hh})$ is convex and an upper semi-continuous correspondence if $W^h(p, q) > 0$ for all (p, q).

This is all that I require concerning households.

IV THE MARKET TECHNOLOGY

For reasons of brevity I shall take all market activities at t to be fully integrated; that is, I shall discuss them as if they were under the control of a single firm. I write M^t as the set of market activities that are technologically feasible at t. A member of M^t is a vector $\tilde{m}^t = (m^t, m^{Ht})$. Here m^t is the vector of net outputs of anonymous goods at t. One takes $m^{Ht} \leq 0$ and regards it as the vector of inputs of named goods at t; If $m^{Ht}_{it'}$ is a component of m^{Ht}, then $m^{Ht}_{it'}$ is the input at t of named good type (it') summed over h. That is, the actual name of the input is irrelevant in specifying the market technology. I shall write $\tilde{m}^t(t) = [m^t(t), m^{Ht}(t)]$ as the subvector of $\tilde{m}^t$ whose components are goods of the type dated t and $\bar{\tilde{m}}^t = (\bar{m}^t, \bar{m}^{Ht})$ as the subvector whose components are goods dated $t' > t$. I postulate the following assumption.

Assumption (M1) (i) For all t, M^t is convex and closed; (ii) $M^t \cap (-M^t) = 0$ (irreversibility); (iii) $M^t \supset (-\Omega)$ (free disposal); (iv) $\tilde{m}^t \neq 0$, $\tilde{m}^t \in M^t$ implies $m^t(t) + m^{Ht}(t) < 0$ and $\bar{m}^t + \bar{m}^{Ht} = 0$; (v) there is $\tilde{m}^1 \in M^1$ with $m^1 \geqslant 0$.

Some of these assumptions are pretty terrible. Assumption (M1(i)) rules out increasing returns when casual observation suggests that set-up costs are an important feature in transaction technologies. The assumptions are made because at present I do not see how to proceed without them. (M1(iv)) is interpreted as follows. If $\tilde{m}(t)$ is feasible at t, then provided $\tilde{m}(t) \neq 0$, (a) it must use more of some good of the type dated t as named input than it produces as anonymous output, and use not less of any such good as named input than it produces as output; (b) the activity transforms quantities of named goods of type dated $t' > t$ equal to the quantities of inputs of named goods of this type. This assumption ensures that a market activity dated t uses some resources dated t but uses no resources dated $t' > t$. For instance, to transact forward butter today uses some good available today but no good, other than the named forward butter, available after today.

There is a further serious assumption embedded in the definitions: the vector $\tilde{m}^t$ has no components bearing the name of the marketing firm. This is tantamount to ruling out durable inputs. The reason this unpalatable assumption is used is that I do not know what to postulate as a proper motive for marketing firms when present values cannot be unambiguously calculated. Recall that the shareholders, that is households, may have different discount factors. One way of overcoming this is to postulate a utility function for firms. I do not do this because it does not seem helpful to sidestep these difficulties so formally. For the same reason I do not allow any firm to engage in storage.

Let $M = \bigtimes M^t$; $\bar{M}$ is a bounded subset of M. Then I define $\tilde{m}(p, q)$, the market correspondence, where

$$\tilde{m}(p, q) = \{\tilde{m} \mid (p, q)\tilde{m} \geqslant (p, q)\tilde{m}', \quad \text{all } \tilde{m}' \in \bar{M}, \tilde{m} \in \bar{M}\}.$$

It is easy to see that if $\tilde{m} \in \tilde{m}(p, q)$, then

$$\tilde{m}^t \in \{\tilde{m}^t \mid (p^t, q^t)\tilde{m}^t \geqslant (p^t, q^t)\tilde{m}'^t, \quad \text{all } \tilde{m}'^t \in \bar{M}^t, \tilde{m}^t \in \bar{M}^t\}.$$

Since all this is closely related to well known production theory, I state without proof the next theorem.

Theorem 4 $\tilde{m}(p, q)$ is an upper semi-continuous correspondence from $\mathscr{P}$.

The following lemma will be useful later.

Lemma 5   For $p^1 > 0$, $0 \notin \tilde{m}^1(p^1, 0)$.
   Proof   By (M1(v)), there is $\tilde{m}^1 \in M^1$, $\tilde{m}^1 \geqslant 0$, from which $(p^1, 0)\tilde{m}^1 > (p^1, 0)0$.

V   EQUILIBRIUM

I define

$$z^t(t) = \sum_h [c^h(t) - s^{h-}(t) - w^{h-}(t)] - m^t(t),$$

$$z^{Ht}(t) = \sum_h [c^{hh}(t) - s^{hh-}(t) - \bar{c}^{hh}(t) - \tilde{s}^{h+}(t)] - m^{Ht}(t),$$

$$\bar{z}^t = \sum x^h(t) - \bar{m}^t, \quad \bar{z}^{Ht} = \sum x^{hh}(t) - \bar{m}^{Ht}(t),$$

$$z^t = [z^t(t), z^{Ht}(t), \bar{z}^t, \bar{z}^{Ht}] \qquad (z = z^1, \ldots, z^T).$$

Then I use the following definition.

Definition (D3)　　An equilibrium of a pure exchange economy with transactions is a price vector (p^*, q^*), a vector of household plans $a^* = (a^{*1} \ldots a^{*H})$, and a market activity vector $\bar{m}^*$ such that (i) $a^{*h} \in a^h(p^*, q^*, \bar{c}^{hh})$ for all h, (ii) $\bar{m}^* \in \bar{m}(p, q^*)$, (iii) $z^* \leqslant 0$.

All this is straightforward and requires no comment. From what has already been established in earlier sections, we suspect that by now traditional methods will show that an equilibrium exists. However, these methods take the price-simplex as the set to be mapped into itself while we have been concerned with the set $\mathscr{P}$.

　　Let $(p, q) \in \mathscr{P}$. By lemma 1(i), $p^1 > 0$. If $q^1 > 0$, then by (H4) $W^h(p, q) > 0$. If $q^1 = 0$, then by lemma 5 $\pi(1) > 0$, whence by (H4) $\pi^h(1) > 0$ and so $W^h(p, q) > 0$. Hence each household has positive wealth for all $(p, q) \in \mathscr{P}$, and so from theorems 3 and 4, $z(p, q)$, the excess demand correspondence for the economy (i.e., a satisfies (D3(i)) and $\bar{m}$, (D3(ii))), is upper semi-continuous and convex at all $(p, q) \in \mathscr{P}$.

　　From $\pi = (p, q)\bar{m}$, (4.6) and (H1), one easily verifies, for $z \in z(p, q)$, that

$$\sum_t [p^t(t) - q^t(t), q^t(t), \bar{p}^t, \bar{q}^t]\hat{z}^t = 0 \qquad (4.7)$$

where $\hat{z}^t = [z^t(t), z^{Ht}(t) + z^t(t), \bar{z}^t, \bar{z}^{Ht}], \hat{z} = (\hat{z}^1 \ldots \hat{z}^T).$

　　One may now proceed as in Debreu (1959). That is, we let $\mu(\hat{z})$ be the set of $(p, q) \in \mathscr{P}$ which maximizes (7) given $\hat{z} \in \bar{E}^N$. Since $\mathscr{P}$ is compact, $(p - q) > 0$, this is a well defined problem and $\mu(\hat{z})$ is convex and upper semi-continuous. The mapping $\mu(\hat{z}) \times z(p, q)$ of $\mathscr{P} \times \bar{E}^N$ into itself has a fixed point (p^*, q^*, z^*). Using (4.7), one verifies from the definition of $\mu(\hat{z})$ that this is an equilibrium for the bounded economy. One then shows that by a suitable choice of bounds this is also the equilibrium for the actual economy. Here the procedure is no different from the usual one, and I simply state the next theorem.

Theorem 5   The pure exchange economy with transactions has at least one equilibrium, with $(p^*, q^*) \in \mathscr{P}$.

There is one comment I should like to make on this now. In establishing the existence of an equilibrium one need only be concerned with (4.7) even though a sequence of 'Walras laws' holds for the economy. When we come to discuss efficiency in the next section, matters will be different.

One would expect that many markets will be inactive in an equilibrium. Some anonymous goods will not be 'produced' or demanded and the corresponding named goods not supplied or demanded. The analysis here is exactly analogous to that of non-produced goods in the conventional model. The abstraction becomes particularly irksome here, however, since one is asked to suppose that prices are established for all possible markets, active or not.

Consider an equilibrium in which all markets after $t = 1$ are inactive, and suppose that all market activities require the input of leisure, and that households cannot consume more leisure than they are endowed with. (This last assumption causes no difficulty for theorem 5.) Then since, by (M1(iv)), market firms will demand only leisure dated $t = 1$, it must be that in this economy the optimum plan of households involves the consumption of all their leisure after $t = 1$ (since the demand for leisure from other sources is zero). On the other hand, of course, the market activities at $t = 1$ must not use more leisure than there is. It is easy to see that such an equilibrium will be rather special, and it is easy by some choice of Cobb–Douglas utility and market activity functions and endowments to construct a large class of examples where this equilibrium is impossible.

The point is, of course, simple: the economy may have active markets at various dates, because this is a sensible intertemporal use of resources. One is accustomed to saying that Debreu assumed all future markets to exist, or at least that this is how his system can be interpreted. In the present constriction of course this makes no sense. The Debreu economy results when only markets of a given date are active.

VI   EFFICIENCY

I am interested in the question of whether an equilibrium for the economy is efficient.

In the present economy the distinction between named and anonymous goods is fundamental. One must therefore expect that, in the definition of the set of feasible allocations, or transactions, the distribution of named goods between households and so the distribution of endowment between them will be essential. This is an important departure from the usual procedure where only aggregate endowments matter. We must also take account of transaction dates. A definition of efficiency will have to be relative to the given endowment matrix, denoted by $\hat{\bar{c}}$, and of course relative to the given market and storage technologies.

Let

$$A^h(\bar{c}^{hh}) = \{a^h \mid c^{hh} \leqslant \bar{c}^{hh} + \bar{s}^{h+} + \bar{x}^{h+}, w^h(T) \nleq 0,$$
$$\bar{s}^h \in S^h, c^{hh}, c^h \geqslant 0\}.$$

Then $A^h(\bar{c}^{hh})$ is the set of activities of h which, given its endowment and storage technology, will not lead it to consume more of a named good of any type than it has, and will not lead it to a net endowment vector at T with every component negative. The set is not empty since $a^h = (0, 0, \bar{c}^{hh}, 0, 0)$ is a member. The set is convex, since S^h is. Write

$$A(\hat{\bar{c}}) = \bigtimes_h A^h(\bar{c}^{hh}),$$

with a an element of $A(\hat{\bar{c}})$. For any a^h, let $v^h(a^h)$ be the vector with components

$$v_{it}^h = (\bar{c}_{it}^{hh} + \bar{s}_{it}^{h+} + \bar{x}_{it}^h - c_{it}^{hh} + s_{it}^{h-})$$

and as usual $v^{h-}(a^h)$ has the components $\min(0, v_{it}^h)$. Also,

$$v^-(a) = \sum v^{h-}(a^h).$$

The components of $v^-(a)$ measure the quantities of the anonymous good of the given type which must be bought if households are to fulfil their forward commitments.

Now let $\hat{a}^h$ be the vector a^h without the components $\bar{s}^h$ and define

$$b(a) = \sum_h (\hat{a}^h - \bar{s}^h) - [v^-(a), 0, \bar{c}, 0].$$

Then a positive element of $b(a)$ is the requirement of anonymous good of given type for the economy with plan a and endowment matrix $\hat{c}$. A negative element is the available quantity of named good of given type.

I now write the set of feasible transactions b as

$$B = \{b \mid b = b(a) \text{ for some } a \in A(\hat{c}), b \leqslant \tilde{m} \text{ for some } \tilde{m} \in M\}$$

but I shall postpone discussion of this set until a little later.

Let $a*$ be an allocation of household activities, $b* = b(a*) \in B$ with $\tilde{m} = \tilde{m}*$. Every activity a^h defines a unique consumption vector

$$\tilde{c}^h(a^h) = c^{hh} + c^h$$

and so one may write the set of activities h prefers to a^{h*} as

$$P^h(a^{h*}) = \{a^h \mid u^h[\tilde{c}^h(a^h)] > u^h[\tilde{c}^h(a^{h*})]\}$$

and also

$$P(a*) = \underset{h}{\text{X}}\, P^h(a^{h*}).$$

Definition (D4) The set of transactions strictly Pareto-superior to $b*$ is

$$\hat{B}(b*) = \{b \mid b = b(a) \text{ for some } a \in P(a*)\}$$

and $(b*, \tilde{m}*)$ is strictly efficient if

$$\hat{B}(b*) \cap B = \emptyset.$$

It is not hard to show, given assumption (H4) (see Arrow and Hahn, 1971), that there is no real loss of generality in considering strictly efficient rather than efficient transactions.

Now let $(a*, \tilde{m}*, p*, q*)$ be an equilibrium. Let

$$\hat{P}^h = P^h(a^{h*}) \cap A^h(\tilde{c}^{hh}).$$

It is easy to see that $\hat{P}^h$ is not empty. Let $\hat{P} = \text{X}_h \hat{P}^h$ and consider $a \in \hat{P}$, $b = b(a)$. By the definition of an equilibrium, a^h cannot be feasible for h under its budget constraints. Since in general h faces a sequence of budget constraints, this does not, however, imply that the budget constraint for every t must be violated.

To be more precise, first note that by the usual arguments

$$(p^*, q^*)\, \bar{m}^* \geqslant (p, q)\, \bar{m}, \quad \text{all } \bar{m} \in M,$$

whence on our assumptions $\pi^{h*} \geqslant \pi^h$, where π^{h*} is the profit received by h in equilibrium and π^h is the profit for any other transactions.

Also, for each h there must be some t such that

$$[p^{*t}(t) - q^{*t}(t), q^{*t}(t), \bar{p}^{*t}, \bar{q}^{*t}]$$
$$\times [z^h(t), z^h(t) + z^{hh}(t), x^h(t), x^{hh}(t)] > \pi^h(t). \tag{4.8}$$

But there may be $t' \neq t$ where the reverse inequality holds. Since this is true for all h, summing over h for every t may give

$$[p^{*t}(t) - q^{*t}(t), q^{*t}(t), \bar{p}^{*t}, \bar{q}^{*t}]\, \hat{z}^t \leqslant 0, \quad \text{all } t.$$

But then we cannot show that $\hat{z}^t$ is not feasible; for $\hat{z}^t \leqslant 0$ for all t is possible, so that $z^t \leqslant 0$ for all t, whence one easily verifies that $a \in \hat{P}$, $b(a) \in B$.

The possibility of inefficient equilibria can be confirmed by simple examples. Suppose that the market technology uses labour and nothing else in transforming any given quantity of named good into the same quantity of anonymous good of the same type. By (M1(iv)), the labour used has the same date as the transaction. For the purpose of this example assume also that labour is both anonymous and named; that is, I treat labour as if it were money. I shall also take the market technologies to be linear and equilibrium profits as zero.

We consider the given equilibrium situation and examine the following reallocation. Let household h be enabled to consume one more unit of leisure at t by reducing the forward transactions in good (k, t') at t, $t' > t$, appropriately. By my special assumptions, giving labour the subscript o, the reduction in forward transactions in this market is given by $p_{ot}^t/(p_{kt'}^t - q_{kt'}^t)$. By this reduction, the stock of named good (k, t') at t' will be reduced for some households, and I suppose that they are compensated for this by an equivalent quantity of anonymous good of that type. (We may suppose that all these households were consuming all of their named good of type (k, t') at t' on their equilibrium plan.) Household h is now required to provide the labour at t' required to make these new transactions at t' possible. We calculate that it must provide $[(p^t_{kt'} - q^t_{kt'})/p^t_{ot'}][p^t_{ot}/(p^t_{kt'} - q^t_{kt'})]$ more units of labour at t' than it did on its equilibrium plan. In our experiment, therefore, we have allocated more labour to h at t and less at t' while changing the allocation of named and anonymous good of type (k, t') at t' to other households in such a manner as to keep their utilities constant. (Recall that household utility depends only on the type of good.)

Now if the equilibrium prices have the Debreu property, the calculations we have just carried out would lead to a substitution rate of labour at t for labour at t' for household h equal to $\lambda(t, t')$. The experiment which we have imagined was not possible for the decentralized economy (since it involves a violation by h of its budget constraint for t and by other households of their budget constraints for t'), although plainly feasible in its resource use, but it could not improve on the equilibrium allocation. For in this case the transformation rate given by the experiment is the same as the one already ruling in the market. This only confirms what is clear from theorem 1 (and equation (4.4)), which can easily be used in the traditional way to show that an allocation that is strictly Pareto-superior to the equilibrium one is not feasible.

However if the equilibrium prices do not have the Debreu property, then the substitution rate established by our experiment may differ from that facing household h when it is constrained by a sequence of budgets. The possibility of equilibrium therefore being inefficient is clear.

The example that I have chosen is only a special case of a large class. When the equilibrium prices do not have the Debreu property, the intertemporal transformation rates that are feasible for any household for a good of given type, given the resources of the economy and the utilities of all other households, will in general not be those that face the household in a decentralized economy. In such an economy these transformation rates will in general differ between households. It is also important to remember that, while a household may, for a given consumption plan, have to engage in forward transactions to meet its budget constraint, the economy is constrained only by the resource use of transactions.

Theorem 6   An equilibrium of the pure exchange economy may be inefficient.

I did not expect this result when I started, but in retrospect it is not surprising once one has understood why, in this economy, households are in general constrained by a sequence of budgets. Considering that all expectational matters and all uncertainty have been neglected, this shows that the recognition of transactions as activities has non-negligible consequences as such.

Let me now briefly take up the postponed discussion of the set B.

Lemma 6 B is a convex set.

   Proof   Let b and $b' \in B$ and a and a' in $A(\hat{\bar{c}})$ be such that $b = b(a)$, $b' = b(a')$. Let $a(\alpha) = \alpha a + (1 - \alpha)a'$, $\alpha \in (0, 1)$, etc. For each h,

$$v^{h^-}[a^h(\alpha)] \geqslant \alpha v^{h^-}(a^h) + (1 - \alpha)\, v^{h^-}(a^h).$$

So

$$v^-[a(\alpha)] \geqslant \alpha v^-(a) + (1 - \alpha)\, v^-(a').$$

Since $A(\hat{\bar{c}})$ is convex $a(\alpha) \in A(\hat{\bar{c}})$ and $b[a(\alpha)] \leqslant b(\alpha)$. But $b(\alpha) \leqslant \bar{m}(\alpha)$ and $\bar{m}(\alpha) \in M$ from which $b[a(\alpha)] \leqslant \bar{m}(\alpha)$ and $b[a(\alpha)] \in B$.

One may now use traditional arguments to show that every efficient point of B has associated with it a separating hyperplane,

$$(\mu^*, \lambda^*)(b^* - \bar{m}^*) = 0. \tag{4.9}$$

Interpreting the first rT components of μ^* as the difference between the spot prices of anonymous and named goods, the remaining components as all forward (buying) prices of anonymous goods, and $\lambda^* = q$, we could obtain (4.7) from (4.9) if $v^-(a) = w^-(a) = \Sigma w^{h^-}(a^h)$. But we may always choose a^* such that this equality holds. For suppose a household is, on the efficient plan, consuming some anonymous good type (i, t) although $w_{it}^h(t) < 0$. Then it must buy that much more of the anonymous good of that type. If instead we make this household consume none of the named good of that type and make it consume more of the anonymous good, its utility would be the same and the transactions would be the same. Hence for every b in B there is an a such that $v^-(a) = w^-(a)$, $b = b(a)$. Hence we can indeed obtain (4.7) from (4.9).

But this does not mean that the economy can be decentralized at these prices. For we are not allowed to redistribute endowments. (If we were allowed to do so, the only efficient point would be one of zero transactions.) Even if at these efficiency prices the endowment of every household were such that the sum of its budget constraints over t were satisfied at the given allocation, that would not be enough, since this would be consistent with the violation of a budget constraint at some t.

I have not been able to show that for any arbitrary $(\hat{c})$ there must exist an efficient allocation such that at its shadow prices the allocation is an equilibrium one. I conjecture that indeed this cannot be done and so that in general every equilibrium of the economy is inefficient.

The exceptional cases must be those for which an equilibrium with the Debreu property is possible.

VII MONEY

In this section the place of money in the kind of model here considered is examined briefly and somewhat discursively. The brevity is due only partly to lack of time. I am not at all clear what an appropriate theory fully articulated, should look like. I hope to return to it at a future occasion.

Money will be written as a good of type (n, t), $t = 1, \ldots, T$. I use the following definition.

Definition (D5) A good of type (n, t), $t = 1, \ldots, T$, is called *money* if it has the following properties:
(i)   For transactions at t, the good of type (n, t) is both named and anonymous. That is, no market is required to transform (n, h, t) into (n, t).
(ii) A given quantity of the good (n, t) can be transformed into an equivalent quantity of the good (n, t'), $t' > t$, by storage without the use of any resources.
(iii) $c_{nt}^h \equiv 0$ for all t and h. The good does not enter the utility function.

Property (i) does *not* abolish the distinction between named and anonymous for transactions at date t of quantities of goods (n, t'),

$t' > t$. That is, the distinction continues to apply to transactions in money dated later than the transaction date. Property (iii) is used because all the interesting questions arise when money is intrinsically worthless and because I cannot appeal to a 'convenience' yield of money when the purpose of the exercise is to discover what this might be from a study of transactions.

One of the consequences of (D5(i)) is that agents, at a positive exchange value of money, are always willing to accept money in exchange for goods. The set of market activities feasible under this regime will in general be larger than the set when there is no such good. That is, the set of marketing activities in a monetary regime will contain the set under barter but not vice versa. I do not think it necessary to discuss this observation. But it gives rise to a technical problem which I can state but not resolve. If one supposes that, in the usual sense, the activities involving a monetary exchange dominate those that do not, then when one considers the transition from a monetary to a non-monetary regime such as would be involved by setting all the prices of money in unit of account equal to zero, the activity transition may not be smooth – that is, there may be a discontinuity. Academic though this problem is, it causes difficulties in the attempt to establish the existence of monetary equilibria.

One can calculate the rate of return in unit of account of buying (n, t') at t as $(p_{nt'}^{t'} - p_{nt'}^{t})/p_{nt'}^{t}$. The rate of return for storing money, given (D5(ii)), is $(p_{nt'}^{t'} - p_{nt}^{t})/p_{nt}^{t}$. If the former rate exceeds the latter, no one will store money. Since money is durable (it cannot be consumed), someone must however store it if money is to have a positive price. Therefore one must show that the equilibrium of the economy does not at any t make the lending rate greater than the implicit storage rate for all $t' > t$ and in particular for t' closest to t. Indeed, in monetary equilibrium it must always be more profitable to some agent to store money between two adjacent intervals than it is to buy forward in any market.

The question is whether an equilibrium with these properties can be shown to be possible or whether this requires one to change (D5(iii)) and allow the storage of money to yield direct or indirect psychic returns.

Let us first of all note that, the more finely time is divided, the more goods and transaction dates there are. If we had allowed for set-up costs (and increasing returns), we could argue that to have markets at every t for all goods dated $t' \geqslant t$ must always use more resources when time is more finely divided. In that case one may be able to show that in any equilibrium many markets will be inactive and in particular all those at any t for goods dated t' when t' is sufficiently close to t. Indeed, the Tobin–Baumol analysis of the transactions demand for money does rest on the assumption that forward purchases of money for short enough periods are always unprofitable. If such transactions do take place, the lending rate is negative.

It will of course also be a requirement that at any t there are agents wishing to transfer resources to t' nearest to t. In my construction this causes a difficulty at $t = T$. But the assumption that all households have the same horizon is inessential (although an economy with an infinite horizon does pose well-known problems), and I do not consider this further. However, a much more interesting question is raised.

Let me say that the economy is *intertemporally connected* if there is no t at which there are no intertemporal transfers between t and t' closest to t, with $t' > t$. In the absence of production there may be difficulties in showing that in every equilibrium the economy is intertemporally connected, in which case there will be obvious difficulties for monetary theory. For money cannot act as a medium of exchange if it does not also act as a store of value for some agent. To avoid these difficulties it seems to me once again that the model which I have discussed must be modified.

If I had allowed for M to be non-convex, I could, for instance, have argued that a contract at t to sell (i, t) and (i, t') uses a different amount of resources than do the sum of separate contracts to sell $((i, t), (it + 1), \ldots, (it'))$. For instance, it is easier in practice to sell labour by the week than by the day and it may be impossible to sell it by the minute. Of course, to integrate this idea into a proper theory I should also have to allow marketing firms to be concerned intertemporally with the attendant difficulties which I have discussed and which I cannot solve. In any event the possibility that the resource cost of a composite contract may be smaller than the resource cost of the sum of the component contracts seems to me to be important for monetary theory. Once again, let me appeal to Tobin–Baumol. They have assumed that the agent's receipts are at discrete time intervals while their purchases are not. A proper money theory must explain why composite contracts of the kind I have been discussing are indeed a feature of an equilibrium; for if they are, the economy will certainly be intertemporally connected. It should be noted that composite contracts introduce new prices and goods.

All these arguments suggest that my description of M must be modified before one can hope to derive a satisfactory monetary theory. For instance, it would have been congenial, one suspects, to many monetary theorists if I had made the number of households concerned in any activity $\bar{m}^t$ a relevant technological variable. For in that case the number of transactions would have been technologically relevant. So far I have not been able to do this without great damage to the result required by a theorist concerned with general equilibrium. But it needs somehow to be done, since most of monetary theory takes it for granted that an equilibrium is possible.

I myself believe that further research on these problems will lead to a rigorous foundation of monetary theory. The alternative, of course, is to allow the holding of money to yield utility. To do this at all sensibly involves the dependence of the utility function on market prices as well.

If I am correct in my view that to obtain a theory in which money is not part of a household's ordering one requires a marketing set which lacks convexity properties, then there are good traditional grounds for the view that an equilibrium, if it exists, may be inefficient. These grounds are, of course, not those of the last section. On the other hand, in such an equilibrium the intertemporal return on holding money is for each household just equal to the opportunity cost and the Friedman-like inefficiency is absent. If, contrarily, we use the model of the previous section and allow the holding of money to yield utility, then Friedman-esque inefficiency can be present while inefficiency arguments connected with non-convexity disappear. However, inefficiencies of the kind discussed in the previous section also remain possible. It should also be noted that, since the opportunity costs of holding money differ between households, the cure of Friedman inefficiency may not be possible in any simple manner.

VIII   EXPECTATIONS

If different states of the economy are possible, we enlarge the space of goods by adding states to their specification. In general, one would not expect all markets to be active at every t for the reasons already discussed earlier. But there are other reasons. Radner (1968) has noted that certain contingent futures contracts may be impossible because the observation of states must be partly deduced from information provided by the action of other agents, and it may be impossible to provide the same information to both parties of a potential contract.

So far I have taken all prices as known to every agent. But of course it will only be the prices ruling in the present which will be known. At any date t the agent may have a hypothesis associating the prices which will rule at $t' > t$, given any state of the economy. He may be taken to have a probability distribution over possible states. Both the hypothesis and the probability distribution may differ between agents if not all possible markets are active at t. Suppose all agents at every t have the same hypothesis but possibly different probability distributions. The following question has recently been studied by Radner (1970) (in a model without transaction costs): Does there exist a set of hypotheses linking prices to states, a price in the current period, and a set of contingent plans by all agents optimal for them such that, for every state, the excess demands for that state at all dates are zero? It will be desirable to study the same question for an economy described in this paper. It will also be very difficult.

One may wish to start far less ambitiously, however, by examining the short-period equilibrium of an economy, that is, the existence of prices at t which, given the agents' expectations, clear all markets at t for the optimal choices made at t. Arrow and I have studied this problem in a rather simple model without transaction costs (Arrow and Hahn, 1971). I have only time to discuss one aspect of this work here.

Radner (1970), in his study to which I have referred, requires that a trader does not plan to deliver at any date–event pair more than he could meet out of his resources or spot purchases without violation of his budget constraint. This assumption, which is quite analogous to my (C3) for the certainty case, rules out the possibility of bankruptcy.

Consider the simplest modification of the model. We examine the economy at t. All prices subsequent to t are expected prices. Suppose $(p^{t'h}, q^{t'h})$ is the single-valued expectation of h at t of prices at $t' > t$. Assume that these are continuous functions of the prices ruling at t, (p^t, q^t). One wants to show that an equilibrium for t exists at every t. Assumption (H3) is now plainly inappropriate. Without a Radner-like postulate, bankruptcy for some h at some (p^t, q^t) cannot be ruled out. Note that by its definition bankruptcy depends on the expectations of h, since it can always borrow at $t < T$. The creditor households may have quite different expectations. Consider a creditor household k which, for the sake of argument, receives all of the endowment of h at (p^t, q^t) where h is bankrupt. Then it is easy to see that the set of feasible choices open to k may fail to be continuous at these prices. Moreover, if h only has to hand over those goods which have a positive price, then its set of feasible choices may also fail to be continuous at these prices. This causes difficulties for an existence of proof. In the present context, particularly in the absence of production, this difficulty may be academic. I believe, however, that it is of considerable interest in more realistic constructions. In any event, the possibility of bankruptcy is one of the main obstacles a short period equilibrium existence proof would encounter in the simple form in which it is here given. It should be noted that this point would be reinforced if we allowed trade in the shares of market firms and if we could also permit intertemporal choices for these firms.

Of course a demonstration, if it is possible, of the existence of equilibrium at every t is quite different from the demonstration of a Radner equilibrium of self-fulfilling expectations. There is no reason to suppose that the first kind of sequence of equilibria will be efficient. Indeed, here is a much more important source of inefficiency than that discussed earlier, in part at least ascribable to transaction costs. In so far as these latter costs are responsible for the sequence of markets, they are also responsible for the inefficiencies which arise at least out of 'Radner-equilibrium'. I do not at present know whether the existence of the latter kind of equilibrium can be established for the economy with transaction costs. But even if it can, I should be rather surprised if such an equilibrium would be a description of an actual economy. Radner himself has drawn attention to the formidable computation requirements which are another species of transaction costs.

REFERENCES

Arrow, K. J. and Hahn, F. H. (1971), *General Competitive Analysis*, Oliver and Boyd, Edinburgh.

Debreu, G. (1959), *Theory of Value*, John Wiley, New York.

Radner, R. (1968), 'Competitive Equilibrium Under Uncertainty', *Econometrica*, **38**.

Radner, R. (1970), 'Existence of Equilibrium of Plans, Prices, and Price Expectations in a Sequence of Markets', parts I and II. Unpublished papers.

5

On Transaction Costs, Inessential Sequence Economies and Money

I INTRODUCTION

In a classical Debreu economy the opportunities open to an agent do not depend on the transaction date; in a sequence economy they may.[1] Moreover, in a Debreu economy households may always be interpreted as facing a 'present-value' budget constraint; in a sequence economy this is not always possible. Roughly speaking, I shall be defining an inessential sequence economy as one in which the sequence makes no difference to what we have already deduced about the equilibrium of a Debreu economy. I shall show that only such economies can be Pareto-efficient relative to a transactions technology and distribution of endowments among households. But there are also non-inessential sequence economies. This leads me to money and forward markets in money. I deal with the question, Why do agents hold money? in a crude way, and comment on other ways, i.e. that of Grandmont and Younes (1972, 1973). I show that no sequence economy in equilibrium with borrowing and lending of money can be efficient if such borrowing and lending is costly; I shall comment on the robustness of these conclusions. It will become plain that, since the classical dichotomy can only fail to hold for economies with sequences which are not inessential, this dichotomy seems to imply that monetary equilibria of this kind are inefficient.

[1] This is one of the technical papers on which I informally reported in a paper delivered to the AUTE at Aberystwyth in March 1972. It was entitled 'On the Foundations of Monetary Theory'. I have made some slight changes in nomenclature. I have benefited from Heller (1972), Kurz (1972) and Starrett (1973). This work was supported by the National Science Foundation Grant GS-3269 at the Institute for Mathematical Studies in the Social Sciences at Stanford University, Stanford, California.

E

I start with a recapitulation of an earlier paper from which this one takes its point of departure, although before that I provide the notation to be used which I hope improves on the very bad one in Hahn (1971). I then construct a sequence economy and a Debreu economy without money so as to be able to define inessentiality, about which certain theorems are proved. I then discuss efficiency. Lastly, the two economies are modified to allow for money and some of the claims made above are substantiated.

Notation

There are H households indexed h and l goods indexed (j, t). The first entry j refers to the physical as well as the locational property, and the second entry t to the date of delivery of the good. I let $t = 1, \ldots, \tau$. Each h will have an endowment $\bar{x}_{hjt} \geq 0$ of (j, t) and I write $\bar{x}_h \in R^{+l}$ as the endowment vector. I distinguish buying from selling and the transactions date. Thus b^v_{hjt}, (s^v_{hjt}) is the purchase (sale) by h at v of (j, t). One takes $b^v_{hjt} \geq 0$, $s^v_{hjt} \leq 0$, and

$$b^v_{hjt} = s^v_{hjt} \equiv 0 \quad \text{for } v > t$$

so that there are no backward transactions. Also, b^v_h, (s^v_h) is the vector of purchases (sales) by h at v while b_h, (s_h) is the vector of purchases and sales by h. I call a^v_h an activity of h and v and

$$a^v_h = (b^v_h, s^v_h), \quad a_h = (a^1_h, \ldots, a^\tau_h).$$

Now at $t = 1$ there is for each good a spot market and $\tau - 1$ forward markets, hence τ markets. At $t = 2$ the good has $\tau - 1$ markets. So each good has $\sum_{t=0}^{\tau-1}(\tau - i) = \tau(\tau + 1)/2$ markets. So $a_h \in R^L$ with $L = l\tau(\tau + 1)$. I define

$$\alpha(\bar{x}_h) = \{a_h \mid b^v_{hjv} + s^v_{hjv} + \bar{x}_{hjv} \geq 0, \text{ all } (j, v)\}.$$

It will also be convenient to have

$$B_{hjt} = \sum_v b^v_{hjt}, \quad S_{hjt} = \sum_v s^v_{hjt}$$

to denote the total purchases (sales) of (j, t) by h. Then B_{ht}, (S_{ht}) is the vector with components B_{hjt}, (S_{hjt}) and B_h, (S_h) the vector with component B_{ht}, (S_{ht}). Given a_h, B_h and S_h are given, and I write

$$A(a_h) = (B_h, S_h) \in R^{2l}.$$

The consumption vector c_h (dimension l) of h is now given by

$$c_h = B_h + S_h + \bar{x}_h \equiv L(a_h)$$

since with given endowments the vector depends only on a_h. The feasible consumption set is taken to be R^{+l} and the set of activities which allow feasible consumption is written as C_h and defined by

$$C_h = \{a_h \mid L(a_h) \in R^{+l}\}.$$

The buying price of anything is denoted by p, the selling price by q. Then p_{jt}^v, (q_{jt}^v) is the buying (selling) price of (j, t) at v. I write p^v, (q^v) as the vector of these prices at v, (p, q) as the vector of prices where $(p, q) \in R^{+L}$. Sometimes I shall want to take the case

$$p_{jt}^v = \hat{p}_{jt}, q_{jt}^v = \hat{q}_{jt}, \quad \text{all } v \quad \text{all } (j, t).$$

I then write $(\hat{p}, \hat{q}) \in R^{+2l}$ as the price vector. Then $\Delta_{2l} \subset R^{+2l}$ is the $2l$ dimensional simplex.

Further notation is introduced as required.

II PRELIMINARIES

I shall not again in detail discuss matters which have been dealt with elsewhere both by myself and by others (e.g. Hahn, 1971; Kurz, 1972; Starrett, 1973). This section is confined to a bare outline.

Households

Each household is taken to have a convex continuous and complete preordering of R^{+l}. This can be represented by a quasi-concave utility function $u_h(c_h)$. In the above notation one may write

$$u_h(c_h) = u_h[L(a_h)] \equiv v_h(a_h).$$

If $a_h(\lambda) = \lambda a_h + (1 - \lambda)a_h'$, $0 \leqslant \lambda \leqslant 1$, then $L[a_h(\lambda)] = \lambda L(a_h) + (1 - \lambda)L(a_h')$ and v_h is quasi-concave in a_h.

I shall throughout employ the unpalatable assumption

$$\bar{x}_h \geqslant 0 \text{ each } h. \tag{5.1}$$

One can relax this somewhat but I do not discuss these matters here.

Transactions

I suppose that for each v there is a T^v of feasible pairs (b^v, s^v) and I define T by

$$T = \underset{v}{\mathsf{X}} \, T^v.$$

For present purposes I shall take T^v to be a closed convex cone for each v. T^v includes the origin. I further postulate when

$$b^v = \sum_h b_h^v, \quad s^v = \sum_h s_h^v.$$

For $(b^v, s^v) \neq 0$, $(b^v, s^v) \in T^v$:

(i) $b^v + s^v < 0$ $\qquad\qquad\qquad\qquad\qquad\qquad$ (5.2)

and

(ii) $b_v^v + s_v^v < 0$.

This ensures that transactions as such cannot increase the amount of any good available for consumption and that transactions at date v use up some input dated v. This last requirement is not essential to what follows, but I like it and it makes it easy to explain why in general not all potential markets at any date are active. The assumptions and in particular convexity are, as noted in Hahn (1971), bad. It may help to think of the transaction technology as representing shops and distribution services; I do not here include the use of transaction resources which may be peculiar to any one agent engaging in transactions.

III THE TWO ECONOMIES

A good deal of what follows turns on a comparison of two economies:[2] the *Debreu Transactions Economy* $\mathcal{E}^d$ and the *Sequence* $\mathcal{E}^s$. The former is distinguished from the latter by two postulates: the relative prices of goods faced by agents are independent of the transaction date, and households do not have to balance their books at each transaction date but only over all dates taken together. The nomenclature is a little misleading, since in general an equilibrium of $\mathcal{E}^d$ will have a sequential structure imposed by T; but households do not face a sequence of budget constraints which justifies the terminology. I now make the distinction precise.

$\mathcal{E}^d$

(i) Each household h as described in section II above faces prices $(\hat{p}, \hat{q}) \in \Delta_{2l}$ and is restrained in its choice of activities by

$$D_h(\hat{p}, \hat{q}) = \{a_h \mid (\hat{p}, \hat{q})A(a_h) \leq 0, \quad a_h \in C_h\}$$

and has the activity correspondence

$$d_h(\hat{p}, \hat{q}) = \{a_h \mid v_h(a_h) \text{ is max on } D_h(\hat{p}, \hat{q})\}.$$

(ii) There is a profit-maximizing transactor (I called him 'marketeer' in Hahn, 1971), one for each v, with the transaction correspondence

$$y_d^v(\hat{p}, \hat{q}) = \{a^v \mid (\hat{p}, \hat{q})a^v \text{ max on } T^v\}.$$

One writes

$$y_d(\hat{p}, \hat{q}) = [y_d^1(\hat{p}, \hat{q}), \ldots, y_d^\tau(\hat{p}, \hat{q})].$$

[2] To one reader at least it appeared wrong to distinguish between two economies which have the same preferences, endowments and technologies. In what I call the Debreu economy there is perfect information for each agent concerning the 'financial probity' of every other agent, while this is not so in the sequence case where books must be balanced at every transaction date. It is precisely our increasing understanding of the relevance of information structures, and indeed of institutional arrangements, to the description of economists which makes it useful to include these in the characterization of any economy.

(iii) An equilibrium $(\hat{p}^*, \hat{q}^*, a_1^*, \ldots, a_H^*)$ of $\mathscr{E}^d$ occurs when, for $(p^*, q^*) \in \Delta_{2l}$,

$$a_h^* \in d_h(\hat{p}^*, \hat{q}^*) \text{ each } h$$

$$a^* = \sum_h a_h^* \in y_d(\hat{p}^*, \hat{q}^*),$$

and I denote by E^d the set of such equilibria.

It is rather easy to show that $\mathscr{E}^d$ has at least one equilibrium since the formal structure of the economy is close to tradition. This demonstration has been provided by Starrett (1973). The following points are worth noting.

1 In every equilibrium of $\mathscr{E}^d$ one has

$$\hat{p}^* \geqslant \hat{q}^*. \tag{5.3}$$

For suppose not, and that say $\hat{p}_{jt}^* < \hat{q}_{jt}^*$: then, by selling only the good (j, t) (and buying it and other goods), the household can attain an unbounded consumption vector. But at any v

$$(\hat{p}^*, \hat{q}^*)a^v = \hat{p}^*(b^v + s^v) + (\hat{q}^* - \hat{p}^*)s^v.$$

By (5.2) the first term on the right is non-positive, and since only (j, t) is sold the last term is negative and this is inconsistent with equilibrium.

2 No household can improve itself by both buying and selling the same good. This follows from (5.3) and from the fact that utility depends only on consumption.

3 If $A(a_h) = A(a_h')$, then, since

$$c_h = e'A(\,\cdot\,) + \bar{x}_h,$$

a_h and a_h' are *consumption-equivalent*. In $\mathscr{E}^d$ any a_h which is consumption-equivalent to a_h^* is also budget-feasible, so that in general $d_h(\hat{p}^*, \hat{q}^*)$ will contain a convex set of activities. This suggests that in an equilibrium with $(\hat{p}^*, \hat{q}^*)$, varying transaction dates may be possible. This is no surprise in an economy where relative prices are independent of transaction dates. But T and in particular (5.2) does place restrictions on possible equilibrium transaction dates, given $(\hat{p}^*, \hat{q}^*)$. Suppose for instance that, for each h, a_h^1 with transactions only in period 1 is consumption-equivalent to a_h^* which has only spot transactions at each date. One knows that $a^* = \Sigma a_h^* \in T$. But then in general $\Sigma a_h^1 \notin T$, for by (5.2) (ii) the substitution of first-period (forward) transactions for spot transactions will require the use of more first-period resources. Hence if the consumption of these is not zero, requiring first-period consumption to be the same in a^1 and a^* makes a^1 infeasible. In general, therefore, an equilibrium of $\mathcal{E}^d$ will have a sequential structure even when there are consumption-equivalent non-sequential activities.

$\mathcal{E}^s$

(i) Each household h as described in section II faces prices $(p, q) \in P \subset R^{+L}$, where P is convex and compact. The household's choices are restrained by

$$\Sigma_h(p, q) = \{a_h \mid (p^v, q^v)a_h^v \leqslant 0 \text{ each } v, a_h \in C_h\}$$

(where the notation Σ_h serves as a mnemonic for 'sequence'). The activity correspondence is

$$\sigma_h(p, q) = \{a_h \mid v_h(a_h) \text{ is max on } \Sigma_h(p, q)\}.$$

(ii) The profit-maximizing transactor at each v has the transaction correspondence

$$y_s^v(p^v, q^v) = \{a^v \mid (p^v, q^v)a^v \text{ is max on } T^v\}$$

and one writes $y_s(p, q) = \{y_s^1(p^1, q^1), \ldots, y_s^\tau(p^\tau, q^\tau)\}$.
(iii) An equilibrium $(p^*, q^*, a_1^*, \ldots, a_H^*)$ of $\mathcal{E}^s$ with $(p^*, q^*) \in P$ occurs when

$$a_h^* \in \sigma_h(p^*, q^*) \text{ each } h$$

$$a^* = \Sigma a_h^* \in y_s(p^*, q^*).$$

I denote by E^s the set of such equilibria.
    That this economy possesses an equilibrium has been shown in Hahn (1971). It can be easily verified that, as in (5.3) above,

$$p^{*v} \geqslant q^{*v}, \text{ all } v. \tag{5.4}$$

If a_h is consumption-equivalent to a_h^* it does not now follow, as it did in $\mathscr{E}^d$, that a_h is budget-feasible for h. The transaction dates consistent with any equilibrium are therefore in some sense more narrowly determined than they are in $\mathscr{E}^d$.

IV   EQUIVALENT AND INESSENTIAL SEQUENCE ECONOMIES

I shall now take $\mathscr{E}^s$ and $\mathscr{E}^d$ always to have identical agents with identical endowments and transactions technologies. Since we know a good deal about economies with the formal structure of $\mathscr{E}^d$ I shall first consider some special cases where the equilibria of the two economies are related in some way.

Definition (D1)[3]   (a) $\mathscr{E}^s$ is said to be *consumption-equivalent* to $\mathscr{E}^d$ (written $\mathscr{E}^s \underset{c}{\subseteq} \mathscr{E}^d$), if for every

$$(p, q, a_1^s, \ldots, a_H^s) \in E^s$$

there is $(\hat{p}, \hat{q}, a_1^d, \ldots, a_H^d) \in E^d$ with a_h^d consumption-equivalent to a_h^s, each h. $(L(a_h^d) = L(a_h^s)$ each $h)$.
   (b) $\mathscr{E}^d$ is said to be *consumption-equivalent* to $\mathscr{E}^s$ (written $\mathscr{E}^d \underset{c}{\subseteq} \mathscr{E}^s$), if for every

$$(\hat{p}, \hat{q}, a_1^d, \ldots, a_H^d) \in E^d$$

there is $(p, q, a_1^s, \ldots, a_H^s) \in E^s$ with $L(a_h^s) = L(a_h^d)$, each h.
   (c) The sequences of $\mathscr{E}^s$ are said to be *inessential* if $\mathscr{E}^s \underset{c}{\subseteq} \mathscr{E}^d$ and $\mathscr{E}^d \underset{c}{\subseteq} \mathscr{E}^s$.

There is an obvious sufficient condition for $\mathscr{E}^s \underset{c}{\subseteq} \mathscr{E}^d$. Suppose that, for every

$$(p, q, a_1^s, \ldots, a_H^s),$$

there is $(\hat{p}, \hat{q}) \in \Delta_{2l}$ and scalars $k^v > 0$, $v = 1, \ldots, \tau$ such that

$$k^v p_{jt}^v - \hat{p}_{jt} \leqslant 0 \quad \text{and} \quad (k^v p_{jt}^v - \hat{p}_{jt})b_{jt}^v = 0$$
$$k^v q_{jt}^v - \hat{q}_{jt} \geqslant 0 \quad \text{and} \quad (k^v q_{jt}^v - \hat{q}_{jt})s_{jt}^v = 0. \tag{5.5}$$

---

[3] The terminology of (a) and (b) of course does not imply an equivalence relationship in the mathematical sense.

When (5.5) holds I shall say that (p, q) has the *Debreu property* (see Hahn, 1971, for a slightly different definition). In this case it is easy to verify that $(\hat{p}, \hat{q}, a_1^s, \ldots, a_H^s) \in E^d$.

Since $a_h^s \in \Sigma_h(p, q)$, multiplying each budget constraint for v by k^v and adding gives $(\hat{p}, \hat{q})A(a_h^s) \leqslant 0$ so that $a_h^s \in D_h(\hat{p}, \hat{q})$. But then $a_h^s \in d_h(\hat{p}, \hat{q})$. For suppose not, and let $a_h^d \in d_h(\hat{p}, \hat{q})$. Then there is $\bar{a}_h^d$ which is consumption-equivalent and budget-feasible in $\mathscr{E}^d$ but where all transactions are concentrated in the same period $v = 1$. But by the Debreu property of (p, q), $\bar{a}_h^d \in \Sigma_h(p, q)$ and is preferred to a_h^s, which contradicts the definition of a_h^s as an equilibrium activity of h in $\mathscr{E}^s$. Lastly, if $a^s \in y_s(p, q)$, then $a^s \in y_d(\hat{p}, \hat{q})$ since for each v, $y_s^v(p^v, q^v) = y_s^v(k^v p^v, k^v q^v)$.

If one interprets $(\hat{p}, \hat{q})$ as $(p^1 q^1)$, then to say that (p, q) has the Debreu property is the same as saying that each agent uses the same discount factor (k^v) to convert prices at v into 'present' prices at 1. There seems no good reason why this should be a property of E^s and I have discussed this at some length in Hahn (1971). However, there may be differently specified sequence economies which do always have this property, and I return to this at length below. But now I want to show that (5.5) is also necessary for $\mathscr{E}^s \underset{c}{\subseteq} \mathscr{E}^d$.

Theorem 1 $\mathscr{E}^s \underset{c}{\subseteq} \mathscr{E}^d$ if and only if, for every $(p, q, a_1^s, \ldots, a_H^s) \in E^s$, (p, q) satisfies (5.5) for every good traded at any v.

Proof Sufficiency has already been established, so let $\mathscr{E}^s \underset{c}{\subseteq} \mathscr{E}^d$ and consider

$$(p, q, a_1^s, \ldots, a_H^s) \in E^s, (\hat{p}, \hat{q}, a_1^d, \ldots, a_H^d) \in E^d$$

with $L(a_h^s) = L(a_h^d)$, each h. Let μ_h be the budget constraint multiplier for h in E^d and λ_h^v the vth budget constraint multiplier for h in E^s. By consumption equivalence, one then gets from the maximization conditions for each h.

If in E^d:

(i) $B_{hjt} > 0, b_{hjt} \geqslant 0: \mu_h \hat{p}_{jt} \leqslant \lambda_h^v p_{jt}^v,$

$\quad (\mu_h \hat{p}_{jt} - \lambda_h^v p_{jt}^v) b_{hjt}^v = 0, \quad$ all v

(ii) $S_{hjt} < 0, s_{hjt} \leqslant 0: \mu_h \hat{q}_{jt} \geqslant \lambda_h^v q_{jt}^v,$

$\quad (\mu_h \hat{q}_{jt} - \lambda_h^v q_{jt}^v) s_{hjt}^v = 0, \quad$ all v

$$(5.6)$$

(iii) $B_{hjt} = S_{hjt} = 0$ and $b^v_{hjt} > 0$: $\mu_h \hat{p}_{jt} \geqslant \lambda^v_h p^v_{jt}$ $\left.\begin{array}{c} \\ \\ \end{array}\right]$ (5.6)

(iv) $B_{hjt} = S_{hjt} = 0$ and $s^v_{hjt} < 0$: $\mu_h \hat{q}_{jt} \leqslant \lambda^v_h q^v_{jt}$.

Then let $k^v_h = \lambda^v_h / \mu_h$ and

$$k^v = \min_h k^v_h.$$

We know from the fact that we are in E^s that $b^v_{hjt} > 0$ some h must mean $s^v_{h'jt} < 0$ some h'. So let a *subscript* v to a vector denote that all entries (j, t) in which there is no trade at v have been deleted. Then from (5.6)

$$\hat{p}_v \geqslant k^v p^v_v$$
$$\hat{q}_v \leqslant k^v q^v_v$$ (5.7)

Suppose that equality does not hold for some element(s) of (5.7). Then since by assumption $a^{sv} \in T^v$ one has

$$(\hat{p}_v, \hat{q}_v)a^{sv}_v > k(p^v_v, q^v_v)a^{sv}_v = (p^v_v, q^v_v)a^{sv}_v = 0.$$

But also

$$(\hat{p}_v, \hat{q}_v)a^{sv}_v = (\hat{p}, \hat{q})a^{sv} \leqslant (\hat{p}, \hat{q})a^{dv} = 0,$$

a contradiction. Hence there must be equality in (5.7).

Corollary 1   A necessary condition for $\mathscr{E}^d \subseteq_c \mathscr{E}^s$ is that (5.7) holds with equality each v, for each $(\hat{p}, \hat{q}, a^d_1, \ldots, a^d_H) \in E^d$ and some $(p, q, a^s_1, \ldots, a^s_H) \in E^s$ with $L(a^d_h) = L(a^s_h)$, each h.
    Proof   The same argument as in theorem 1.

On the other hand, Debreu property (5.7) is not sufficient for $\mathscr{E}^d \subseteq_c \mathscr{E}^s$. For suppose (p, q) satisfy this condition with respect to $(\hat{p}, \hat{q})$. Then there may be, for some h, no $a^s_h \in \Sigma_h(p, q)$ with $L(a^s_h) = L(a^d_h)$. For instance, h in E^d may have $(\hat{p}, \hat{q})a^{dv}_h > 0$. But then suppose that the only consumption-equivalent activity vector which is transaction-feasible is $(a^d_1, \ldots, a^d_H)$ itself. Then (5.7) implies $(p^v, q^v)a^v_h > 0$ and it cannot be an equilibrium for $\mathscr{E}^s$. This then leads to

Theorem 2 Necessary and sufficient conditions for $\mathcal{E}^d \underset{c}{\subseteq} \mathcal{E}^s$ are (a) that the conditions of corollary 1 hold, (b) that for every equilibrium set of prices $(\hat{p}, \hat{q})$ in $\mathcal{E}^d$ there is $(a_1^d, \ldots, a_H^d)$ such that $(\hat{p}, \hat{q}, a_1, \ldots, a_H^d) \in E^d$ and for each h and v

$$(\hat{p}, \hat{q})a_h^{dv} \leqslant 0. \tag{5.8}$$

Proof (i) In view of corollary 1, necessity is obvious. (ii) Let (p, q) satisfy condition (a). Let $a_h^{sv} = a_h^{dv}$ all v and h where $(a_1^d, \ldots, a_H^d)$ satisfies (b). Then $(p^v q^v)a_h^{sv} \leqslant 0$ all v and h and so $(p, q, a_1^d, \ldots, a_H^d) \in E^s$.

Corollary 2 The conditions of theorem 2 are necessary and sufficient for $\mathcal{E}^s$ to have inessential sequences.
  Proof Theorems 1 and 2.

Let us briefly consider condition (b) of theorem 2. It is convenient to say that E^d is *stationary* if in every equilibrium of $\mathcal{E}^d$

$$c_{hjt} = c_{hj} \text{ all } t \text{ and } h.$$

It is then easy to see that, in a stationary equilibrium of $\mathcal{E}^d$, there are consumption-equivalent activities which satisfy (5.8). But they may not be equilibrium activities if for instance transactors are willing to transact (j, t) forward at v and (p, q) but not spot. Therefore a stationary equilibrium of $\mathcal{E}^d$ will satisfy (5.8) if $a^d \in y_d(\hat{p}, \hat{q})$ when a^d consists only of spot transactions. This observation will come in useful presently, and we shall call $\mathcal{E}^d$ which satisfies both these requirements *spot-stationary*.

Alternatively, of course, (b) may be satisfied with $a_h^{dv} = 0$ all $v > 1$. If that is the case, that is if it is possible to concentrate all the transactions of any equilibrium of $\mathcal{E}^d$ into the first period, I shall say that $\mathcal{E}^d$ is *pure*.

V   EFFICIENCY

Let us now write $\hat{a} = (a_1, \ldots, a_H)$ and use the notation $\hat{a}R\hat{a}'$ to denote that $\hat{a}$ is Pareto-superior to $\hat{a}'$; i.e., $v_h(a_h) \geqslant v_h(a_h')$ all h and strict inequality some h.

The following result is obvious and is stated for completeness.

Lemma 1   Every equilibrium of $\mathscr{E}^d$ is Pareto-efficient.

Of course Pareto efficiency here must be relative to both the transaction technology and the matrix of endowments. To make this precise let us consider the linear projection from R^L to R^{2l} to define the appropriate feasibility set F:

$$F = \left\{ A \mid A = \sum_h A_h, A_h = A_h(a_h) \quad \text{some} \right.$$

$$\left. a_h \in \alpha(\bar{x}_h), a_h \in C_h, \sum_h a_h \in T \right\}.$$

It is easily verified that F is convex and that it is bounded (Heller, 1972). In obvious notation let $A = A(\hat{a})$ and suppose $A^* = A(\hat{a}^*) \in F$. Then

$$G(A^*) = \left\{ A \mid A = \sum_h A_h, A_h = A_h(a_h) \text{ each } h \text{ with } \hat{a}R\hat{a}^* \right\}$$

so that this is the set of A (and hence $\hat{a}$ in R^L) that is Pareto-superior to A^*, $(\hat{a}^*)$. It too is evidently convex. Pareto efficiency is then defined as usual by $F \cap G(A^*) = \emptyset$. By routine argument there is $(\hat{p}, \hat{q})$ such that A^* efficient gives

$$0 = (\hat{p}, \hat{q})A(\hat{a}^*) \geqslant (\hat{p}, \hat{q})A(\hat{a}) \text{ when } \hat{a}R\hat{a}^*. \tag{5.9}$$

One can now prove

Theorem 3 $\mathscr{E}^s \underset{c}{\subseteq} \mathscr{E}^d$ is both necessary and sufficient for every element of E^s to be Pareto-efficient.
   Proof   (i) Suppose $\mathscr{E}^s \underset{c}{\subseteq} \mathscr{E}^d$. By lemma 1 and consumption equivalence, every element of E^s is Pareto-efficient. (ii) Let $(p, q, a_1^s, \ldots, a_H^s) \in E^s$ be Pareto-efficient. Then there exists $(\hat{p}, \hat{q})$ which satisfies (5.9) with $\hat{a}^* = (a_1^s, \ldots, a_H^s)$. Let $\mathscr{E}^{*d}$ be the Debreu economy obtained when each household is given a lump-sum tax or subsidy in unit of account of T_h, so that

$$(\hat{p}, \hat{q})A(a_h^s) + T_h = 0, \quad \text{all } h.$$

Of course, $\Sigma T_h = 0$. Then $(p, q, a_1^s, \ldots, a_H^s)$ is consumption-equivalent to

$$(\hat{p}, \hat{q}, a_1^s, \ldots, a_H^s),$$

an equilibrium of $\mathscr{E}^{*d}$. By theorem 1 it follows that (p, q) has the Debreu property for $(\hat{p}, \hat{q})$. Multiplying each budget constraint in $\mathscr{E}^s$ by k^v and adding, we then find

$$(\hat{p}, \hat{q})A(a_h^s) = 0.$$

hence $T_h = 0$ each h and $(\hat{p}, \hat{q}, a_1^s, \ldots, a_H^s) \in E^d$.

On the other hand, unless $\mathscr{E}^s$ has inessential sequences, there are efficient equilibria in $\mathscr{E}^d$ not attainable in $\mathscr{E}^s$. One of the main differences between the two economies is that in $\mathscr{E}^s$ all agents must balance their books each v while in $\mathscr{E}^d$ they need not, and this may appear to be a fortuitous instutitional requirement which has nothing to do with the 'real' part of the economy. It is also of course the case that this is the point of the story where we should turn to 'financial' considerations. That is what I now do.

VI   A SEQUENCE ECONOMY WITH MONEY

In this section money will perform only as a store of value. I assume (1) that money does not enter the utility function, (2) that spot transactions in money are costless so that there is no difference between the spot buying and selling price of money, (3) that each household has a positive initial endowment of money, and (4) that each household must at τ return (to the 'government') whatever money it has been endowed with.

The assumption (4) is of course objectionable, although one could tell a sort of taxation story about it. But in a finitely lived economy it is plain that I shall not be able to do without it. It is extremely likely that, when one considers an infinitely lived economy with overlapping generations, this postulate can not only be abandoned but the conclusions which follow will remain intact. I am aware that (4) provides an artificial motive for holding money, but this problem of monetary theory is not my present concern.

I shall write m for money so that (m, t) is the suffix for money dated t and

$$b^v_{hmt}, b^v_{hm}, b_{hm}, s^v_{hmt}, s^v_{hm}, s_{hm}$$

have the usual meaning. One takes $b^v_{hmt} \geqslant 0$ and $s^v_{hmt} \leqslant 0$, as well as $b^v_{hmt} = s^v_{hmt} \equiv 0$ for $v > t$. Also,

$$a^v_{hm} = (b^v_{hm}, s^v_{hm}), a_{hm} = (a^1_{hm}, \ldots, a^\tau_{hm}), B_{hmt} = \sum_v b^v_{hmt},$$

$$S_{hmt} = \sum_v s^v_{hmt}.$$

I also write m_{ht} as the amount of money held at the end of period t and interpret $m_{h0} > 0$ as the endowment of money h has. (The household has no exogenous sources of money thereafter.) Since storage transforms money of one date costlessly into money at another date, one has

$$m_{ht} = B_{hmt} + S_{hmt} + m_{ht-1}. \tag{5.10}$$

The household must obey the restrictions

$$m_{ht} \geqslant 0 \text{ all } t \tag{5.11}$$

$$m_{h\tau} \geqslant m_{h0}. \tag{5.12}$$

One writes $\bar{a}_h = (a_h, a_m)$ where a_h has the same meaning as before. Also

$$A(\bar{a}_h) = [A(a_h), B_{hm1} + S_{hm1}, \ldots, B_{hm\tau} + S_{hm\tau}]$$

$$f_h = \{\bar{a}_h \mid a_h \in C_h, a_h \in \alpha(\bar{x}_h), a_{hm} \text{ satisfies } (5.11), (5.12)\}.$$

The notation for the price of money is the natural one p^v_{mt}, q^v_{mt}, etc., but it is postulated throughout that

$$p^v_{mv} = q^v_{mv}, \quad \text{all } v.$$

No Forward Market in Money

I start by postulating that the transactions technology allows no forward trading in money. I write $\mathscr{E}^{sm}$ and $\mathscr{E}^{dm}$ as the Sequence and Debreu transactions economies which one can now derive.

Define

$$\Sigma_{hm}(p, q, p_m, q_m) = \{\bar{a}_h \mid (p^v, q^v, p_m^v, q_m^v)\bar{a}_h^v \leqslant 0 \text{ all } v, \bar{a}_h \in f_h\}$$

as the set of activities h must choose from all the given prices. The price vector is taken to be in $P_m \subset R^{+L'}$ with $L' = \tau[(\tau + 1)/2] + L$. One then defines the new activity correspondence in $R^{L'}$, $\sigma_{hm}(p, q, p_m, q_m)$ in the usual way. Since storage is costless and in this section T is unchanged, one now specifies $\mathscr{E}^{sm}$, with the given modifications, as $\mathscr{E}^s$ was specified.

In exactly the same way, let

$$D_{hm}(\hat{p}, \hat{q}, \hat{p}_m, \hat{q}_m) = \{\bar{a}_h \mid (\hat{p}, \hat{q}, \hat{p}_m, \hat{q}_m)A(\bar{a}_h) \leqslant 0, a_h \in f_h\},$$

where the price vector is in $\Delta_{2(l+\tau)}$. The activity correspondence $d_{hm}(\hat{p}, \hat{q}, \hat{p}_m, \hat{q}_m)$ is found in the usual way.

The following is pretty obvious.

Lemma 2   Let $\hat{E}^d$ be the set of activity vectors a^d which occur in some E^d and define $\hat{E}^{dm}$ analogously. Then $\hat{E}^d = \hat{E}^{dm}$.

Proof   (i) We may set $\hat{p}_m = \hat{q}_m$ since in $\mathscr{E}^{dm}$ the prices of everything are independent of transaction date and spot money transactions are costless.

(ii) Let $\hat{a}^d \in \hat{E}^d$ at $(\hat{p}, \hat{q})$. Let $\hat{p}_{mt} = \hat{p}_m > 0$ all t and choose $\hat{p}_m$ so that $2\tau\hat{p}_m = r < 1$. Let

$$(\hat{p}', \hat{q}') = (\hat{p}, \hat{q})(1 - r).$$

Then $\hat{a}^d \in \hat{E}^{dm}$ at $(\hat{p}', \hat{q}', \hat{p}_m, \hat{p}_m)$. For by (5.12) one has for every h in $\mathscr{E}^{dm}$ at the prices as constructed

$$(\hat{p}', \hat{q}', \hat{p}_m, \hat{p}_m)A(\bar{a}_h) = (\hat{p}', \hat{q}')A(a_h) \leqslant 0 \tag{5.13}$$

and so that at these prices there cannot be a_h preferred to $\hat{a}_h^d$ without contradicting $\hat{a}^d \in \hat{E}^d$. Lastly of course, $\hat{a}^d$ is transaction-feasible in both economies.

(iii) Let $\hat{a}^{dm} \in \hat{E}^{dm}$ at $(\hat{p}, \hat{q}, \hat{p}_m, \hat{p}_m)$. It is easily verified that, unless $\hat{p}_{mt}$ is constant all t, there cannot be an equilibrium. Set $\hat{p}_{m\tau} > 0.$[4] If $\hat{p}_{m\tau-1} < \hat{p}_{m\tau}$ there would be an excess demand for

---

[4] One can choose $p_m^* > 0$ because (5.12) when summed over h introduces a linear dependence in addition to the Walras' law. The case $p_m^* = 0$ is excluded for obvious reasons. See Heller (1972).

money at $\tau - 1$ since everyone would want unlimited amounts. If $\hat{p}_{m\tau-1} > \hat{p}_{m\tau}$ there would be an excess supply. Recursion then proves the statement. But then (5.13) holds in the equilibrium of $\mathscr{E}^{dm}$ which is sufficient to establish that $\hat{a}^{dm} \in \hat{E}^d$ at $(\hat{p}, \hat{q})$. It is of course no surprise that money does not matter in a Debreu transactions economy. None the less, E^{dm} is a valuable reference. We now prove

Theorem 4 $\mathscr{E}^d \subsetneq_c \mathscr{E}^{sm}$.

When we have proved this we shall have shown (1) that $\mathscr{E}^{sm}$ has at least one equilibrium and (2) that $\mathscr{E}^{sm}$ has at least one Pareto-efficient equilibrium.

Proof   (i) Let $(\hat{p}, \hat{q}, \hat{a}^d) \in E^d$. Let $\hat{p}_{mt} = \hat{p}_m$ all t and choose $\hat{p}_m$ and $(\hat{p}', \hat{q}')$ as in (ii) of lemma 2 for some $r < 1$. Suppose that we can find some value of r and some a_{hm}, $h = 1, \ldots, H$ so that

$$\bar{a}_h = (a_h^d, a_{hm}) \in f_h \text{ and } (\hat{p}_v', \hat{q}_v', \hat{p}_{mv}, \hat{p}_{mv})\bar{a}_h^v \leqslant 0, \quad \text{all } v \text{ and } h.$$

$$(5.14)$$

Certainly, by lemma 2, $(\hat{p}', \hat{q}', \hat{p}_m, \hat{p}_m, \bar{a}_1, \ldots, \bar{a}_H) \in E^{dm}$. Now determine p_v^v, q_v^v, p_{mv}^v by

$$k_v(p_v^v, q_v^v, p_{mv}^v) = (\hat{p}_v', \hat{q}_v', p_m)k_v > 0, \quad \text{all } v$$

and write (p, q, p_m, q_m) as the price vector derived in this way. (Note that in q_m the components $q_{mv}^v = p_{mv}^v$). Then by theorem 1, which here can be applied go $\mathscr{E}^{sm}$ and $\mathscr{E}^{dm}$, one has

$$(p, q, p_m, q_m, \bar{a}_1, \ldots, \bar{a}_H) \in E^{sm}.$$

(ii) It remains to show that (5.14) can be met. Suppose that

$$p_m m_{h0} \geqslant (\hat{p}', \hat{q}') \sum_{v=1}^{t} a_h^{dv} \text{ all } t = 1, \ldots, \tau, \quad \text{all } h. \tag{5.14'}$$

Then there would be a choice of a_{hm} satisfying (5.11). For recalling that there is no forward market, set

$$p_m(B_{hmv} + S_{hmv}) = -(\hat{p}', \hat{q}')a_h^{dv}$$

so that, in view of (5.14′),

$$p_m m_{ht} = p_m m_{h0} - (\hat{p}', \hat{q}') \sum_{v=1}^{t} a_h^{dv} \geq 0, \quad \text{all } t. \tag{5.15}$$

Moreover, taking $t = \tau$ in (5.15) and recalling $(\hat{p}', \hat{q}')\Sigma^\tau a_h^{dv} \leq 0$, (5.12) will be satisfied. Hence if (5.14′), $(a^d, a_{hm}) \in f_h$ for this choice of a_{hm}. But there certainly exists $0 < r < 1$ such that

$$m_{h0} \geq \max_{h,t} \left(\frac{1-r}{2\tau r}\right) (\hat{p}, \hat{q}) \sum_{v=1}^{t} a_h^{dv}, \quad \text{all } h,$$

which thus ensures the possibility of (5.14).

It is easy to see how $\mathscr{E}^{dm}$ has been used. By introducing money, it is possible to find a 'price level' in terms of money such that every equilibrium activity of $\mathscr{E}^d$ is possible in $\mathscr{E}^{dm}$ with all books balancing in each period. But this we know will allow us to find a consumption-equivalent equilibrium in $\mathscr{E}^{sm}$. The introduction of money, therefore, improves on $\mathscr{E}^s$ in the sense that we now know that some of the equilibria of $\mathscr{E}^{sm}$ are efficient. Indeed, one has at once

Corollary 4 If $\mathscr{E}^{sm}$ has a unique equilibrium for $\hat{p}_{ms} > 0$ then it is Pareto-efficient.

On the other hand, in general there is no reason for $\mathscr{E}^{sm}$ to have inessential sequences.[5] Indeed, it is possible for $\mathscr{E}^s$ to have inessential sequences when $\mathscr{E}^{sm}$ has not, in which case the intro-duction of money 'worsens' things in the sense that it permits insufficient sequence equilibria which were not possible before its introduction. However, one can prove

Theorem 5 If in every member of E^{sm}, $m_{hv} > 0$ all h and v then $\mathscr{E}^{sm}$ is inessential (and hence Pareto-efficient).

---

[5] There may be equilibria of $\mathscr{E}^{sm}$ where some households hold no money in some period and are constrained by (5.11). They do not sell more of any good forward because the implied borrowing rate is too high. Other households who hold all the money do not use it to buy goods forward because of the low implied lending rate. Starrett (1973) has modified his examples to illustrate such a case, and other examples can be constructed.

Proof   For each h, if $m_{hv} > 0$ all v there are Lagrangean multipliers $\lambda_h^v > 0$ such that

$$\lambda_h^{v+1}/\lambda_h^v = p_{mv}^v/p_{mv+1}^{v+1} \quad v = 1, \ldots, \tau - 1.$$

Hence $\lambda_h^{v+1}/\lambda_h^v$ must be independent of h and one writes

$$k_v = \lambda^v/\lambda^1 \quad v = 1, \ldots, \tau$$

and defines $(\hat{p}_v', \hat{q}_v', p_m)$ by

$$(\hat{p}_v', \hat{q}_v', p_m) = k_v(p^v, q^v, p_{mv}^v)c,$$

where $c > 0$ is a normalizing constant. Then each h will make the. same choices at

$$(\hat{p}', \hat{q}', p_m, p_m)$$

as it did at the sequence prices, and the usual argument establishes the theorem.[6]

At the moment there is nothing to ensure the condition of theorem 5. It may be thought that this is because we have not given money any work to do, and no doubt that is right. On the other hand, when we do give money work to do the condition of the theorem will be met but the theorem will no longer be true.

To see this, take the crudest case first, where we take the short cut of arguing that our transaction model implicitly involves the use of money and is not defined when households are not *constrained* by $m_{hv} > 0$ all v. This constraint, the reader can verify, will make no difference to theorem 4. On the other hand, $m_{hv} > 0$ does not now imply the relationship between the Lagrangean multipliers which we used to establish theorem 5

---

[6] The economics and mathematics of this result seem sufficiently obvious, but experience suggests that it may help to be explicit. If, in a sequence economy equilibrium, each household has the same intertemporal marginal rates of substitution between wealth, then each household must face the same marginal intertemporal rates of transforming wealth. These latter can be interpreted as discount factors. Since they are the same for all h we can use them to calculate 'the present price' of any good in the sequence economy and the present value budget constraints for each h. Households faced with this constraint will act in the same way as they were doing in a sequence. If in a sequence equilibrium each household holds money at every date, then the conditions we started with must plainly hold. The whole point is, as was fully discussed in Hahn (1971), that in general, the marginal intertemporal transformation rates in a non-money sequence economy with transaction costs are not the same for all h.

unless the constraints are ineffective all h and v. But then either we are no better off or theorem 5 ceases to hold. Hence the modified $\mathscr{E}^{sm}$ may in general fail to have inessential sequences.

It may be argued that this route is exceedingly crude. So let us instead use the *ad hoc* constraint employed by Grandmont and Younes (1973). For its justification in a completely different model the reader is referred to their work. In our sequence economy their constraint reads:

$$p^v b_h^v + kq^v s_h^v \leqslant p_m^v m_{hv-1}, \quad \text{all } v, k < 1, \tag{5.16}$$

while in the Debreu transactions economy it becomes

$$\hat{p}_v' b_h^v + k\hat{q}_v' s_h^v \leqslant \hat{p}_{mv} m_{hv-1} \quad k < 1, \quad \text{all } v, \tag{5.17}$$

Let $\mathscr{E}^{dm}$ be the Debreu transactions economy modified by (5.17). Then one finds, setting $\hat{p}_{mv} = p_m$ all v,

$$p_m m_{ht} = p_m m_{h0} - (\hat{p}', \hat{q}') \sum_{v=1}^{t} a_h^{dv} + (1-k)\hat{q}_t s_{ht}$$

in any equilibrium in which (5.17) holds with equality for all v. But then it is easy to verify that it is possible for any $\hat{a}^d \in E^d$ to find $\hat{a}^{dm}$ and p_m so that (i) $m_{ht} > 0$ all h and t and (ii) (5.17) is ineffective. But then certainly theorem 4 will continue to hold. In particular, if $\bar{\mathscr{E}}^{sm}$ is $\mathscr{E}^{sm}$ modified by (5.16), then $\bar{E}^{sm}$ will contain activities which are Pareto-efficient, and for which (5.16) does not bind. On the other hand, it is once again plain that, from $m_{hv} > 0$ all h, v in any $\bar{E}^{sm}$ we cannot conclude that $\bar{\mathscr{E}}^{sm}$ has inessential sequences and it may therefore have inefficient equilibria.

To this conclusion there is an exception summarized in the following. It arises when in every equilibrium of $\bar{\mathscr{E}}^{sm}$, (5.16) is ineffective. For then, if all h trade at each v, the condition of theorem 5 will indeed be met. For instance, if in every equilibrium the marginal utility of wealth is independent of v, then in $\bar{E}^{sm}$ one has

$$\lambda_h^{v+1} p_{mv+1} - \lambda_h^v p_{mv} + k\mu_h^{v+1} p_{mv+1} = 0, \quad \text{each } h \text{ and } v$$

where μ_h^v is the 'shadow price' of (5.16) at v. Since $\lambda_h^{v+1} = \lambda_h^v$, the conclusion follows that $\mu_h^v = 0$. This is the case discussed in a different context by Grandmont and Younes.

But there are other examples of $\bar{\mathscr{E}}^{sm}$ with inessential sequences. For instance, if each h has a utility function additive over consumption at different dates with discount factor δ. Suppose first that the equilibrium in $\bar{\mathscr{E}}^{sm}$ has (5.16) ineffective. Then one easily finds that $(p^v, q^v)\delta^v = (\hat{p}_v, \hat{q}_v)$ gives (p, q), which allows the goods activities of $\mathscr{E}^{sm}$ in $\mathscr{E}^d$. But then these activities will also be in $\mathscr{E}^{dm}$ and so indeed by an application of theorem 4 the constraint (5.16) will be ineffective on an equilibrium of $\bar{\mathscr{E}}^{sm}$.

I am not at all sure how interesting these *ad hoc* constraints are. But in any event we have seen that it is not necessary to work with a model of the sort where all transaction costs are zero in an equilibrium in which the transaction constraints are not binding. In particular it need not be true – as in Grandmont and Younes – that in an efficient equilibrium the marginal rate of substitution between goods of the same date must be the same for all h. It may also be remarked that the fact that I have taken a finite economy (and so need (5.12)), while Grandmont and Younes take an infinite economy (and so do not), is of no significance for the qualitative results.

The following conclusion emerges from the analysis so far. To say that $\mathscr{E}^{sm}$ or $\bar{\mathscr{E}}^{sm}$ have essential sequences is equivalent to saying that it is Pareto-efficient and that the same equilibrium is attainable in $\mathscr{E}^d$ without money. In particular, then, it means that the 'classical dichotomy' is valid.[7] If on the other hand this dichotomy is not valid, then the sequences of $\mathscr{E}^{sm}$ are not inessential and so not Pareto-efficient. This is of some interest.

Foward Market in Money

We now write

$$T^{mv} \text{ and } T^m = \underset{v}{\bigtimes} T^{mv}$$

as the transaction sets when forward transactions in money are included. One writes $\mathscr{E}^{sm}$ as the sequence economy which results.

The special case investigated by Starrett (1973) arises when in every member of E^{sm} one has

$$p^v_{mt} = q^v_{mt} \quad \text{all } v \text{ and } t.$$

[7] The 'classical dichotomy' asserts that all real magnitudes and exchange rates have equilibrium values which can be determined without the introduction of monetary variables. This is the case here.

That is, in effect, forward transactions in money are costless. But then it is clear that in such an equilibrium $m_{hv} = 0$ must mean, if $m_{hv} \geq 0$ is a binding constraint, that h is selling money forward at v. Since there can be no difference (in equilibrium) in the return in unit of account between selling forward for one or several periods, one has

$$\lambda_h^{v+1}/\lambda_h^v = p_{mv+1}^v/p_{mv+1}^{v+1}.$$

Since in equilibrium there must be a forward buyer and he cannot prefer to hold money to forward-buying, one has at once

$$p_{mv+1}^v/p_{mv+1}^{v+1} = p_{mv}^v/p_{mv+1}^{v+1}.$$

But then $\lambda_h^{v+1}/\lambda_h^v$ is independent of h and by the usual argument $\bar{\mathscr{E}}^{sm}$ is inessential.[8]

But of course there is no reason to suppose that forward transactions in money are costless, and indeed supposing this to be the case loses a good deal of economic interest. So let me make the reverse assumption and assume that, in every equilibrium of $\mathscr{E}^{sm}$,

$$p_{mt}^v > q_{mt}^v \quad v < t, \quad \text{all } v \text{ and } t \tag{5.18}$$

but of course retain

$$p_{mv}^v = q_{mv}^v \quad \text{all } v. \tag{5.19}$$

But then one can prove

Theorem 6 Every equilibrium of $\mathscr{E}^{sm}$ satisfying (5.18) and (5.19) and in which at least one futures market for money is active is not Pareto-efficient.

Proof Since spot transactions in money are costless, no equilibrium of $\mathscr{E}^{dm}$ will use a costly forward market in money. But then the equilibrium of $\mathscr{E}^{sm}$ in question cannot be consumption-equivalent to any of the Pareto-efficient equilibria of $\mathscr{E}^{dm}$; for if it were forward transactions in money would not be costly.

It is not difficult to understand this result. We have already seen that the mere presence of money allows any equilibrium of $\mathscr{E}^d$ to

---

[8] There is an alternative interpretation. Let each h be able (costlessly) to increase his endowment of money at each v on the understanding that everything is returned at τ. This would be equivalent to a costless futures market in money.

be realized in $\mathscr{E}^{sm}$ with books balancing in each v for each h at Debreu prices. Hence if borrowing and lending money uses resources, such resources are ill-used in borrowing and lending money.

It is here that I have made some contact with recent discussions. It is well known that it has been claimed that money should earn a rate of return equal to 'the rate of interest' if a sequence economy is to be Pareto-efficient. But when there are, say, brokerage fees, the lending and borrowing rates differ. Hence the recommendation makes sense only when in fact there is no lending and borrowing of money and when people borrowing from themselves (buying up money which eventually must be returned to the government) costs them the appreciation of this money and this is equal to the gain of the household which accumulates the money. The rate of return on money is hence derived from the common marginal rate of substitution between present and future wealth.

Theorem 6 is interesting but care is required in the weight which is put on it. First of all it is clear that (5.12) and the 'as if story' about it is not very convincing. There is in practice no 'initial endowment of money' which is known to a government. Hence the taking of an arrangement like (5.12) as costless must be treated with a large grain of salt. If indeed it were costly in resources, then lemma 2 would no longer hold and we would lose much of the subsequent analysis. It is important to understand what is going on here: in $\mathscr{E}^{sm}$ we were able to ensure a costless balancing of books period by period, and so such balancing can be ignored in thinking of the feasible activity set for the economy. But when balancing can be achieved only at a cost in resources, we are in serious trouble if we also maintain that every decentralized economy must have such balancing. What is the feasible activity set now? I do not know.

Secondly, I have ignored production and have in any case taken a rather special transactions technology. Third, I have ignored uncertainty. Since transactions costs will certainly lead to some contingent futures markets being inactive, there are likely to be difficulties in defining the efficiency of sequence economies. For all these reasons it would be unwise to regard anything that has been said as more than suggestive to an eventual proper theory of monetary economies. But I think that there can be no doubt that what will make such a theory interesting will be that the appropriate sequence economy will not be inessential.

REFERENCES

Grandmont, J. M. and Younès, Y. (1972). 'On the Role of Money and the Existence of a Monetary Equilibrium', *Review of Economic Studies*, **39**.

Grandmont, J. M. and Younès, Y. (1973), 'On the Efficiency of a Monetary Equilibrium', *Review of Economic Studies*, **40**.

Hahn, F. H. (1971), 'Equilibrium with Transaction Costs', *Econometrica*, **39**.

Heller, W. H. (1972), 'The Holding of the Idle Money Balances in General Equilibrium', University of Pennsylvania Discussion Paper 243.

Kurz, M. (1972), 'Equilibrium in a Finite Sequence of Markets with Transaction Costs', Technical Report no. 52, IMSSS, Stanford University.

Starrett, D. (1973), 'Inefficiency and the Demand for "Money" in a Sequence Economy', *Review of Economic Studies*, **40**.

Part II

Non-Walrasian Equilibria

6

On Non-Walrasian Equilibria

I INTRODUCTION

I shall call an economy non-Walrasian whenever the trading possibilities of agents cannot be described as the set of trades which at given prices make the value of purchases no greater than the value of sales.[1]

There are many reasons for being interested in non-Walrasian economies. My own immediate reason comes from an attempt to study more precisely the meaning one might give to the old proposition that the division of labour depends on the extent of the market. In the usual Walrasian context it is not easy to define 'the extent of the market'. But there are of course many other reasons, among which the desirability of studying 'Keynesian' propositions in the context of general equilibrium analysis ranks high. If non-Walrasian models are rejected on whatever grounds, then so it would seem must properly formulated Keynesian models. This is not because of difficulties of reconciling unemployment with equilibrium – it is not at all obvious that Keynes' theory requires it – but rather because, as long as market opportunities are described only in the Walrasian way, no distinction can be drawn between demand and effective demand (Clower, 1965, and Leijonhufvud, 1960). But this distinction seems so central to the Keynesian theory that it seems impossible to proceed without it. There are also sound reasons for arguing that one must abandon the Walrasian

[1] This work was supported by National Science Foundation Grant SOC74-11446 at the Institute for Mathematical Studies in the Social Sciences, Stanford University. I have benefited from discussions with Robert Aumann, Kenneth Arrow, Jean-Michel Grandmont, and Roger Witcomb. My greatest debt is to Douglas Gale, Oliver Hart and Eric Maskin, who spotted mistakes in an earlier version. Douglas Gale also supplied the argument of the appendix, and Oliver Hart convinced me that it was necessary to proceed as there indicated. The muddled mind indicated by the mistakes which were spotted must leave a suspicion that there are others.

hypothesis that agents treat prices parametrically if one is to make sense of Keynesian doctrines.

To all of this one must add that the Walrasian procedure runs into both logical and empirical difficulties. The former arise when one wishes to study an economy out of equilibrium. Then, not only does the Walrasian theory provide no logical way in which actual agents could change prices (Arrow, 1959), but the theory also runs into trouble should there be constant returns to scale (Arrow and Hahn, 1971). The empirical difficulties are not only that for many actual firms a perfect competition postulate is plainly wrong and incapable of yielding explanations of such phenomena as advertising, but also that it is wrong for almost all agents. Thus it is not possible to explain the wide requirement of collateral when borrowing or the wide support for unemployment insurance.

The central difficulty in studying non-Walrasian economies, which to some extent it shares with Walrasian sequence economies, is the distinction between the trading possibilities as perceived by an agent and the 'true' trading possibilities. This difficulty is recognized for instance when we distinguish between expectations and rational expectations, but it is rather more severe in the non-Walrasian case. For instance, in a Walrasian sequence economy with single-valued price expectations we say that the expectations are rational when they are confirmed by the sequence of equilibrium prices. Compare this with the non-Walrasian case studied by Negishi (1960). The trading possibilities as perceived by some agents included a conjectural demand curve for the goods sold by them. In an equilibrium of the economy they sell what at the going price and the conjectured demand curve is most profitable. There will be no further experience suggesting that their conjectures should be revised. But the demand curve which is conjectured may not be the 'true' demand curve, if indeed the latter can be defined. Here the circumstance that the market signals that the agent has not made a mistake does not ensure that he is in fact not mistaken. The difficulty then is that these Negishi-like equilibria will be 'boot-strap' equilibria, that is, dependent on unexplained conjectures of agents, and that there will be many of them depending on what the conjectures of agents actually are. It is the *ad hoc* element in the theory, which of course also occurs in the study of short-period Walrasian equilibria, which in the usual model we try to avoid by studying rational expectations. In the non-Walrasian context it is not always clear what rational expectations are, and even when it is we may find that we finish with an implausibly exacting concept of equilibrium. To this must be added the rather obvious point that the existence of rational non-Walrasian equilibria is by no means easy to establish.

Although there is much recent literature on this topic, it cannot be claimed that we are very close to the kind of understanding which we have gained of the Walrasian economy. What follows is essentially an attempt to gain some insight into the main difficulties in the hope that this will be of use in the eventual construction of more general models.

I begin section II with the extreme case studied by Drèze (1975) and by Grandmont and Laroque (1976). Here it is supposed that prices are fixed and that agents are rationed. One considers certain quantity-constrained equilibria which one can think of as resulting from non-tâtonnement. The equilibria one wants to show to exist have two features: only one side of the market is restrained by rationing (Hahn and Negishi, 1962) and some trade occurs. I call such equilibria orderly and non-trivial. The existence of an orderly and non-trivial equilibrium for this case has already been provided by Drèze and others. So why do it again? Here are the answers:

1   The proof is different and very natural since it uses implicit prices for rations. It is also very simple.
2   Orderly and non-trivial equilibria may be Pareto-inefficient relative to the requirement that each agent satisfies his budget constraint (Arrow and Hahn, 1971; Younès, 1975). The method of proof allows one to understand this better. In particular, it shows that quantity constraints give rise to an essential externality. This understanding is underlined by showing that there would exist rationing schemes (by means of coupons) at fixed money prices, in which the externality would be overcome.

In section III I relax the fixed-price assumption. I replace it by allowing agents to have conjectures of how a given perceived ration might be relaxed by their willingness to offer a different price. The idea here is closely related to the pioneering work of Negishi (1960), although it is different. *In particular, I do not wish to make imperfect competition intrinsic to the model. The conjectures I consider always permit a Walrasian equilibrium. What I show is that there are also non-Walrasian equilibria.* This seems to me of some interest since it shows that an economy can settle into a quantity-constrained equilibrium even when prices are not fixed *a priori* and in particular a Walrasian equilibrium is available. This section is related to Benassy (1976) and to Malinvaud and Younès (1975).

But neither of these authors showed that the Walrasian equilibrium was also a possible equilibrium for their economy. This is what makes section III of interest. For once agents change prices (and not the auctioneer), an economy, which with given conjectures has a competitive equilibrium, may 'get stuck' in a non-Walrasian one. If one starts with monopolistic competition this is not the case. There are some objections to this result which depends on the class of conjectures I have chosen. The objections will be discussed in their proper place (see section III).

However, it may be thought that a fundamental objection is the arbitrariness of conjectures, an objection which I have already touched upon. As a first reply I would suggest that it is not obvious that one is justified in treating preferences as given and quite unjustified in treating conjectures as given. Certainly, almost any feasible allocation can be a Walrasian equilibrium for some preferences, and certainly we do not believe that we emerge from the womb with formed preferences or that the latter are independent of economic experiences. We treat preferences as exogenous for the very good reason that we have no good and manageable theory of an economy in which they are treated as endogenous. In any case, I would not be alarmed if conjectures, at least in the short period, are taken as formed by history. One would have to look at what conjectures they are for applications; but the theory would still be useful.

But one must keep on trying. So in section IV I examine a notion of rational conjectures (evidently I am here inspired by rational expectations). I show that for a class of conjectures no rational conjectural equilibrium exists.

An editor of *The Review of Economic Studies* believes that there may be a relationship between the negative result of section IV and the negative results of the literature on incentive compatibility. He is almost certainly right. On the other hand, his further suggestion that one could sail into 'positive' waters by considering a large economy is less helpful. If agents are of measure zero, then one cannot make them responsible for price adjustments.

II FIXED PRICES

In this section I consider an economy in which agents receive both price and quantity signals which they treat parametrically. One asks, Do there exist quantity signals, given a fixed-price signal, which are compatible with an equilibrium? To give this question some interest we shall look for a *non-trivial* and *orderly* equilibrium. By non-trivial we mean that some trade is permitted and occurs. By orderly we mean that in any one market in equilibrium quantity signals restrain either demand or supply but not both.

The notation is as follows. There is a finite number, A, of agents indexed by a, and a finite number, l, of goods, indexed by i. The agent's consumption set is R_+^l and $x_a \in R_+^l$ is a consumption, $e_a \in R_{++}^l$ an endowment. One defines $t_a \in R^l$ by

$$t_a = x_a - e_a$$

and calls it a trade of a. The agent receives signals $\sigma_a \in R_+^{3l}$ where

$$\sigma_a = (p, b_a, s_a)$$

and $p \gg 0$ is a price vector and b_a, s_a are quantity signals restricting the purchases and sales of a. The precise interpretation is given by a's trading correspondence: $T_a: R_+^{3l} \to R^l$, where

$$T_a(\sigma_a) = \{t_a | pt_a \leqslant 0, b_a \geqslant t_a, s_a \geqslant -t_a\}.$$

To keep matters simple I shall use

Assumption (2.1) For all a, preferences on R_+^l are representable by a Cobb–Douglas utility function.

This could easily be replaced by more usual postulates on the convexity and continuity of preferences. Its merit here is that it allows one to simplify as follows:

(i) For b_{ai} finite, b_{ai} will be a 'biting' constraint as $p_i \to 0$.
(ii) When the agent has maximized utility on

$$F_a(p, b_a, s_a) = T_a(p, b_a, s_a) \cap \{t_a | e_a + t_a \in R_+^l\}$$

a unique choice $t_a(\sigma_a)$ results.
(iii) There will be a unique $p^* \gg 0$ in the simplex $\Delta \subset R_+^l$ for which there exist (b_a^*, s_a^*), each a, such that each a gives the quantity constraints zero shadow prices and $\Sigma_a t_a(p^*, b_a^*, s_a^*) = 0$. (So p^* is a unique Walrasian equilibrium.)

Now let $t(\sigma) = \Sigma_a t_a(\sigma_a)$, where $\sigma = (p, b_1, \ldots, b_a, s_1, \ldots, s_a)$. Then

Definition (2.1) σ^0 is a *non-Walrasian equilibrium* if (i) $p^0 \neq p^*$ and (ii) $t(\sigma^0) = 0$.

Let α_{ai} be the shadow price of the constraint $b_{ai} \geqslant t_{ai}$ and β_{ai} the shadow price of the constraint $s_{ai} \geqslant -t_a$. Then

Definition (2.2) σ^0 is a *non-trivial* and *orderly* non-Walrasian equilibrium if (D2.1(i)–(ii)) are satisfied and

(i) $t_a(\sigma_a^0) \neq 0$ some a (i.e., equilibrium is non-trivial).
(ii) For all i: either $\alpha_{ai} = 0$, all a, or $\beta_{ai} = 0$, all a (i.e., equilibrium is orderly).

A non-trivial equilibrium may not exist (theorem XIII.1, Arrow and Hahn, 1971) even when the trivial equilibrium is Pareto-inefficient relatively to $pt_a = 0$, all a. So one will need some assumption.
     I shall use the following.

Definition (2.3) Let $A(i)$ be the set of agents who are not quantity-constrained in market i, when $p \gg 0$. The economy satisfies *strong tradability* if there exists $\epsilon > 0$ such that

$$\Sigma_{A(i)} |t_{ai}| \geqslant \epsilon \qquad \text{all } i.$$

This assumption is somewhat strong. I discuss in the appendix the consequence of using a weaker version. One now has

Theorem (2.1) Let $p \neq p^*$, $p \gg 0$ and let the strong tradability condition be satisfied. Then there exists σ^0 with $p^0 = p$ which is a non-trivial orderly non-Walrasian equilibrium.

To establish this I consider an interesting fictional economy. In that economy a central agency sells rights to buy and to sell for a special currency. Let $v_i \geqslant 0$, $w_i \geqslant 0$, respectively denote the prices of the right to buy and to sell one unit of good i denominated in the special currency. Each a is allocated λm_a units of the currency $0 \leqslant \lambda \leqslant 1$, $m_a > 0$. The trading set of agent a is, when $v = (v_1, \ldots, v_l)$, $w = (w_1, \ldots, w_l)$,

$$T_a^0(p, v, w, \lambda) = \{t_a \,|\, pt_a \leqslant 0,\, b_a \geqslant t_a,\, s_a \geqslant -t_a$$

$$\text{with} \quad vb_a + ws_a \leqslant \lambda m_a\}.$$

The set of feasible choices, in view of assumption (2.1), can be written

$$F_a^0(p, v, w, \lambda) = T_a^0(p, v, w, \lambda) \cap \{t_a | t_a + e_a \geqslant 0\}.$$

The strategy is to show that the fictional economy has an equilibrium and thence that this equilibrium corresponds to an orderly non-trivial Drèze equilibrium.

To this end, let $G \subset R_+^l$ where

$$G = \{g | \sum_i |g_i| \leqslant 1, g_1 \equiv 0\}$$

and define the map from G to R_+^{l+1} by

$$v_i(g) = \max(0, g_i), \; w_i(g) = \max(0, -g_i), \; \lambda(g) =$$
$$= \max(\epsilon^1, 1 - \sum|g_i|)$$

where $\epsilon^1 = \epsilon/m$, ϵ given from strong tradability and $m = \Sigma m_a$.

The feasible set is now written as $F_a^0(p, g)$. It is continuous on G. Let $t_a(p, g)$ be the 'best' trade at (g). It is unique and continuous. Now some budget arithmetic. For $t_a \in F_a^0$ one has

$$\lambda m_a \geqslant v(g) b_a + w(g) s_a \geqslant v(g) t_a^+ - w(g) t_a^- =$$
$$= g \cdot t_a + w(g) t_a^+ - v(g) t_a^-. \qquad (6.1)$$

Here $t_a^+ = \{\max(0, t_{ai})\}$, $t_a^- = \{\min(0, t_{ai})\}$, two l-vectors. Suppose $g_i < 0$. Then $w_i = -g_i$ and $-g_i t_{ai}^+$ is the amount of fictional currency suppliers of good i need if they are to be able to meet the demand for i by a. Similarly, if $g_i > 0$, $-g_i t_{ai}^-$ is the amount of fictional currency required by demanders of good i if they are to be able to take up a's supply. So if

$$R(p, g) = w(g) \sum_a t_a^+(p, g) - v(g) \sum_a t_a^-(p, g)$$

then $R(\cdot)$ measures the fictional currency requirement if markets are to clear. Notice that

$$R(p, g) \geqslant \epsilon^1 m \quad \text{for all } g \in G \quad \text{with} \quad \Sigma |g_i| = 1. \qquad (6.2)$$

For if say $g_i > 0$, then $-g_i \Sigma t_{ai}^-(p, g) = |g_i| \Sigma_{A(i)} |t_{ai}|$ so that, by summing over i, (6.2) follows at once.

F

On the other hand, if

$$\mu_a(p, g) = v(g) t_a^+(p, g) - w(g) t_a^-(p, g)$$

then $\mu_a(\cdot)$ is the minimum amount of fictional currency required to finance the given trades. Of course $\mu_a(p, g) \leqslant \lambda m_a$. Then if

$$M(p, g) = \Sigma_a \mu_a(p, g)$$

we obtain, from summing (6.1) over agents and rearranging,

$$Z(p, g) \equiv M(p, g) - R(p, g) = g \cdot t(p, g).$$

We can now use the well known method of Debreu (1959) to show the existence of g^0 such that

$$Z(p, g^0) = g^0 t(p, g^0) \geqslant g \cdot t(p, g^0), \quad \text{all } g \in G. \tag{6.3}$$

Suppose $t(p, g^0) \neq 0$. Then, since

$$g^0 t(p, g^0) \leqslant \sum_i |g_i^0| \, |t_r(p, g^0)|$$

where $|t_r(p, g^0)| \geqslant |t_i(p, g^0)|$ all i, it follows from (6.3) that $\Sigma |g_i^0| = 1$ and so from (6.2) *and strong tradability* that $R(p, g^0) \geqslant \lambda(g^0) m \geqslant \Sigma_a \mu_a(p, g^0)$.[2] Also $\lambda(g^0) = \epsilon^1$ so $Z(p, g^0) \leqslant 0$. But then in (6.3), setting $g_i = \pm 1$, we obtain

$$0 \geqslant |t_i(p, g^0)| \quad \text{all } i,$$

a contradiction. Hence $t(p, g^0) = 0$. Summing up,

---

[2] For suppose not; i.e., suppose $\Sigma |g_i^0| < 1$. Since (6.3) holds for all $g \in G$, let g be the unit vector with 1 as its rth element; i.e., $g = (0, 0, \ldots, 1, 0, \ldots, 0)$. Then (6.3) can be written as

$$g^0 t(p, g^0) \geqslant t_r(p, g^0). \tag{1}$$

But also, since $\Sigma |g_i^0| < 1$, we have that

$$t_r(p, g^0) > \Sigma |g_i^0| t_r(p, g^0). \tag{2}$$

Combining (1) and (2), we get

$$g^0 t(p, g^0) > \Sigma |g_i^0| |t_r(p, g^0)|,$$

a contradiction.

Lemma (2.1)   Under the conditions of theorem (2.1), there exists (v^0, w^0, λ^0) such that $t^0(p, v^0, w^0, \lambda^0) \equiv \Sigma_a t_a^0(p, v^0, w^0, \lambda^0) = 0$; i.e., the fictional economy has an equilibrium.

Lemma (2.2)   The equilibrium of the fictional economy is orderly and non-trivial.
   Proof   (i) It is orderly since one of $(v_i(g^0), w_i(g^0))$ is zero each i. (ii) By strong tradability.

Lemma (2.3)   The actual economy shares at least one equilibrium with the fictional economy.
   Proof   In the actual economy let

$$b_{ai}^0 = +\infty \quad \text{if} \quad g_i^0 \leqslant 0 \quad \text{and} \quad = \max[0, t_{ai}^0(p, g^0)] \text{ otherwise}$$

$$s_{ai}^0 = +\infty \quad \text{if} \quad g_i^0 \geqslant 0 \quad \text{and} \quad = \max[0, -t_{ai}^0(p, g^0)] \text{ otherwise.}$$

Then certainly $t_a^0(p, g^0) \in T_a(p, b_a^0, s_a^0)$. On the other hand, if $t_a \in T_a(p, b_a^0, s_a^0)$, then $t_a \in T_a^0(p, g^0)$ which suffices for the proof.
   These three lemmas prove theorem (2.1).

It should be emphasized that this theorem proves the existence of an orderly non-trivial equilibrium and that the rationing scheme of the fictional economy is to be regarded as no more than a mathematical device. It plays the same role as do, say, personalized prices in the theory of general equilibrium where public goods are paid by taxes. If one is interested in showing that in general there may be many orderly non-trivial equilibria, then one modifies the fictional economy by letting agents receive different amounts of the fictional currency. This was noted by a referee who is interested in showing that there are many such equilibria. In an earlier version of this proof I proceeded differently and, as it turned out, mistakenly.[3] However, one mistake had a lesson which I now discuss.
   One is interested in whether there are rationing schemes such that the resulting fixed-price equilibria are Pareto-efficient relative to each agent a being constrained by $p \cdot t_a \leqslant 0$. In the economy so far considered, agents receive the signal (p, b_a, s_a) and they are constrained by $t_a \leqslant b_a, -t_a \leqslant s_a$. The agent then receives no signal which would tell him that if he, say, bought more in a market in which he has no biting quantity constraint, he might, by enabling

---

[3] Eric Maskin discovered one mistake and a referee the other.

some other agent to trade more, relax a biting constraint in some other market. In equilibrium there may then be Pareto-improving trades at fixed prices which are not revealed by the signals.

So let me begin by formulating the notion of an orderly non-Walrasian equilibrium more generally. Let $R_a \subset R^l$ be thought of as a's rationing constraint. So if

$$B_a(p) = \{t_a | p \cdot t_a \leqslant 0, t_a + e_a \in R^l_+\},$$

the agents' choice must be in $R_a \cap B_a(p)$.

Definition (2.4)   For $p \neq p^*, R^0_a, R^0_b \ldots, t^0_a, t^0_b \ldots$ is a *generalized non-Walrasian equilibrium* if (i) t^0_a is not dominated in a's preferences on $R^0_a \cap B_a(p)$, all a, (ii) $\Sigma t^0_a = 0$.

Again, it is of interest to restrict the class of admissible equilibrium rationing constraints:

Definition (2.5)   A generalized non-Walrasian equilibrium is *orderly* if, for every i with $t^0_{ai} \neq 0$, some a:

(i) *either*, all t_a, with $[t_{ai} \geqslant t^0_{ai}, t_{ak} = t^0_{ak}, (k \neq i)] \in R^0_a$, all a
(ii) *or* all t_a, with $[t_{ai} \leqslant t^0_{ai}, t_{ak} = t^0_{ak}, (k \neq i)] \in R^0_a$, all a.

So orderliness requires that for any good traded in equilibrium the rationing constraint should either not restrict purchases or not restrict sales for any a.

Proposition (2.2)   There exists a rationing scheme for which the orderly non-Walrasian equilibrium is Pareto-efficient relative to the constraints $p \cdot t_a = 0$, all a.
  Proof   (i) Let $\bar{G} = \{\bar{g} \in R^{l-1} \times R_+ | \Sigma |\bar{g}_i| = 1, \bar{g}_1 \geqslant 0\}$ and define

$$R_a(\bar{g}) = \{t_a | \bar{g} \cdot t_a \leqslant 0\}, \quad \text{all } a.$$

A generalized non-Walrasian equilibrium (if it exists) is now $\bar{g}^0$ (i.e., $R_a(\bar{g}^0) = R^0_a$) all a and t^0_a, t^0_b etc. such that $\Sigma_a t^0_a = 0$ and $t_a \succ_a t^0_a$ implies $t_a \notin R_a(\bar{g}^0) \cap B_a(p)$, all a. Such an equilibrium is orderly since $\bar{g}_i > 0$ does not restrict sales of i in any $R_a(\bar{g}^0)$ and $\bar{g}_i < 0$ does not restrict any a.

(ii) Let $\hat{t} \in XR^l$ denote a trade allocation $(t_a, t_b \ldots)$. Suppose that $\hat{t}$ is Pareto-superior to $\hat{t}^0$ under the constraint $t_a \in B_a(p)$, all a. Let A_0 be the subset of agents for whom $\bar{g}^0 t^0_a < 0$. Then for

$a \in A_0$, t_a^0 is optimal in $B_a(p)$. Hence given assumption (2.1), which ensures $p \cdot t_a^0 = 0$, all a, if $t_a \neq t_a^0$ (some $a \in A_0$) it must be true that $p \cdot t_a > 0$. So we need only consider $\hat{t}$ which are Pareto-superior to $\hat{t}^0$ under the budget constraints and for which

$$t_a = t_a^0, \quad \text{all } a \in A_0.$$

(iii) Let A' be the complement of A_0 in the set of agents. Then we now have[4]

$$\bar{g}^0 t_a \geq 0 \text{ all } a \in A', \quad \bar{g}^0 t_a > 0, \text{ some } a \in A'$$

whence

$$\bar{g}^0 \Sigma_{A'}(t_a - t_a^0) > 0.$$

Hence $\bar{g}_i^0 \Sigma_{A'}(t_{ai} - t_{ai}^0) > 0$ some i. If $\bar{g}_i^0 > 0$ then $\Sigma_{a \in A'}(t_{ai} - t_{ai}^0) > 0$. But we know $\Sigma_{a \in A_0}(t_{ai} - t_{ai}^0) = 0$. Therefore $\Sigma_a(t_{ai} - t_{ai}^0) > 0$; i.e., $t_i > t_i^0$. But by feasibility $t_i^0 = 0$, so $t_i > 0$ and $\hat{t}$ is not, therefore, feasible. If $\bar{g}_i^0 < 0$, then by the same argument $t_i < 0$ which does not violate feasibility. But since $p \cdot t = 0$, $\exists$ some j subject to $t_j > 0$ so that $\hat{t}$ is not feasible. So $\hat{t}$, which is Pareto-superior to the orderly non-Walrasian equilibrium $\hat{t}^0$, is not feasible. Hence $\hat{t}^0$ is Pareto-efficient.

An interpretation of the rationing scheme is as follows. Under this scheme an agent buying one unit of good i has to pay $v_i \geq 0$ units of a coupon. However, by buying he is supplying one unit of the right to sell good i, for which he receives $w_i \geq 0$ units of a

---

[4] For suppose not; i.e., suppose

$$\bar{g}^0 t_a < 0 \quad \text{all } a \in A', \quad \bar{g}^0 t_a \leq 0 \quad \text{some } a \in A'.$$

Since $\bar{g}^0 t_a^0 = 0$ all $a \in A'$, then $t_a < t_a^0$ all $a \in A'$ and $t_a \leq t_a^0$ some $a \in A'$. Since $\bar{g}^0 t_a < 0$ all $a \in A_0$, it follows that

$$t_a \in R_a(\bar{g}^0), \forall a. \tag{1}$$

But also, $p \cdot t_a \leq p \cdot t_a^0$ some $a \in A'$, $p \cdot t_a < p \cdot t_a^0$ all $a \in A'$, whereas $p \cdot t_a = 0$ all $a \in A_0$ and $p \cdot t_a^0 = 0$ all a. Therefore

$$t_a \in B_a(p) \text{ all } a. \tag{2}$$

Hence (1) and (2) imply $t_a \in R_a(\bar{g}^0) \cap B_a(p)$ all a, a contradiction with $t_a \succ_a t_a^0$.

coupon. The net coupon cost of buying one unit of good i is thus $v_i - w_i$. The analogous map in lemma (2.1) gives us $\bar{g}_i$. It should be noticed that this scheme signals the externalities involved in quantity constraints. For instance, suppose $\bar{g}_i < 0$. Then in deciding how much of i to buy, agent a, if he is a buyer of i, will take account of the fact that his purchase will increase his coupon income and thereby improve his ability to buy rights to buy or sell other goods.

Lastly, one wants to know whether an equilibrium for the rationing scheme exists. Since for all $\bar{g} \in \bar{G}$, $B_a(p) \cap R_a(\bar{g})$ has a non-empty interior, theory, together with assumption (2.1), gives us all the continuity we require. Together with $\bar{g}t(p, \bar{g}) \leq 0$, where $t(p, \bar{g}) = \Sigma t_a(p, \bar{g})$ and $t_a(p, \bar{g})$ is the optimum choice of agent a at $(p, \bar{g})$, this allows the good old Debreu method to do the rest.

It is of course obvious that there will be many other equilibria of the kind here discussed which are not Pareto-efficient in the above sense. Indeed, if one continues to put a short-period inter-pretation on the model with fixed prices, then it is not at all clear that the equilibria will be orderly, leave alone Pareto-efficient. For it takes time and information to find such equilibria. So none of the above is very interesting as such under this interpretation. But there is another possible interpretation: prices are fixed because no agent wishes to change them in spite of being 'rationed'. It is to this far more interesting case that I now turn.

III CONJECTURES

In this section I consider the implication of the fact that an agent whose transactions are constrained at p must abandon the postu-late that he can trade whatever he wishes to at p (Arrow, 1959). It is then difficult to continue with the postulate that the agent treats all signals parametrically. In the spirit of Negishi (1960), I shall therefore suppose that agents conjecture a relationship between the prices they offer and the quantity signals which they receive. My programme differs from Negishi's as follows. *I do not assume that the economy is intrinsically one of monopolistic competition.* The economy to be studied always has a Walrasian equilibrium. I shall show that it also has non-Walrasian equilibria. Hence the 'price flexibility' implied by the conjectures does not ensure a competitive equilibrium.

The class of conjectures which I consider is restricted in the following way. First, I suppose that agents who do not encounter a quantity constraint take the price at which they must trade as given. Second, I suppose that agents who are quantity-constrained in a market conjecture that they must raise price in order to be allowed to buy more than they are buying and that they must lower price in order to be allowed to sell more than they are selling. In view of a referee's comments and an important observation of Maskin's, it is worth while emphasizing the following.

1   The formulation is designed in order to avoid straightforward monopolistic competition. An agent believes he can affect price only when he has had a signal that he is not a perfect competitor, i.e., experiences a quantity constraint. This signal is endogenous to the economy. All this is done in order to consider economies which always do have Walrasian equilibria. A referee asked me to relate this to the literature. Well, it is not the model Negishi (1960) considered. I have not found it in Benassy. The kink which my formulation gives rise to has recently been used by Negishi (1974) in a different context. Since I had not seen it when I wrote this, and since Negishi is concerned with a special case, that is all I can say on the matter.

2   On the other hand, Maskin has made an important point when he points out to me that I have cooked the story in favour of the result I am looking for, viz. the possibility of non-Walrasian equilibria when Walrasian ones are available. This I do by not allowing an agent to consider that he could trade at prices other than the ones ruling when he notices that other agents are constrained. Most vividly, Why, when labour is rationed and employers are not rationed in the labour market, do not employers respond to the observation that labour is rationed, by lowering price? There may be an answer to this: agents cannot observe the constraints on other agents but at best only their constrained trades; e.g., unemployment statistics are not published. But it may also be that my present hypotheses can be sensibly maintained only by introducing further features, such as informational imperfections, into the story. I hope to examine this on a future occasion.

I now turn to the more formal account.

Interpret b_{ai} as the signal received by a that he cannot buy more of good i than that at the given price. Interpret s_{ai} analogously. Let

$$\zeta_{ai} = \max(0, t_{ai} - b_{ai}), \quad \zeta_a \in R_+^l$$

$$\xi_{ai} = \min(0, t_{ai} + s_{ai}), \quad \xi_a \in R_-^l.$$

Definition (3.1) C_a: $R_+^l \times R_-^l \times \Delta \to R_+^l$ is called the *conjecture* of *a*. It shows, given *p*, the price vector at which *a* believes he must trade as a function of (ζ_a, ξ_a) the excess of his trade over the amount indicated by the quantity signals.

I shall stipulate

Assumption (3.1) (i) C_a is a continuous function and for given $s_a, b_a, C_a(\cdot) t_a$ is a convex function in t_a.

(ii) $C_{ai}(p, \zeta_{ai}, \xi_{ai}) = p_i$ when $\zeta_{ai} = \xi_{ai} = 0$.

(iii) $C_{ai}(\cdot)$ is an increasing function of ζ_{ai} and ξ_{ai} for $p_i > 0$.

The set of feasible choices under the conjecture is F_a^c where

$$F_a^c(p, b_a, s_a) = \{t_a | C_a(p, \zeta_a, \xi_a) t_a \leqslant 0\} \cap \{t_a | e_a + t_a \geqslant 0\}. \tag{6.4}$$

By assumption (3.1) this is a convex set, since $C_a(\cdot) t_a$ is a convex function in t_a. The agent chooses his best trade in (6.4). By assumption (2.1) he chooses a unique $t_a^c(p, b_a, s_a)$ satisfying

$$C_a(p, \zeta_a, \xi_a) t_a^c(p, b_a, s_a) = 0. \tag{6.5}$$

Now define $\hat{c}_a(p, b_a, s_a) \in R_+^l$ as having components

$$\hat{c}_{ai}(p, b_a, s_a) = C_{ai}\{p, \max[0, t_{ai}^c(p, b_a, c_a) - b_{ai}],$$
$$\min[0, t_{ai}^c(p, b_a, s_a) + s_{ai}]\}.$$

Then $\hat{c}_{ai}(\cdot)$ is the price for good *i* at which *a* offers to trade. One has

$$\hat{c}_{ai}(p, b_a, s_a) > 0, \quad \text{for all } i, \quad p \in \Delta . \underset{}{\times} b_a \geqslant 0, \underset{}{\times} s_a \geqslant 0. \tag{6.6}$$

The reason for (6.5) is clear: By assumption (2.1) the optimum trade at a zero price for *i* must be an unbounded purchase of good *i*. If that is restrained by b_{ai}, then $\zeta_{ai} > 0$ and so via assumption (3.1 (iii)) one has (6.6). (It is assumed here that C_{ai} is differentiable at $p_i = 0$.)

An equilibrium of an economy now requires two conditions to be fulfilled: markets must clear, and agents must accept current prices as optimal. Formally,

Definition (3.2) $(p^0, \hat{b}, \hat{s})$ with $p^0 \in \Delta$, $\hat{b}^0 \in \bigtimes_A R^l_+$, $\hat{s}^0 \in \bigtimes_A R^l_+$ is a *conjectural equilibrium* if:

(i) $t^c(p^0, \hat{b}^0, \hat{s}^0) = \Sigma_a t^c_a(p^0, b^0_a, s^0_a) = 0$.

(ii) $\hat{c}_a(p^0, b^0_a, s^0_a) = p^0$ all a.

The motivation is clear. If (ii) but not (i), then the quantity signals cannot be what they are. If (i) but not (ii), agents will offer prices other than what they are. It will be clear that the Walrasian equilibrium with $b^*_{ai} \geqslant t_i(p^*)$, $s^*_{ai} + t_i(p^*) \geqslant 0$, all a and i, is also a conjectural equilibrium. I show that, with two additional assumptions, there are other conjectural equilibria. Since the Walrasian equilibrium is unique, this suffices for the main contention that 'conjectural price flexibility' is consistent with non-Walrasian conjectural equilibrium.

In what follows, write

$$t^+_i = \Sigma_a \max(0, t_{ai}), \quad t^-_i = \Sigma_a \min(0, t_{ai})$$

and for notational ease the superscript c is omitted. I shall use

Assumption (3.2) There is ϵ in the open interval $(0, 1)$ and $r \in R^A_{++}$ with $\Sigma r_a = 1$ such that when $p_1 > 0$

(i) $t_1(p, \hat{b}, \hat{s}) < 0$ and

(ii) $\Sigma \zeta_{a1}(p, b_a, s_a) \leqslant \epsilon' t^+_1(p, \hat{b}, \hat{s})$, $0 < \epsilon' \leqslant \epsilon$

then also:

$$\Sigma_a r_a \hat{c}_{a1}(p, b_a, s_a) < p_1. \tag{6.7}$$

The interpretation is as follows. If at $(p, \hat{b}, \hat{s})$ good 1 is in excess supply, then if the 'short-fall' in desired purchases is small relatively to the total desired purchases a weighted average of the offered prices for market 1 is less than the prevailing price. This postulate is not very restrictive. I also use

Assumption (3.3) For $p \gg 0$, $p \in \Delta$ and all $\hat{b}, \hat{s}$ which are admissible $t_{ai}(p, b_a, s_a) > 0$, some a, each i.

This stipulates that at all the specified signals every good has a buyer. It is somewhat stronger than assumption (3.2) but one can live with it. We now have

Theorem (3.1)   Given assumptions (2.1), (3.1)–(3.3), there exists a non-Walrasian conjectural equilibrium, when one good is not rationed.

Before giving the formal proof it will be convenient to give a preliminary discussion. For this purpose let B_a and S_a be two large compact cubes in R^l_+ and $B = X_A B_a$, $S = X_A S_a$. I shall construct a continuous map $\theta = \theta^p \times \theta^b \times \theta^s$: $\Delta \times B \times S \to \Delta \times B \times S$. As in earlier sections let $\sigma = (p, \hat{b}, \hat{s})$.

(i) θ^p: $\Delta \times B \times S \to \Delta$ is given by

$$\theta^p_i = \frac{\hat{c}^*_i(\sigma)}{c_0(\sigma)} \quad i = 1 \ldots l, \tag{6.8}$$

where $\hat{c}^*_i = (1/A) \Sigma_a \hat{c}_{ai}$ for $i \neq 1$, $\hat{c}^*_1 = \Sigma_a r_a \hat{c}_{a1}$, $c_0 = \Sigma_{i=1} \hat{c}^*_i$. From (6.6) one has $\theta^p \geqslant 0$ and $\theta^p \in \Delta$.

(ii) θ^s: $\Delta \times B \times S \to S$ is given by

$$\left. \begin{aligned} \theta^s_{ai} &= \frac{t^-_{ai}(\sigma)}{\mu_i(\sigma)} \quad i = 1 \ldots l-1, \text{ all } a \\[2mm] \theta^s_{al} &= k \qquad \text{all } a, \text{ where } k \text{ is very large} \end{aligned} \right\} \tag{6.9}$$

where

$$\mu_i(\sigma) = \frac{t^-_i(\sigma) - m}{t^+_i(\sigma) + m}, \quad m > 0$$

so

$$\left. \begin{aligned} t_i &< 0 \Leftrightarrow -\mu_i > 1 \\ t_i &> 0 \Leftrightarrow -\mu_i < 1 \end{aligned} \right\}. \tag{6.10}$$

Summing (6.5) over a and using (6.6) confirms that $-\mu_i$ is bounded above and below for all σ in the domain. Since, for each a, t^-_{ai} is bounded below by finite endowment, one has $\theta^s \in S$ if S is chosen large enough.

(iii) θ^b: $\Delta \times B \times S \to B$ is given by

$$\left. \begin{aligned} \theta^b_{ai} &= -\mu_i(\sigma) t^+_{ai}(\sigma), && \text{all } a \text{ and all } i \neq 1 \text{ and } i \neq l \\ \theta^b_{al} &= k, && \text{all } a \text{ and } k \text{ very large} \\ \theta^b_{a1} &= -\lambda(p) \mu_1(\sigma) t^+_{a1}(\sigma), && \text{all } a \end{aligned} \right\} \tag{6.11}$$

where

$$\lambda(p) = 1 - \epsilon + \min[\epsilon, d(p, p^*)]. \tag{6.12}$$

In (6.12) ϵ is given by assumption (3.2) and $d(p, p^*)$ is the Euclidean distance in Δ of p from the unique Walrasian equilibrium p^*. From (6.12),

$$0 < \lambda(p) \leqslant 1 \quad \text{all } p \in \Delta. \tag{6.13}$$

By routine argument $\theta^b \in B$ if B is chosen large enough.

Proof of theorem (3.1) Let σ^0 be a fixed point of the map θ just given.

(i) $c_0(\sigma^0) = 1$. Since good l is not rationed one has, by assumption (3.1),

$$p_l^0 = \hat{c}_i^*(\sigma^0).$$

(ii) It follows from (i) that

$$p_i^0 = \hat{c}_i^*(\sigma^0) \quad \text{all } i.$$

Hence, for $i \neq 1, l$, one has $t_i(\sigma^0) = 0$. For suppose, say $t_i(\sigma^0) > 0$. Then by (6.11)

$$b_{ai}^0 \leqslant t_{ai}^+(\sigma^0), \quad \text{all } a$$

with strict inequality, some a. But then by assumption (3.1), $p_i^0 < \hat{c}_i^*(\sigma^0)$.

(iii) By the same argument, $t_1(\sigma^0) > 0$ is impossible since $\lambda(p^0) \leqslant 1$. So suppose $t_1(\sigma^0) < 0$ but $p_1^0 = \hat{c}_1^*(\sigma^0)$. Then for some a one must have, by assumption (3.3),

$$b_{a1}^0 < t_{a1}^+(\sigma^0), \quad \text{i.e., } \lambda(p^0) < 1. \tag{6.14}$$

By (6.11),

$$t_{a1}^+(\sigma^0) - b_{a1}^0 = [1 + \mu_1(\sigma^0)\lambda(p^0)]t_{a1}^+(\sigma^0) \leqslant [1 - \lambda(p^0)]t_{a1}^+(\sigma^0).$$

But

$$\lambda(p^0) = \{1 - [\epsilon - d(p^0, p^*)]\} = 1 - \epsilon'$$

so

$$t_{a1}^+(\sigma^0) - b_{a1}^0 \leqslant \epsilon' t_{a1}^+(\sigma^0).$$

This must be true for all a constrained in their buying. So the conditions of assumption (3.2) are satisfied whence

$$p_1^0 > \hat{c}_1^*(\sigma^0), \qquad (6.15)$$

a contradiction.

(iv) So by (6.5) $t_i(\sigma^0) = 0$, all i. But then certainly $\lambda(p^0) = 1$ since otherwise (6.14) holds for some a and so (6.15). But then from the definition of λ, $d(p^0, p^*) \geqslant \epsilon$.

I have now shown that an economy can get stuck in a non-Walrasian equilibrium even when prices are free to vary. Price-setting is now part of a story of rationally acting agents. This involves conjectures, and one must ask where they come from or, at least, whether they must be restricted in some way. Before I turn to this there is a piece of tidying up yet to be done in the present account. For I have not demanded of the conjectural non-Walrasian equilibrium that only one side of each market should be constrained.

For each good i define $\sigma(i, b)$ as having the components of σ except that b_{ai} is replaced by a large positive scalar k_b each a. Similarly $\sigma(i, s)$ has the components of σ except that s_{ai} is replaced by a large positive scalar k_r, each a. Then one writes $t_a[\sigma(i, b)]$ as the best choice in $F_a^c[\sigma(i, b)]$ and $t_a[\sigma(i, s)]$ as the best choice in $F_a^c[\sigma(i, s)]$. Suppose

$$t_{ai}^+[\sigma(i, b)] < t_{ai}^+(\sigma).$$

Then from the definitions, $t_a[\sigma(i, b)] \in F^c(\sigma)$, which contradicts the definition of $t_a(\sigma)$ as the unique choice in $F^c(\sigma)$. So in general

$$t_{ai}^+[\sigma(i, b)] \geqslant t_{ai}^+(\sigma), \quad t_{ai}^-[\sigma(i, s)] \leqslant t_{ai}^-(\sigma), \quad \text{all } a \text{ and } i. \quad (6.16)$$

Now alter the map of the proof of theorem (3.1) as follows.

1   In (6.9), for each $i \neq l$, replace $\mu_i(\sigma)^{-1}$ by

$$r_i^s(\sigma) = \frac{t_i^+[\sigma(i, b)] + m}{t_i^-(\sigma) - m}.$$

2   In (6.11), for each $i \neq 1, l$ replace $\mu_i(\sigma)$ by

$$r_i^b(\sigma) = \frac{t_i^-[\sigma(i, s)] - m}{t_i^+(\sigma) + m} .$$

Otherwise make no change in the map, which remains continuous and has a fixed point which I again write as σ^0. I sketch a proof that σ^0 is an equilibrium on the lines of the previous proof.

(i′) As in (i).

(ii′) Suppose $t_i(\sigma^0) < 0$, for some $i \neq 1, l$. In view of (6.16) this gives $-r_i^b(\sigma^0) > 1$ and so $b_{ai}^0 - t_{ai}^+(\sigma^0) > 0$ all a, which must mean

$$t_{ai}^+(\sigma^0) = t_{ai}^+[\sigma^0(i, b)], \quad \text{all } a$$

and so $-r_i^s(\sigma^0) < 1$, from which $s_{ai}^0 + t_{ai}^-(\sigma^0) = 0$, all a, with strict inequality, some a. Hence one deduces $c_0(\sigma^0) < 1$. One deals with $t_i(\sigma^0) > 0$ analogously.

(iv′) Proceed as in (iv).

But now notice

(v) For all $i \neq 1$: $\min[-r_i^s(\sigma^0), -r_i^b(\sigma^0)] \geqslant 1$. If the strict inequality holds then neither side of the market is restricted. If, say, $-r_i^s(\sigma^0) = 1$, then, in view of $t_i(\sigma^0) = 0$ and (6.16), $t_i^+[\sigma^0(i, b)] = t_i^+(\sigma^0)$, and so while sellers may be restricted, buyers are not. Symmetrically, $-r_i^b(\sigma^0) = 1$ implies that sellers are not restricted.
One now has

Theorem (3.2) Given the assumption of theorem (3.1), there exists a non-Walrasian conjectural equilibrium where in $(l-1)$ markets at most one side of the market is quantity-constrained.

IV   RATIONAL AND REASONABLE CONJECTURES

The objection to a conjectural equilibrium is the arbitrariness of the conjecture. It should be emphasized that the traditional perfectly competitive Walrasian economy with a finite number of participants is open to the same objection. For it is an equilibrium relative to the conjecture that an agent can trade what he wishes to at given prices which is only correct for the equilibrium trade. Similarly in the conjectural non-Walrasian equilibrium which I have discussed: the equilibrium prices confirm the equilibrium conjecture. Put crudely, the conjectured demand curve coincides with the 'actual' demand curve which one can consider.

When one attempts to tie down permissible conjectures it is natural to think first of the requirement that they be 'correct'. For instance, one is familiar with the reason for considering rational expectations in Walrasian sequence models (Radner, 1972). But here matters are harder. For in the Walrasian case agents observe discrepancies between their conjectures and outcomes, while in the present case agents may be in a situation where they trade what they wish at the terms they expect and yet their wishes may be based on conjectures the falsity of which they could only discover by varying their trades. That is, experiment rather than observation would be required to verify conjectures (see Rothschild, 1974).

These are much deeper waters for general equilibrium theory, and I go only a small way in a number of small steps.

I start with some definitions.

Definition (4.1)   Call $\sigma^0(t_a)$ a conjectural equilibrium relative to t_a, an arbitrary trade vector of agent a, if

   (i) For all $a' \neq a$: $p^0(t_a) = C_{a'}[\sigma^0(t_a)]$

   (ii) $t_a + \Sigma_{a' \neq a} t_{a'}[\sigma^0(t_a)]_{\text{def}} = t[\sigma^0(t_a), t_a] = 0$

   (iii) $b_a^0(t_a) \geqslant t_a^+$ and $s_a^0(t_a) + t_a^- \geqslant 0$.

Notice that by (i), $p^0(t_a) \Sigma_{a' \neq a} t_{a'}[\sigma^0(t_a)] = 0$, whence from (ii) and (iii), if a's conjectures satisfy assumption (3.1),

$t_a \in F_a^c[\sigma^0(t_a)]$.

It seems that it would be useful to give a verbal account of definition (4.1) so here it is. Consider an agent a who fixes his trade at t_a and does not just now worry about his budget constraint. We shall be interested to know whether t_a is consistent with some conjectural equilibrium of the economy. Since, however, t_a has been taken as given, such an equilibrium cannot also insist on a being in conjectural equilibrium. Hence a conjectural equilibrium relative to t_a is a price vector $p^0(t_a)$ and a set of rations to all agents such that (1) all agents other than a are in conjectural equilibrium, (2) the net trade of the economy excluding a makes t_a possible and (3) the rations allocated to a are consistent with the given t_a. Hence if this equilibrium exists, the arbitrary t_a is consistent with an equilibrium of all agents other than a, and t_a can be carried out in such an equilibrium. Arithmetic then ensures that t_a also satisfies the budget constraint for a at $p(t_a)$.

Now it seems a first sensible step to suppose that, if no conjectural equilibrium exists relative to t_a, then t_a cannot be carried out. This of course is not a proposition but an assumption. I refer to t_a as *equilibrium-infeasible* if no conjectural equilibrium relative to t_a exists. I now try

Definition (4.2) Let σ^0 be a conjectural equilibrium and let

$$\tau_a(\sigma^0) = \{t_a | t_a \succ_a t_a(\sigma^0)\}.$$

Then C_a is called a *rational conjecture* for a at σ^0 if all $t_a \in \tau_a(\sigma^0)$ are equilibrium-infeasible. One calls σ^0 a *rational conjectural equilibrium* if the conjectures of all agents are rational for σ^0.

Once again I put this into words. For a conjectural equilibrium to be rational, there should be no other conjectural equilibrium in which all agents other than a given one are in conjectural equilibrium and markets clear with the given agent's trade being higher in his preferences. It is perhaps worth noting why this somewhat complicated concept is used.

Some authors, e.g., D. Gale in his Cambridge thesis, postulate at given prices a rationing mechanism which is a map from the trade of all agents to the rations for each agent. One can, in this context, then ask of an equilibrium that, given this mechanism, and given the trades of all other agents, no agent should be able to choose a preferred trade. This then is a straightforward Nash requirement. I, however, want to consider a situation where an agent by changing a price may change his ration. The mechanism here is hard to specify. For that reason, and also because I want to take the conjectures rather than the trades of other agents as given, I look simply at whether there is an equilibrium where $t_a \succ_a t_a^0$, all agents other than a being in conjectural equilibrium.

If conjectures are rational for σ^0, then one might argue that experiments will confirm them, although this would be a rather weak argument since one would require experiments on the part of one agent only. In particular, of course, a rational conjectural equilibrium does not imply that there is no equilibrium, when two agents attempt arbitrary trades, preferred to those at σ^0. The reverse argument is also rather weak: if σ^0 is not a rational equilibrium it does not follow that agents' conjectures are likely to change. In spite of these arguments, the notion is sufficiently interesting to study a little further.

Consider the following case where $A(a)$ is the set of agents excluding a.

Assumption (4.1)   It is possible to choose an a such that for every market i there are at least two agents $a', a'' \in A(a)$ with

$$t_{a'i}(\sigma)\, t_{a''i}(\sigma) < 0, \quad \text{for all } \sigma \text{ with } p \geqslant 0, \hat{b} \in B, \hat{s} \in S.$$

This assumption of 'variety' among agents does not seem very strong. It has, however, the unpleasant consequence that the class of conjectures satisfying assumption (3.1) is incompatible with the existence of rational conjectural equilibrium.

To establish this take agent a of assumption (4.1) and let

$$\bar{t}_a \in \tau_a(\sigma^0), \, |\bar{t}_a - t_a(\sigma^0)| \leqslant \epsilon.$$

If u_a is a's utility function, write $u_a(\bar{t}_a) = \bar{u}_a$. Define

$$t^a(\sigma) = \Sigma_{A(a)} t_{a'}(\sigma)$$

and

$$\tilde{t}_a(\sigma) \text{ solves:} \quad \min_{u_a(t_a) \geqslant \bar{u}_a} W(\Sigma_i |t_i^a(\sigma) + t_{ai}|), \qquad (6.17)$$

where W is a strictly convex increasing function. Hence, given the concavity of u_a, (6.17) defines $\tilde{t}_a(\sigma)$ uniquely. Given the continuity of $t^a(\sigma)$, one has $\tilde{t}_a(\sigma)$, continuous over the domain. Lastly, let

$$\tilde{t}(\sigma) = t^a(\sigma) + \tilde{t}_a(\sigma).$$

Theorem (4.1)   Given assumption (4.1), there exists no rational conjectural equilibrium for the class of conjectures satisfying assumption (3.1).

Proof   Let $B(a) = \mathsf{X}_{A(a)} B_{a'}$, $S(a) = \mathsf{X}_{A(a)} S_{a'}$ and $\bar{\theta} \colon \Delta \times B(a) \times S(a)$ into itself where $\bar{\theta}$ is defined as follows.

(i) For all $a' \in A(a)$, $\bar{\theta}^{s_i}_{a'}$ is the mapping (6.9), where $\tilde{\mu}_i(\sigma)$ replaces $\mu_i(\sigma)$. Here $\tilde{\mu}_i(\sigma)$ is derived from $\mu_i(\sigma)$ by replacing $t^-_i(\sigma)$ and $t^+_i(\sigma)$ by $\tilde{t}^-_i(\sigma)$ and $\tilde{t}^+_i(\sigma)$.

(ii) For all $a' \in A(a)$ let (6.11) be the map of $\bar{\theta}^b_{a'}$ except that (a) $\tilde{\mu}_i(\sigma)$ replaces $\mu_i(\sigma)$ and (b) $\tilde{\lambda}(p) \equiv 1$, all p, replaces $\lambda(p)$. (We are not now specially concerned with non-Walrasian equilibria.)

(iii) The map $\bar{\theta}^p$ is given by

$$\bar{\theta}^p_i = \frac{\hat{c}^*_i(\sigma, a)}{c_0(\sigma, a)}, \quad i = 1 \dots l \tag{6.18}$$

where

$$\hat{c}^*_i(\sigma, a) = \frac{1}{A-1} \Sigma_{A(a)} \hat{c}_{a'i}(\sigma), \quad i = 1 \dots l,$$

$$c_0(\sigma, a) = \Sigma_i \hat{c}^*_i(\sigma, a).$$

(iv) The map certainly has the fixed-point property. Let $\sigma^0(a)$ be such a fixed point.

(a) $\tilde{t}[\sigma^0(a)] = 0$. Suppose not, and $\tilde{t}_i[\sigma^0(a)] > 0$. Then by assumption (4.1) $t_{a'i}[\sigma^0(a)] < 0$, all $a' \in A(a)$, is not possible. Hence by (ii), $b^0_{a'i}(a) < t^+_{a'i}[\sigma^0(a)]$ some $a' \in A(a)$, and by (iii), $s^0_{a'i}[\sigma^0(a)] + t^-_{a'i}[\sigma^0(a)] \geq 0$ all $a' \in A(a)$. Hence by assumption (3.1),

$$p^0_i(a) < \hat{c}^*_i[\sigma^0(a), a], \tag{6.19}$$

whence $c_0[\sigma^0(a), a] > 1$. But this now implies that (6.19) holds for all $i = 1 \dots l$ and so by assumption (3.1) again

$$\tilde{t}[\sigma^0(a)] \gg 0. \tag{6.20}$$

(b) But now, since

$$\Sigma c_{a'i}[\sigma^0(a)] t_{a'i}[\sigma^0(a)] > p^0(a) t_{a'}[\sigma^0(a)]$$

and (6.5), one has

$$p^0(a) t^a[\sigma^0(a)] < 0$$

and $p^0(a) \gg 0$ by assumption (2.1). Hence for at least one i,

$$t_i^q [\sigma^0(a)] < 0.$$

But then by (6.17) it must be that

$$\tilde{t}_i [\sigma^0(a)] = 0$$

since if not then $W(\cdot)$ has not been minimized under the given constraint. Hence (6.20) is impossible. The case $\tilde{t}_i [\sigma^0(a)] < 0$ some i is treated symmetrically.

(c) By (i) and (ii), (a) implies

$$p_i^0(a) = c_{a'i} [\sigma^0(a)], \quad \text{all } a' \text{ and } i.$$

Hence we have shown that the fixed point is a conjectural equilibrium. But by construction $\tilde{t}_a [\sigma^0(a)]$ is attainable and

$$\tilde{t}_a [\sigma^0(a)] \succ_a t_a(\sigma^0).$$

Even so, the class of conjectures considered is small, but I believe sensible for a decentralized economy. By sensible I mean two things. (1) A small agent must not be expected to have 'general equilibrium theories' embodied' in his conjectures. Thus, he believes that the change in his budget situation consequent upon his wishing 'to break a ration' in any one market can be conjectured with reference to events in only that market. (2) An agent does not have 'perverse' conjectures; i.e., he does not believe that getting a larger purchase allocation of good i goes with a lower price of that good or that getting a larger sale allocation goes with a higher price of that good. This 'separability' of conjectures and their lack of perverseness I consider sensible on the grounds that postulating conjectures violating these conditions would result in models even more remote from the world than the present one.

On the other hand, the result of theorem (4.1) may simply be that our definition of rational is too demanding and in particular is bound to conflict with what I have just called sensible conjectures. It must now also be noted that the requirement of rationality places no weight on the *action* of agents. To put it starkly, there may indeed at σ^0 exist an equilibrium relative to t_a with $t_a \in \tau_a(\sigma^0)$, but there may still be no action of agent a which would ensure him t_a. In general, the action open to an agent is a change in the price at which he offers to trade in some market. Whether such an action leads to a preferred equilibrium will depend not only on the existence of the latter but also on the dynamic behaviour of the economy. Indeed, I now believe that the latter is crucial in narrowing down the conjectures to those which are likely to persist. But I cannot at present contribute to this problem.

The following two further remarks may be made.

Let us say that an agent has *competitive conjectures* if, for all a and i

$$c_{ai} = p_i \text{ identically in } p, b_{ai}, s_{ai}.$$

Evidently the Walrasian p^* is the only conjectural equilibrium. On present assumptions it is unique. Now suppose there to be a continuum of agents. Then it is intuitive that p^* will be the equilibrium of the economy whatever t_a. For agent a is of measure zero. But then, $p^* t_a > 0$ for all t_a preferred to t_a^* and the Walrasian equilibrium is a rational conjectural equilibrium. I do not give a formal account of this result since it does not belong to the study of economies in which price adjustments are to be, at least in principle, deducible from the rational action of agents.

The second remark concerns the relationship between rational and 'correct' conjectures. If conjectures are correct, then one supposes that the agent correctly conjectures the prices at which a given trade could be carried out. But this causes some difficulties. At σ^0, $t_a \in \tau_a(\sigma^0)$ implies $pt_a > 0$ where p are the prices conjectured by a for trade t_a. But then at these conjectured prices no equilibrium relative to t_a exists. There is thus no correct conjecture for such trades. So let us restrict 'correct' to refer to price conjectures for trades relative to which equilibria exist. The difficulty is now changed to that deriving from the non-uniqueness of such equilibria. One is therefore driven to a yet weaker formulation: conjectures are not incorrect when, for every t_a relative to which an equilibrium exists, the conjecture p belongs to the set of equilibrium prices. But then, conjectures which are not incorrect are rational. For suppose an equilibrium relative to t_a exists with $t_a \prec_a t_a^0$. So the conjectured p is not such an equilibrium. Then the conjecture is incorrect but it does not preclude it from being rational. For the agent may still be perfectly right in the general conjecture that $t_a \succ_a t_a^0$ is not available.

As I have already noted, the requirement of rationality, as I have defined it, is in view of theorem (4.1) not only too strong but perhaps also misguided. I conclude this section therefore with an alternative which is more appealing but for which I have no theorems.

Let me now choose good l as numeraire by putting $p_l \equiv 1$. I continue to write p for the price vector, it being understood that $p \notin \Delta$. Consider σ^0 a conjectural equilibrium. Let p_a be a price vector announced by a where p_a differs from p^0 in at *most* one coordinate, say the rth. So agents other than a receive the price signals (p^0, p_a). Let $p(a, r)$ be a price vector with $p_r = p_{ar}$. Lastly, let $P(a, r)$ represent the set of $p(a, r)$ consistent with an equilibrium of the economy when agent a chooses his trades which are best for him under his conjecture for $i \neq r$ and for $p_r = p_{ar}$ whatever his trades or rations. Then

Definition (4.4) Agent a's rth conjecture will be said to be *reasonable* at σ^0 if, for all p_a different from p^0 only in the rth coordinate, *either* (i) $P(a, r)$ is empty, *or* (ii) there is no conjectural equilibrium σ, with $p \in P(a, r)$, for which agent a's optimal choice is higher in his preference than is t_a^0, *or* (iii) the response mechanism of the economy from the initial condition (σ^0, p_a) leads to an equilibrium inferior in a's preference to t_a^0.

It will be seen that I have included a number of ideas under the heading 'reasonable'. I believe (iii) to be the most interesting but it is also the most difficult. The definition excludes strategic considerations. Indeed, it is Nash-like in taking the conjectures of agents other than a as given. But I have nothing of a formal nature to report on reasonable conjectures.

APPENDIX TO SECTION II

In this appendix I consider a weaker tradability assumption. It will have the consequence that I can no longer ensure that one can confine attention to the case $\lambda > 0$, i.e., where agents have positive coupon wealth. But when $\lambda = 0$ the feasible set of an agent is not continuous and so the Debreu fixed-point argument would fail there.

Definition (2.3*) Let $\mu_{ai}(e_a)$ be a's marginal rate of substitution, at e_a, between good i and good 1 minus the price of good i in terms of good 1. Then the economy satisfies *tradability* if there are agents a and b such that

$$\mu_{ai}(e_a)\,\mu_{bi}(e_a) < 0 \quad \text{some } i.$$

If an economy satisfying tradability has an orderly equilibrium it must be non-trivial. For by orderliness, either $\mu_{ai}(e_a) \geqslant 0$ all a or $\mu_{ai}(e_a) \leqslant 0$ all a each i.

Now let $v_i(q)$, $w_i(q)$ be defined as in the text but fix $\lambda > 0$ arbitrarily. The Debreu map has a fixed-point q^λ, t^λ:

$$\lambda m \geqslant z(p, q^\lambda, \lambda) \geqslant q^\lambda t^\lambda \geqslant q t^\lambda \quad \text{all } q.$$

A problem arises if $z(p, q^\lambda, \lambda) > 0$ all $\lambda > 0$ which I now assume to be the case. Note that $z(\cdot)$ is not continuous at $\lambda = 0$. But if we take $\lambda \to 0$ we may take a convergent subsequence q^λ such that $v_i(q^\lambda) = 0$ all λ *or* $w_i(q^\lambda) = 0$ all λ. Along this subsequence let $q^\lambda \to \bar{q}$, $t^\lambda \to \bar{t}$. It is clear that $\bar{t} = 0$. On the other hand, $\bar{t}$ need not be $\lim_{\lambda \to 0} t(p, q^\lambda, \lambda)$ because of lack of continuity.

However, consider the *actual* economy where

$$\bar{b}_{ai} = \bar{t}_{ai}^+, \quad \bar{s}_{ai} = \infty \text{ for } \bar{q}_i > 0, \quad \bar{b}_{ai} = \infty, \quad \bar{s}_{ai} = \bar{t}_{ai}^- \text{ for } \bar{q}_i < 0.$$

If agent a faced this quantity constraint, $\bar{t}_a$ would be his choice. For if not there would be $t_a \succ_a \bar{t}_a$ where we may take t_a interior to his set of feasible trades given the quantity constraints. But then for λ small, $t_a \succ_a t^\lambda$, a contradiction. Hence the quantity rations $(\bar{b}_a, \bar{s}_a)$ all a gives a Drèze equilibrium at p. It is of course orderly and non-trivial.

This proof, which is due to Douglas Gale, shows that there are Drèze equilibria which cannot be mimicked by a coupon economy or, better, that the coupon economy is not well defined at zero coupon wealth.

REFERENCES

Arrow, K. J. (1959), 'Towards a Theory of Price Adjustment', in *The Allocation of Economic Resources*, ed. A. Abramovitz, Stanford University Press.

Arrow, K. J. and Hahn, F. H. (1976), *General Competitive Analysis*, Holden Day, San Francisco.

Benassy, J. P. (1976), 'The Disequilibrium Approach to Monopolistic Price Setting and General Monopolistic Equilibrium', *Review of Economic Studies*, **43**.

Clower, R. W. (1965), 'The Keynesian Counterrevolution: A Theoretical Appraisal', in *The Theory of Interest Rates*, ed. F. H. Hahn and F. P. R. Brechling, Macmillan, London.

Debreu, G. (1959), *Theory of Value*, John Wiley, New York.

Drèze, J. (1975), 'Existence of Exchange Equilibrium under Price Rigidities', Core no. 7326, *International Economic Review*, **16**.

Grandmont, J. and Laroque, G. (1976), 'On Temporary Keynesian Equilibria', *Review of Economic Studies*, **43**.

Hahn, F. H. and Negishi, T. (1962), 'A Theorem on Non-Tâtonnement Stability', *Econometrica*, **30**.

Leijonhufvud, A. (1960), *On Keynesian Economics and the Economics of Keynes*, Oxford University Press.

Malinvaud, E. and Younès, Y. (1975), 'A New Formulation for the Microeconomic Foundations of Macroeconomics', paper presented at a Conference of the International Economic Association at S'Agaro, Spain, July 1975. Reprinted in Harcourt, G. C. (ed.) (1977), *The Microeconomic Foundations of Macroeconomics*, Macmillan, London.

Negishi, T. (1960), 'Monopolistic Competition and General Equilibrium', *Review of Economic Studies*, **28**.

Negishi, T. (1974), 'Unemployment Equilibrium', unpublished paper.

Radner, R. (1972), 'Existence of Equilibrium of Plans, Prices and Price Expectations in a Sequence of Markets', *Econometrica*, **40**.

Rothschild, M. (1974), 'A Two-armed-bandit Theory of Market Pricing', *Journal of Economic Theory*, **9**.

Younès, Y. (1975), 'On the Role of Money in the Process of Exchange and the Existence of a Non-Walrasian Equilibrium', *Review of Economic Studies*, **42**.

7

Exercises in Conjectural Equilibria

I INTRODUCTION

In orthodox theory an agent is described by his endowment, tastes and the technological production possibilities which are open to him.[1] One does not enquire how these characteristics of the agent came to be what they are, nor, in general, does one allow the characteristics to be affected by the economic environment. The characteristics are arbitrarily given by the history of the economy and of the agent and so, for instance, there are many equilibria depending on the characteristics. In particular, if the total endowment of goods is given, *any allocation* of these between agents (in a pure exchange economy), will be an equilibrium for some tastes and endowment distribution. There does not seem to me anything wrong with the conclusion that equilibria are not history-free (they are not independent of initial conditions). Indeed, one may adduce rather strong arguments to support the view that history-free theorems in the social sciences are bogus. To say that the equilibrium set depends on history is not to make equilibrium theory vacuous: the reverse is the case. For one is thereby taking the view that empirical evidence is required to generate interesting propositions. The relevance of these remarks to what follows will be seen below.

The orthodox description of the agent is however incomplete on several counts. The most important omission concerns the information available to the agent. For instance, if one considers the set of all physical objects in an economy, a partition of this set will define the goods which one agent can distinguish. The partition may differ between agents and need not be independent of economic signals. One need only think of second-hand motor

[1] This work was supported by National Science Foundation Grant SOC74-11446 at the Institute for Mathematical Studies in the Social Sciences, Stanford University.

cars or different qualities of labour to see that an assumption that
all agents have identical fine partitions is not satisfactory. *Pari passu*,
the same remarks apply to the partitioning of states of nature;
see Radner (1968). A great deal of work has recently been
undertaken, mainly in the context of very simple models, to
study the consequences of enriching the agent's description by
endowing him with an information structure and taking account
of the possibility that this structure may be only partly a characteristic, i.e. may in part at least depend on economic events
(e.g. Rothschild, 1974).

Related to this is the observation that agents have, in general,
to deduce their economic environment from the signals which
they receive. Thus, in orthodox theory the agent does not know
the production possibility set of the economy but only relative
prices. One of the beautiful aspects of the theory is that this is all
he needs to know. Yet even in this simple orthodox world there
is a theoretical lacuna: there is no description in terms of the
decisions of agents of how prices come to be what they are. It is
true that there is a very special account of exchange processes
between agents which terminate in allocations which can be
supported by competitive prices. But that is hardly satisfactory,
although even such special constructions may be superior to the
auctioneer. For most markets it is simply the case that the description of the agent and of the signals which he receives is not rich
enough for a theory of price formation by the agents. I have now
come to the central issues to be studied in this paper. Since they
are easy to misunderstand, I shall discuss them further before
introducing technicalities.

The proposal to study an economy which is sufficiently well
described to answer the question, Why are the signals received by
agents what they are?, is not at all to embark on 'dynamics',
except in a very weak sense. The weak sense is that an equilibrium must be recognizable as a stationary state of a dynamic
system, the finer characteristics of which may be unknown. For
instance, in the orthodox tâtonnement matters are normally too
complicated to give a precise account of the evolution of prices
from a given starting point. But the dynamic equations induce
the definition of an equilibrium as stationary points. If the
auctioneer is replaced by the agents who change the prices at
which they are willing to trade whenever they consider this to be
profitable, then the stationary point of the dynamic system will
have to be a set of signals at which agents do not see profits to
be made by changing price. The set of stationary points or

equilibria may include those of the tâtonnement but clearly need not coincide with the set of equilibria of the latter. I am making the obvious point that the states which we designate as equilibria cannot be independent of the theory of how signals and allocations change. The underlying axiom of the Arrow–Debreu theory is that (at positive prices), prices are stationary if and only if target excess demand is everywhere zero. If this assumption is changed, and nothing else in the description of the economy is changed, we may expect to find states which previously did not, and now do, qualify as equilibrium states.

At prices which are not in the stationary set of prices for a tâtonnement it is true by definition that not all agents can carry out their intended transactions. One postulates that this gives rise to a further set of signals which tell some of the agents that the transactions which are open to them at these prices are restricted in size. One now requires a theory or rule of the generation of such *quantity signals* (e.g. a 'rationing scheme'), and one requires a theory of the agents' adjustments to these signals. It is in this second stage that one needs the notion of *conjectures.* If we include in the actions of an agent not only the amounts of each good which he wishes to trade but also the prices which he will announce as those at which he is willing to trade, then in the first instance we are looking for a correspondence from the signals received by an agent to the set of actions he conjectures to be available to him. Call it the *action correspondence.* The equilibrium notion is fairly clear: it is signals received by agents such that the best action for each of the set of possible actions again induces the original signals. A formal definition is found below. Such an equilibrium I want to call a *conjectural equilibrium.*

I can now return to my opening paragraph. Certainly in the above description of a conjectural equilibrium the designated equilibrium states depend on the conjectures with which we have endowed the agents – e.g., their beliefs of the relation there might be between their ration and their announced price. But the conjectures are unexplained, and to that extent conjectural equilibria appear to be arbitrary. As a first reply one is tempted to say that this is no different from the arbitrary tastes of orthodoxy. Certainly this is not entirely unjustified. But there is an objection to this, namely that it may be more convincing to believe that there is no clear inducement to discover which are 'correct' tastes. I am not at all sure that this objection has much force. A person brought up on hamburgers may continue with this unpleasing diet even if it is the case that if he tried fish and chips he would discover that he preferred that. Just in the same way, a person may continue to find himself unemployed every so often at a given wage and conjecture wrongly that he can do nothing about it by proposing a lower wage, and never undertake the experiment which would reveal this mistake. The belief of the orthodox that given sufficient time men discover their true environment suggests a certain ignorance of both anthropology and history. Children were sacrificed for good harvests for centuries, and many people believe that the quantity of money determines the level of money income. Both are wrong conjectures.

That conjectures may be the outcome of past experience, and that they may be 'given' for the theorist and discoverable by empirical enquiry, is to me acceptable. It is a view which decisively divides both Keynesians and Marxists from orthodoxy. The world is to be explained at least partly by the way agents perceive it, and the way in which they perceive it is partly for history, partly for sociology and partly for psychology. To the orthodox, perception does not enter in the story. That is of course why they are so sanguine about the working of the Invisible Hand.

None the less, the orthodox pose an interesting problem when they suggest that the arbitrariness of conjectures be removed by the requirement that they be 'correct'. As we shall see, that requirement is not unambiguously defined and may be impossible to satisfy. In what follows I shall be concerned mainly with that problem.

II A SIMPLE CONJECTURAL ECONOMY

Let there be H households, F firms and $(l + 1)$ goods. The generic subscript of an agent is a and $a = h$ refers to a household and $a = i$ to a firm producing good i. Each firm produces only one good and each good is produced by a different firm; i.e., $F = l$. The subscript $i = 0$ refers to leisure. The production sets $Y_i \subset R^{l+1}$ of all firms are strictly convex and $y_i \in Y_i$ is the vector with $y_{ii} \geqslant 0$, $y_{i0} \leqslant 0$ and $y_{ij} = 0$, $j \neq i$. Good i is produced by only the input of leisure. All Y_i are compact and $y_i \in Y_i$, $y_{ii} \neq 0$ implies $y_{i0} < 0$. Households have strictly convex closed preferences on R_+^{l+1}, are endowed with $l_{h0} > 0$ units of leisure (and nothing else) and receive the profit of firms which are distributed among them according to a fixed rule. One writes $x_h \in R^{l+1}$ as the demand vector of h, $x = \Sigma_h x_h$. Lastly, let $\hat{y} \in X_l R^{l+1}$ be the allocation of production among firms, where X stands here for the Cartesian product.

I shall assume here that households have perfectly competitive conjectures. By this I mean that households choose x_h which is best in their preferences from the budget set.

$$B_h(p, \hat{y}) = \left\{ x_h \mid px_h \leqslant p_0 l_{h0} + \sum_i \beta_{hi} p \cdot y_i \right\}$$

where $0 \leqslant \beta_{hi} \leqslant 1$ each i,

By my assumption this gives rise to the demand functions:

$$x_h = x_h(p, \hat{y}) \text{ all } h.$$

Let firm i observe the price vector $p \in R_+^{l+1}$, the demand x_i and a labour ration $L_{i0} < 0$. The latter is a signal that firm i must choose its production at p from $Y_i \cap \{ y_i \mid y_{i0} \geqslant L_{i0} \}$. We stipulate

$$\sum_i L_{i0} = \sum_h (x_{h0} - l_{h0}).$$

Now write

$$\pi_i(p, x_i, L_{i0}, y_i)$$

as the conjectured profit function of firm i. We postulate the following properties:

$(\pi.1)$ $\pi_i(p, x, L_{i0}, y_i) = p \cdot y_i$ for y_i with $y_{ii} = x_i, y_{i0} = L_{i0}$.
$(\pi.2)$ $\pi_i(p, x_i, L_{i0}, y_i) < p \cdot y_i$ for $y_{ii} \geqslant x_i, y_{i0} \leqslant L_{i0}$ and at least one inequality strict.
$(\pi.3)$ $\pi_i(p, x_i, L_{i0}, y_i) > p \cdot y_i$ for $y_{ii} \leqslant x_i, y_{i0} \geqslant L_{i0}$ and at least one inequality strict.
$(\pi.4)$ Given (p, x_i, L_{i0}), π_i is concave in y_{ii} and $-y_{i0}$.

Each firm i chooses $y_i \in Y_i$ given the signal (p, x_i, L_{i0}) to attain the highest conjectural profit. Notice that $(\pi.2)$ for instance implies that the firm conjectures that it must sell at a lower price than p_i if it wants to produce more than x_i, and/or buy labour at a higher price than p_0 if it wants to employ more than L_{i0}. We may write the production choice of firm i as

$$y_i = y_i(p, x_i, L_{i0}).$$

Lastly, write $L_0 = \{ L_{10} \ldots L_{F0} \}$.

Definition (2.1)   We say that p^0, L^0_0, $(x^0_1 \ldots x^0_H)$, $\hat{y}^0$ is a *conjectural equilibrium* if

(a) $x^0_h \geqslant_h x_h$ all $x_h \in B_h(p^0, \hat{y}^0)$ all h

(b) $p^0 y^0_i = \pi_i(p^0, x^0_i, L^0_{i0}, y^0_i) \geqslant \pi_i(p^0, x^0_i, L_{i0}, y_i)$

all $y_i \in Y_i$ all i

(c) $y^0_{ii} = x^0_i$ all $i = 1 \ldots l$

(d) $\sum_i y^0_{i0} = \sum_i L^0_{i0}$ when $\sum_i L^0_{i0} = \sum_h (x^0_{h0} - l_{h0})$.

The definition is straightforward. Of course, the economy considered is somewhat special, in particular in insisting that households are endowed with competitive conjectures. In the sequel I shall follow tradition and not ask that these conjectures of households correspond to what is the case.

Now the profit functions $\pi_i(\cdot)$ embody the conjectures of firms and at the moment are arbitrary up to $(\pi.1)–(\pi.4)$. In studying the notion of rational conjectures, it will be as well not to be too ambitious at the outset. In particular, I shall start with considering the possibility of imposing *local* restrictions on conjectures.

To do this I need to define a conjectural equilibrium relatively to the production of firm i. Let p^0, L^0_0, $(x^0_1, \ldots, x^0_H)$, $\hat{y}^0$ be a conjectural equilibrium and consider $y_i \in N(\epsilon, y^0_i)$ where $N(\cdot)$ is a small (ϵ), neighbourhood of y^0_i in R^{l+1}. Then

Definition (2.2)   Let $p(y_i)$, $L_0(y_i)$, $[x_1(y_i), \ldots, x_H(y_i)]$, $\hat{y}(y_i)$ be called[2] an *ϵ-conjectural equilibrium* relatively to $y_i \in N(\epsilon, y^0_i)$ if

(a) $x_h(y_i) \gtrsim_h x_h$ all $x_h \in B_h[p(y_i), \hat{y}(y_i)]$ all h

(b) $p(y_i)y_k(y_i) = \pi_k[p(y_i), x_k(y_i), L_{k0}(y_i), y_k(y_i)]$

$\geqslant \pi_k[p(y_i), x_k(y_i), L_{k0}(y_i), y_k]$

all $y_k \in Y_k$ and all $k \neq i$.

(c) $y_{kk}(y_i) = x_k(y_i)$ all $k = 1 \ldots l$

---

[2] The ith vector of $\hat{y}(y_i)$ is y_i.

(d) $\sum_k y_{k0}(y_i) = \sum_k L_{k0}(y_i)$ and

$$\sum_k L_{k0}(y_i) = \sum_h [x_{h0}(y_i) - l_{k0}].$$

It will be seen that the difference between a conjectural equilibrium and a conjectural equilibrium relatively to y_i is that in the former we do, and in the latter we do not, demand that firm i should have maximum profits under its conjectures. The reason for this construction will become clear almost at once.

Let $E_i(y_i, y_i^0, \epsilon) \subset R^{l+1} \times R^F \times R_+^{H \cdot (l+1)} \times R^{(F \cdot 1)(l+1)}$ be the set of ϵ-conjectural equilibria relative to y_i when $y_i \in N(y_i^0, \epsilon)$. An element of $E_i(\cdot)$ is $\{p(y_i), L(y_i), [x_1(y_1) \ldots x_H(y_i)], \hat{y}(y_i)\}$. I write $E_{ip}(\cdot)$ as the projection of $E_i(\cdot)$ on to the price space.

Definition (2.3) I call $(p^0, x_1^0 \ldots x_H^0, L_0^0, \hat{y}^0)$ an ϵ-*reasonable* conjectural equilibrium if, for all $i = 1 \ldots l$ and given ϵ, either

(a) $p_i y_i \leqslant \pi_i(p^0, x_i^0, L_{i0}^0, y_i^0), p_i \in E_{ip}(y_i, y_i^0, \epsilon)$,

   $y_i \in Y_i \cap N(y_i^0, \epsilon)$,   or

(b) $E_i(y_i, y_i^0, \epsilon)$ is empty.

Let me explain the idea of (D2.3). One considers a given conjectural equilibrium and asks what would happen to the equilibrium profits of a firm i if it deviated slightly in its production plan from what, under its conjectures, is an optimum plan. If such a slight deviation is inconsistent, given the conjectures of *all other firms*, with an equilibrium (D2.3(b)), we argue that it is reasonable for firm i not to undertake that deviation. If it is consistent with such an equilibrium but profits are no higher for firm i than they were without that deviation (D2.3(a)), we also argue that the firm i is reasonable in not making the deviation. In this of course (D2.3(b)) is the least attractive. But unless one is willing to open the Pandora's box of dynamics there is not much alternative.

I use the terminology 'reasonable' to distinguish the case where a firm may be right in its belief that it cannot locally improve profits for the 'wrong' reason, from that where the firm is right in that belief for the 'right' reason (which I shall call 'rational'). Thus a firm may wrongly predict the relevant elements of $E_i(\cdot)$ and yet be correct in its conclusion that it cannot improve itself by small changes in production. A more stringent requirement is that, in a conjectural equilibrium, each firm i should correctly predict the element of $E_i(\cdot)$. Thus

Definition (2.4) I call $(p^0, x_1^0 \ldots x_H^0, L^0, \hat{y}^0)$ an ϵ-*rational* conjectural equilibrium if

   (a) it is an ϵ-reasonable equilibrium,   and

   (b) for all i and $y_i \in Y_i \cap N(\epsilon, y_i^0)$,

$$p_i y_i = \pi_i(p, x_i, L_{i0}, y) \quad \text{where}$$

$$(p, x_1, \ldots, x_H, L_0, \hat{y}) \in E_i(y_i, y_i^0).$$

Thus, in an ϵ-rational conjectural equilibrium not only is there no other conjectural equilibrium consistent with $y_i \in N(y_i^0, \epsilon)$ in which i's profits are higher than they are in the given equilibrium, but also, the profits attained in any conjectural equilibrium relatively to y_i are those which i's conjectures predict.

Both of the definitions of ϵ-reasonable and ϵ-rational conjectural equilibrium are in the general equilibrium spirit, and it may be thought that they are too demanding even before one has considered the problem of their existence. So let me consider one last alternative formulation which is more in the spirit of Nash equilibria.

Let $\hat{y}_N^0(y_i)$ be the vector $\hat{y}^0$ with y_i replacing y_i^0. (The subscript N reminds us of the Nash feature that the production vectors of firms other than i are fixed.) We require the notion of an ϵ-Nash deviation from a conjectural equilibrium relatively to y_i.

Definition (2.5) Let $(p^0, x_1^0, \ldots, x_H^0, L_0^0, \hat{y}^0)$ be a conjectural equilibrium. Then $p^N(y_i) \in R_+^{l+1}$, $x_H^N(y_i) \in R_+^{l+1}$, $(h = 1, \ldots, H)$, $L_0^N(y_i) \in R^F$ is called an ϵ-*Nash deviation* from the given conjectural equilibrium relatively to y_i if when $y_i \in Y_i \cap N(\epsilon, y_i^0)$:

   (a) $x_h^N(y_i) \succsim_h x_h$ all $x_h \in B_h[p^N(y_i), \hat{y}_N^0(y_i)]$ all h

   (b) $\sum_h x_{hk}^N(y_i) = y_{kk}^0$ all $k \neq i$

   (c) $\sum_h x_{hi}^N(y_i) = y_{ii}$

(d) $\sum_h (x_{h0}^N(y_i) - l_{h0}) = \sum_k L_{0k}^N(y_i) = \sum_{k \neq i} y_{k0}^0 + y_{i0}.$

Thus, in an ϵ-Nash deviation we calculate the equilibrium of the economy on the supposition that all firms other than i keep their productions as it is in conjectural equilibrium and therefore ignore the fact that this constancy of production may not be profit-maximizing for these firms under their conjectures. One may say that this is an interesting concept either because no firm i could calculate anything more elaborate or, more speculatively, that, for a small enough firm i at ϵ, the ϵ-Nash deviation is a good approximation to an ϵ-conjectural equilibrium relatively to y_i. One now has

Definition (2.6) The conjectural equilibrium $(p^0, x_1, \ldots, x_H^0$ $L_0^0, \hat{y}^0)$ is *ϵ-Nash rational* if for all i and $y_i \in Y_i \cap N(\epsilon, y_i)$ there exists an ϵ-Nash deviation relatively to y_i such that

$$p^N(y_i)y_i = \pi_i[p^N(y_i), x_i^N(y_i), L_{0i}^N(y_i), y_i].$$

That is, in an ϵ-Nash rational conjectural equilibrium the conjectural profit functions of firms correctly predict the profits to be made from an ϵ-Nash deviation.

We now have a good many candidates for tying down conjectures. One wants to ask two questions: (a) Are there good economic grounds for supposing conjectural equilibria to have one or more of the characteristics captured by ϵ-reasonable, ϵ-rational and ϵ-Nash rational? and (2) Are all of these equilibria non-vacuous – that is, could they exist? Until we have explored question (2) it is not worthwhile arguing about (1).

III EXISTENCE PROBLEMS

Given the assumptions in section II, one can show that a conjectural equilibrium exists,[3] and I shall here take this for granted. To proceed to the next task it will be convenient to simplify the model in the non-essential way of letting firms have competitive

---

[3] A proof for closely related models will be found in Hahn (1978) [reprinted as chapter 6 of the present volume] and Negishi (1961).

conjectures in the labour market. That is, we now remove the quantity signals L_{i0} from the profit functions. I shall also suppose that a conjectural equilibrium with $p_0 > 0$ exists and henceforth, without change of notation, take $p_0 = 1$ in p. Lastly, I postulate that all functions that interest me are of class C^2 (i.e., twice continuously differentiable).

Let $\hat{\pi} = (\pi_1, \ldots, \pi_i)$ be the vector of profits $p \cdot y_i$. Let us also now write

$$y_{i0} = f_i(y_{ii})$$

for the input of labour required to produce y_{ii}. One takes $f_i(\cdot)$ as convex. From what has already been said, one may write

$$x_i = x_i(p, \hat{y})$$

and also

$$x_i - y_{ii} \equiv g_i(p, \hat{y})$$

where, without change of notation, I now take $\hat{y} \in R_+^l$ to be the vector of outputs. Also, if $\pi_i(p_i, x_i, y_{ii})$ is the conjectural profit function, let

$$h_i(p_i, x_i, y_{ii}) \equiv \bar{h}_i(p, \hat{y}) \equiv \frac{\partial \pi_i}{\partial y_{ii}}$$

Then $(p^0, \hat{y}^0)$ is a conjectural equilibrium if

(a) $g(p^0, \hat{y}^0) = 0$
(b) $\bar{h}(p^0, \hat{y}^0) = 0$ $\Big\}$.   (7.1)

Suppose that $(p^0, \hat{y}^0) \gg 0$, and let the superscript 0 to a function denote that it is evaluated at $(p^0, \hat{y}^0)$. Then the conjectural equilibrium is called *regular* if

$$M(p^0, \hat{y}^0) = \begin{bmatrix} g_p^0 & g_y^0 \\ \bar{h}_p^0 & \bar{h}_y^0 \end{bmatrix}$$

is of full rank (i.e. of rank $2l$).

It will be convenient to state the regularity condition in a different form. Let H always denote an $l \times l$ diagonal matrix where

$$H_p^0 = [h_{ip_i}^0], H_x^0 = [h_{ix_i}^0], H_y^0 = [h_{iy_{ii}}^0]. \ H_z^0 = [h_{ix_i}^0 + h_{iy_{ii}}^0].$$

Then

$$\bar{h}_p^0 = H_p^0 + H_x^0 x_p = H_p^0 + H_x^0 g_p^0$$

$$\bar{h}_y^0 = H_y^0 + H_x^0 x_y = H_y^0 + H_x^0 + H_x^0 [x_y - I]$$

$$= H_y^0 + H_x^0 + H_x^0 g_y^0.$$

Hence, if $M(p^0, \hat{y}^0)$ is non-singular, so is $M^*(p^0, \hat{y}^0)$ where

$$M^*(p^0, \hat{y}^0) = \begin{bmatrix} g_p^0 & g_y^0 \\ H_p^0 & H_z^0 \end{bmatrix}.$$

Definition (3.1) A conjectural equilibrium $(p^0, \hat{y}^0)$ will be called *regular* if $(p^0, \hat{y}^0) \gg 0$ and $M^*(p^0, \hat{y}^0)$ is of full rank.

Now consider a regular conjectural equilibrium and take a small variation in the production of firm k. We want to find the conjectural equilibrium (if it exists), relatively to $(y_{kk}^0 \pm \epsilon)$ where ϵ is very small. Suppose this conjectural equilibrium is $(p, \hat{y})$. Then it must satisfy

$$g_p^0(p - p^0) + g_y^0(\hat{y} - \hat{y}^0) = 0$$

and

$$\bar{h}_{ip}^0(p - p^0) + \bar{h}_{iy}^0(\hat{y} - \hat{y}^0) = 0 \quad \text{all } i = k. \tag{7.2}$$

Also, one has

$$y_{kk}^0(p_k - p_k^0) + [p_k^0 + f_k'(y_{kk}^0)](y_{kk} - y_{kk}^0) = \pi_k - \pi_k^0. \tag{7.3}$$

So if $H_p^0(k)$ is the matrix H_p^0 with its kth diagonal element replaced by y_{kk}^0 and $H_z^0(k)$ is the matrix H_z^0 with its kth diagonal element replaced by $[p_k^0 + f_k'(y_{kk}^0)]$, one is interested in the equations

$$M_k^*(p^0, y^0)(p - p^0, y - y^0) = [\delta_{ik+l}(\pi_k - \pi_k^0)] \tag{7.4}$$

where

$$M_k^*(p^0, \hat{y}^0) = \begin{bmatrix} g_p^0 & g_y^0 \\ H_p^0(k) & H_z^0(k) \end{bmatrix}.$$

Proposition (3.1) A necessary and sufficient condition for a regular conjectural equilibrium to be ϵ-rational for ϵ arbitrarily small is that *either* the matrix $M_k^*(p^0, \hat{y}^0)$ be singular for all $k = 1, \ldots, l$, or no equilibria relatively to $(y_{kk}^0 \pm \epsilon)$ exist for any k.[4]

Proof (a) *Necessity.* If $(p^0, \hat{y}^0)$ is a conjectural equilibrium and $M_k^*(p^0, \hat{y}^0)$ is of full rank for some k, then (7.4) has a solution with $\pi_k > \pi_k^0$ so that the equilibrium would not be ϵ-reasonable and so not ϵ-rational.

(b) *Sufficiency.* If at $(p^0, \hat{y}^0)$ the condition of the proposition is satisfied, then one can solve

$$M_k^*(p^0, \hat{y}^0)(p - p^0, \hat{y} - \hat{y}^0) = \{0\}$$

for all the conjectural equilibria $(p, \hat{y})$ relatively to $(y_{kk}^b \pm \epsilon)$. In all such equilibria $\pi_k = \pi_k^0$ and there exists no such equilibrium with $\pi_k > \pi_k^0$.

The proposition is of course trivial – indeed, it is almost a definition of an ϵ-rational conjectural equilibrium. None the less, it is of some help with the rather intractable problem of whether ϵ-rational equilibria exist. To see this I consider an example.

Suppose that the conjectural profit function of each firm is derived from the conjectural inverse demand function:

$$p_i + \beta_i(y_{ii} - x_i). \quad \beta_i < 0 \text{ all } i. \tag{7.5}$$

Also assume that

$$f_i(y_{ii}) = -c_i y_{ii} \quad c_i > 0 \text{ all } i. \tag{7.6}$$

Then one verifies that $H_p^0 = I$, $H_z^0 = \{\beta_i\}$ while $H_p^0(k)$ has y_{kk}^0 in the kth diagonal place and, since $c_i = p_i^0 + \beta_i y_i^0$, all i, $H_z^0(k)$ has $-\beta_k y_{kk}^0$ as the kth diagonal element.

[4] I shall henceforth in this section ignore the second contingency. Throughout I am strictly concerned with 'infinitesimal rationality' i.e. with $\epsilon \to 0$. But the exposition will serve if sufficient regularity is granted.

Let us consider only regular conjectural equilibria for this economy, so that, writing small letters for the determinant of the matrix, $m^*(p, \hat{y}) \neq 0$ at any conjectural equilibrium $(p, \hat{y})$. In the present economy one has

$$m^*_{l+k,k} + \beta_k m^*_{l+k,\,l+k} = m^*$$

where I now omit the arguments $(p, \hat{y})$ and where m^*_{ij} are co-factors in the usual notation. If the conjectural equilibrium is ϵ-rational and we use proposition (3.1) in the present case, one must have

$$m^*_{l+k,k} - \beta_k m^*_{l+k,\,l+k} = 0$$

and since this must hold for all k one now has

$$m^*_{l+k,k} = \tfrac{1}{2} m^* \quad \text{all } k. \tag{7.7}$$

Now let us specialize somewhat further by assuming (i) $l = 2$, (ii) all households have parallel linear Engel curves, and (iii) labour is supplied inelastically and leisure does not enter the utility function.

It is a consequence of (ii) that g_p becomes a matrix of substitution terms which in view of (iii) is singular. Also, a typical element of g_y is $x_{iyj} - \delta_{ij}$, where $\delta_{ij} = 1$ for $i = j$ and $\delta_{ij} = 0$ for $i \neq j$. If μ is the sum of profits and wages, then

$$x_{iyj} = x_{i\mu}(p_j - c_j) = -\beta_j x_{i\mu} y_{jj}; \quad i,j = 1, 2$$

by (iii) where $x_{i\mu} = \partial x_i/\partial \mu$. Also by (iii), $\Sigma p_i x_{i\mu} = 1$. Using all of this and (7.7), one finds that we require a regular conjectural equilibrium that[5]

(A) $c_1 \beta_2 S_{12} + c_2 \beta_1 S_{11} = 0$

where S_{ij} is a substitution term. From this and (iii) one has

$$\frac{c_1 \beta_2}{p_2^0} = \frac{c_2 \beta_1}{p_1^0} = k. \tag{7.8}$$

---

[5] See appendix for manipulations.

We also require

(B) $\quad x_{1\mu}(\beta_1 c_2 x_1 - \beta_2 c_1 x_2) + c_2 = 0$

or, using (7.8),

$$kx_{1\mu}(p_1^0 x_1 - p_2^0 x_2) + c_2 = 0. \tag{7.9}$$

These two conditions must be satisfied if the conjectural equilibrium is to be ϵ-rational. But now suppose the common utility function to be Cobb–Douglas with exponents α_i $(i = 1, 2)$. Then (7.9) becomes

$$k\mu x_{i\mu}(\alpha_1 - \alpha_2) + c_2 = 0. \tag{7.9'}$$

Since one wants $k < 0$, it now follows that, should $\alpha_2 > \alpha_1$, no ϵ-rational regular conjectural equilibrium exists.

As a second example, consider profit conjectures based on the following conjectural inverse demand functions:

$$p_i(y_{ii}/x_i)^{\beta_i} \text{ where } -1 < \beta_i < 0. \tag{7.10}$$

Then one verifies that $H_p^0 = \{1 + \beta_i\}$, $H_z^0 = \{0\}$, $H_p^0(k)$ has y_{kk}^0 in the kth diagonal place and, since $c_i = p_i^0(1 + \beta_i)$ all i, $H_3(k)$ has $-\beta_k p_k^0$ as the kth diagonal element. We now assume that $c_1 = c_2 = c$ and continue the assumptions (i)–(iii) of the previous example.

The rather tedious manipulations will be found in the appendix. Using proposition (3.1), one shows that if a given conjectural equilibrium is to be ϵ-rational one requires

$$-\frac{\sigma_{21}}{\sigma_{11}} = \frac{\beta_1(1 + \beta_2)}{\beta_2(1 + \beta_1)} \tag{7.11}$$

and also that

$$-\frac{\sigma_{21}}{\sigma_{11}} > 1 \tag{7.12}$$

where σ_{ij} is the compensated elasticity of demand for good i for a change in the price of good j. From elementary theory then (7.12) can also be written as

$$\frac{x_1^0}{x_2^0} > 1. \tag{7.13}$$

From (7.11) also $|\beta_1| > |\beta_2|$, and so, since $p_i^0(1 + \beta_i) = c, i = 1, 2$, one has

$$p_1^0 > p_2^0. \tag{7.14}$$

But now it is easy to find a hypothesis which makes the fulfilment of these conditions impossible. For instance, let the common, strictly quasi-concave, function be homothetic with the indifference curves having a unitary slope where they cross the 45° line. Then (7.13) and (7.14) together are not possible.

If one has enough patience, one can construct other 'well-behaved' economies which have no regular ϵ-rational conjectural equilibrium. Thus one can relatively easily find examples with three goods where the requirements of proposition (3.1) conflict with the concavity of the conjectured profit function.

The examples suggest that there will be considerable difficulty in describing an economy with simple enough conjectures which also possesses an ϵ-rational equilibrium. My present view is that the conditions will turn out to be sufficiently restrictive to make the result uninteresting. But there is another lesson which seems important.

In the examples I gave conjectures of a particular form. Now if one takes ϵ small enough, what one is roughly concerned with is the existence of an equilibrium where the conjectured slope of the inverse demand curve at the equilibrium output accurately predicts the price in an equilibrium relatively to a very small deviation in a producer's output. But as we have seen, this will depend not only on the conjectured slopes of other producers but also on their rates of change (the terms h_p, h_y). In the examples, in trying to discover whether conjectured slopes can be 'tied down' by asking that they be 'correct' in a proper sense, we made these higher order terms *arbitrary*. So even had our conclusion been positive we should have shown that there exists an equilibrium in which conjectured slopes are 'correct' only at the cost of arbitrarily imposing a form on the conjectured demand function. Indeed, I think that under fairly general assumptions one may be able to show that there always exists a conjectural equilibrium with 'correct' slopes provided one can arbitrarily specify the form of the conjecture. But this means that we do not escape the arbitrariness of conjectures.

Evidently there are quite hard technical problems, and they require further investigation. But I think there is enough evidence in this section to warrant the preliminary conclusion that ϵ-rationality is not a hopeful way of avoiding the arbitrariness – i.e. the exogenous nature – of conjectures.

IV NASH ϵ-RATIONALITY

I shall be brief in this section, for the matter requires more investigation than I can give it here. Indeed, I shall only consider an example of $l = 2$.

Suppose that $(p^0, \hat{y}^0)$ is a conjectural equilibrium and consider a small ϵ deviation from y_{11}^0 by producer 1. We are in the first instance interested in the equilibria (if they exist), relatively to that deviation on the supposition that the output of producer 2 stays at y_{22}^0. Notice that such equilibria will not in general be conjectural equilibria, since producer 2 will not be maximizing relatively to his conjectures. Now p will be an equilibrium relatively to $(y_{11}^0 \pm \epsilon)$ when ϵ is small enough if it satisfies

$$g_p^0(p - p^0) = -g_{y_1}^0(y_{11} - y_{11}^0)$$

where g_p^0 has the usual meaning and $g_{y_1}^0 \in R^2$ is the vector $(x_{1y_1} - 1, x_{2y_1})$.

This equation can be solved, when $(y_{11} - y_{11}^0) \neq 0$ iff g_p^0 is not singular. But in one of our examples, where households supply labour inelastically and where they have parallel linear Engel curves, g_p^0 is a singular matrix of substitution terms. Let us call an economy where households satisfy these assumptions 'Hicksian' (cf. Arrow and Hahn, 1971). Then

Proposition (4.1) Any conjectural equilibrium of a Hicksian economy where labour is supplied inelastically is ϵ-Nash rational for ϵ small enough.

This result is a direct consequence of our general decision to call conjectures rational if deviations in the actions of one agent are not compatible with equilibrium (D2.3(b)). Of course, this is open to argument. Yet it is not easy to see what alternative route should be followed in this case. One could, for instance, relax the purely Walrasian equilibrium notion (and consider equilibria with rationing), or one could try to model the 'true' dynamics of the economy which would give an answer to the agent's question, What will be the case if I deviate slightly from my present actions? But not only is this procedure technically and conceptually hard; it is one which makes it even more impossible to suppose that agents can carry out correct calculations.

So let me now suppose that g_p^0 is not singular, which I achieve in the Hicksian economy by dropping the assumption that labour is inelastically supplied (i.e. that it does not enter the utility function). Let

$$N_1^0 = \begin{bmatrix} g_p^0 & g_{y_1}^0 \\ y_{11}^0 & p_1^0 - c_1 \end{bmatrix}.$$

Then if the conjectural equilibrium is ϵ-Nash rational one wants N_1^0 to be singular. The argument here is exactly as in the previous section, the only difference being that $y_{22} = y_{22}^0$ by construction.

To see the difficulties one may now encounter, let the common utility function be Cobb–Douglas with exponents α_i ($i = 0 \ldots 2$) where the subscript 0 refers to leisure. Suppose further that conjectures have the form of (7.9), and choose units so that $c_i = 1, i = 1, 2$.

Then the condition that N_1^0 be singular reduces in this special case to

$$\alpha_0 + \alpha_1 \alpha_2 - (1 - \alpha_2)\alpha_1 = \frac{1 + \beta_1 (\alpha_2 - 1)}{\beta_1} \frac{}{\alpha_1}.$$

For $(\pi.1)$–$(\pi.4)$ to hold, one wants $-1 < \beta_1 < 0$ and hence

$$\frac{\alpha_0}{1 - 2\alpha_2} > \alpha_1. \tag{7.15}$$

If (7.15) is violated, then no ϵ-Nash rational conjectural equilibrium is possible. For with $\beta_1 > 0$ no profit-maximizing choice of the firm exists, while for $\beta_1 < 0$, N_1^0 cannot vanish.

Once again it is rather doubtful that one can find sufficiently general conditions which would ensure the existence of an ϵ-Nash rational conjectural equilibrium. But this is a matter for further study.

V   SOME CONCLUSIONS

To a practical economist, it will be no surprise that the notions of rationality in conjectures explored here are very unpromising.

Indeed, he would argue that the questions are incorrectly formulated. For either the typical firm is 'small', and hence one should ignore the general equilibrium repercussions of its own actions, or it is significant, in which case the proper approach is either game-theoretic or a rule of thumb.

There evidently is some force in this objection. On the other hand, unless a firm is so small (strictly of measure zero) as to make a perfectly competitive conjecture ϵ-rational in my sense, it will make mistakes when it acts on a conjectured demand curve derived from partial equilibrium hypotheses. By this I mean that it correctly calculates the slope of the demand curve on the hypothesis that all other prices and outputs other than its own are fixed. The question of course is whether these mistakes are small enough to be 'sensibly' ignored.

With sufficient assumptions (which certainly must exclude the Cobb–Douglas utility function) one can almost certainly establish the existence of a 'Marshallian ϵ-conjectural equilibrium'. That would be an equilibrium in which producers have chosen optimally relatively to observed demand and price and have correctly calculated the slope of their demand curve at this point on the assumption that all other prices and outputs remain constant. There will be some technical difficulties since one will not be sure without special hypotheses that conjectural profit functions are concave everywhere. But there certainly is a class of utility for which this will be true. Such equilibria will not be ϵ-reasonable or ϵ-rational. Hence in an actual experiment a firm may discover that it is mistaken. Depending on cross-elasticities, these mistakes may be 'large' for a 'small' firm.

All of this requires further study, and the present paper is no more than an introduction to some of the questions which arise. My present view is that, if it will prove possible to make conjectures less arbitrary, it will have to be done in a Marshallian way. This is not a conclusion congenial to a general equilibrium man.

APPENDIX

Linear Conjectures

$$m_i(p, y, x) = p_i y_{ii} + \beta_i y_{ii}(y_{ii} - x_i) + y_{i0}, \quad i = 1, 2$$

Then

$$\bar{h}_i(\cdot) \equiv \frac{\partial m_i(\cdot)}{\partial y_{ii}} = p_i + 2\beta_i y_{ii} - \beta_i x_i - c_i.$$

Clearly, at a conjectural equilibrium $(p^0, \hat{y}^0)$, we get

$$H_p^0 = I, \quad H_z^0 = \{\beta_i\}$$

and

$$c_i = p_i^0 + 2\beta_i y_{ii}^0 - \beta_i y_{ii}^0 = p_i^0 + \beta_i y_{ii}^0$$

Since $g_i(p, \hat{y}) = x_i - y_{ii}, i = 1, 2$ we get

$$\frac{\partial g_i(\cdot)}{\partial y_i} = \frac{\partial x_i(p, y)}{\partial y_i} - 1$$

and $\qquad\qquad\qquad i = 1, 2$

$$\frac{\partial g_i(\cdot)}{\partial y_j} = \frac{\partial x_i(p, y)}{\partial y_j}$$

But $\mu(p, y) = y_{11}(p_1 - c_1) + y_{22}(p_2 - c_2)$. Thus

$$x_{iyj} \equiv \frac{\partial x_i(p, y)}{\partial y_j} = \frac{\partial x_i(p, y)}{\partial \mu} \frac{\partial \mu(p, y)}{\partial y_j} = x_{i\mu}(p_j - c_j), \quad i = 1, 2$$

So

$$x_{iyj} = x_{i\mu}(p_j - c_j) = -x_{i\mu}\beta_2 y_{jj}, \quad i, j = 1, 2$$

which is the expression given on p. 171. Using all of this, we get:

$$m^* = \begin{vmatrix} S_{11} & S_{12} & x_{1\mu}(p_1 - c_1) - 1 & x_{1\mu}(p_2 - c_2) \\ S_{21} & S_{22} & x_{2\mu}(p_1 - c_1) & x_{2\mu}(p_2 - c_2) - 1 \\ 1 & 0 & \beta_1 & 0 \\ 0 & 1 & 0 & \beta_2 \end{vmatrix}.$$

Adding p_1 times first row to p_2 times second row gives

$$m^* = \begin{vmatrix} S_{11} & S_{12} & x_{1\mu}(p_1 - c_1) - 1 & x_{1\mu}(p_2 - c_2) \\ 0 & 0 & -c_1 & -c_2 \\ 1 & 0 & \beta_1 & 0 \\ 0 & 1 & 0 & \beta_2 \end{vmatrix}.$$

Let Δ be the top right-hand 2×2 determinant. Then

$$m^* = S_{11}\beta_1 c_2 - S_{12}\beta_2 c_1 + \Delta$$

$$m_{31}^* = -S_{12}c_1\beta_2 + \Delta$$

$$m_{41}^* = S_{11}c_2\beta_1 + \Delta.$$

From (7.7), $m_{31}^* = m_{41}^*$ gives

$$S_{11}c_1\beta_1 + S_{12}c_1\beta_2 = 0$$

which is (A) of the text. For (7.7) also $2m_{31}^* = m^*$ or

$$S_{11}\beta_1 c_2 + S_{12}\beta_2 c_1 - \Delta = 0$$

and so

$$\Delta = c_2 - c_2 x_{1\mu}(p_1 - c_1) + c_1 x_{1\mu}(p_2 - c_2)$$

$$= c_2 + x_{1\mu}(c_2\beta_1 x_1 - c_1\beta_2 x_2) = 0$$

which is (B) of the text.

Constant Elasticity Conjectures

$$m_i(p, y, x) = p_i(y_{ii})^{\beta+1} x_1^{-\beta} + y_{i0}$$

So

$$\bar{h}_i(\cdot) \equiv \frac{\partial m_i(\cdot)}{\partial y_{ii}} = (\beta + 1)p_i(y_{ii})^{\beta} x_1^{-\beta} - c_i$$

Then at a conjectural equilibrium we get

$$H_p^0 = \{1 + \beta\}, \quad H_z^0 = \{0\}$$

and

$$c_i = (1 + \beta)p_i^0$$

Therefore we have

$$M^* = \begin{bmatrix} g_p^0 & g_y^0 \\ \{1 + \beta_i\} & 0 \end{bmatrix}$$

whence

$$m^* = \prod^i (1 + \beta_i)|g_y^0|.$$

Proceeding as in the previous example and using $p_k^0 - c = -\beta_k p_k^0$, one finds

$$|g_y^0| = x_{1\mu}(\beta_1 c p_1^0 - \beta_2 c p_2^0) + c. \tag{A7.1}$$

Also

$$M_1^* = \begin{bmatrix} g_{p_1}^0 & g_{p_2}^0 & g_{y_1}^0 & g_{y_2}^0 \\ y_{11}^0 & 0 & -\beta_1 p_1^0 & 0 \\ 0 & (1 + \beta_2) & 0 & 0 \end{bmatrix}$$

and similarly for M_2^*. One finds

$$m_1^* = (1 + \beta_2)[x_1^0|g_y^0| - \beta_1 p_1^0 m_{33}^*]$$

$$m_2^* = (1 + \beta_1)[x_2^0|g_y^0| - \beta_2 p_2^0 m_{44}^*].$$

Calculating further yields

$$m_{33}^* = -S_{11}(1 + \beta_2)c, \quad m_{44}^* = S_{12}(1 + \beta_1)c. \tag{A7.2}$$

By proposition (3.1) one wants $m_1^* = m_2^* = 0$ if the equilibrium is to be ϵ-rational. So

$$\beta_1 p_1^0 m_{33}^*/x_1^0 = \beta_2 p_2^0 m_{44}^*/x_2^0 \tag{A7.3}$$

or, by (A7.2),

$$-\beta_1(1 + \beta_2)c\sigma_{11} = \beta_2(1 + \beta_1)c\sigma_{12} \tag{A7.4}$$

which then yields (7.11) of the text.

Next, since $m_{33}^* > 0$, $m_{44}^* > 0$, $\beta_i > 0$, one must have

$|g_y^0| < 0.$

So from (A7.1)

$$\frac{\beta_1 p_1^0}{\beta_2 p_2^0} = \frac{\beta_1(1 + \beta_2)}{\beta_2(1 + \beta_1)} > 1. \tag{A7.5}$$

This confirms (7.12) of the text.

REFERENCES

Arrow, K. J. and Hahn, F. H. (1971), *General Competitive Analysis*, Holden Day, San Francisco.

Hahn, F. H. (1978), 'On Non-Walrasian Equilibria', *Review of Economic Studies*, 45. [Reprinted as chapter 6 of the present volume.]

Negishi, Y. (1961), 'Monopolistic Competition and General Equilibrium', *Review of Economic Studies*, 28.

Radner, R. (1968), 'Competitive Equilibrium under Uncertainty', *Econometrica*, 36.

Rothschild, M. (1974), 'A Two-armed bandit Theory of Market Pricing', *Journal of Economic Theory*, 9.

Part III

Stability

8

On Some Propositions of General Equilibrium Analysis

It turns out that the proofs of a number of interesting propositions in Walrasian general equilibrium analysis can be made simpler than they now are. My main task is to show this.

Notations and Assumptions

The perfectly competitive economy has $(n + 1)$ goods, labelled $0 \ldots n$. I write P as the $(n + 1)$ vector of prices in unit of account and $S(P)$ as the $(n + 1)$ vector of excess supply functions at P. Row and column vectors are distinguished by their context. Other notations will be introduced as required.

I assume that $S(P)$ is a continuous vector valued function over $P \geqslant 0$ and that it is homogeneous of degree zero (H), in P. (When $S(P)$ is differentiable, I write $S_{ij}(P)$ as the partial differential coefficient of $S_i(P)$ with respect to its jth argument.) It is natural to take $S(P)$ as bounded from above, (B). Lastly, I stipulate Walras' Law:

(W): $PS(P) = 0$, all $P \geqslant 0$.

P^* is an equilibrium of the economy if $S(P^*) \geqslant 0$.

I THE WEAK AXIOM OF REVEALED PREFERENCE

From (W), one has for P^* an equilibrium:

$$0 = PS(P) \leqslant PS(P^*), \quad \text{all } (P \neq kP^*, k > 0). \tag{8.1}$$

Write, $S(P) = y(P) + \bar{x} - x(P)$, where $y(P)$ is the supply vector of producers, at P; $x(P)$, the demand vector of households, at P; and

$\bar{x}$ the stock of goods owned by agents, $(\bar{x} \geqslant 0)$. From profit maximization, $Py(P) \geqslant Py(P^*)$; and so, from (8.1),

$$Px(P) \geqslant Px(P^*), \quad \text{all } P \neq kP^*, k > 0. \tag{8.1'}$$

The above inequality refers, of course, to households as a whole and need not hold for any given household. However, if also

$$P^*x(P) > P^*x(P^*), \quad \text{all } P \neq kP^*, k > 0, \tag{8.2}$$

then, by an obvious extension, we may say that the Weak Axiom of Revealed Preference (WA), holds for all households taken together, for comparisons *in which one of the situations is always an equilibrium*. Using (W) and profit maximization, (8.2) may also be written as

$$P^*S(P) < P^*S(P^*) = 0, \quad \text{all } P \neq kP^*, k > 0. \tag{8.2'}$$

I am now interested in finding sufficient conditions for (8.2') for if (8.2') holds, it enables one to show quite easily the stability of the classical tâtonnement process (Arrow and Hurwicz, 1958), and also to deduce a number of useful propositions in comparative statics.

1   If all households have parallel linear Engel curves through the origin, then the inequality (8.1') must hold for all households. For there is always a redistribution of initial endowments which ensures this inequality for all households. But by assumption, $x(P)$ and $x(P^*)$ are independent of this distribution. Hence (8.2), and so (8.2'), must hold since households have a consistent ordering. This is the case first investigated by Hicks (1939), where 'all income effects cancel'.

2   Suppose $S(P)$ to be differentiable and to have the property

$$(GS): \quad S_{ij}(P) < 0, \quad \text{all } j \neq i, i = 0 \dots n; P \geqslant 0.$$

Then all goods are said to be *gross substitutes*. The following implications of (GS) for the functions $S_i(P)$ are well known (Arrow and Hurwicz, 1958; Arrow *et al.*, 1959).

(a) For all i, as $P_i \to 0$, $S_i(P) \to -\infty$. Consequently it must be true that P^*, the equilibrium, is strictly positive.

(b) Let $P_r/P_r^* \leqslant P_i/P_i^*$ all i; then $S_r(P) < S_r(P^*) = 0$.

It is now easy to show that (GS) implies (8.2′). To do so, I write $g(P) = P^*S(P)$ and prove that $g(P)$ has a unique maximum at P^* (where, of course, $g(P^*) = 0$). By (B), a maximum exists. In view of (a), it must be that this maximum occurs where P is strictly positive. Hence a necessary condition is

$$\partial g(P)/\partial P_j = \sum_i P_i^* S_{ij}(P) = 0 \qquad (j = 0, \ldots, n). \tag{8.3}$$

Because of (a), this condition is also sufficient. By (W) and $P_j^* > 0$ all j, (8.3) certainly holds at P^*. Suppose it is also satisfied at $P \neq kP^*$. By (W),

$$\sum_i P_i S_{ij}(P) = - S_j(P) \qquad (j = 0, \ldots, n). \tag{8.4}$$

Let $k = P_r/P_r^* \leqslant P_i/P_i^*$, all i. Then by (GS) implication 2 and (8.4),

$$\left[P_r^* S_{rr}(P) + \sum_{i \neq r} P_i^* S_{ir}(P) \right] k \geqslant P_r S_{rr}(P) + \sum_{i \neq r} P_i S_{ir}(P)$$

$$= - S_r(P) > 0,$$

and so (8.3) cannot hold, and P^* (up to a positive multiple) is the only solution to the problem.

This demonstration is a considerable simplification of that given in Arrow and Hurwicz (1958). It also makes it obvious that a necessary condition for (WA) in comparisons involving P^* is that $g(P^*)$ be strictly concave in a small neighbourhood of P^*. The present case and implication 1 above are the only economically meaningful assumptions which ensure this.

3   Suppose that we weaken (GS) to (WGS): $S_{ij}(P) \leqslant 0$, all $j \neq i$, $i = 0, \ldots, n$, $P \geqslant 0$. One says that all goods are *weak gross substitutes*. This restriction on the form of the excess supply functions does not enable us to establish WA as in implications 1 and 2 above. However, let E be the set of equilibrium prices. Then I show that (WGS) suffices for the following:

(WA)*: $P^*S(P) < 0$,   all $P \notin E, P^* \in E$.

Evidently (WA)* is weaker than (WA), but it is worth having. For the proof I take the following result as given (Arrow and Hurwicz, 1960; McKenzie, 1960). (i′): Let $P_{(r)}$ be the vector P with zero in the rth place. Let (WGS) be postulated. Then if $S_r(P_{(r)}) \geqslant 0$ some $P_{(r)}$, $S_r(P) \geqslant 0$ all $P \geqslant 0$. With this result in mind let

$$R = \{i \mid P_i^* > 0\}, \qquad R' = \{i \mid P_i^* = 0\},$$

where P^* is the equilibrium used in formulating (WA)*. It is convenient to think of R as containing the first m indices. In obvious notation, I now write: $P = (P_R, P_{R'})$, $S(P) = [S_R(P), S_{R'}(P)]$. By (WGS) one has

$$S_i(P_R, P_{R'}) \leqslant S_i(P_R, 0). \quad \text{all } i \in R,$$

and so (WA)* is proved if

$$g(P_R) = P_R^* S_R(P_R, 0) < 0, \quad \text{all } (P_R, 0) \notin E.$$

I shall show that $g(\cdot)$ can attain a maximum only on E (where it is zero).

By (B) a maximum exists, but one cannot now exclude the possibility that, at this maximum, some component of P_R is zero. The necessary condition accordingly becomes:

$$\sum_{i \in R} P_i^* S_{ij}(P_R, 0) \leqslant 0, \qquad j \in R, \tag{8.5}$$

where a strict inequality implies $P_j = 0$. By (W), (8.5) evidently holds at $P_R = P_R^*$, and I must show that it cannot hold at $(P_R, 0) \notin E$. Let $k_r = P_r / P_r^*$, $r \in R$ and take, without loss of generality, $k_0 \geqslant k_1 \geqslant \ldots \geqslant k_m$. One may certainly take $k_0 > 0$. By (WGS), (H) and $P_0^* > 0$, one has

$$0 = S_0(P_R^*, 0) = S_0(k_0 P_R^*, 0) \leqslant S_0(P_R, 0) \tag{8.6}$$

If this inequality is strict, then by (W)

$$k_0 \sum_{i \in R} P_i^* S_{i0}(P_R, 0) \leqslant P_0 S_{00}(P_R, 0) + \sum_{i \neq 0} P_i S_{i0}(P_R, 0)$$

$$= -S_0(P_R, 0) < 0. \tag{8.7}$$

But $P_0 > 0$ means that (8.5) must hold with equality for $j = 0$; and this (8.7) shows to be impossible.

So suppose that (8.6) holds with equality. Then surely $S_{ij}(P_R, 0) P_j = 0$, all $j \in R$. For if not, (WGS) and continuity would ensure the strict inequality in (8.6). But then if it is asserted that (8.7) does not violate (8.5), it must also be the case (in view of WGS) that $P_i S_{i0}(P_R, 0) = 0$, all $i \in R$. But then if $k_1 > 0$, one has at once

$$k_1 \sum_{i \in R} P_i^* S_{i1}(P_R, 0) \leqslant P_1 S_{11}(P_R, 0) + \sum_{i \neq 1} P_i S_{i1}(P_R, 0)$$

$$= -S_1(P_R, 0), \qquad (8.7')$$

and $S_1(P_R, 0) \geqslant 0$, so that (8.7) is violated for $j = 1$ if $S_1(P_R, 0) > 0$. If $k_i > 0$ all $i \in R$, we may evidently proceed in this way, should $S_1(P_R, 0) = 0$ to k_2 etc. Since $(P_R, 0) \notin E$ by assumption, there must be an $r \in R$ such that $S_r(P_R, 0) > 0$, and (8.5) is violated for $j = r$. The only remaining possibility is the existence of $0 < h < m$ such that $k_h = 0$ (also $k_i = 0$ all $i > h$).

Suppose then that $S_i(P_R, 0) = 0$ for $i < h$. (If not, then by the above argument, there would be nothing left to prove.) Then I claim

$$S_i(P_R, 0) \leqslant 0, \quad \text{all } i \geqslant h. \qquad (8.8)$$

For if not, i.e. if, say, $S_h(P_R, 0) > 0$, it follows from (i′) that $S_h(P_R^*, 0) > 0$, contradicting the definition of $(P_R^*, 0)$ as an equilibrium. Since the strict inequality must hold for some i in (8.8) (else $(P_R, 0) \in E$) and P_R^* is strictly positive, one now has $P_R^* S(P_R, 0) < 0$, and so $(P_R, 0)$ cannot maximize $P^* S(P_R, 0)$ (since $(P_R^*, 0) = 0$). This concludes the proof. Although it has been a little more complex than that of implication 2 above, it is still a good deal simpler than existing proofs (Arrow and Hurwicz, 1960).

II THE UNIQUENESS OF EQUILIBRIUM

One of the advantages of (WA) is that it implies trivially that equilibrium is unique. It is also easy to see that (WA)* implies that E is convex. Both of these results can be put to good use in comparative statics analysis, as is done by Morishima (1964). However, one can establish the uniqueness of an equilibrium for cases which do not imply either (WA)* or (WA). This section is designed to provide a simple proof of a uniqueness proposition due to Gale and Nikaidô (1965).

Let A be a matrix the principal minors of which are all positive. Then one needs the following result due to Gale:

(G): $Av \leqslant 0, v \geqslant 0$, only has the solution $v = 0$.

In what follows one will wish to apply (G) to the Jacobian of the excess supply functions. However, it is well known that, because of (H) (and/or (W)), this Jacobian vanishes for all P. It is therefore necessary to deal with a system in which one good can be specified as numeraire so that the order of the relevant Jacobian can be reduced by one. But a good can serve as a numeraire only if in every equilibrium it has a positive exchange value. I find the following assumption therefore necessary:

Assumption (A) There is a good, label it 0, with the property that $S_0[P(0)] = -\infty$ all $P(0)$. ($P(0)$ is P with zero in the 0th place.) Certainly (A) will ensure that the economy cannot have an equilibrium with $P_0 = 0$. It is not clear that weaker forms of this postulate are available.

In what follows I shall wish to argue by induction on the number of goods, and for this purpose I make use of the fact that an economy with $(n + 1)$ goods, in which the relative prices of any two are fixed, may be treated like an economy with n goods. To be precise, let $Q_i = P_i$, $i = 2 \ldots n$; $Q_1 = P_0 + P_1$. Let $\alpha = P_0/(P_0 + P_1)$, and $\underline{S}_i(Q, \alpha) = S_i(P)$, $i = 2 \ldots n$; $\underline{S}_1(Q, \alpha) = \alpha S_0(P) + (1 - \alpha) S_1(P)$, where Q is an n vector. Then if $\underline{S}(Q, \alpha)$ is the n vector of $\underline{S}_i$'s, one verifies from $PS(P) = 0$, that $Q\underline{S}(Q, \alpha) = 0$, so that (W) holds for the economy $\underline{S}$. From (H) for $S(P)$ one deduces that $\underline{S}(Q, \alpha)$ has (H) in Q. Clearly, (B) will hold for $\underline{S}$, For given α, I call the economy $\underline{S}$ with prices Q, a reduced economy, $R(\alpha)$. It is now possible to prove the main result.

Theorem If (A) and if for all $P \geqslant 0$, the $(n \times n)$ Jacobian $[S_{ij}(P)]$, $(i, j \neq 0)$, has positive principal minors, then there is at most one vector[1] P^* in $S(n + 1) = \{P | P \geqslant 0, \Sigma P_i = 1\}$ for which $S(P^*) \geqslant 0$. In the statement of this result I have taken advantage of (H) to normalize prices to lie in the $(n + 1)$-dimensional simplex. The reader should note that $Q \in S(n)$.

[1] $S(n + 1)$ is thus the $(n + 1)$-dimensional simplex. In general, $S(i)$ will stand for the i-dimensional simplex.

To prove the theorem one first notes that it is trivially true for $n = 1$ (i.e. two goods); for $S_{11}(P) > 0$, all $(P_0 + P_1) = 1$. Now I suppose that the theorem is true for an n-good economy, and show that it must also hold for an $(n + 1)$-goods economy. First reduce the $(n + 1)$-goods economy to $R(\alpha)$. Then by the induction hypothesis it has a unique equilibrium $Q(\alpha)$. I need to show that $Q(\alpha)$ is continuous in α, $\alpha \in (0, 1)$.

Without change of functional notation I write $\underline{S}[Q(\alpha)]$ as the vector of excess supply functions when Q takes on its equilibrium value for $R(\alpha)$. Let $\alpha^v \to \alpha$ and $Q^v = Q(\alpha^v)$, $v = 1, 2 \ldots$. By the continuity of $\underline{S}(\cdot)$,

$$\lim_{v \to \infty} \underline{S}(Q^v) = \underline{S}(\lim_{v \to \infty} Q^v).$$

But $\underline{S}(Q^v) \geqslant 0$ all v, and by the induction hypothesis it must then follow that $\underline{S}(\lim_{v \to \infty} Q^v) = \underline{S}[Q(\alpha)]$, else there would be two equilibria for $R(\alpha)$. Moreover since $\underline{S}(\cdot)$ is differentiable, $Q(\alpha)$ can be shown to be differentiable almost everywhere.

Now suppose the theorem is false so that the $(n + 1)$-goods economy has two equilibria, $[Q(\alpha), \alpha]$ and $[Q(\alpha'), \alpha']$. Take $\alpha' > \alpha > 0$. It is convenient to write: $q = [1/(1 - \alpha)Q_1]Q$. By (H), $[q(\alpha), \alpha]$ and $[q(\alpha'), \alpha']$ are also equilibria. (Note that $q_1 = 1/(1 - \alpha)$.) Let $R = \{i \mid \underline{S}_i[q(\alpha)] > 0\}$. By (A), $i = 1$ is not R. For if it were, $q_1(\alpha) = 0$ and using (B), $\underline{S}_1[q(\alpha)] = -\infty$, a contradiction. Moreover, by continuity, $q_i(\alpha)$ will remain equal to zero for small changes in α, for $i \in R$ since $\underline{S}_i[q(\alpha)]$ will remain positive.

Now let $J[q(\alpha)]$ be the Jacobian of $S_i[q(\alpha)]$ for $i \notin R$. Let $\partial q(\alpha)/d\alpha$ and $\partial S[q(\alpha)]/d\alpha$ be vectors the components of which do not have suffixes in R. Then

$$J[q(\alpha)] \frac{dq(\alpha)}{d\alpha} = \frac{dS[q(\alpha)]}{d\alpha}. \tag{8.9}$$

Since the reduced system is in equilibrium for all α, it must be that

$$\frac{dS_i[q(\alpha)]}{d\alpha} \frac{dq_i(\alpha)}{d\alpha} \leqslant 0, \quad \text{all } i \notin R, i \neq 1. \tag{8.10}$$

(For instance, should the change in α make S_i positive, then its price must either remain at, or fall to, zero.) Moreover, from the definition of q,

$$dq_1(\alpha)/d\alpha > 0. \tag{8.11}$$

But now let T be the diagonal matrix with -1 or $+1$ on the diagonals, such that $T \cdot dq(\alpha)/d\alpha = v \geqslant 0$. Note that, by (8.11), $T_{11} = +1$. Also, of course, $T = T^{-1}$. I can now write (8.9) as

$$TJ[q(\alpha)] Tv = T \frac{dS[q(\alpha)]}{d\alpha}. \tag{8.9'}$$

By (8.10), all the components of the right-hand vector, other than $i = 1$, are now positive. But then by (G) and $T_{11} > 0$, one concludes that

$$\frac{dS_1[q(\alpha)]}{d\alpha} > 0 \tag{8.12}$$

(else (8.9') could only be satisfied with $v = 0$).

If one now takes a sequence, $\alpha^v \to \alpha'$ with $\alpha^0 = \alpha$ and $\alpha^v < \alpha^{v+1}$, and argues as above for every $q(\alpha^v)$, one finds that (8.12) holds for all $q(\alpha^v)$, and so $S_1[q(\alpha')] > 0$. Since $q_1(\alpha') > 0$, it follows at once that the $(n + 1)$-economy cannot have a second equilibrium at $[Q(\alpha'), \alpha']$. Hence if the n-goods economy has a unique equilibrium, so does the $(n + 1)$-goods economy, and the proof of the theorem is complete.

It is clear that the conditions of the theorem are weaker than those required for (WA). For instance, there is no reason to suppose that $[S_{ij}(P)]$ is definite or quasi-definite at P^*, while (GS) or identical households clearly imply the conditions of the theorem. On the other hand, there seems only one instance in which the requirements of the theorem can be given a satisfactory economic interpretation, and that is the case of diagonal dominance.

III   EXISTENCE OF EQUILIBRIUM: A DIGRESSION

I have taken it for granted, so far, that an equilibrium exists. The procedure for proving this (for given assumptions) is well-known, although there cannot be many economists who do not take 'fixed-point theorems' on trust. It may therefore be not without interest to have a simple demonstration for the case in which the conditions of the theorem of the previous section hold. Once again, the procedure is by induction.

Since one is taking the supply functions as differentiable, they are continuous. Consider the two-goods economy: S_0, S_1, $P = (P_0, P_1)$. Normalize so that $P \in S(2)$. Suppose that the economy does not have an equilibrium at $(0, 1)$ or at $(1, 0)$. (If it has, there is no more to prove.) Thus $S_0(0, 1) < 0$, since by (W), $S_1(0, 1) = 0$. If for all P with $0 < P_0 < 1$, one has $S_0(P) < 0$, then by (W) also $S_1(P) > 0$ for this range. But then by continuity, $S_1(1, 0) \geqslant 0$ while by (W), $S_0(1, 0) = 0$, so that, contrary to assertion, $(1, 0)$ is an equilibrium. Hence for some P^* with $0 < P_0^* < 1$, one has $S_0(P^*) = S_1(P^*) = 0$, an equilibrium. Suppose then that the n-goods economy has an equilibrium. I want to show that then the $(n + 1)$-goods economy has an equilibrium also. To do so, form the reduced economy $R(\alpha)$ of the previous sections. By the theorem it has a unique equilibrium $Q(\alpha)$. By (A) it must be that $Q_1(\alpha) > 0$, $\underline{S}_1[Q(\alpha)] = 0$, for $\alpha > 0$, where we recall definition

$$\underline{S}_1 = \alpha S_0 + (1 - \alpha) S_1. \tag{8.13}$$

I have already shown $Q(\alpha)$ to be continuous in α. If, contrary to assertion, the $(n + 1)$-goods economy does not have an equilibrium, then certainly at $\alpha = 1$, $S_1[Q(1)] < 0$, for by construction $S_0[Q(1)] = 0$, $S_i[Q(1)] \geqslant 0$, all $i \geqslant 2$. Let $\alpha \to 0$. Then by (A), $S_0[Q(\alpha)] \to -\infty$. Since $Q(\alpha)$ is continuous in α and $S_i(\cdot)$ are all continuous functions, there must then, by (8.13), be an α^* such that $S_0[Q(\alpha^*)] = S_1[Q(\alpha^*)] = 0$. But then the $(n + 1)$-goods economy does have an equilibrium.

REFERENCES

Arrow, K. J. and Hurwicz, L. (1958), 'On the Stability of the Competitive Equilibrium, I', *Econometrica*, **26**, 522-52.

Arrow, K. J., Block, H. D. and Hurwicz, L. (1959), 'On The Stability of the Competitive Equilibrium, II', *Econometrica*, **27**, 82-109.

Arrow, K. J. and Hurwicz, L. (1960), 'Competitive Stability under Weak Gross Substitutability: The "Euclidean Distance" Approach', *International Economic Review*, **1**, 38-49.

Gale, D. and Nikaidô, H. (1965), 'The Jacobian Matrix and Global Univalence of Mappings', *Mathematische Annalen*, **159**, 81-93.

Hicks, J. R. (1939), *Value and Capital*, Oxford University Press.

McKenzie, L. W. (1960), 'Stability of Equilibrium and the Value of Positive Excess Demand', *Econometrica*, **28**, 606-17.

Morishima, M. (1964), *Equilibrium, Stability and Growth*, Oxford University Press.

9

On the Stability of Pure Exchange Equilibrium

In this paper I propose to show that, under some not too unreasonable assumptions, a pure exchange equilibrium is always quasi-stable.[1] By this I mean that, starting from any arbitrary initial stocks and prices at $t = 0$, the system will approach a Pareto optimum (contract locus), arbitrarily closely as $t \to \infty$. Before substantiating this claim a general outline is in order.

I INTERPRETATION OF TÂTONNEMENT

Until recently, all work on the stability of general equilibrium systems made use of the notion of a tâtonnement. This notion can be interpreted in at least two ways. We may suppose a process by which prices are 'cried' in the market according to certain rules, but no transactions take place until, if ever, the prices called just clear all markets. Alternatively, we may imagine a world in which no stocks of goods exist but where there is a continuous flow of perishable goods going to each individual.[2] Transactions here take place, but because of the perishability of goods they have no effect on the distribution of welfare between individuals; thus we may take all excess demand functions as independent of transactions. The reason for imagining such rather artificial situations was two-fold. On the one hand, they make it possible to investigate models where the final (equilibrium) outcome is independent

[1] This paper was first read to the Berkeley–Stanford Joint Seminar in Mathematical Economics. I gained greatly from discussions there, and in particular I am indebted to K. J. Arrow, T. Negishi, R. Radner and H. Uzawa. Of course, they bear no responsibility for this paper. I am also greatly indebted to helpful comments by the referees of this paper.

[2] I owe this view of the tâtonnement to Professor Arrow.

of the path to equilibrium; on the other, they were thought to make the problem of stability simpler than it would otherwise be. Yet it would clearly be desirable to pass to less restricted models.

Now if we imagine all individuals at time $t = 0$ to be in possession of a stock of non-perishable goods and some arbitrary prices are called, it is reasonable to postulate that some exchange will take place at these prices provided that at least one individual gains and no individual loses thereby. It seems legitimate to argue that this condition is not only sufficient for exchange to take place but also necessary. But it may now happen that, at the prices called, this condition is not met, so that no exchange can take place. As long as this is so, we are restricted to a tâtonnement. This suggests the following idea. If we argue that a tâtonnement takes place, i.e., no exchange, if and only if no individual can 'gain' by exchanging at the called prices without some other individual 'losing', then this condition itself may help to determine whether the tâtonnement process is stable. As it turns out, it does.

But we must now recognize that the rule for calling prices may be such that at some of the prices called no trading is possible while at some others it is. Here we can, however, call to our aid the fact that, by assumption, the utility of at least one individual is increased by exchange while that of no individual is diminished. This suggests the use of a Liapounov criterion defined as the sum of the utilities of all individuals. Uzawa (1962), Negishi (1961) and Radner (1960) all have noted this and have made varied use of it. Here we employ this notion to establish, with the aid of a number of rather weak assumptions, the following. If, starting with some initial distribution of stocks between individuals and some arbitrary prices, the pricing rule leads to a development of prices which never allow trading, the system is stable. If it does allow trading, either continuously or at discrete intervals, the system is still stable and so it approaches a Pareto optimum arbitrarily closely. The point of departure of our procedure is that we postulate a tâtonnement only when we are forced to, i.e., when no trading is possible.

II ASSUMPTIONS AND RULES

Notation

There are n goods and m individuals or households. We write $x_\alpha = \{x_{\alpha 1}, \ldots, x_{\alpha n}\}$ as the αth demand vector, $\bar{x}_\alpha = \{\bar{x}_{\alpha 1}, \ldots, \bar{x}_{\alpha n}\}$

as the αth 'stock' vector and $z_\alpha = x_\alpha - \bar{x}_\alpha$ as the αth excess demand vector. $z = \Sigma_\alpha z_\alpha$ is the aggregate excess demand vector with components $z_i (i = 1, \ldots, n)$. $\bar{x} = \{\bar{x}_1, \ldots, \bar{x}_m\}$ is a matrix showing the distribution of stocks among m individuals. We write $\Sigma_\alpha \bar{x}_\alpha = \bar{x}^* > 0$, where $\bar{x}^*$ is the vector of total stocks of the n goods available in the economy. We shall also sometimes write $\hat{x}_\alpha$ as the vector of goods held by α after trading at given prices, and $x = \{x_1, \ldots, x_n\}$ as any vector in the commodity space. $p = \{p_1, \ldots, p_n\}$ is a price vector in unit of account and $q = (1/p_n)p, p_n > 0$. $S = \{p | p_i \geqslant 0, \Sigma p_i = 1\}$. All vectors are column vectors, and a prime denotes transposition. Further notation will be introduced as required.

Utility

Assumption (A1) (i) Let X_α be the set of all possible consumption vectors for α. X_α is assumed convex.

(ii) For each α we may define a strictly quasi-concave[3] utility function $U_\alpha(x_\alpha)$ on X_α which is continuously differentiable over this set.

(iii) Let $A_\alpha(p, \bar{x}_\alpha) = \{x | x \in X_\alpha, p'x \leqslant p'\bar{x}_\alpha\}$, and write the αth demand vector as $x_\alpha = x_\alpha(p, \bar{x}_\alpha)$. Then

   (a) $x_\alpha(p, \bar{x}_\alpha) \in A_\alpha(p, \bar{x}_\alpha)$, and
   (b) for all $x \in A_\alpha(p, \bar{x}_\alpha)$, $x \neq x_\alpha$, $U_\alpha(x) < U_\alpha(x_\alpha)$ (utility maximization).

(iv) If $\bar{x}_\alpha > 0$ then for all x such that $U_\alpha(x) \geqslant U_\alpha(\bar{x}_\alpha)$, $x > 0$.[4]

(v) If an individual α can acquire $\hat{x}_\alpha$ by trading at p and $\bar{x}_\alpha$, then he will trade if and only if $U_\alpha(\hat{x}_\alpha) \geqslant U_\alpha(\bar{x}_\alpha)$.

(vi) For all p and $\bar{x}_\alpha > 0$, there exists some $x \in X_\alpha$ such that $U_\alpha(x) > U_\alpha[x_\alpha(p, \bar{x}_\alpha)]$.

(A1(i)), (A1(ii)) and (A1(iii)) require no comment. (A1(iv)) is quite strong. In more familiar language, it supposes that all indifference surfaces are asymptotic to the axes. The reason for introducing it is similar to introducing a somewhat analogous postulate into the proof of the existence of a pure exchange equilibrium. Its use will become apparent presently (see Arrow and Debreu,

---

[3] A utility function is strictly quasi-concave if $U(x) = U(\bar{x})$ then $U[x(\lambda)] > U(x)$, where $x(\lambda) = \lambda(x) + (1-\lambda)\bar{x}, 0 < \lambda < 1$.

[4] We employ the usual vector inequality conventions. That is, $x_\alpha \geqslant 0$ means $x_{\alpha i} \geqslant 0$ for all i; $x_\alpha \geqslant 0$ means $x_{\alpha i} \geqslant 0$ for all i, and $x_{\alpha i} > 0$ for some i. When we write $\bar{x} > 0$, where $\bar{x}$ is a matrix, we mean that every element of $\bar{x}$ is strictly positive.

1954). (A1(v)) seems to be quite reasonable. It says that α will only trade at the going prices if he can *gain* by so doing. (A1(vi)) states that no individual can be 'satiated' by exchange.

Trading

Assumption (A2) Trade will take place if and only if, at p and $\bar{x}$, there exists some $\hat{x} = \{\hat{x}_1, \ldots, \hat{x}_m\} \neq \bar{x}$, $\hat{x}_\alpha \in A_\alpha(p, \bar{x}_\alpha)$ for all α such that $U_\alpha(\hat{x}_\alpha) \geqslant U_\alpha(\bar{x}_\alpha)$ for all α, with strict inequality for at least one α, and $\Sigma_\alpha \hat{x}_\alpha \leqslant \Sigma_\alpha \bar{x}_\alpha$.

This assumption states that trade will take place *if and only if* at least one individual gains by exchange and no individual loses. This seems to be a reasonable hypothesis to make.

We are interested in characterizing situations where no trade consistent with (A2) is possible.

Let

$$U_{\alpha i}(\bar{x}_\alpha) = \frac{\partial U_\alpha(\bar{x}_\alpha)}{\partial \bar{x}_{\alpha i}}; \quad \bar{R}_{\alpha i} = \frac{U_{\alpha i}(\bar{x}_\alpha)}{U_{\alpha n}(\bar{x}_\alpha)}.$$

Write

$$q_i = p_i/p_n,$$

and define

$$\mu_{i\alpha} = \frac{\bar{R}_{\alpha i}}{q_i} - 1 \quad (i = 1, \ldots, n-1, \alpha = 1, \ldots, m).$$

Definition (D1) Let

$$|\mu_{r\alpha}| \geqslant |\mu_{i\alpha}|. \quad \text{for all } i. \tag{9.1}$$

(i) We shall say that r *dominates* for α if $\mu_{r\alpha} > 0$, that r is *dominated* for α if $\mu_{r\alpha} < 0$, and that α is in *equilibrium* if $\mu_{r\alpha} = 0$.

(ii) We shall say that r *dominates* if $\mu_{r\alpha}$ satisfies (9.1) for *all* α, $\mu_{r\alpha} \geqslant 0$ for *all* α, and $\mu_{r\alpha} > 0$ for *some* α. We shall say that r is *dominated* if $\mu_{r\alpha}$ satisfies (9.1) for *all* α, $\mu_{r\alpha} \leqslant 0$ for *all* α, and $\mu_{r\alpha} < 0$ for at least one α. We shall say that there is *equilibrium* if $\mu_{r\alpha}$ satisfies (9.1) for *all* α, and $\mu_{r\alpha} = 0$ for all α.

(iii) We define the following two sets:

$$R(p, \bar{x}) = \{r \mid |\mu_{r\alpha}| \geq |\mu_{i\alpha}| \text{ for all } i \text{ and } \alpha, \text{ and either } \mu_{r\alpha} \geq 0,$$

$$\text{or } \mu_{r\alpha} \leq 0 \text{ for all } \alpha\},$$

$$E(\bar{x}) = \{p \mid \mu_{i\alpha} = 0 \text{ for all } i \text{ and } \alpha\}.$$

We shall now establish the following.

Lemma 1 A necessary condition for no trade to be possible at $(p, \bar{x}) > 0$, given (A1) and (A2), is $R(p, \bar{x}) \neq \emptyset$, where $\emptyset$ is the null set.

Proof Suppose the contrary, i.e., that no trade is possible, but $R(p, \bar{x}) = \emptyset$. Then by the definition of $R(p, \bar{x})$ one of the following possibilities arises:

(i) There exists some r such that $|\mu_{r\alpha}| \geq |\mu_{i\alpha}|$ for all i and α, but for some α and β, sign $\mu_{r\alpha} = -\text{sign } \mu_{r\beta}$.

(ii) There exists no r such that $|\mu_{r\alpha}| \geq |\mu_{i\alpha}|$ for all i and α.

If (i), then the marginal rate of substitution of r for n exceeds their relative prices for some individual and falls short of those for another. Since $\bar{x} > 0$, and since we assume continuity of the utility function, some exchange between these two individuals is clearly possible. If (ii), then suppose without loss of generality that (9.1) is satisfied by r for individual α and by s for individual β. If r *dominates* for α ($\mu_{r\alpha} > 0$), and s *dominates* for β ($\mu_{s\beta} > 0$), then individual α can clearly gain by an exchange of r for s and individual β by an exchange of s for r, at the going prices. Exchange is thus possible. If r *dominates* for α and s is *dominated* ($\mu_{s\beta} < 0$) for β, then the situation is analogous to (i) and exchange must also be possible.

Hence, for no trade to be possible it must be true that $R(p, \bar{x}) \neq \emptyset$. The common sense of the lemma is self-evident. If no 'profitable' exchange is possible, then the maximum rate at which any individual is willing to exchange one good for another (his marginal rate of substitution) must bear the same relation (i.e., 'greater than', 'equal to' or 'less than') to the market rate of substitution (relative prices) that it does for any other individual. If $R(p, \bar{x}) = \emptyset$, this is not so.

The lemma will play a considerable part in what follows. In order to utilize it we introduce the following further postulates.

Assumption (A3) If $t_2 \geq t_1$, then $\Sigma_\alpha \bar{x}_\alpha(t_2) \leq \Sigma_\alpha \bar{x}_\alpha(t_1)$. It is evident that $\Sigma_\alpha \bar{x}_\alpha(t_1) - \Sigma_\alpha \bar{x}_\alpha(t_2)$ stands for consumption in period (t_1, t_2).

Excess Demand

Assumption (A4)   (i) If *r dominates* at $(p, \bar{x}) > 0$, then $z_r(p, \bar{x}) > 0$.
    (ii) If *r* is *dominated* at $(p, \bar{x}) > 0$, then $z_r(p, \bar{x}) < 0$.
    (iii) If $p \in E(\bar{x} > 0)$, then $z(p, \bar{x}) = 0$.

The rationalization of (A4) is fairly clear. If, for instance, no one is willing to exchange the *r*th good for any other good at $(p, \bar{x}) > 0$, while some are willing to exchange any good for the *r*th, then it seems reasonable to suppose the *r*th good to be in excess demand. However, this must be assumed rather than deduced from what went before, since the $\bar{R}_{\alpha i}$, on which the notion of dominance depends, are defined for given $\bar{x}_\alpha$. It is thus possible, because of 'perverse' income effects, that at the utility-maximizing position which α hopes to reach, he wants less of the *r*th good rather than more.[5]

Assumption (A5)   There exists some small $\epsilon > 0$ such that $z_i > 0$ if $p_i \leq \epsilon$, $i = 1, \ldots, n$, whatever (non-negative) values we give to the other components of $p \in S$.

This assumption is introduced in order to allow us to deal with strictly positive prices (see rule 1 below). This, in turn, makes it possible to consider a numeraire process of price adjustment and to ignore possible inequalities in the first-order conditions of a utility maximum.

Trading and Pricing Rules

We shall lay down the following rules.

Rule 1 $\dot{p}_i = k_i z_i, \quad k_i > 0 \qquad (i = 1, \ldots, n-1)$.

    $\dot{p}_n \equiv 0$.

This numeraire rule is familiar and requires no comment.

Rule 2   If at $[p(t), \bar{x}(t)] > 0$, $R[p(t), \bar{x}(t)] = \emptyset$, then $\dot{\bar{x}}_\alpha(t) \neq 0$ for all α. If $R[p(t), \bar{x}(t)] \neq \emptyset$ then $\dot{\bar{x}}_\alpha(t) = 0$ for all α.

---

[5] This was pointed out to me by Professor Arrow. Mr Negishi has also shown that complementarities between goods may invalidate assumption (A4).

This rule states that if at some t exchange is definitely possible, consistent with (A2), then some trade will take place. No trade will take place if trade is not definitely possible.[6]

III   A STABILITY THEOREM

The following theorem can now be established.

Theorem   If (A1)–(A5) and rules 1 and 2 hold, and if $\bar{x}(0) > 0$, $0 < p(0) \in S$, then the system will approach a Pareto optimum (equilibrium) arbitrarily closely as $t \to \infty$.

  Proof   (a) Suppose

$$R[p(0), \bar{x}(0)] \neq \varnothing,$$

and consider

$$V[p(0), \bar{x}(0)] = \frac{1}{2} \sum_{\substack{\alpha \\ r \in R}} (\mu_{r\alpha})^2$$

By rule 2, $\dot{\bar{x}}_\alpha(0) = 0$ for all α; so by rule 1

$$\dot{V}[p(0), \bar{x}(0)] = -\sum_{\substack{\alpha \\ r \in R}} \mu_{r\alpha} \frac{k_r z_r \bar{R}_{r\alpha}}{q_r^2 p_n} \ .^7$$

---

[6] See below for a relaxation of this rule.

[7] Since

$$V[p(0), \bar{x}(0)] \stackrel{\text{def.}}{=} \frac{1}{2} \sum_{\substack{\alpha \\ r \in R}} (\mu_{r\alpha})^2$$

then

$$\frac{dV(\cdot)}{dt} \equiv \dot{V}(\cdot) = \frac{dV(\cdot)}{d\mu_{r\alpha}} \frac{d\mu_{r\alpha}}{dt} = \frac{dV(\cdot)}{d\mu_{r\alpha}} \frac{d\mu_{r\alpha}}{dp_r} \frac{dp_r}{dt} \ .$$

By rule 2 one gets

$$\dot{V}(\cdot) = \sum_{\substack{\alpha \\ r \in R}} \mu_{r\alpha} k_r z_r \frac{-p_r - p_n \bar{R}_{r\alpha} + p_r}{p_r^2} = -\sum_{\substack{\alpha \\ r \in R}} \mu_{r\alpha} k_r z_r \frac{\bar{R}_{r\alpha}}{q_r^2 p_n}$$

which is the expression in the text.

By (A4) sign $z_r = $ sign $\mu_{r\alpha}$ for some $\mu_{r\alpha} \neq 0$. Hence $\dot{V} \leqslant 0$. But if $\dot{V} = 0$, then $\mu_{r\alpha} = 0$ for all α and $r \in R$; so $p(0) \in E[\bar{x}(0)]$. Alternatively, if $p(0) \in E[\bar{x}(0)]$, then by definition $\mu_{r\alpha} = 0$ for all α and all r. Hence $\dot{V}[p(0), \bar{x}(0)] = 0$ if and only if $p(0) \in E[\bar{x}(0)]$.

(b) Suppose that $R[p(t), \bar{x}(0)] \neq \emptyset$ for all $t \geqslant 0$. Then our rule 2 never allows any trade to take place. It is known that assumption (A1) is sufficient to ensure the continuity of the excess demand functions over X_α and S. Also, by assumption (A5) and rule 1, $q_r > 0$ for all $t \geqslant 0$. Hence using (a) we may treat V as a Liapounov norm which has a negative derivative for all $p \notin E[\bar{x}(0)]$ and which converges on 0 as $t \to \infty$. But then if $p[t, p(0), \bar{x}(0)] = p(t)$ is the solution of the 'no trade' process, the limit point of this solution belongs to $E[\bar{x}(0)]$. Thus, if by rule 2 we are forced to have a tâtonnement for all $t \geqslant 0$, the tâtonnement is stable.[8]

(c) Now suppose that at some $t \geqslant 0$, $R[p(t), \bar{x}(t)] = \emptyset$. Consider $W(t) = \Sigma_\alpha U_\alpha[\bar{x}_\alpha(t)]$. By rule 2 and assumption (A2) we now have

$$\dot{W}(t) > 0 \text{ for } R[p(t), \bar{x}(t)] = \emptyset.$$

But $\dot{W} > 0$ if and only if trade is possible; otherwise $\dot{W} = 0$. Since by (A3) W is bounded, it follows that if trade is possible for all $p(t) \notin E[\bar{x}(t)]$, W will approach a limit which is an equilibrium.

(d) There remains the mixed case where for some t trade is possible and for others not. If at $T > 0$, $R[p(T), \bar{x}(T)] \neq \emptyset$, then $\dot{W}(T) = 0$. But by (a) and (b), $\dot{V}(T) < 0$. Hence either trade is impossible for all $t \geqslant T$, and then we already know that we approach an equilibrium arbitrarily closely as $t \to \infty$, or at some $T^* > T$, $R[p(T^*), \bar{x}(T^*)] = \emptyset$ and $\dot{W}(T^*) > 0$. We then consider all $t \geqslant T^*$. If trade is possible for all $\infty > t \geqslant T^*$, then by (c) we once again approach an equilibrium arbitrarily closely. If for some $T^{**} > T^*$, trade becomes impossible, then we are back in the same argument as in the case of T. Hence for all $p(t) \notin E[\bar{x}(t)]$,

---

[8] It is an immediate consequence of (a) and (b) that $R[p(t), \bar{x}(0)] \neq \emptyset$ for all $t \geqslant 0$ only if $\mu_{i\alpha} = \mu_{i\beta} = \ldots = \mu_{im}$ for all i. For suppose $\mu_{r\alpha} < \mu_{r\beta}$, say. Suppose, without loss of generality, that r dominates. Then by (a) there will be some t for which $\mu_{r\alpha} = 0$ while $\mu_{r\beta} > 0$. Hence by (A4) and for h small, $r \in R[p(t+h), \bar{x}(0)]$, since by rule 1, $\mu_{r\alpha}$ will become negative in this interval while $\mu_{r\beta}$ will stay positive. Hence if $R[p(t+h), \bar{x}(0)] \neq \emptyset$, there exists some $s \in R[p(t+h), \bar{x}(0)]$. But then at t, by the continuity of the process, $|\mu_{s\alpha}| = |\mu_{r\alpha}|$, and $|\mu_{s\beta}| = |\mu_{r\beta}|$. But this is impossible. For if $\mu_{s\beta} > 0$ at t, then $\mu_{s\alpha} < 0$ at $t+h$. Lastly, if $\mu_{s\beta} = 0$ at t, then $\mu_{r\alpha} = \mu_{r\beta}$ by definition and contrary to assumption. Hence it follows that $s \in R[p(t+h), \bar{x}(0)]$, and so $R[p(t+h), \bar{x}(0)] = \emptyset$.

at least one of the Liapounov norms has a non-zero derivative, and V cannot increase and W cannot diminish at any t. The system will therefore approach an equilibrium arbitrarily closely as $t \rightarrow \infty$.

A Relaxation of Rule 2

The condition $R[p(t), \bar{x}(t)] \neq \emptyset$ is necessary if, in a market with perfect information, *no* trade is to take place. It is, however, not sufficient. It is perfectly possible that some trade can take place even if there exists some good r which either *dominates* or *is dominated*. There is no reason why we should not weaken our rule 2 to take account of this.

Rule 2a   If at $[p(t), \bar{x}(t)] > 0, \dot{x}_\alpha(t) = 0$ for all α, then

$$R(p(t), \bar{x}(t)) \neq \emptyset.$$

Rule 2a is weaker than rule 2. It is also evident that our theorem will none the less continue to hold. For by this new rule, if in a non-equilibrium situation W has a zero derivative, V must have a negative derivative. (See (a) and (b) of the above proof.) Hence once again it is certain that at least one of the Liapounov norms has a non-zero derivative for $p(t) \notin E[\bar{x}(t)]$. Moreover, V cannot increase, and W cannot diminish, so that the same argument can be carried through just as before.

IV   CONCLUSION

We have shown that, if it is possible to assume each individual to have a positive stock of each good at each moment of time, and if the association between 'dominance' and the sign of the excess demand functions as postulated in assumption (A4) is valid, the pure exchange system is always stable. It would be nice to do without these restrictions. There is good ground for believing that this will be possible if we relax our rules somewhat. For all we require to establish the stability of a pure exchange system using the rather inoffensive (A2) is the following: if $p(t) \notin E[\bar{x}(t)]$, then there should exist some $T > t$ such that $\bar{x}(T) \neq \bar{x}(t)$. That is, some trade should eventually become possible. For then at some T, W has a positive derivative so that W will never diminish and always increase (eventually) as long as the system is out of equilibrium.

Since *W* is bounded it must approach a limit which is an equilibrium. One can construct rules and cases where that is not so, i.e., where trade never becomes possible and the tâtonnement is unstable. So far, I have not found any which are not entirely artificial and unrealistic.

REFERENCES

Arrow, Kenneth J. and Debreu, Gerard (1954), 'Existence of an Equilibrium for a Competitive Economy', *Econometrica*, **22**, 265-90.

Hahn, F. H. and Negishi, T. (1962), 'A Theorem on Non-tâtonnement Stability', *Econometrica*, **30**, 463-9. [Reprinted as chapter 10 in the present volume.]

Negishi, T. (1961), 'On the Formation of Prices', *International Economic Review*, **2**, 122-6.

Radner, R. (1960), 'A Paper on a Stochastic Bargaining Process', presented to the Berkeley–Stanford Joint Seminar in Mathematical Economics, April, 1960.

Uzawa, H. (1962), 'On the Stability of Edgeworth's Barter Process', *International Economic Review*, **3**, 218-32.

10

A Theorem on Non-tâtonnement Stability

with Takashi Negishi

In recent years some not inconsiderable progress has been made in finding conditions sufficient to ensure the stability of competitive equilibrium (Arrow and Hurwicz, 1958; Arrow et al., 1959; Uzawa, 1961). Most of this work shares the following two characteristics: (1) restrictions are placed on the forms of the excess demand functions aggregated over the market participants, and (2) the dynamic process investigated is a tâtonnement. In this paper, the latter is not assumed. That is to say, trading is permitted even if some markets are not in equilibrium. It will then be shown that, provided certain not unreasonable rules of trading are postulated, the system always approaches some equilibrium arbitrarily closely, quite irrespective of the forms of the excess demand functions. This proposition is here proved for a pure exchange economy only.

It will be useful to give an intuitive account of the formal model which we shall use. Imagine certain prices to be 'called' and suppose that at those prices trading leads to the following result: if good i was in excess demand before trading, then after trade there is no market participant who holds more of this good than he desires to hold; if good i was in excess supply before trading, then after trade no market participant holds less of this good than he desires to hold. In other words, trade is such that there is never an individual with any unsold good on his hand when that good is in excess demand or with an unpurchased good

[1] This is the outcome of two papers by Frank H. Hahn and Takashi Negishi, each written independently. Hahn's paper (1960) formulated the process of adjustment and proved some theorems, which were then generalized by Negishi to the theorem in this paper. Negishi's contribution, which is a sequel to Negishi (1961), was supported by the Office of Naval Research (Contract Nonr-255 (50), NR-047-004) at Stanford University. We are indebted to our referees for valuable comments.

when that good is in excess supply. This, on the face of it, seems a reasonable postulate. Trading having taken place, prices change according to the customary rule: the prices of goods still in excess demand after trade rise, those of goods still in excess supply, fall (unless the good is free). Then once again prices are 'called' and trade takes place. The model just stated is in discrete form. In what follows it will be assumed that trading and prices change continuously after an initial interval during which prices remain constant while trading takes place.

I PRELIMINARIES

Notation

There are n goods (items) and m individuals. Prices are expressed in terms of units of account.

Latin subscripts (e.g., i or j) refer to goods; Greek subscripts (e.g., α or β) refer to individuals. A variable followed by t enclosed in parentheses is measured at time t. This reference to time is often omitted.

p denotes price, $\bar{x}$ stock, x (without a bar above it) gross demand, z excess demand. Thus $p_i(t)$ denotes the price of the ith item at time t, $\bar{x}_{\alpha i}(t)$ the stock of the ith item held by the αth individual at time t, $x_{\alpha i}(t)$ the corresponding gross demand, while $z_{\alpha i}(t) = x_{\alpha i}(t) - \bar{x}_{\alpha i}(t)$ is the corresponding excess demand of the αth individual for the ith item at time t.

A column vector with components $a_1, a_2, \ldots, a_N$ is written as $a = \{a_1, \ldots, a_N\}$. Transposition is indicated by a prime, so that a' is the corresponding row vector. Thus we introduce the column vectors

$$p(t) = \{p_1(t), \ldots, p_n(t)\},$$
$$\bar{x}_\alpha(t) = \{\bar{x}_{\alpha 1}(t), \ldots, \bar{x}_{\alpha n}(t)\},$$
$$x_\alpha(t) = \{x_{\alpha 1}(t), \ldots, x_{\alpha n}(t)\},$$
$$z_\alpha(t) = \{z_{\alpha 1}(t), \ldots, z_{\alpha n}(t)\} \equiv x_\alpha(t) - \bar{x}_\alpha(t).$$

The aggregate excess demand for the ith item at time t (a scalar) is written as

$$z_{.i}(t) = \sum_{\alpha=1}^{m} z_{\alpha i}(t).$$

The corresponding vector of aggregate excess demands for all goods is written

$$z(t) = \{z._1(t), \ldots, z._n(t)\} \equiv \sum_{\alpha=1}^{m} z_\alpha(t).$$

Also we write

$$\bar{x} = (\bar{x}_1, \ldots, \bar{x}_m) = \|\bar{x}_{\alpha j}\|,$$

a matrix of n rows and m columns.

In what follows, a dot over a symbol denotes the operation d/dt. An asterisk marks equilibrium values.

Assumption (A1)　For each $\alpha = 1, \ldots, m$ there is a function $Z_{\alpha i}$ associating with each pair of vectors $(p, \bar{x}_\alpha)$ a number $z_{\alpha i}$, so that

(i) $z_\alpha = Z_\alpha(p, \bar{x}_\alpha)$ for $\alpha = 1, \ldots, m$, and, hence, $z = Z(p, \bar{x})$.

(ii) $Z(p, \bar{x}) = Z(kp, \bar{x})$ for all $k > 0$ (positive homogeneity of order zero).

(iii) $Z(p, \bar{x})$ is single-valued and continuous over a (fixed) closed subset H of positive points in its $n(m + 1)$-dimensional domain.

(iv) For any $p \geqslant 0$, and any $\bar{x}$, $p'Z(p, \bar{x}) = 0$ (Walras identity).

Definition (D1)　$p^* \geqslant 0$ is called an equilibrium price vector[2] (relative to x^*) if $Z(p^*, x^*) \leqslant 0$. The set of all p and x satisfying this vector inequality will be denoted E.

Adjustment Hypothesis (AH)　There exists $h > 0$ such that

(i) (a) $\dot{p}(t) = Kz(t)$ for $t \geqslant h$, where K is a diagonal matrix with positive diagonal elements $K_1, \ldots, K_n$;

(b) $\dot{p}(t) = 0$ for $t < h$;

(ii) $\dot{\bar{x}}_\alpha(t) = F_\alpha[p(t), \bar{x}(t)]$, $\alpha = 1, \ldots, m$, $t \geqslant 0$, where F_α has the following properties:

(a) it is single-valued and continuous over the set H given in (A1(iii));

(b) $\sum_\alpha F_\alpha[p(t), \bar{x}(t)] = 0$, $t \geqslant 0$;

(c) $p'(t) F_\alpha[p(t), \bar{x}(t)] = 0$, $t \geqslant 0$;

---

[2] $p \geqslant 0$ means that all components of p are non-negative and at least one component of p is positive.

(d) $z_{\alpha j}(h)z_j(h) \geqslant 0$ for all j, and each α;

(e) $z_{\alpha j}(t)z_j(t) \geqslant 0$, $t > h$ for all j, and each α;

(iii) functions $Z(p, \bar{x})$ and $F(p, \bar{x})$ satisfy the Lipschitz condition. This implies the existence of the solutions (paths) of the above mentioned differential equations,

$$p(t) = p[t: p(0), \bar{x}(0)],$$

$$\bar{x}(t) = x[t: p(0), \bar{x}(0)],$$

which are unique and continuous with respect to initial values $p(0)$, $\bar{x}(0)$. These solutions will remain in the set H introduced in (A1(iii)).

We will explain this hypothesis and then give an example of the process which satisfies (AH).

Let us call $z_{\alpha j}$ 'individual α's excess demand for good j'. It is supposed that in the time interval $(0, h)$, prices remain unchanged (AH(i)(b)). In that interval trade takes place in such a way that the sign of the individual excess demand for any good and any participant is not the opposite of the sign of the corresponding total excess demand (AH(ii)(d)). Thus if we imagine, in that interval, trade to take place on a 'first come, first served' basis, it will certainly be possible to satisfy this condition although some plans may have to be overfulfilled. This 'overfulfilment' occurs because individuals may be forced by shortages to spill over from one market to the next to satisfy their budget constraints. This seems agreeable to common sense.

It is clear that trade as such cannot change the total amount of the good available, and this explains (AH(ii)(b)). At h, prices start changing in the usual manner (AH(i)(a)), and trade takes place in such a way as never to permit opposite signs between any individual and the corresponding total excess demands (AH(ii)(e)). Exchange as such, however, cannot change the value of an individual's stock holdings – a simple balance sheet point – and hence we have (AH(ii)(c)).

Assumption (A2)   (i) The initial endowment of the αth individual (household) denoted by $\bar{x}_\alpha(0)$ is positive; i.e., $\bar{x}_\alpha(0) > 0$ for all $\alpha = 1, \ldots, m$.

(ii) For each $\alpha = 1, \ldots, m$, the αth household has a continuously differentiable strictly quasi-concave[3] utility function $U_\alpha(x_\alpha)$.

---

[3] A function $F(x)$ is said to be strictly quasi-concave if the equality $F(x') \leqslant F(x'')$ implies the inequality $F[\theta x' + (1 - \theta)x''] > F(x')$ whenever $0 < \theta < 1$.

The demand at any time t maximizes the utility function subject to the budget constraint. That is, for each t and each α,

$$p'Z_\alpha(p, \bar{x}_\alpha) = 0$$

and

$$U_\alpha[Z_\alpha(p, \bar{x}_\alpha) + \bar{x}_\alpha] \geqslant U_\alpha(w + \bar{x}_\alpha)$$

for any w such that

$$p'w = 0.$$

An example We now construct an example of the process which satisfies (AH).

(E(i))   The same as (i)(a) and (i)(b) of (AH).

(E(ii)) $p_n(0) > 0$ and $Z_n(p_1, \ldots, p_{n-1}, 0, \bar{x}) > 0$ for all non-negative p_i ($i = 1, \ldots, n-1$) and $\bar{x}$.

(E(iii))

$$\dot{\bar{x}}_{\alpha j} = \sum_{s=1}^{n} \frac{\partial x_{\alpha j}}{\partial p_s} K_s z_s - \bar{K}_\alpha \sum_{\beta=1}^{m} \sum_{s=1}^{n} \frac{\partial x_{\beta j}}{\partial p_s} K_s z_s$$

where $\bar{K}_\alpha > 0$, $\sum_\alpha \bar{K}_\alpha = 1$ ($\alpha = 1, \ldots, m; j = 1, \ldots, n-1$), it being understood that all entities are evaluated at time $t > h$.

(E(iv))

$$p_n(t) \dot{\bar{x}}_{\alpha n}(t) = - \sum_{j \neq n} p_j(t) \dot{\bar{x}}_{\alpha j}(t) \qquad (\alpha = 1, \ldots, m)$$

(E(v))

$$z_{\alpha j}(h) = \bar{K}_\alpha z_j(h) \qquad (j = 1, \ldots, n; \alpha = 1, \ldots, m).$$

Verification of the requirements of (AH(ii)) By (E(iv)) we have $\sum_j p_j(t) \dot{\bar{x}}_{\alpha j}(t) = 0$, all α, $t > 0$, and so (ii)(c) of (AH) holds.

We suppose (E(ii)) in order to ensure $p_n(t) > 0$ for all $t > 0$. Then the assumptions (E(iii)) and (E(iv)) define a set of stock adjustment functions F_α which depend only on $p(t)$ and $\bar{x}(t)$.

If we sum (E(iii)) over α, we have, for all $j \neq n$,

$$\sum_{\alpha=1}^{m} \dot{\bar{x}}_{\alpha j} = \sum_{\alpha=1}^{m} \sum_{s=1}^{n} \frac{\partial x_{\alpha j}}{\partial p_s} K_s z_s - \sum_{\alpha=1}^{m} \bar{K}_\alpha \sum_{\beta=1}^{m} \sum_{s=1}^{n} \frac{\partial x_{\beta s}}{\partial p_s} K_s z_s = 0,$$

since $\Sigma_{\alpha=1}^{m} \bar{K}_{\alpha} = 1$ by (E(iii)). Then we have, by (E(iv)),

$$\sum_{\alpha=1}^{m} \dot{\bar{x}}_{\alpha n} = -\frac{1}{p_n} \sum_{j \neq n} p_j \sum_{\alpha=1}^{m} \dot{\bar{x}}_{\alpha j} = 0.$$

Hence, (AH(ii)(b)) is obtained.

Let us write

$$x_{\alpha j} = X_{\alpha j}(p, \bar{x}_\alpha) = \hat{X}_{\alpha j}(p, r_\alpha)$$

where r_α is the 'income' of the αth individual; i.e., $r_\alpha = p'\bar{x}_\alpha$. We have from (AH(ii)(c)), which is already established,

$$\Sigma_s \frac{\partial X_{\alpha j}}{\partial \bar{x}_{\alpha s}} \dot{\bar{x}}_{\alpha s} = \Sigma_s \frac{\partial \hat{X}_{\alpha j}}{\partial r_\alpha} \frac{\partial r_\alpha}{\partial \bar{x}_{\alpha s}} \dot{\bar{x}}_{\alpha s} = \frac{\partial \hat{X}_{\alpha j}}{\partial r_\alpha} \Sigma_s p_s \dot{\bar{x}}_{\alpha s} = 0,$$

since demand depends on stock holdings only through 'income' r_α. Then it follows from (E(i)) that

$$\dot{x}_{\alpha j}(t) = \Sigma_s \frac{\partial X_{\alpha j}}{\partial p_s} \dot{p}_s + \Sigma_s \frac{\partial X_{\alpha j}}{\partial \bar{x}_{\alpha s}} \dot{\bar{x}}_{\alpha s} = \Sigma_s \frac{\partial X_{\alpha j}}{\partial p_s} K_s z_s(t)$$

$$(t \geqslant h, \alpha = 1, \ldots, m, j = 1, \ldots, n).$$

Now from (E(iii)) we have[4]

$$\dot{\bar{x}}_{\alpha j}(t) = \dot{x}_{\alpha j} - \bar{K}_\alpha \dot{z}_j \qquad \text{for all } \alpha, j \neq n, t \geqslant h.$$

This, together with (E(v)), gives us

$$z_{\alpha j}(t) = \bar{K}_\alpha z_j(t) \qquad (t \geqslant h, j \neq n).$$

For $j = n$, let $z_{\alpha n} = \bar{K}_\alpha z_n + \epsilon$. Then we have

$$\sum_{j=1}^{n-1} p_j z_{\alpha j} + p_n z_{\alpha n} = \sum_{j=1}^{n-1} p_j \bar{K}_\alpha z_j + p_n(\bar{K}_\alpha z_n + \epsilon),$$

i.e.,

$$\sum_{j=1}^{n} p_j z_{\alpha j} = \bar{K}_\alpha \sum_{j=1}^{n} p_j z_j + p_n \epsilon.$$

---

[4] Since $\dot{z}_j = \Sigma_\alpha \dot{x}_{\alpha j} - \Sigma_\alpha \dot{\bar{x}}_{\alpha j} = \Sigma_\alpha \dot{x}_{\alpha j}$, by (AH(ii)(b)) already established.

But the budget constraint (A2(ii)) is $\Sigma_{j=1}^n p_j z_{\alpha j} = 0$, and their summation yields $\Sigma_j p_j z_j = 0$ (Walras identity, A1(iv)). Since (E(ii)) ensures that $p_n > 0$, we have $\epsilon = 0$. Thus we have established (AH(ii)(e)).

Lastly, by (A2(ii)), condition (ii)(a) of (AH) is seen to be satisfied.

Remark   It is very likely that other, perhaps more acceptable, examples of (AH) can be found; here we only wish to demonstrate the possibility of (AH).

We shall prove the following lemma.

Lemma   Let $U_\alpha[x_\alpha(t)] = U_\alpha(t)$. Then for $(p, \bar{x}) \notin E$, and assuming (AH), we have $\dot{U}_\alpha(t) \leq 0$ for all α and $\dot{U}_\alpha(t) < 0$ for some α $(t \geq h)$.

Proof   (a) Consider the αth budget constraint:

$$B_\alpha(t) = p'[x_\alpha(t) - \bar{x}_\alpha(t)] = 0.$$

Then

$$\dot{B}_\alpha(t) = \dot{p}'z_\alpha(t) + p'[\dot{x}_\alpha(t) - \dot{\bar{x}}_\alpha(t)] = 0.$$

By (AH(i)(a)) and (AH(ii)(e)), $\dot{p}'z_\alpha(t) \geq 0$ for all α, and $\dot{p}'z_\alpha(t) > 0$ for some α, for $(p, \bar{x}) \notin E, t \geq h$.

By (AH(ii)(c)), $p'\dot{\bar{x}}_\alpha(t) = 0$. Therefore we have

$$p'\dot{x}_\alpha(t) \leq 0 \text{ for all } \alpha, \ p'\dot{x}_\alpha(t) < 0, \text{ for some } \alpha, \text{ for } (p, \bar{x}) \notin E,$$

$$t \geq h. \tag{10.1}$$

(b) But from elementary utility theory we have[5]

$$\dot{U}_\alpha(t) = \lambda_\alpha(t)\, p'\dot{x}_\alpha(t) \tag{10.2}$$

where $\lambda_\alpha(t) > 0$ (the 'marginal utility' of income r_α). So, by (10.1),

$$\left.\begin{array}{l} \dot{U}_\alpha(t) \leq 0 \text{ for all } \alpha \\ \dot{U}_\alpha(t) < 0 \text{ for some } \alpha \end{array}\right\} (p, \bar{x}) \notin E, t \geq h. \tag{10.3}$$

We can now easily prove the theorem mentioned in the introduction.

---

[5] Since $\dot{U}_\alpha = \Sigma_j(\partial U_\alpha/\partial x_{\alpha j})\,\dot{x}_{\alpha j}$ and $\partial U_\alpha/\partial x_{\alpha j} = \lambda_\alpha p_j$.

Theorem If (A1), (A2) and (AH) hold, then the general equilibrium system is quasi-stable, i.e., every limit point of $p[t: p(0), \bar{x}(0)]$ and $\bar{x}[t: p(0), \bar{x}(0)]$ belongs to E for all $p(0), \bar{x}(0)$ (see Uzawa, 1961).

Proof We shall use the method of Liapounov (Hahn, 1959) with which we shall assume the reader to be familiar. Consider

$$V = V(p, \bar{x}) = \Sigma_\alpha U_\alpha(x_\alpha).$$

It is clear that $p(t)$ is bounded. This can be seen by taking d/dt of $\Sigma_i p_i^2/K_i$ which gives, by (AH), $\Sigma_i p_i z_i = 0$. Also, $\bar{x}$ is bounded since $\bar{x}_\alpha(t) \geqslant 0$ and $\Sigma_\alpha \dot{\bar{x}}_\alpha(t) = 0$ from (AH(ii)(b)) and (AH(iii)). Hence if $\dot{V} < 0$ for all $t \geqslant h$, since $U_\alpha(t)$, and therefore $V(t)$, is bounded from below, it will approach a limit, say, $V^* = V(p^{**}, \bar{x}^{**})$ such that $\dot{V}(p^{**}, \bar{x}^{**}) = 0$. But we know by the lemma that $\dot{V} < 0$ for all $(p, \bar{x}) \notin E$ and $\dot{V} = 0$ for $(p, \bar{x}) \in E$. Thus quasi-stability is established.

REFERENCES

Arrow, Kenneth J. and Hurwicz, Leonid (1958), 'On the Stability of the Competitive Equilibrium, I', *Econometrica*, **26**, 522-52.

Arrow, Kenneth J., Block, H. D. and Hurwicz, Leonid (1959), 'On the Stability of Competitive Equilibrium', II', *Econometrica*, **27**, 82-109.

Hahn, Frank H. (1960), 'On the Stability of Competitive Equilibrium', Working Paper no. 6, Bureau of Business and Economic Research, University of California at Berkeley.

Hahn, Wolfgang (1959), *Theorie und Anwendung der Direkten Methode von Ljapunov*, Springer-Verlag, Berlin; Göttingen, Heidelberg.

Negishi, Takashi (1961), 'On the Formation of Prices', *International Economic Review*, **2**, 122-6.

Uzawa, Hirofumi (1961), 'The Stability of Dynamic Processes', *Econometrica*, **29**, 617-31.

11

Uncertainty and the Cobweb

I

There has in the past ten years been a very rapid development in the analysis of stability conditions both in simple and multiple-market models.[1] Most of these developments have this in common: they make hardly any allowance for expectational factors and uncertainty. This is not meant as a reproach; it is very important to obtain a clear insight into the working of simple economic systems first. But sufficient progress has now been made in this field to encourage us to hope that the exclusion of some of the simplifying assumptions will not wreck the whole analysis. Indeed, it may well be that it will fortify some of the known conclusions.

That expectations may act as stabilizers and destabilizers is well known, although not many satisfactory methods of taking formal account of them exist. The effect of uncertainty however is, so far as I am aware, as yet unnoticed in the literature. By 'the effects of uncertainty' we mean to specify the following kinds of question: Given any way in which the unit of decision formulates its expectations concerning future events, what will be the comparative stability of the model if (i) the uncertainty of these expectations has no influence on action and (ii) uncertainty does have such an influence?

For the most part of our work we shall say that uncertainty as such exerts an influence on decisions if there is a difference (positive or negative) between the expected utility of income and the utility of expected income. The paper itself is a first attempt to look the effect of uncertainty on stability squarely in the face, although, as the reader will soon discover, we will protect ourselves from the full gaze by a number of more or less heroic assumptions.

[1] This paper is greatly indebted to discussions with my colleague, W. M. Gorman.

II

An analysis of behaviour under uncertainty must answer three main questions: (i) How are uncertain prospects formulated by the unit of decision? (ii) How does the actual occurrence of contemplated events affect the estimation of prospects? and (iii) How is the choice between uncertain prospects, arrived at? The first question asks, 'How is knowledge acquired?' and the third, 'How is knowledge acted upon?'

It would be idle to pretend that we have at this time any set of answers to these questions on which we could place any very great reliance. It may also be argued that these questions present a field of enquiry to psychologists rather than to economists. But unfortunately, psychologists seem either unwilling or unable to supply the answers in a useful way, and economists must for the present do as best they may, without their aid.[2] In this I believe that they 'should stick to their last' and use methods with which they are familiar and which have proved fruitful. Their hypotheses may turn out to be wrong, but as long as this possibility is not excluded by the very framing of the assumptions, that is as it should be.

III

At present we have only two reasonably worked out hypotheses available: (i) the hypothesis that knowledge is organized and acquired probabilistically, and acted upon by seeking maximum expected utility (see von Neumann and Morgenstern, 1944), and (ii) the hypothesis that knowledge is organized and acquired by a potential surprise ordering of events and the selection of focus outcomes, and that this knowledge is acted upon by seeking to maximize utility as a function of these focus outcomes (see Shackle, 1949). We shall apply each hypothesis in turn to examine the effect of uncertainty on stability conditions in simple situations.

IV

We must however confess at the outset that in one particular we shall shirk the application of either of the hypotheses in their full

---

[2] The notable exception is the work of Katona (see Katona, 1951). But even here there remains a considerable gap between the psychological propositions and the kind of rather precise analysis economists are accustomed to.

rigour, namely in the matter of acquiring knowledge. To apply the theories, we should have to assume that the individual has at any moment of time some hypothesis about each of a large number of events occurring over the indefinite future, so that the effect of the occurrence of any one event on the potential surprise or probability attached to the occurrence of other events can be established from the basic laws and axioms of probability and potential surprise theory. The reasons for shirking this task are threefold: first, the calculations and tabulations involved are both tedious and complicated; second, for this very reason it seems to me to be the least plausible part of the hypotheses; and third, in an analysis of stability conditions, as I hope to show, a simpler hypothesis concerning learning seems more appropriate.

V

The following assumptions will be made throughout.

(i) There is perfect competition in the sense that suppliers are concerned only with estimates of the market price and not with quantity demanded.

(ii) The economic horizon is one period. Hence suppliers hold no speculative stocks.

(iii) Demand reactions are instantaneous so that decisions to demand involve no uncertainty.

(iv) The prices of all commodities other than the one supplied are fixed, and there is no uncertainty with respect to these.

VI

We shall now examine some of the implications of hypothesis III(i) for our problem of stability conditions. We must first set out the special assumptions of III(i).

(i) Individual behaviour obeys the axioms which lead to a cardinal measure of utility, unique except for origin (von Neumann and Morgenstern, 1944).

(ii) Because of V(iv), utility can be regarded as an increasing function of profit only; 'entrepreneurial effort', etc., are excluded from the function.

(iii) The individual unit of decision acts as if it were maximizing expected utility.

VII

Let

$$\lambda_1, \ldots, \lambda_n \text{ with } \sum_{i=1}^{n} \lambda_i = 1$$

be the probabilities of prices $p_1 \ldots p_n$ for the commodity x being established.[3] Let k = total cost of production, and let

$$g_i(p_i, x) = p_i x - k(x). \tag{11.1}$$

By section VI(ii),

$$U = U(g_i), \quad \frac{dU(g_i)}{dg_i} > 0 \tag{11.2}$$

and by section VI(iii) the producer acts as if

$$\max_{x} \bar{U} = \sum_{i} \lambda_i U(g_i). \tag{11.3}$$

And thus,

$$\frac{d\bar{U}}{dx} = \Sigma_i \lambda_i Ug_i \frac{dg_i}{dx} = 0 \tag{11.4}$$

where $Ug_i = dU(g_i)/dg_i$, $i = 1 \ldots n$. Using (11.1), (11.4) can be written as

$$\frac{\Sigma Ug_i \lambda_i p_i}{\Sigma Ug_i \lambda_i} = \frac{dk}{dx}. \tag{11.5}$$

In words, the output produced will be such that the weighted sum of contemplated prices equals marginal cost, the weights used being the ratio of the expected marginal utility of profit if the ith

[3] Because of 5 (i), the prices are indices of the position of the demand curve.

price materializes to the total expected marginal utility of producing x.

VIII

If there were no utility or disutility of uncertainty, then the expected utility of income should equal the utility of expected income, and we could maximize either to obtain our equilibrium condition. Thus,

$$\max_{x} U' = U\left[\sum_i \lambda_i p_i x - k(x)\right] \tag{11.6}$$

yields

$$U'g\left(\Sigma \lambda_i p_i - \frac{dk}{dx}\right) = U'g\left(E(p) - \frac{dk}{dx}\right) = 0 \tag{11.7}$$

where $g = [E(p)x - k]$, $E(p) = \Sigma \lambda_i p_i$, $U'g = dU'/dg$; and since $U'g > 0$,

$$E(p) = \frac{dk}{dx}. \tag{11.8}$$

In words, expected price equals marginal cost in equilibrium.

If now P^e is the equivalent certain price which will induce the same production as when expected utility is maximized, we can measure uncertainty by the difference between $E(p)$ and P^e. This difference we shall call the risk premium R.

IX

It has always been assumed, in the literature of the subject which uses the probabilistic approach to uncertainty, that the entrepreneur's procedure is as follows. He calculates expected prices $(E(p) = \Sigma \lambda_i p_i)$ and from these deducts a positive risk premium R to arrive at the equivalent certain price P^e.[4] We shall now establish the, for us, rather important proposition that R may be

[4] This procedure is as old as Knight's (1921).

positive, negative or zero. This proposition was first put forward in a different context by Friedman and Savage (1948).

If there were no uncertainty, price would equal marginal cost, hence:

$$P^e = \frac{dk}{dx} \tag{11.9}$$

and therefore, by (11.5),

$$R \equiv E(p) - P^e = \sum_i \lambda_i \left(1 - \frac{Ug_i}{\Sigma_i Ug_i \lambda_i}\right) p_i. \tag{11.10}$$

Let us consider a simple special form of the utility function and write

$$U = A + ag + \frac{b}{2}g^2 \quad g, A, a > 0, b > -\frac{a}{g} \tag{11.11}$$

so that

$$dU/dg = a + bg \tag{11.12}$$

$$d^2U/dg^2 = b. \tag{11.13}$$

By definition, $R \gtrless 0$ according as $E[U(g_i)] \lessgtr U[E(g)]$. We are therefore interested in the sign of

$$\Delta U = E[U(g_i)] - U[E(g)] = \frac{b}{2}\left(\sum_i \lambda g_i^2 - \sum_i \lambda_i g_i^2 + \sigma^2\right) = \frac{b\sigma^2}{2} \tag{11.14}$$

where σ^2 = variance of the distribution of g_i. By (11.13) we know that b measures the rate of change of the marginal utility of profit. Hence for $b = 0$ (constant marginal utility), $\Delta U = 0$; $R = 0$. For $b > 0$ (increasing marginal utility), $\Delta U > 0$ and hence $R < 0$, for $-a/g < b < 0$ (diminishing marginal utility), $\Delta U < 0$ and $R > 0$.

Normally we shall be interested in utility functions of a higher order than (11.11). This would then introduce higher moments of the probability distribution into the picture. But for small changes it will be legitimate to regard (11.11) as describing a segment of the utility function, in the vicinity of equilibrium.

Thus the normal statement that $R > 0$ must be attributed, as Friedman and Savage have pointed out, to the implicit, and in economic analysis strongly embedded, assumption that the marginal utility of income is always declining with higher incomes. It should, however, be fairly obvious, after the discussions of the last 14 years or so, that there is nothing in theory, intuition or experience to bear out, and considerable evidence (viz. gambling-cum-insurance) to contradict, the universal applicability of this assumption. The fact that different socioeconomic classes exist, and that movement between these both takes place and · is attempted, provides by itself sufficient basis for the hypothesis that there are at least ranges of the utility function for which the marginal utility of income is an increasing function of income.

X

Let us now suppose that the number of firms in the industry we are interested in is fixed. (That is, we shall be concerned with that short-run period for which abnormal profits have not yet attracted entrants or losses have not yet caused firms to drop out.) We also assume, but only for the moment, that all firms in the industry are exactly alike. Let us also postulate that at the ruling price, which has been established for a considerable time past, the number of firms is the equilibrium number (in Mrs Robinson's sense) and that each firm is in equilibrium. The ruling price is assumed by the producers to continue indefinitely, and this assumption is held with certainty. We wish to investigate the stability of this equilibrium.

XI

The numerous published papers on the Cobweb have familiarized us with the proposition that the stability of a static supply and demand equilibrium depends on the relative slopes (in the vicinity of equilibrium) of the demand and supply curves. These papers, and especially recent ones, have also drawn attention to the possible stabilizing influence of 'inelastic price expectations'. If a static equilibrium described in section X exists and is established, it is highly unlikely that a small, *unexpected* change in price will lead to the expectation that the new price will be permanent (as is assumed in most models). But even if that is the case, further stabilizers (or destabilizers) may be at work, which have so far not been considered. This will be clear from the modifications in the following familiar model. The notation is as in section VII; in addition, S = supply, D = demand, α is a 'shift parameter' and the subscripts t, $t-1$, etc., have the normal meaning. The superscript 0 refers to the equilibrium value of the functions and variables.

We know from our previous analysis, and especially from (11.11), that supply will depend on expected prices and on some function of the variance of expected prices. Quite generally we could write:

$$S_t = S[E(P_t) + b\sigma^2].$$

(11.15)

But σ^2 is itself a function of price. By the assumptions of section X,

$$\sigma^2 = \sigma(P^0) = 0$$

(11.16)

(where P^0 is the equilibrium price). We now introduce the further simplifying assumption that

$$\frac{d\sigma^2}{dP^0} = r = \text{constant}.$$

(11.17)

In words, we assume that the variance changes at a constant rate as the price moves away from its equilibrium value. The assumption of constancy is made for mathematical convenience; other hypotheses, while slightly more complicated, can readily be incorporated in what follows.

On intuitive grounds, it seems reasonable to assume that the variance increases with deviations from the equilibrium price, so that $r > 0$ when prices are rising above P^0 and $r < 0$ when prices are falling below P^0.

Having made assumption (11.17), the further assumptions,

$$\left. \begin{array}{l} E(P_t) = f(P^0) = P^0 \\ \dfrac{dE(P_t)}{dP^0} = \epsilon = \text{constant} \end{array} \right\}$$

(11.18)

naturally follow. That they are 'heroic' will not be denied, but we are interested in the effects of uncertainty, and are therefore to some extent justified in making our expectational assumptions as simple as possible.

Writing our demand equation in the familiar form,

$$D_t = D(P_t, \alpha) \qquad (11.19)$$

(where α = shift parameter) and combining with (11.15) and writing the assumptions just made, we obtain an equation in x_t the divergence of actual from equilibrium output at moment t:

$$x_t = \mu(\epsilon + br) x_{t-1} \qquad (11.20)$$

where μ is the ratio of the 'slopes' of the supply and demand curves.

If the coefficients of (11.20) are independent of time, (11.20) can be solved very easily. Stability then requires that these coefficients be numerically smaller than unity. Unfortunately, the coefficients are not always so well behaved in our model. In the following section we investigate the cases where the coefficients are independent of time, and in section XIII the cases where that is not so.

XII

We wish to discover whether uncertainty exercises a 'stabilizing' influence or not. This term requires rather careful definition. Let $\hat{x}_t$ = the deviation from equilibrium output at time t when $r = 0$. Let

$$d_{0t}^2 = \frac{\hat{x}_{t-1}^2 + \hat{x}_t^2}{x_0^2} ; \quad d_{rt}^2 = \frac{x_{t-1}^2 + x_t^2}{x_0^2} . \qquad (11.21)$$

(a) r will be said to be *perfectly stabilizing* if, for every t, $x_t < \hat{x}_t$.

(b) r will be said to be *imperfectly stabilizing* if not (a) but for some $t = T$ and every subsequent $t = T+1$, $T+2$, etc., $d_{rT}^2 < d_{0T}^2$.

In words, r is perfectly stabilizing if, in the absence of a risk premium different from zero, every deviation from equilibrium at any moment of time is greater than it would have been with a risk premium different from zero. r is said to be imperfectly stabilizing if the ratio of the sum of the squares of the deviations from equilibrium in every two consecutive periods after the Tth to the square of the initial deviation is smaller for $r \neq 0$ than it is for $r = 0$. We are now ready for our main task.

(i) It is obvious, and it is only mentioned for the sake of completeness, that if the marginal utility of income is constant ($b = 0$), uncertainty plays no part in influencing stability.

(ii) If $br < 0$, then it can easily be verified that uncertainty will exert a perfectly stabilizing influence.

Now from our assumption that σ^2 increases with every (i.e., positive or negative) deviation from the equilibrium price, it follows that $br < 0$ implies $b < 0$ when prices rising above P^0 ($r > 0$) and $b > 0$ when prices falling below P^0 ($r < 0$). If then we assume (as seems sensible) that $\epsilon > 0$, so that expected profits change in the same direction as prices, the requirement $br < 0$ implies that the marginal utility of profits is increasing for profits below, and is falling for profits above, the equilibrium level.

We thus conclude that, given our assumptions, uncertainty is perfectly stabilizing if, at the equilibrium profits, the marginal utility of profit is at a (local) maximum. (Practical interpretation of this and other results is held over until section XV.)

(iii) If $br > 0$ then uncertainty is found to be perfectly destabilizing. By an exactly analogous argument to the one just given, this occurs when at the equilibrium profit the marginal utility of profit is at a (local) minimum.

XIII

We must now face the difficulty alluded to in the last paragraph of section XI. If b is always of the same sign whatever the deviation from equilibrium, then br will fluctuate in sign, as prices fluctuate about the equilibrium level.

To solve (11.20) in these circumstances, let us regard $br < 0$ by convention. Thus if $b < 0$ for all prices, we write the expression of (11.20) in brackets as $(\epsilon + br)$ when prices are rising above P^0 and as $(\epsilon - br)$ when prices are falling below P^0. In this case ($b < 0$) we obtain two solutions according as $x_0 > 0$ or $x_0 < 0$ (x_0 = initial deviation from equilibrium):

$$x_0 > 0: \quad x_t = \mu^t (\epsilon - br)^{f^i(t)} (\epsilon + br)^{f^j(t)} \tag{11.22}$$

$$x_0 < 0: \quad x_t = \mu^t (\epsilon - br)^{f^j(t)} (\epsilon + br)^{f^i(t)} \tag{11.23}$$

where

$$f^i(t) = t - \sum_{i=0}^{t-1} \frac{(-1)^{t-i}+1}{2} \; ; \quad f^j(t) = t - \sum_{i=0}^{t-1} \frac{(-1)^{t-i+1}+1}{2} \, .$$

If b is always negative, then (11.22) is the solution for $x_0 > 0$, and (11.23) that for $x_0 < 0$.

It can now easily be verified that uncertainty will in general be only imperfectly stabilizing. To avoid a further plethora of algebra, we will as far as possible only give the intuitive reason for this result. Suppose that $b > 0$, $r < 0$ and $x_0 > 0$, so that prices have fallen below their equilibrium level. That means that suppliers subtract a (positive) risk premium from the lower (expected) price to arrive at their supply. Hence for prices below the equilibrium value, the supply curve will be flatter, and hence the divergence from equilibrium output greater, than it would otherwise have been. In the following period, prices rise above the equilibrium value. This time the deduction of a positive risk premium makes the supply curve steeper than it would otherwise have been and hence the divergence from equilibrium output less than it would otherwise have been (at the same expected price). The supply curve thus has a kink at the equilibrium output. It is clear that in this case r cannot be perfectly stabilizing.

On the other hand, consider any even $t = T$. Then the equation in x_T involves a term such as $(\epsilon + br)^{T/2} (\epsilon - br)^{T/2}$. Since $(\epsilon^2 - b^2 r^2)/\epsilon^2 < 1$, it is easily seen that the following expression approaches zero with higher values of T:

$$m = \frac{d^2 r, T+1}{d^2 0 T+1} = \frac{(\epsilon + br)^T (\epsilon - br)^T [1 + (\epsilon^2 - b^2 r^2) \mu^2]}{\epsilon^{T+2}(\mu^2 + \epsilon^{-2})} . \quad (11.24)$$

It is seen that, for T high enough, $m < 1$, and hence r, will be imperfectly stabilizing.

Since a uniformly positive risk premium implies (by section IX) that the marginal utility of profit is uniformly diminishing, and the reverse for a uniformly negative risk premium, we conclude that uncertainty has an imperfectly stabilizing influence whenever the total utility curve is either concave (diminishing marginal utility) or convex (increasing marginal utility) on either side of the equilibrium position.

XIV

Our results naturally depend on our assumptions; these certainly are no more restrictive than those normally found in general equilibrium analysis. None the less, it may be of some interest (as Mr Roy has suggested to me) to relax the assumption that input prices are expected with certainty.

If input prices are uncertain, let us write g_{ij} as the profit which will be obtained at a given output and input combination if the ith output and jth input price materializes. (We are assuming that only the price of one input is uncertain.) If μ_j is the probability of the ith input price occurring, the producer now maximizes

$$E[U(g)] = \sum_i \sum_j \mu_j \lambda_i U(g_{ij}). \tag{11.25}$$

If we proceed as before we shall find that, in all cases where a positive risk premium is added to expected prices, it will be subtracted from expected costs and vice versa. That means that the results of the previous section, provided we continue to make all the assumptions there made, will continue to hold.

It must, however, be admitted that for practical purposes certain of these assumptions (making for linear difference equations) would have to be modified. This is so for the following reason. The uncertainty of input prices will lead to input substitution when expected output price changes. This occurs because the rate of change in the marginal cost of employing any input, and thus the rate of change in the variance of profit for employing any input, are not generally the same for all inputs. Although I have not investigated the consequences of this in a completely general model (mainly because of the difficulties of solving non-linear difference equations), such investigations as I have carried out led me to suppose that our results would not be seriously affected.

XV

We are now ready to sum up and then to interpret our conclusions.

1   Except for the case where the point of equilibrium is associated with a (local) minimum marginal utility of income, uncertainty will exert a stabilizing influence.

2 If the point of equilibrium lies on a section of the utility curve exhibiting diminishing marginal utility (positive risk premium), the fluctuations about equilibrium will be asymmetric; prices will always rise by more, and output increase by less, above the equilibrium price and output than prices fall and output falls below it.

3 If the point of equilibrium lies on a section of the utility curve exhibiting increasing marginal utility (negative risk premium), then the reverse of 2 will be true.

These results are all very fine, but it may now be argued that they represent just another vicious aspect of 'armchair economics': how, it may be asked, are we ever to find which industry is characterized by what segment of a utility function? Some answer to this must be given. Moreover, as Mr Gorman has pointed out to me, if the utility function is continuously differentiable, then the risk premium involves only second-order terms of the utility function (11.14) and hence r may be very small in relation to the other terms entering into (11.20). Some answers to these objections must now be given.

XVI

First of all, it should be repeated that, unlike more conventional utility analysis, the assumptions of a cardinal index and the maximization of expected utility can certainly be contradicted by experiment. It is *not* an empty tautological formulation.

Second, once the existence of a cardinal index has been established, we can infer from a number of observations (by attitude to gambling and insurance, etc.) on which part of the utility curve any one firm finds itself.

There is thus little reason to fear that our formulation is 'meaningless' in the sense that it cannot conceivably be contradicted. We may, however, stick our neck out a little further and make an additional hypothesis which has a certain plausibility, is capable of verification and has the additional merit of doing away with the necessity of elaborate aggregation formulae.

XVII

The analysis of the stability of static equilibrium implicitly goes on the assumption that the equilibrium has persisted over some time. No firm in the industry for quite some time past has felt any inducement to expand or contract its operations. Certain routines have been established, certain dividends normally paid.

My hypothesis is now as follows. If the actual profit is below the equilibrium profit, firms would be willing to pay for the chance of a gamble the 'satisfactory' outcome of which would bring them closer to their (accustomed) equilibrium position, and the expected outcome of which leaves their position unaltered; while if actual profits are above their equilibrium value firms would have to be paid to take the chance of a gamble the expected value of which leaves their position unaltered, and the 'satisfactory' outcome of which gives them a higher profit than they are earning at present. That is, firms act as 'gamblers' when they are receiving less than their accustomed profit, and as 'insurers' when they are receiving more than that.

The rationalization of the hypothesis is related (although not directly) to Duesenberry's hypothesis concerning the utility function of households. It is argued:

(i) that to fall below the accustomed ('normal') level of profits reduces utility by more than an equivalent rise above the normal level. A contraction in operations causes more alarm and despondency in the firm than equivalent expansion gives rise to exhilaration and rejoicing. Both processes involve the upsetting of established routines which may be regarded as a negative item. But the contraction is itself unpleasant, and thus reinforces the 'routine-upsetting' effect;

(ii) that, as long as the firm's attention remains focused on its 'normal' position, it seems reasonable to suppose that increments in profits are valued by the firm with reference to the gap this increase leaves between the actual and normal position. Thus, if profits are a little less than normal a firm may be willing to make considerable efforts to increase them, while if they are considerably less than normal the same effort will still leave them far from normal; a small increase would still leave routines greatly upset and do relatively little towards re-establishing them. Conversely, the greater the excess of actual over normal profits becomes, the greater is the upset in routine, etc., and the smaller the value placed on further increments in profit.

Let us depart from our strict assumption that there is a unique equilibrium price. The demand curve is subject to small random displacements. The expected price has remained constant for some time, and the risk premium is zero. Firms have adapted themselves to these fluctuations by evolving a routine; that is, they produce an output at which expected price is equal to marginal cost. Let us call this expected price again simply the equilibrium price. Actual income now fluctuates from period to period, but as long as the equilibrium price remains the same, output remains the same. If now expected price falls below the equilibrium price or rises above it, it seems reasonable to suppose that the disruption caused to accustomed behaviour will be considerable. It is the occurrence of events outside the range of normal experience which is responsible for this.

It is clear that 'plausible' is the most favourable term that can be applied to the above speculations. But it seems desirable to pass from classification to hypothesis, and this is one which may either be ruled out of court very easily by those with more practical knowledge than I possess or, if not, may be at least a useful starting point, which would also have some interesting implications for the theory of investment decisions.

In any case, speculation (iii) suggests (1) that the utility curve has a kink at the equilibrium expected profit, and (2) that the marginal utility of profits is increasing and is higher than the equilibrium marginal utility, for profits less than normal, and the reverse for profits higher than normal. This is the condition for r to be perfectly stabilizing.

XVIII

If our hypothesis is at all correct, we avoid most of the problems of aggregation. For our results depend on the position each firm occupies on its utility function, where this position is defined by its rate of change in its marginal utility at the equilibrium point.

If the hypothesis is not correct, and some firms are on a segment of increasing, and others on one of decreasing, marginal utility, then aggregation does indeed become a problem in the sense that our classification of outcomes now depends on the relative number and costs of firms on different positions of their utility curve. This is an empirical rather than a theoretical difficulty.

But for what it is worth, we may put forward the alternative hypothesis that firms whose output is less than the average output of all firms are on a segment of their utility curve exhibiting increasing marginal utility, those whose output is the average are on the kink (described previously), and those whose output is greater than the average are on a segment exhibiting constant marginal utility. The rationale for this hypothesis is again given by general 'Duesenberry considerations'. In this case, unless the rate of change of the marginal costs of the smallest firm are greatly different from those of the average firms, the latter will dominate the situation if they produce more than the small firms.

The classification of cases becomes more involved. But this is due to the fact that we are not certain whether any one simplifying hypothesis is correct, i.e., appropriate. Aggregation as such presents no intellectual problems in this case, but it is tiresome to classify all the possible outcomes.

One last point. If the expectations of different firms differ, no new difficulty of principle is introduced. We simply find how each firm behaves on the two alternative assumptions that uncertainty does or does not influence its actions. Addition will then tell us whether the industry as a whole behaves like a gambler or an insurer or both.

XIX

We shall now give a necessarily brief outline of a possible approach to the problems raised in this paper via Professor Shackle's theory. To do this we shall make certain assumptions, which I have found necessary for simplicity's sake, and with which Professor Shackle may well disagree. The assumptions in section V above are retained.

Once a decision as to how much to produce has been taken, then possible profits depend on the prices which will be established in the market. We now make the following assumptions.

(i) The potential surprise function is defined for prices and *not* for profits.

(ii) The 'two branches' of this function refer to prices higher and lower than the equilibrium price, respectively.

(iii) The ϕ function is defined in terms of prices and their potential surprises, and accordingly there are two focus prices: the highest price P^H, and the lowest price P^L, which attract most attention, or 'stimulate the imagination most'.

(iv) The ϕ functions are linear so that 'standardization' of P^L and P^H proceeds by multiplying each of them with a constant. We shall omit this and let P^L and P^H stand for standardized focus prices.

(v) Utility is a function of two possible profits for each level of output: the profit which would be earned at that output if $P = P^H$ and the profit which would be earned if $P = P^L$. This utility is maximized.

XX

On the basis of these assumptions, we have

$$\max_{x} U = U(P^H x - k, P^L x - k) \qquad (11.26)$$

and hence

$$U_H\left(P^H - \frac{dk}{dx}\right) + U_L\left(P^L - \frac{dk}{dx}\right) = 0$$

or

$$\frac{U_H P^H + U_L P^L}{U_H + U_L} = \frac{dk}{dx} \qquad (11.27)$$

where U_H and U_L are first derivatives of U with respect to the first and second argument of U.

It should be noted that the coefficients of P^H and P^L add up to unity, so that in words (11.27) reads: output will be such that marginal cost is equal to a convex linear combination of P^H and P^L, the coefficients being the ratio of the marginal utility of profits at high and low prices respectively to the total marginal utility of producing.

XXI

In this paper we are interested in the effect of uncertainty on stability. In our previous work there was no difficulty in isolating the attitude to uncertainty from the formation of expectations. In the present case we must however adopt a somewhat special procedure.

Suppose that we offered the following choice to our producer: (a) to produce what he has decided to produce and take his chance on the market, or (b) to toss a fair coin, and to give him the standardized focus gains and losses of producing if heads or tails come up, respectively. Clearly, the potential surprise of heads or tails in alternative (b) must be zero. Hence the focus gains and losses in (b) must be the same as those in (a), and our producer will be indifferent between the two alternatives. We can therefore, if we wish, use the utility of alternative (b) instead of the utility of alternative (a) (producing).

Moreover, since we are offering a 'toss', there is no objection to using probability in defining expectations, since Professor Shackle's strictures against the use of probability do not apply in this case. (A probability distribution, with only two alternatives, is clearly defined.) Suppose now that we offer the further choice of (i) (b) or (ii) the certain receipt of the expected outcome of (b); that is, suppose we compare the following two utilities:

$$U^1 = U(G, L) \text{ with } U(\tfrac{1}{2}G + \tfrac{1}{2}L) = U^2$$

$$(G = \text{focus gain}, L = \text{focus loss}). \quad (11.28)$$

Then it seems reasonable to say that, if $U^1 = U^2$, our entrepreneur gets neither utility nor disutility from uncertainty; if $U^1 > U^2$, then he derives some utility from uncertainty (gambles); and if $U^1 < U^2$ he derives disutility from uncertainty (insures).

It should be emphasized that we are *not* implying that the entrepreneur takes production decisions probabilistically; what we are saying is that there exists a probabilistical experiment, after production decisions have been taken, to allow us to disentangle the entrepreneur's attitude to uncertainty.

XXII

The remainder is now simple. Let

$$E(P) = \tfrac{1}{2}P^H + \tfrac{1}{2}P^L \qquad (11.29)$$

and

$$P^e = \frac{U_H P^H + U_L P^L}{U_H + U_L} \quad (\text{see } (11.27)). \qquad (11.30)$$

Then

$$R = [E(P) - P^e] \quad \begin{cases} = 0 \text{ if } U_H = U_L \\ > 0 \text{ if } U_H < U_L \\ < 0 \text{ if } U_H > U_L \end{cases} . \tag{11.31}$$

Since by definition now,

$$U(G, L) = U(\tfrac{1}{2}G + \tfrac{1}{2}L + R) \tag{11.32}$$

and U is an increasing function of income, we can say that

(i) risk premium is zero if $U^1 = U^2$ and this implies a constant marginal utility of income;

(ii) risk premium is positive if $U^1 < U^2$ and this implies a declining marginal utility of income;

(iii) risk premium is negative if $U^1 > U^2$ and this implies an increasing marginal utility of income.

Since these are the same results as in section IX above, the analysis can now, with obvious minor modifications, proceed as before.

REFERENCES

Friedman, M. and Savage, L. S. (1948), 'The Utility Analysis of Choices Involving Risk', *Journal of Political Economy*, **56**.

Katona, G. (1951), *Psychological Analysis of Economic Behaviour*, McGraw-Hill, New York.

Knight, F. H. (1921), *Risk, Uncertainty and Profit*, Houghton Mifflin Company, Boston.

Shackle, G. L. S. (1949), *Expectations in Economics*, Cambridge University Press, Cambridge.

von Neumann, J. and Morgenstern, O. (1944), *Theory of Games and Economic Behaviour*, Princeton University Press, Princeton, NJ.

Part IV

Growth

12

On Two-sector Growth Models

I INTRODUCTION

The two-sector growth story (see list of References) has been unwinding slowly and is not always easy to read. It seems desirable to have a simple account of the whole matter. Although Matthews and I have already elsewhere given a more or less simple translation of the story (Hahn and Matthews, 1964), its connection with ordinary general equilibrium analysis was not given the prominence which, I now think, it deserves. To do so is one of the main purposes of this note.

II THE PROBLEMS

We are to consider a world in which only two goods are produced: a consumption good and an investment good. At every moment of time all markets are cleared and everyone has maximized what he is supposed to maximize. The capital good is perfectly malleable and freely transferable between sectors. If net investment is not zero the stock of capital will be changing through time. The supply of labour services is also changing, either because people are breeding through thick and thin or because the real wage is such as to cause them to reproduce at a certain rate. One is interested in that path of the system for which all relative prices and quantities remain constant through time – the steady-state path. It need not exist. One way of making sure is to postulate constant returns to scale everywhere, although this is not quite enough. Since Harrod-neutral innovations are akin to population growth, they can be introduced into the model without any difficulty.

The world here considered does not use money. An act of saving by a household always implies a corresponding demand for the only asset there is: the capital good. It is then easiest to suppose that all stocks of capital good are owned by households who rent them to producers who use them in production.

The story starts with a given stock of capital inherited from the past. Since there are constant returns to scale we might just as well start with a given capital–labour ratio. The first question, familiar to general equilibrium theorists, is, Does there exist a momentary equilibrium for any given capital–labour ratio? The second question asks, Is such an equilibrium unique? The answer to this is important for the simple reason that multiple momentary equilibria would make it impossible without further postulates to predict the subsequent development of the system from the initial conditions. Supposing momentary equilibrium to be uniquely determined by the capital–labour ratio, we now ask, Where is the system going? Here we want to know whether a steady state is approached or not. Answering this question involves an examination of the existence of a steady-state solution, possibly also the uniqueness of this and of course rather straightforward stability analysis.

The questions may be answered in varying degrees of generality.

III THE MODEL

We are to suppose that the two goods are produced separately under constant returns to scale. The production functions are strictly concave and differentiable where required. From this, it follows at once that for any given wage, (w), and rental on capital, (q), there is only one set of goods prices such that no producer makes a profit or loss. This can be seen easily: if at $p_i' > p_i$ the ith producer makes zero profit in both situations, then the unit cost in one must exceed that in the other. In view of constant returns to scale and profit maximization, this is not possible.

The technique of production chosen by the ith producer is fully described by the chosen capital–labour ratio, (k_i). Since there are constant returns to scale, the least-cost technique depends only on the ratio of w to q, (μ). Because of strict concavity, there can be only one k_i associated with each μ. For if not, i.e. if both k_i and k_i' minimize unit cost at μ, then a convex combination of the two techniques must give lower unit cost still, contradicting the hypothesis that they were cost-minimizing techniques. We may therefore assert that to each μ there corresponds a unique price ratio, (p), of the two goods. We take the consumption good as numeraire.

Compare two situations where $\mu' > \mu$. If there were no choice of alternative techniques it is clear that the price of the more labour-intensive good must be higher in terms of the other good if the zero profit condition is to hold for μ' as well as for μ. The choice of alternative techniques, however, cannot affect this prediction if μ' is close to μ. For by continuity and strict concavity of the production functions, if $k_i > k_j$ at μ, this inequality will also hold for μ' close to μ. This result is much used in the simple stories which follow.

One assumes that producers plan to supply as much of each good as is demanded at a given μ and associated p. There are two kinds of income: wages and rental on capital. A given proportion of each kind of income is spent on each kind of good. The underlying utility theory giving this result has rarely been explored in this context and we ignore it until the next section. Since the initial capital–labour ratio, (k), is known, and since p is uniquely determined by μ, it is clear that the ratio in which the two goods are demanded may be written as a function of μ. Evidently this function will be single-valued and continuous. It now also follows that the ratio in which capital and labour are demanded can also be written as a function of μ.

One may normalize w and q, by requiring that they be non-negative and that they add up to one. This can be done since we have seen that only their ratio μ matters. A normalized w^* and q^* are called a momentary equilibrium if at these values the excess demands for capital and labour are each non-positive. This is so because by our assumptions Walras' Law[1] takes the form:

$$w(L'-L) + q(K'-K) = 0 \qquad (12.1)$$

(where L' and K' are the demands for labour and capital and L, K their given supplies). It follows from (12.1) that a factor can be in equilibrium excess supply only if its price is zero. Since the excess demand functions are continuous over the normalized price space, it is trivial to prove that an equilibrium exists.[2]

---

[1] The income of households is $wL + qK$. This must equal the value of their total demand for goods which must in turn equal the cost of producing these: $wL' + qK'$.

[2] Let $w + q = 1, w \geqslant 0, q \geqslant 0$ and let $u = (w, q)$. If no equilibrium exists at $u = (0, 1)$ one must have $L'-L > 0$ there. If no equilibrium exists at $u = (1, 0)$ one must have $K'-K > 0$ there. Let μ^q be a sequence of μ converging on $(1, 0)$ as $q \to \infty$ with $\mu^0 = (0, 1)$. Then if for all μ^q one had $L'-L > 0$ it would follow from (1) of the text that for all μ^q, $K'-K < 0$, contradicting $K'-K > 0$ as $q \to \infty$. Hence for some μ^q, $L'-L = 0$ and equilibrium is attained.

IV   THE UNIQUENESS OF MOMENTARY EQUILIBRIUM

As we have seen, the two-sector model at a moment of time can be completely described in terms of the excess demand function for labour and capital. In such a situation it is easy to state a necessary and sufficient condition for the uniqueness of a momentary equilibrium.

Uniqueness Proposition   If $w^* > 0$, $q^* > 0$ is a momentary equilibrium, then it is unique if and only if for all $w \neq w^*$, $q \neq q^*$, $w + q = 1$:

$$(w - w^*) X_L(w, q) + (q - q^*) X_K(w, q) > 0 \tag{12.2}$$

where $X_L(w, q)$, $X_K(w, q)$, are the excess demand functions for labour and capital.

Condition (12.2) may be interpreted as stating that the Weak Axiom of Revealed Preference holds with respect to (w^*, q^*) in the labour-capital space.[3]

The proof of the proposition is quite straightforward and can be partially accomplished by means of a simple diagram.

Sufficiency   Suppose without loss of generality $w > w^*$ (hence $q < q^*$). Then if (w, q) were an equilibrium it must be that $X_L(w, q) = 0$, (since $w > 0$). But then, by (12.2), $X_K(w, q) > 0$ and so (w, q) cannot be an equilibrium.

Necessity   In figure 12.1 we measure w from left to right and q from right to left along the horizontal axis of unit length. If the graph of X_L looks like the solid curve, i.e., cuts E from above, then in view of (12.1), (12.2) must certainly hold.

---

[3] Let L' and K' be the demand for labour and capital at w and q and $L^{*'}$, $K^{*'}$ the demand for these factors at the equilibrium prices w^*, q^*. Now, from (12.2),

$$wL' + qK' \geqslant wL^{*'} + qK^{*'} \tag{1}$$

as can be seen by subtracting $wL + qK$ from both sides of (1), noting (12.1) of text and using the definition of an equilibrium.

But also, using (12.1), condition (12.2) may be written

$$w^*L' + q^*K' > w^*L^{*'} + q^*K^{*'} \tag{2}$$

(as can be seen by subtracting $w^*L + q^*K$ from both sides of (2)). But (1) and (2) are indeed the Weak Axiom of Revealed Preference for L and K.

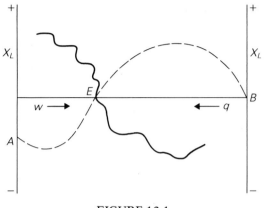

FIGURE 12.1

Now suppose $X_L > 0$ for all points between E and B. By (12.1) it must be that $X_K < 0$ for all these points and so by continuity $X_K \leqslant 0$ at B. But by (12.1) also, $X_L = 0$ at B (since $w = 1, q = 0$), and so B is another equilibrium, contradicting the uniqueness of the equilibrium at E. Using the same argument, it would follow, from the supposition that $X_L \leqslant 0$ for all points to the left of E, that there would be another equilibrium distinct from E at $w = 0$, $q = 1$. Hence the graph of X_L cannot look like the dotted curve, but must cut E from above. Hence (12.2) must hold. Clearly, this also implies that the graph of X_K must cut E from below.)

It is natural to enquire what meaningful economic assumptions there are to ensure that (12.2) holds.

From what has been said earlier, it is clear that X_L and X_K are homogeneous of degree one in K and L. Suppose that $\mu > \mu^*$ always implies that the ratio in which capital and labour are demanded (k') exceeds the ratio in which they are available (k). Reduce K and L in the same proportion until the amount of capital demanded at μ is the same as it was at μ^*. This cannot change the signs of X_L and X_K. But evidently after this reduction $X_L < 0$ and $X_K > 0$ so that (12.2) holds. Certainly therefore assumptions which ensure that k' is an increasing function of μ will also ensure uniqueness.

Now when $\mu > \mu^*$, producers will be induced to choose more capital-intensive techniques at μ than they had at μ^* and so the 'substitution effect' is always favourable to uniqueness. If then the demand for the capital-intensive good relatively to the other is no lower at μ than at μ^*, the 'income effect' will also be of the 'right' kind. Two types of hypothesis ensure this:

(i) if the ratio of expenditures of the two goods is independent of μ (the proportional savings hypothesis): for then, since the price of the capital-intensive good in terms of that of the other is lower at μ than at μ^*, the demand for the former good must be relatively higher, and so k' is greater at μ than it is at μ^*;

(ii) if the constant proportion of wage income spent on the capital-intensive good is higher than the constant proportion of profits spent on that good: for then, when $\mu > \mu^*$, the share of wages (μ/k), is higher at μ and so the expenditure on the capital-intensive good is relatively higher at μ than it was at μ^*. But the price of that good is relatively lower, and so the demand for it must be relatively higher. But the k' is greater at μ than it is at μ^*.

It is clear that (i) and (ii) are somewhat stronger than they need be. For it is possible that the 'substitution effect' is strong enough to outweigh an 'income effect' which is unfavourable to uniqueness. We consider one such case.

Suppose wage-earners spend the whole of their income on the labour-intensive good (good 1) and capitalists the whole of their income on the other good (good 2). Then the argument of (ii) suggests that we have made the income effect as unfavourable as we can for uniqueness. However, suppose that σ_1, the elasticity of substitution in sector 1, is never less than unity.

We note that the proportion of the labour force employed in producing good 1 (L_1/L) is equal to the share of wages in sector 1 (since wL = expenditure on good 1). Since $\sigma_1 \geqslant 1$, a rise in μ cannot increase this share, and so the weight given to the labour-intensive good either declines or remains constant. But then the desired capital–labour ratio must increase with μ, and uniqueness follows.

This is the simplest case. More generally, the desired capital–labour ratio k_i' may, under the present savings assumptions, be written as[4]

$$k' = k_1 \frac{\mu + k_2}{\mu + k_1}$$

[4] Since L_1/L is equal to the share of labour in sector 1, it is given by $\mu/(\mu + k_1)$. But then $L_2/L = k_1/(\mu + k_1)$ at full employment. So

$$\frac{L_1}{L} k_1 + \frac{L_2}{L} k_2 = k_1 \frac{\mu + k_2}{\mu + k_1}.$$

where k_i ($i = 1, 2$) is the capital–labour ratio in the ith sector. Differentiating logarithmically with respect to μ, writing $\sigma = \sigma_2 + \sigma_2$, one easily verifies that k' is increasing in μ provided $\sigma > 1$.[5] This, considering the high degree of aggregation implicit in a two-sector model, does not seem a very stringent uniqueness condition.

Lastly, it is possible to ensure that momentary equilibrium is unique by postulating a common utility function for all members of the economy. This point however is more conveniently taken up at a later stage (p. 239).

Before leaving this part of the problem, it is worthwhile drawing attention to one obvious implication of the 'Uniqueness Proposition'. If we imagine short-period equilibrium to be established by a series of (rather rapid) adjustments of the kind

$$\dot{w} = h_L X_L, \dot{q} = H_K X_K, h_L, h_K > 0 \tag{12.5}$$

then it is evident that uniqueness implies that this adjustment process converges on to the unique momentary equilibrium. Hence in this simple model, the uniqueness of momentary equilibrium not only ensures a well-defined equilibrium accumulation path for the economy, but also allows us to tell some kind of story (e.g., (12.5)) of how it comes about that the economy follows a path consisting of momentary equilibria.

V   THE STEADY STATE

If we write s as savings per head in terms of investment good and abstract from depreciation, then one evidently has the following equation to describe the manner in which the economy's capital-labour ratio is changing:

$$\frac{\dot{k}}{k} = \frac{s}{k} - n \tag{12.6}$$

where n is the rate of growth of the labour force.

[5] $\text{Log } k' = \log k_1 + \log (\mu + k_2) - \log (\mu + k_1)$

$$\frac{\partial \log k'}{\partial \mu} = \frac{1}{\mu}\sigma_1 + \frac{1}{\mu}\frac{\mu + \sigma_2 k_2}{\mu + k_2} - \frac{1}{\mu}\frac{\mu + \sigma_1 k_1}{\mu + k_1} = \frac{1}{\mu}\left(\frac{\sigma_2 \mu + \mu + k_2 \sigma}{\mu + k_2} - \frac{\mu + \sigma_1 k_1}{\mu + k_1}\right) > 0$$

if $\sigma > 1$.

It is customary to define a steady state by such values of k for which $s/k = n$ (s is of course a function of k). But this is unnecessarily restrictive. A value of k for which $s/k \geqslant n$ but $q = 0$ ($\mu = \infty$), or one for which $s/k \leqslant n$ but $w = 0$ ($\mu = 0$), has an equally good claim to be regarded as a long-run equilibrium, since changes in the quantity of a 'free' factor are of no economic significance.

Consider the problem of whether a steady-state equilibrium exists. Suppose $K = 0$, $L > 0$ (i.e., $k = 0$), and that the associated momentary equilibrium value of μ, say $\underline{\mu} > 0$. Then evidently for $\mu < \underline{\mu}$, k cannot diminish further, but either remains constant or increases. But then (12.2) is violated and the momentary equilibrium cannot be unique for $k = 0$. Similarly, if $K > 0$, $L = 0$ ($k = \infty$) and the associated μ, call it $\bar{\mu} < \infty$, raising μ above $\bar{\mu}$ either leaves k unchanged or reduces it so once again violating the condition for the uniqueness of momentary equilibrium. Hence, in general, if momentary equilibrium is unique for all $0 \leqslant k \leqslant \infty$, then there must be some $\underline{k}$ such that $\mu = 0$ and some $\bar{k}$, such that $\mu_1 = \infty$. Inada (1963) has taken $\underline{k} = 0$, $\bar{k} = \infty$, but this is required only if we wish to ensure a steady-state equilibrium where all factor prices are positive.

The existence of a steady state under the extended uniqueness assumption (momentary equilibrium is unique for all k), is now easy. If $s/k > n$ all k, then $\bar{k}$ a steady state where capital is free exists; if $s/k < n$ all k, then $\underline{k}$ a state where labour is free exists; if neither of these eventualities occur, then for some k^*, $\underline{k} < k^*$, $< \bar{k}$, $s/k^* = n$, a steady state, and both factors have a positive price. It is quite clear from this that the system will also always approach some steady state, whatever the initial conditions.

There remains the question of whether the steady state is unique. A necessary and sufficient condition for this to be so is that $V(k)(k - k^*) < 0$ where $V(k) = s/k - n$ and k^* is a given steady state value of k. That the condition is sufficient is obvious. We prove necessity by diagram.

In figure 12.2 we have plotted $V(k)$, first as a solid curve, which satisfies the uniqueness condition and where a steady state with positive factor prices exists. If $V(k) > 0$ all k we have a unique steady state at $\bar{k}$, and if $V(k) < 0$ all k a unique steady state at $\underline{k}$ and evidently once again the uniqueness condition holds. If $V(k) < 0$ for points to the left of E, then the uniqueness condition is violated but then also both $\underline{k}$ and E are equilibria. If $V(k) > 0$ to the right of E, both $\bar{k}$ and E are equilibria. The condition is thus necessary.

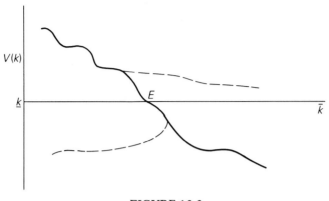

FIGURE 12.2

The condition will hold when $V(k)$ is a diminishing function of k. This in turn is assured if only capitalists save or if, when savings are proportional to income, the consumption sector is the more capital-intensive. (For simple proofs, see Hahn and Matthews, 1964.)

An Extension

If the production set of the economy is convex, then the uniqueness of the momentary equilibrium can also be established if one assumes that all individuals have the same strictly quasi-concave homogeneous utility functions of degree one. In that case community indifference fields which do not intersect exist and they are strictly convex. This is an elementary result which I shall take for granted. The main question arises in the specification of the common utility function.

It would seem absurd to postulate that the utility depends only on current consumption and additions to the stock of assets. In that case the actual level of assets is not valued, and that seems more far-fetched than even these exercises warrant. Instead I shall assume that utility depends on current consumption and the permanent consumption embodied in the capital stock.

Let K^* be the capital stock held t moments from now, where t is as small as desired. If q is the rental on capital in terms of consumption good, then we write $Q = qK^*$. Q is then the permanent consumption embodied in K^* with stationary expectations. We postulate the utility function:[6]

$$U = Q^a C^b \qquad a + b = 1, b > 0$$

where C = current consumption. This function is evidently more specialized than required by the introductory paragraph of this section, but it is convenient. The budget constraint is written as

$$p(K^* - K) + C = qK + wL$$

where all prices are in terms of consumption good. We maximize U subject to this and also $K^* - K \geqslant 0$. It is not possible to decumulate capital. Proceeding in the normal way, one finds for t small

$$\dot{K}/K = \max(o, ay/k - b)$$

where y = output per head, k = capital per head in numeraire. If we subtract n, the rate of increase in the labour supply, from both sides of this expression, we obtain a differential equation in k, the capital–labour ratio. This equation is well defined for any initial conditions. For evidently the ratio of expenditure on consumption to the desired value of capital is a constant and hence the arguments of (i) with minor modifications apply. Existence of a steady state is proved as before.

We may now also note that the production assumptions can be made less restrictive for this model. What is required is a convex production set, which is additive, contains the origin and does not permit the output of anything in positive amount without input. We may write the members of this set as the vectors x, the positive components of which measure outputs of the two goods and the negative components of which measure inputs. With any momentary equilibrium there will be associated some efficiency price vector v such that, if x is a momentary equilibrium vector, $vx \geqslant vx'$

[6] Strictly speaking, Q should be defined in terms of permanent consumption from all sources, i.e., including from prospective labour income. If expectations are taken as static, i.e., if rising labour income is not anticipated, no difficulties arise and the reader can easily modify the account in the text. If however permanent consumption is defined in terms of the present value of wealth from all sources, with perfect foresight, then the whole model is converted into a Ramsay kind problem. The assumption of the text may be rationalized by supposing that no expectations of future labour income are formulated.

all feasible x'. Of course there may be a whole cone of these v's satisfying this inequality, but the strict convexity of the community indifference curves ensures that only one of these will be compatible with momentary equilibrium. None of these postulates excludes the possibility of joint production. The Inada condition may now be stated in terms of the efficiency prices of the capital input. Keeping labour constant, one requires that this price should go to zero as k goes to infinity and that it should go to infinity as k goes to zero.

VI   CONCLUDING REMARKS

It is evident that in all these constructions the condition that the equilibrium at a moment of time be unique is crucial. The rest of the story is really concerned with ensuring that there is a steady state with positive factor prices. But the assumptions required to establish uniqueness of momentary equilibrium are all terrible assumptions. People differ in the assets they hold in their age and, alas, in their tastes. Simple proportional savings assumptions no doubt have their place in political arithmetic but seem rather desperate at this level. Moreover, assuming all these uniqueness problems away prevents us from facing the interesting, although admittedly philosophical, question of what is supposed to happen when the assumptions do not hold. After all, some decisions are taken at any moment of time.

It seems likely that the way out of many of these problems is to examine paths which are not equilibrium paths. Of course this will be a good deal more difficult. It will also mean that we shall want to abandon the malleability assumption. There is a great deal to learn.

REFERENCES

Drandakis, E. M. (1963), 'Factor Substitution in the Two-sector Growth Model', *Review of Economic Studies*, **30**.

Hahn, F. H. and Matthews, R. C. O. (1964), 'The Theory of Growth: A Survey', *Economic Journal*, **74**.

Inada, K. (1963), 'On a Two-sector Model of Economic Growth: Comments and a Generalization', *Review of Economic Studies*, **30**.

Meade, J. E. (1961), *A Neo-Classical Theory of Economic Growth*, Oxford University Press.

Solow, R. M. (1961-2), 'Note on Uzawa's Two-sector Model of Economic Growth', *Review of Economic Studies*, **29**.

Takayama, A. (1963), 'On a Two-sector Model of Economic Growth: A Comparative Statics Analysis', *Review of Economic Studies*, **30**.

Uzawa, H. (1961-2), 'On a Two-sector Model of Economic Growth', *Review of Economic Studies*, **29**.

Uzawa, H. (1963), 'On a Two-sector Model of Economic Growth: II', *Review of Economic Studies*, **30**.

13

Equilibrium Dynamics with Heterogeneous Capital Goods

I INTRODUCTION

It is now almost ten years since Solow (1956) showed that, in a one-good world with a 'well-behaved' neoclassical production function, all full-employment equilibrium paths approach the steady-state path.[1] An equilibrium path is one where at all times there is no *ex ante* excess demand in the markets for goods and factors and where producers have at all times that combination of inputs which they would wish to have at the going prices. Indeed, it is what Harrod called a 'warranted' path. The possibility of factor substitution means that there is a variety of warranted paths depending on initial conditions, and Solow showed that all such paths would, under suitable assumptions, approach a particular one.

Solow's work was soon extended to an economy producing one capital, and one consumption good (Hahn and Matthews, 1964). Once again, for all cases where the initial conditions defined a unique path and where production functions were 'well behaved', it could be shown that all equilibrium paths would converge to one particular such path (the 'golden age' path).

It is widely believed that these results are crucially related to the postulate that factor proportions are variable. No doubt in the context of these models this is so. But it would appear that the assumption that there is only one single capital good is of equal importance. Indeed, it is the purpose of this paper to show that the 'Solowesque' results for equilibrium paths do not extend to a

[1] I am much indebted to discussions with Professors Meade and Solow and with Dr J. A. Mirrlees. They cleared away cobwebs and nonsense. They are not responsible for what remains.

world with heterogeneous capital goods. I postpone until the end of the exercise a more general discussion of why this should be the case.

II THE ASSUMPTIONS

Assumption (A1) There is one consumption good and there are m different kinds of capital goods.

Assumption (A2) The production functions everywhere are Cobb–Douglas. No output of any good is possible without the input of some labour and the input of at least one capital good. Every capital good is used in at least one industry and there is no joint production.

Assumption (A3) Capital lasts for ever and there are no intermediate goods.

Assumption (A4) The labour force grows at a constant proportionate rate n.

Assumption (A5) Workers do not save; capitalists do not consume.

Some of these assumptions are stronger than strictly required. Thus, if there is more than one consumption good but the proportion of wage income spent on each is constant, the story would not be much changed. Again, (A3) could be replaced by the supposition of 'radio-active' decay and (A4) by the postulate of uniform 'Harrod-neutral' technical change everywhere. But not much would be gained and some simplicity lost.

(A2) has been introduced for two reasons. First, the Cobb–Douglas production function is a 'well-behaved' neoclassical function and it allows substitution between all finite levels of input, and since we wish to concentrate on the consequences of heterogeneity of capital goods, these are desirable properties. Second, although the differential equations we shall have to consider are by no means simple, they are a great deal simpler than they would have been for a less special class of production function. Moreover, it is my strong impression that nothing of what follows is crucially dependent on the special form of production function chosen, and should carry over to other 'well-behaved' functions.

III NOTATION

We shall give the consumption good the subscript 0 and let $i = 1, \ldots, m$ be the subscripts of the capital goods. A Latin symbol without a subscript always denotes an m-vector with components whose subscripts run from 1 to m. We take the wage as identically equal to unity (labour is the numéraire) and we write P_i as the *supply* price of the ith good in terms of labour and Q_i as the *demand* price of the ith good in terms of labour. R_i will be the rate of profit on the ith capital good.

One defines Y_i as the output *per man* employed in the ith industry and K_{ij} as the amount of the jth capital good used in the ith industry *per worker* employed there. Also K_i is the total amount of the ith kind of capital divided by the total labour force, while L_i is the *proportion* of the labour force employed in the ith industry.

We adopt the following conventions:

(a) small letters denote the log of capital letters; e.g.,

$$p_i = \log P_i; \quad p = \{\log P_1, \ldots, \log P_m\};$$

(b) all summation are over $i = 1, \ldots, m$ or $j = 1, \ldots, m$;
(c) a dot over a symbol denotes the operation d/dt.
Other notation will be introduced as required.

IV THE MODEL

In the notation just introduced, (A2) is formulated as:[2]

[2] The 'original' production function is of the form

$$\bar{y}_i = \prod_j \bar{K}_{ij}^{a_{ij}} \bar{L}_i^{a_{i0}}, \quad a_{i0} = 1 - \sum_j a_{ij}$$

where $\bar{y}_i$ is output of good i, $\bar{K}_{ij}$ is capital of the jth kind employed in the ith industry, and $\bar{L}_i$ is labour force employed in the ith industry. Hence

$$\frac{\bar{y}_i}{\bar{L}_i} = \frac{\prod_j \bar{K}_{ij}^{a_{ij}}}{\bar{L}_i^{\sum_j a_{ij}} \bar{L}_i^{a_{i0}}} \bar{L}_i^{a_{i0}} \Rightarrow y_i = \prod_j K_{ij}^{a_{ij}}$$

where y_i, K_{ij} are as defined in the text. Hence (13.1) follows immediately by taking the log.

$$y_i = \sum_j \alpha_{ij} k_{ij} \quad i = 0, \ldots, m, \alpha_{ij} \geqslant 0 \text{ all } j, \alpha_{ij} > 0 \text{ some } j, \quad (13.1)$$

$$\sum_j \alpha_{ij} + \alpha_{i0} = 1, \quad \text{all } i = 0, \ldots, m.$$

Suppose that inputs are bought at the 'demand' price, Q. Then cost minimization gives, for $P_i > 0$, $Q_i > 0$,

$$p_i + y_i = \text{constant} \qquad i = 0, \ldots, m \qquad (13.2)$$

$$k_{ij} + r_j + q_j = \text{constant} \qquad i = 0, \ldots, m, j = 1, \ldots, m. \qquad (13.3)$$

Here (13.2) and (13.3) are the usual marginal product–reward relationships for a Cobb–Douglas world.[3] Substituting for k_{ij} in (13.1) from (13.3) and the result into (13.2) gives

$$p_i - \sum_j \alpha_{ij} q_j - \sum_j \alpha_{ij} r_j = \text{constant} \qquad i = 0, \ldots, m. \qquad (13.4)$$

The last m equations of (13.4) may be written more compactly. Let $e_i + q_i = p_i$ and let $e = \{e_1, \ldots, e_m\}$. Then if A is the $(m \times m)$ matrix (α_{ij}) we obtain

$$e + (I - A)q - Ar = \text{vector of constant, say } b. \qquad (13.5)$$

If a good is to be newly produced, then its supply price cannot be more than its demand price. Indeed, because of perfect competi-

---

[3] Notice that (13.2) is the log of the inverse of the share of wages in the profits in the ith industry since

$$P_i y_i = \frac{P_i \bar{y}_i}{w \bar{L}_i} = \frac{1}{a_{i0}} (w = 1)$$

since the production function is Cobb–Douglas. Similarly, (13.3) is the log of the ratio of the share of the jth kind of capital over the share of the wages in the ith industry since

$$K_{ij} Q_j R_j = \frac{\bar{K}_{ij}}{\bar{L}_i} \frac{Q_j}{w} R_j = \frac{a_{ij}}{a_{i0}}$$

since

$$\frac{K_{ij} Q_j R_j}{P_i \bar{y}_i} = a_{ij} \qquad \text{and} \qquad \frac{w \bar{L}_i}{P_i \bar{y}_i} = a_{i0} (w = 1).$$

tion considerations we shall require $e_i = 0$ when $L_i > 0$ and $e_i > 0$ if and only if $L_i = 0$. That is, we shall require

$$e_i L_i = 0, e_i \geqslant 0 \qquad i = 1, \dots, m. \tag{13.6}$$

Since (as we shall see) $L_0 > 0$ always, we also require

$$P_0 = Q_0. \tag{13.7}$$

We now turn to the market for goods. The markets for capital goods are cleared when

$$K_i = \sum_j K_{ji} L_j + K_{0i} L_0 \qquad i = 1, \dots, m.$$

Multiplying both sides by $R_i Q_i$, this becomes

$$R_i Q_i K_i = \sum_j c_{ji} L_j + c_{0i} L_0 \qquad i = 1, \dots, m \tag{13.8}$$

where

$$c_{ji} = R_i Q_i K_{ji} = \frac{\alpha_{ji}}{\alpha_{j0}}.$$

The labour market is cleared when

$$\sum_j L_j + L_0 = 1. \tag{13.9}$$

Lastly, the market for consumption goods is cleared when[4]

$$L_0 = \alpha_{00}. \tag{13.10}$$

[4] By (A5), market-clearing for the consumption good implies

$$w\bar{L} = P_0 \bar{y}_0. \tag{1}$$

Also, we have from the Cobb–Douglas production function that in perfect competition

$$\frac{w\bar{L}_0}{P\bar{y}_0} = a_{00}. \tag{2}$$

(1) and (2) imply that $w\bar{L}_0 / w\bar{L} = a_{00}$; i.e., $L_0 = a_{00}$ since $L_0 = \bar{L}_0 / \bar{L}$ by definition.

This last equation follows from (A5) whereby the proportion of labour employed in the consumption goods industry is equal to labour's share in that industry which by (A2) is constant.

If we consider equation (13.4) with $i = 0$, and then the equations (13.5), (13.6), (13.7), (13.8), (13.9) and (13.10), we find that we have $3(m + 1) + 1$ relationships. Our unknowns are q, e, r, L, L_0, p_0, q_0; i.e., there are $4(m + 1) - 1$ of these. Hence we have $(m - 1)$ degrees of freedom. This is just as it should be, since precisely $(m - 1)$ demand conditions have remained unspecified by our savings assumption.

Now the rate of return on holding the ith capital good is given by

$$R_i + \dot{q}_i \qquad i = 1, \ldots, m.$$

In a world of perfect competition which is also in equilibrium, individuals must be indifferent between the various capital goods they hold, and so one has

$$R_1 + \dot{q}_1 = R_2 + \dot{q}_2 = \ldots R_m + q_m = \mu \text{ (say)} \tag{13.11}$$

or

$$R_i = \mu - \dot{q}_i \qquad i = 1, \ldots, m.$$

Here $\dot{q}_i$, etc., must be interpreted as the expected rate of change in the ith price. However, when attention is focused on equilibrium paths, expected and actual prices coincide. The model will tell us at a moment of time $t = 0$ that given, say, the expectations $(\dot{q}_i - \dot{q}_m)$, $i = 1, \ldots, m - 1$, what the capital–labour ratios in various activities must be in order that for all newly produced goods production costs be covered and also for (13.11) to be satisfied. However, once initial expectations have been specified, since they must be fulfilled, the development of the system through time should also be determined.

This will become clearer when the main equations have been cast into recursive form. Here we simply note that, when the story starts, we are given no information as to the distribution of investment between the various capital assets. If such information were to be provided by, say, the introduction of suitable investment demand functions, then this would 'close' the system, but by the same token it would determine what price expectations would have to be.

V BALANCED GROWTH

We consider a path for which (a) $e = 0$ all t, i.e., $P_i = Q_i$ all i; (b) $\dot{p} = 0$, $\dot{p}_0 = 0$, and (c) $\dot{K} = 0$. We call this the balanced growth path.

From (13.11) one has $R_1 = R_2 = \ldots = R_m$ along such a path. By (A4) the common rate of profit is equal to n, the rate of population growth. Let r^* be a vector with all components equal to $\log n$. Then we solve

$$(I - A)p^* - Ar^* = b \tag{13.5'}$$

for the prices ruling on a balanced growth path. Since the matrix A satisfies the Hawkins–Simon condition (see Hahn and Matthews, 1964) by (A2), $(I - A)^{-1}$ exists and is a positive matrix. The typical component of the vector of constants on the right-hand side of (13.5') is easily found to be

$$\sum_j \alpha_{ij} \log \alpha_{ij} - \alpha_{i0} \log \alpha_{i0}.$$

On solving, we find that the system determines a unique strictly positive P^*. Substituting this and r^* in the equation $i = 0$ of (13.4), we solve for $P_0^* > 0$.

Next we note that

$$L_j/\alpha_{j0} = L_j P_j Y_j \qquad j = 1, \ldots, m.$$

So that (13.8), in view of the definition of c_{ji}, may also be written

$$R_i P_i K_i = \sum_j \alpha_{ji} L_j P_j Y_j + c_{0i} L_{0j} \qquad i = 1, \ldots, m. \tag{13.8'}$$

But on any equilibrium path one has

$$L_j P_j Y_j = P_j(\dot{K}_j + nK_j) \qquad j = 1, \ldots, m.$$

Substituting this into (13.8') and using (13.10), one has

$$R_i P_i K_i = \sum_j \alpha_{ji} P_j(\dot{K}_j + nK_j) + c_{0j}\alpha_{00} \qquad i = 1, \ldots, m. \tag{13.8''}$$

On a balanced growth path $R_i = n$ all i and $\dot{K}_j = 0$ all j. Using this and the P^* already solved for, $(13.8'')$ can be used to find K^*, the vector of balanced growth capital–labour ratios. In matrix notation this is found from

$$\{P_i^* K_i^*\} = \frac{1}{n} (I - A') c^{-1}$$

where the left-hand side is the vector with components $P_i^* K_i^*$ and c is the vector with components c_{0i}, α_{00}. Since c is semi-positive, $(I - A')^{-1}$ is a positive matrix and $P_i^* > 0$, we find $K_i^* > 0$ all i.

That the balanced growth path is unique seems self-evident. In particular, there cannot be another path in which some of the capital goods are not produced. For suppose the rth kind of capital not to be produced. Then if it is used in the production of, say, the sth kind which is produced, the marginal product of the rth kind of capital in the production of the sth would tend to infinity, which is impossible. But if the sth kind of capital is not produced then a similar argument applies to say the tth kind, into the production of which s enters. Proceeding in this way and recalling that the production of the consumption good requires some kind of capital, we easily see that all types of capital goods must be produced on a balanced growth path.

VI   MOMENTARY EQUILIBRIUM

We consider a moment $t = 0$ with an arbitrarily given capital–labour ratio vector $K(0)$. We wish to examine the equilibrium at this moment of time. To do so, we already know that $(m - 1)$ unknowns of the model must be arbitrarily specified. Let us do so by fixing

$$R_i(0) - R_m(0), \qquad i = 1, \ldots, m - 1, R_i > 0 \text{ all } i,$$

$$R_m(0) \leqslant R_i(0) \qquad \text{all } i.$$

This then is equivalent to supposing that at $t = 0$ there are given certain expectations of changes in the relative prices of capital goods. The first question we consider is the existence of an equilibrium at $t = 0$.

Although it is tiresome, it will be convenient and necessary to have further notation. We shall write $\hat{R}(0)$ for the $(m - 1)$ vector with components $[R_i(0) - R_m(0)]$ and we write $V_i \equiv R_i Q_i$, $v = \{v_1, \ldots, v_m\}$. One also defines the set S by

$$S = \{L/L_i \geqslant 0, \Sigma L_i = 1 - \alpha_{00}\}$$

and C as the $m \times m$ matrix $[c_{ji}]$ and c as the $m -$ vector: $\{c_{01}, \ldots, c_{0m}\}\alpha_{00}$. We continue to use lower-case letters to denote the log of capital letters.

For what follows we shall now suppose that c is a strictly positive vector. This, of course, means that the consumption good sector uses every capital good in its production. This is less restrictive than appears at first sight, since we can think of the consumption good as a composite good in which the various individual goods are in fixed proportions.

The argument establishing the existence of momentary equilibrium now proceeds by stages. Since $\hat{R}(0)$ and $K(0) > 0$ are constant, they will be omitted as arguments from functions which depend on them.

(a) Combining (13.8) and (13.10) yields:

$$\{V_i K_i(0)\} = CL + c. \tag{13.12}$$

Evidently for every $L \in S$ there exist values of V_i, call them $V_i(L)$, such that (13.12) is satisfied and $V(L) > 0$ since $c > 0$.

(b) We may write (13.5) as

$$\alpha + q - Av(L) = b \tag{13.5''}$$

where V takes the value determined by (a). For L fixed, $V(L)$ is fixed. Since $\hat{R}(0)$ is given, knowledge of R_m determines $R_1, \ldots, R_{m-1}$. From the definition of $V(L)$, knowledge of R_m gives Q. Hence we may write

$$Q = Q(R_m, L). \tag{13.13}$$

Since $R_i > 0$ all i, $V(L) > 0$, $Q > 0$ and is strictly diminishing in R_m. We may now write (13.5'') as

$$\alpha(R_m, L) + q(R_m, L) - Av(L) = b. \tag{13.14}$$

By the above argument e is strictly increasing in R_m.

(c) Consider the function

$$F_i(L_i, R_m) = \max\{0, L_i + [1 - E_i(R_m, L)]\} \tag{13.15}$$

(where, of course, $\log E_i = e_i$). Clearly, $F_i \geqslant 0$ all i. We wish to confirm that for some value of R_m one has $F(L, R_m) \in S$; i.e.,

$$\sum_i F_i(R_m, L_i) = 1 - \alpha_{00}.$$

By our choice of R_m such that $\hat{R}_i \geqslant 0$ all i, we may let $R_m \to 0$. But then $Q_m(R_m, L) \to +\infty$ and so by (13.14) $E_m(R_m, L) \to 0$. But then certainly there is some value of R_m small enough[5] so that $\Sigma F_i(L_i, R_m) > 1 - \alpha_{00}$. On the other hand, as $R_m \to \infty$, $Q_i(R_m, L) \to 0$ all i, and by the same argument as before, $E_i(R_m, L) \to +\infty$. Hence for some R_m large enough,

$$\sum_i F_i(L_i, R_m) < 1 - \alpha_{00}. \tag{13.16}$$

Since E is monotonic in R_m, we know that there is only one value of R_m satisfying (13.16). Since $V(L)$ is evidently continuous in L and Q is continuous in R_m, one has $R_m(L)$ continuous in L.

(d) Consider now the mapping

$$f_i(L) = \max\langle 0, L_i + \{1 - E_i[R_m(L), L]\}\rangle \quad i = 1, \ldots, m. \tag{13.17}$$

Then, by construction, $L \in S$ implies $f(L) \in S$. Thus (13.17) is a continuous map of S into itself, and so there is a fixed point L^* such that

$$L_i^* = \max\langle 0, L_i^* + \{1 - E_i[R_m(L^*), L^*]\}\rangle \quad i = 1, \ldots, m.$$

If $L_i^* > 0$ then it must be that $E_i = 1$ (and so $Q_i^* = P_i^*$). If $L_i^* = 0$ then it must be that $E_i > 1$ (and so $Q_i^* < P_i^*$).

All this is just as it should be to satisfy (13.5) and (13.6). By inserting Q^*, r^*, into the equation $i = 0$ in (13.4) we obtain $P_0^* > 0$, the price of the consumption good. Thus, on our assumptions a momentary equilibrium does indeed exist.

Now let us suppose (we return to the point shortly) that the equilibrium for $K(0)$, $\hat{R}(0)$ is unique at $t = 0$, and let us consider the system at a very short interval after $t = 0$, i.e., at $t = 0 + \epsilon$.

From (13.11) we know that the equilibrium of $t = 0$ has determined $\dot{q}_i(0) - \dot{q}_m(0)$, $(i = 1, \ldots, m-1)$, and since expectations

---

[5] Since then $F_m(\ ) \to L_m + 1$ and all $F_i(\ ) > 0$.

are to be correct, this means that $q_i(0 + \epsilon) - q_m(0 + \epsilon)$, $(i = 1, \ldots, m - 1)$, are also fully determined. Moreover, since the equilibrium at $t = 0$ determined $\dot{K}_i(0)$ $(i = 1, \ldots, m)$, we also know $K_i(0 + \epsilon)$, $i = 1, \ldots, m$. It follows that at $t = 0 + \epsilon$ we have lost the $(m - 1)$ degrees of freedom we had at $t = 0$. We conclude that, once the expectations at $t = 0$ are known, and provided equilibrium is unique at every moment of time, the whole subsequent development of the system is known.

Quite clearly, the uniqueness assumption is crucial here (as indeed it was found to be in the 'two-sector' models). Unfortunately there seems to be no simple economically meaningful or appealing restriction available to ensure that the initial conditions determine a unique path.

For instance, suppose $K(0)$, $\hat{R}(0)$ to be such as to yield one momentary equilibrium with L^* strictly positive (all goods are newly produced). The question asked may now be, Does there exist some other equilibrium L^{**} where once again all goods are newly produced? Since we are only interested in situations where $Q_i = P_i$ all i, one has $e = 0$ in (13.5) and each $R_iQ_iK_i$ may be written as a function of R_m, say $\pi_i(R_m)$, since (13.5) determines Q as a function of R_m. We may then write (13.12) as

$$\pi_i(R_m) - CL = c. \tag{13.12'}$$

Moreover, we are only interested in situations for which

$$\Sigma L_i = 1 - \alpha_{00}. \tag{13.18}$$

We are told that (13.12') and (13.18) have at least one solution R_m^* and $L^* \gg 0$. The question of whether this type of solution is unique turns then on the global properties of the Jacobian

$$\begin{bmatrix} \left\{ \dfrac{\partial \pi_i(R_m)}{\partial R_m} \right\} - C \\ 0 \qquad i' \end{bmatrix} \tag{13.19}$$

where $\{\partial \pi_i / \partial R_m\}$ is an m vector and i' the unit row vector. It is known for instance that, if the principal minors of (13.19) are all one-signed over a given domain, then the solution over a specified range will also be unique. Inspection of (13.19) quickly convinces one that there just are no simple or appealing assumptions to make on C and the functions $\pi_i(\ )$ to ensure this result. Since only (rather strong) sufficient conditions for uniqueness (univalence) are available, nothing much further can be said. However, it should be noted that one may readily construct theoretical examples of the model here presented, where equilibrium is definitely not unique.

In the 'two-sector' story (i.e., $m = 1$), since the savings assumption fixes L_0, (13.18) means that L_1 is also fixed, and it is then easy to see that the system would have only one solution. Here, however, there is always the possibility of a reallocation of production between the various capital goods so that multiple equilibria cannot be excluded. Moreover, of course, we have to take account of situations where equilibrium gives $L_i = 0$ for some i, so that the equilibrium price of that good is not equal to its unit cost of production.

Since there may be a number of equilibrium solutions, one cannot predict future events from initial conditions and given expectations. But we shall now simplify sufficiently drastically to remove this difficulty and show that we are even then not much better off.

VII   TWO CAPITAL GOODS

We shall now suppose there to be two capital goods only, and we shall introduce an assumption which allows us to suppose for $0 \leqslant t \leqslant T$, a unique momentary equilibrium in which both capital goods are newly produced.

From (13.12'), we have

$$CL = \{\pi_i(R_m) - c_i\} \tag{13.12''}$$

where it will be recalled that $\pi_i(R_m) = V_i K_i$ on the supposition that the price of i just covers its unit costs and $R(0)$, $K(0)$ are given. It is easily verified that $\pi_i(R_m)$ is strictly increasing in R_m, and so we may always find R_m such as to give $\pi_i(R_m) > c_i$ ($i = 1, 2$).

Now if (13.12'') has a solution with $L \geqslant 0$ and $\Sigma L_i = 1 - \alpha_{00}$ and if we suppose $c_{ii}/c_{ji} < 1$ ($i = 1, 2$), then, in view of the monotonicity of π_i in R_m, that solution must be unique. For if both R_m^* and R^{**} are equilibria with, say, $R_m^{**} > R_m^*$, then $\pi_i(R_m^{**}) - c_i >$

$\pi_i(R_m^*) - c_i$ $(i = 1, 2)$, and we easily find that on this assumption

$$C(L^{**} - L^*) \geqslant 0$$
$$i'(L^{**} - L^*) = 0$$

has no solution.

We therefore stipulate

Assumption (A6) There are only two capital goods $(m = 2)$. Each of these two capital goods industries always uses the output of the other more intensively than it does its own. Moreover, $K(0) \geqslant 0$ and $\hat{R}(0)$ are such as to allow our equilibrium with $L \geqslant 0$ at $t = 0$.

Occasionally we shall wish to vary the first part of (A6) to read:

Assumption (A7) The elasticity of production of each capital good with respect to an input of itself is less than the elasticities with respect to the input of the other capital good.

Neither of these assumptions is particularly 'reasonable' or the reverse. They are made to permit us to continue the story which in any case is coming to a sad end.

We are now supposing that the initial conditions and price expectations allow us to determine a unique equilibrium path for $0 \leqslant t \leqslant T$ where the prices of capital goods continuously cover unit production costs. To see what happens, let us differentiate (13.5), with $e = 0$, with respect to t to obtain

$$A^{-1}(I - A)\dot{p} = \dot{r}. \qquad (13.20)$$

Let the left-hand matrix be written as G having elements g_{ij}. Routine calculations give

$$g_{11} - g_{21} = \frac{1 - \alpha_{20}}{|A|} - 1$$

$$g_{12} - g_{22} = \frac{\alpha_{10} - 1}{|A|} + 1.$$

Suppose for a moment that $\alpha_{10} = \alpha_{20}$, so that (A6) implies (A7). Then, in subtracting the second from the first equation in (13.20), we obtain

$$\left(\frac{1 - \alpha_{20}}{|A|} - 1\right)(\dot{p}_1 - \dot{p}_2) = \dot{r}_1 - \dot{r}_2.$$

Or, using (13.11),

$$\left(1 + \frac{\alpha_{20} - 1}{|A|}\right)(R_1 - R_2) = \dot{r}_1 - \dot{r}_2. \tag{13.21}$$

Let us call the coefficient of $(R_1 = R_2)$, h, and note that $h > 0$ since certainly $\alpha_{20} < 1$ and $|A| < 0$ by (A6). Now consider the expression

$$W = 1/2(R_1/R_2 - 1)^2 \qquad R_1 > 0, R_2 > 0.$$

Evidently $W > 0$ for all $R_1 \neq R_2$. Certainly also in the vicinity of a balanced growth path we may take $R_1 > 0$, $R_2 > 0$. Using (13.21), we find

$$\dot{W} = (R_1/R_2 - 1)hR_1/R_2(R_1 - R_2) > 0 \quad \text{for } R_1 \neq R_2. \tag{13.22}$$

It follows that, if the two rates of profit diverge at $t = 0$ and both goods continue to be produced, then they cannot come together again and the balanced growth path will not be attained; nor can it be approached asymptotically.

Similar conclusions can be derived from rather less special examples. By suitable manipulations we may cast (13.20) into the following form:

$$R_1 - R_2 = f_1 \dot{r}_1 - f_2 \dot{r}_2 \tag{13.23}$$

where, taking $f = |1 - A|/|A|$, one defines

$$f_1 = -\frac{1}{f}\left(\frac{\alpha_{11} - \alpha_{21}}{|A|} - 1\right)$$

$$f_2 = -\frac{1}{f}\left(\frac{\alpha_{22} - \alpha_{12}}{|A|} - 1\right).$$

Given (A7), one has $-1/f > 0$. The first term in brackets is also positive, and if α_{11} is small we may take the whole expression as positive, which we proceed to do.

Suppose $f_1 \leqslant f_2$. Then $R_1^{f_1} > R_2^{f_2}$ implies $R_1 > R_2$. If $R_1^{f_1}(0) \geqslant R_2^{f_2}(0)$, it then follows from (13.23) that $R_1^{f_1}/R_2^{f_2}$ is increasing, and so the two rates of profits continue to diverge. Suppose $f_1 > f_2$. Then $R_1^{f_1}(0) < R_2^{f_2}(0)$ implies $R_1(0) < R_2(0)$ and, again by (13.23), the two rates of profit will continue to diverge. We conclude that, as in the more special case, there is a wide class of initial conditions for which, on the supposition that we may determine prices by unit production costs, the system does not approach a balanced state.

Lastly, let us consider what happens if, at some $t = T$, one or the other of the capital goods ceases to be produced and its unit production costs exceed its market (demand) price.

Let us now use $V_i = R_i Q_i$ and suppose $L_2(T) = 0$ (henceforth we omit time subscripts). Then evidently (13.8), (13.9) and (13.10) determine V_1 and V_2. Moreover, as long as L_2 remains zero it must be true that

$$V_i K_i = \text{constant} \qquad i = 1, 2.$$

But since the second good is not produced, we have $\dot{k}_1 = -n$ and so

$$\dot{v}_2 + \dot{k}_2 = \dot{v}_2 - n = 0. \tag{13.24}$$

So the rental–wage ratio of the non-produced good must be rising. Subtracting (13.24) from $\dot{v}_1 + \dot{k}_1 = 0$, and noting that $\dot{k}_1 + n > 0$, since the first good is produced, we have, using (13.11),

$$\dot{v}_1 - \dot{v}_2 + \dot{k}_1 + n = 0 \tag{13.25}$$

or

$$\dot{v}_1 - \dot{v}_2 = (\dot{r}_1 - \dot{r}_2) + (\dot{p} - \dot{q}_2)$$
$$= (\dot{r}_1 - \dot{r}_2) - (R_1 - R_2) < 0.$$

Now it follows from (13.25) that, if $R_1(T) < R_2(T)$ and $f_1 > f_2$, then the rates of profit will continue to diverge even when the second good is no longer being produced. There is nothing in the story to prevent $L_2(T) = 0$ being a solution for $R_2(T) > R_1(T)$.

For instance, suppose $\alpha_{ii} = 0$ $(i = 1, 2)$. Then (A6) and (A7) certainly hold. One has $\alpha_{12} > g_{21}$ when $f_1 > f_2$. The rate of change of production costs is given by

$$\dot{p}_i(T) = \alpha_{ij}\dot{v}_j \qquad i = 1, 2, j \neq i. \tag{13.26}$$

Evidently $\dot{p}_1(T) - \dot{p}_2(T) > 0$, since $\dot{v}_2 - \dot{v}_1 > 0$. At the point of time at which the second good ceases to be produced, $P_2(T) = Q_2(T)$, and if thereafter the production cost exceeds the demand price, $P_2(T) > Q_2(T)$ so $\dot{p}_1(T) - \dot{q}_2(T)$ certainly > 0 and $R_1(T) - R_2(T) < 0$.

If at (T) the first good ceases to be produced, then if $R_1(T) > R_2(T)$, the reader can verify that the same unpleasant conclusions emerge for $f_1 < f_2$.

In contrast to the two-sector case (one consumption and one capital good), one must therefore conclude that not all equilibrium paths, where they exist, approach a balanced growth path. Indeed, many behave in a way which puts considerable strain on one's credulity and raises considerable doubts concerning the model.

VIII   SOME COMMENTS

It is time to take stock and to interpret the results. There are two main conclusions to be considered. First, in the case of heterogeneous capital goods, the problem of the non-uniqueness of momentary equilibrium is much more acute than in the two-sector case. Even when the initial expectations are given, the system may pursue a variety of equilibrium paths. Second, even when (in the two-capital case) a single equilibrium path is found, there is a wide class of initial conditions and values of the parameters for which such equilibrium paths do not approach the balanced growth path.

The first conclusion is largely ascribable to the fact that neo-classical growth models do not incorporate any explicit investment functions. The condition that the holding of all assets should be equally profitable (13.11) does not determine how much of each asset should be produced. It is thus possible that a given volume of savings may find a widely different allocation between the different kinds of investment at different price constellations, which are compatible with equilibrium. When there is only one capital good and we are concerned with full employment equilibrium paths, an investment function is not only unnecessary but may actually prevent the system having a solution. The question asked is, What must investment be in order to take up full employment savings? Having found it, since there is only the asset to hold, we may presume that that amount of investment will take place. With two capital goods this procedure is evidently not possible.

However, it is not clear how 'investment functions' can be grafted on to the model. The world considered is one of perfect competition, so that individual producers have no 'volume of demand for their product' to estimate, on which to base their investment decisions. At the same time, households, provided only that the rate of return of holding any asset is that of any other, must be regarded as indifferent as to whether their savings are invested in one or the other direction. Having stated this, we have also already provided sufficient reason for regarding the neo-classical equilibrium path as not very interesting as a description of the world, and it does not seem worthwhile pursuing the story much further.

On the other hand, if we consider an economy which is planned,[6] then many of these difficulties would disappear – and we return to this point presently.

The second of our conclusions is essentially ascribable to the fact that an equilibrium with heterogeneous capital goods is not specified for any moment of time unless it also includes expectations as to the relative capital goods prices at a subsequent moment of time. Given an investment allocation, we can find a set of expectations which must rule if equilibrium is to be possible. Alternatively, given the expectations, we can find a set of consistent investment allocations. The fact that the description of the present involves the future in an essential way must bear the responsibility for the unsatisfactory behaviour of the equilibrium path. For if expectations should turn out to be correct, then this requirement by itself to a large extent determines the subsequent evolution of the system. But, not surprisingly, there is only a restricted set of expectations for every given situation, which is consistent with an evolution of the system towards the balanced growth path. Once again, the supposition that expectations are not only correct but consequently that they are identical for all

---

[6] See Samuelson (1960). Here it is shown that the balanced growth path is a local saddle-point (in phase space) for all finite horizon efficient paths. Evidently this result is closely related to the one of the previous section – but the problem is different.

economic agents is a hard postulate to swallow, and undoubtedly makes equilibrium dynamics less attractive once we admit that there are hoes as well as shovels.

There remains an alternative interpretation, used by Meade in the two-sector case, of equilibrium paths. On this interpretation the government somehow ensures that the economy always follows a full-employment path with planned savings equal to planned investment. In the two-sector case this is not entirely unacceptable; in our case we must evidently suppose the government to be involved in far greater detail in the economy. In particular, if the government were to enforce any particular, detailed accumulation plan which is also 'efficient', then associated with such a plan will be a set of shadow prices (including their rate of change), which will satisfy the relationships of our model. If the efficient plan is one for which the balanced growth path is approached, then one particular equilibrium path out of a large number of possible ones has been chosen. This, however, is quite another story.

REFERENCES

Hahn, F. H. and Matthews, R. C. O. (1964), 'The Theory of Economic Growth: A Survey', *Economic Journal*, **74**.

Samuelson, P. A. (1960), 'Efficient Paths of Capital Accumulation in Terms of the Calculus of Variations', in *Mathematical Methods in the Social Sciences*, Stanford University Press.

Solow, R. M. (1956), 'A Contribution to the Theory of Economic Growth', *Quarterly Journal of Economics*, **70**.

14

On Warranted Growth Paths

Recently I showed (Hahn, 1966) that the steady-state path of an economy with more than one capital good was not the asymptotic state of all equilibrium paths. For some special cases I demonstrated that, indeed, all equilibrium paths diverged. This is in marked contrast to the well-known result of Solow for the one-sector world and to the equally familiar two-sector propositions. Partly through discussions with Mirrlees, I had become aware that my analysis bore a family resemblance to the 'local turnpike theorems' of Dosso, Samuelson (1959) and McKenzie (1963), which exploit the fact that the Neumann ray is a saddle-point[1] in the phase space of all intertemporally efficient paths. However, I could not make a firm connection, since my construction allowed for a separate consumption sector, a descriptive consumption function and an exogenously given labour force. The 'turnpike' results had none of these features. But further study of the problem has enabled me to clarify the connection between the descriptive and the 'planning' model, and it is the first purpose of this paper to report on this.

It has been shown by Kurz (1968) and Goldman (1968) that in the case of one capital good a descriptive model of a neoclassical economy can be converted into one where the equilibrium path taken by the economy is the same path it would take if its rate of change of consumption were governed by the Euler equations for an appropriately chosen Ramsey objective function. If that conclusion were to hold for any number of capital goods, then, since for many cases the Ramsey paths have a unique singular point which is also a saddle-point, it would follow that the same is true for a large class of descriptive economies. The second purpose of this paper is to examine this question.

---

[1] This is inexact terminology for the case where the differential equations in the vicinity of the steady state have roots which come in pairs $(+\lambda, -\lambda)$. These need not be real, which is *the* saddle-point case. We shall sometimes just call these motions catenary.

Lastly, I should like to take the opportunity to offer some rather general remarks on the economics of the problem discussed. These should be taken as supplementing the excellent recent analysis of Shell and Stiglitz (1967).

I THE MODEL

Consider a world of one consumption good (indexed '0') and m capital goods (indexed $1, \ldots, m$). Let $Y_i(t)$ ($i = 0, \ldots, m$) be the output *per man* at time t and $K_i(t)$ ($i = 1, \ldots, m$), the stock *per man* of the ith capital good at time t. Time arguments will be omitted when the context makes this safe.

Assumption (A1)   There exists a twice differentiable, concave efficiency frontier:

$$Y_1(t) = F[Y_0(t), Y_2(t), \ldots, Y_m(t), K_1(t), \ldots, K_m(t)]. \quad (14.1)$$

The choice of the output (per man) of the first capital good as the dependent variable is of course arbitrary.[2] Note that constant returns have been stipulated. We shall write F_i as the partial differential coefficient of F with respect to its ith argument and F_{ij} as the partial differential coefficient of F_i with respect to its jth argument.

Assumption (A2)   (a) capital goods last for ever; (b) the labour force grows at a given rate n; (c) there is no technical change.

Part (a) of this assumption is introduced for tidiness' sake only. Part (c) could be replaced by the supposition of a given and identical rate of Harrod-neutral technical change in all sectors.
   In view of (A2(b)), we may write

$$Y_i = \dot{K}_i + nK_i \quad i = 1, \ldots, m \qquad (14.2)$$

---

[2] For many purposes the analysis which follows could have been simplified by writing:

$$Y_0 = F[Y_1(t), \ldots, Y_m(t), K_1(t), \ldots, K_m(t)].$$

The reason I have not done so is that (14.1) makes comparison with the literature easier. I also felt there to be an expositional advantage in having the own rate of return of one capital good independent of price expectations.

and substitute this into (14.1). (A dot over a symbol denotes the operation d/dt.)

Assumption (A3) Let $P_i(t)$ be the price of the ith good, in terms of the first, at t and $\dot{P}_i^e(t)$ the rate at which, at t, this price is expected to change. Then (a) for all $i = 1, \ldots, m$, $\dot{P}_i(t) = \dot{P}_i^e(t)$ and (b) for all $i = 1, \ldots, m$, the own rates of return (including expected changes in capital values), in terms of good 1, are the same. This assumption is made because we are interested in the behaviour of warranted paths. It has nothing to recommend it on the grounds of realism and I return to it below (see section V).

Assumption (A4) At every t the economy is in competitive equilibrium.

This assumption is made for the same reasons as is (A3). It implies that, for all t,

$$P_i(t) = -F_i(t) \quad i = 0, \ldots, m$$

(where $F_i(t)$ is the shorthand notation for $F_i[Y_o(t), Y_2(t), \ldots, Y_m(t), K_1(t), \ldots, K_m(t)]$). From (A3(a) and (b)) we then have[3]

$$F_i(t)\, F_{m+1}(t) + F_{m+i}(t) = \dot{F}_i(t) \quad i = 2, \ldots, m \tag{14.3}$$

which is a well-known (Samuelson, 1959) necessary condition for the intertemporal efficiency of an accumulation path.

Assumption (A5) There is no saving out of wages and no consumption out of profit.

I make this assumption because the 'proportional' savings case has already been investigated by Samuelson (1959), because it is the

---

[3] Suppose I own one unit of good 1 and use it in production to gain $\partial Y_1/\partial K_1 = F_{m+1}$ units of good 1. I could also have bought $-1/F_i$ units of good i and gained

$$-F_i[-(1/F_i)\,(\partial Y_i/\partial K_i)] = F_{m+i}/F_i$$

units of good 1 by producing good i as well as the capital gain (loss) of $\dot{F}_i/F_i$. To be indifferent between these two courses of action we must have

$$F_{m+1} = -\frac{F_{m+i}}{F_i} + \frac{\dot{F}_i}{F_i},$$

which gives (14.3) of the text.

case in which the 'inverse optimum' approach would encounter the greatest difficulties, and because I used it in my earlier paper. In view of (A4), this assumption implies[4]

$$F - F_{m+1}K_1 - \sum_{i=2} (nF_i + F_{m+i}) K_i - \sum_{i=2} F_i \dot{K}_i = 0 \qquad (14.4a)$$

which it will be more convenient to write, using (14.2), as

$$(F_{m+1} - n) K_1 + \sum_{i=2} (nF_i + F_{m+i}) K_i + \sum_{i=2} F_i \dot{K}_i - \dot{K}_1 = 0.$$
$$(14.4)$$

Now, from (14.3) we have

$$F_{m+1} = \dot{F}_i - F_i F_{m+1} \quad i = 2, \dots, m.$$

So on substituting in (14.4) we have

$$(F_{m+1} - n)\left(K_1 - \sum_{i=2} F_i K_i\right) + \left(\sum_{i=2} \dot{F}_i K_i + \sum_{i=2} F_i \dot{K}_i - \dot{K}_1\right) = 0.$$
$$(14.4')$$

We note that the second term on the LHS is the value of capital in terms of capital good 1 and that the term in the last bracket is the rate of change in that value. However, for reasons which will become clear, we shall be interested in the behaviour of 'wealth' measured in terms of the consumption good. Let w represent this. Then on revaluation, (14.4') may be written[5]

---

[4] Let L be labour. Then since $-F_0$ is the price of consumption good in numeraire we have, from (A5), $-F_0 Y_0 = \partial(LY_1)/\partial L$. But using (14.2) in (14.1), we find

$$\frac{\partial(LY_1)}{\partial L} = F - F_{m+1}K_1 - \sum_{i=2} (nF_i + F_{m+i}) K_i - \sum_{i=2} F_i \dot{K}_i - F_0 Y_0,$$

and so (14.4a) follows.

[5] In steady state we can choose units in which to measure goods so that

$$F_0 = F_2 = F_m = -1.$$

Hence $\partial Y_i/\partial K_i = n, i = 1, \dots, m$ is a sufficient condition for (14.4'') to hold.

$$\left(F_{m+1} - n - \frac{\dot{F}_0}{F_0}\right) = \frac{\dot{w}}{w}. \tag{14.5}$$

I shall have more to say concerning this version of (14.4$'$) below.

Consider the systems (14.1), (14.3) and (14.4) with $K_i(0)$ ($i = 1, \ldots, m$) given (i.e., 'momentary' equilibrium). The unknowns are: $\dot{K}_i$ ($i = 1, \ldots, m$), $\ddot{K}_i$ ($i = 2, \ldots, m$), Y_0 and $\dot{Y}_0$. There are ($m + 1$) equations and ($2m + 1$) unknowns; this gives m degrees of freedom. However, we are only interested in paths along which expectations can be fulfilled, and so we require that (14.4a) should hold at all t. Differentiating (14.4a) with respect to t yields one further equation and no additional unknowns. Taking this into account, we have ($m-1$) degrees of freedom. Their significance was discussed in Hahn (1966). In a descriptive model such as this, they can be made good by stipulating the price expectations: $\dot{P}_i(0)/P_i(0)$, $i = 2, \ldots, m$. In a finite planning model the transversality conditions provide the missing information.

II   THE STEADY STATE

The system (14.1), (14.3) and (14.4) is said to be in steady state when

$$Y_i(t) = nK_i(t) \quad i = 1, \ldots, m \quad t \geqslant 0.$$

Clearly, the 'endowment', $K_i(0)$ ($i = 1, \ldots, m$), must be treated as an unknown in solving for the steady state of the economy. The equations in (14.4) provide the necessary extra information. Since we have $\ddot{K}_i = 0$ ($i = 2, \ldots, m$), we lose all degrees of freedom.

Assumption (A6)   The system (14.1), (14.3) and (14.4) has a unique steady-state solution

$$K_i^* (i = 1, \ldots, m), Y_0^*, \text{ with } K_i^* > 0 \text{ all } i.$$

This assumption implies a certain connectedness property of the production set, but it is sufficiently familiar to require no elaboration here.

K

In a steady state, (14.4) becomes

$$(n - F_{m+1}) K_1^* - \sum_{i=2} (nF_i + F_{m+i}) K_i^* = 0, \qquad (14.4'')$$

which will certainly be satisfied if all the terms in brackets are zero. By (A6) this must be the only steady-state solution; i.e.,[6]

$$\frac{\partial Y_i}{\partial K_i} = n \quad i = 1, \ldots, m.$$

It is painfully obvious that this is also the 'golden rule' path of the system; i.e.,

$$\frac{\partial Y_0}{\partial K_i} = 0 \text{ all } i.$$

III STABILITY

The question which now concerns us is this: consider the system (14.1), (14.3) and (14.4) with given endowments $K_i^*(0)$ and given expectations $\dot{P}_i(0)/P_i(0)$. We can trace its subsequent development on the assumption (A3) that all expectations are fulfilled. Will this development tend to the steady state?

In answering the question we shall consider an economy in the vicinity of a steady state, which, as it turns out, will mean that no complete answer can be provided. If it is true that, for all 'starting points' in this neighbourhood, the economy does not approach the steady state, then we can certainly assert that this state will not be approached from any starting point (since to do so it would have to pass through this small neighbourhood). Unfortunately, so strong a result is not generally available.

It will be convenient to adopt the following further notation and conventions:

$$R_i \equiv F_{m+1} F_i + F_{m+i} \quad i = 2, \ldots, m$$

---

[6] Let W be the value of capital in terms of the first capital good. Then (14.4') gives $(F_{m+1} - n) = \dot{W}/W$. But $-(1/F_0)$ is the price of good 1 in terms of the consumption good, and so $\dot{w}/w = \dot{W}/W - \dot{F}_0/F_0$.

where of course R_i depends on the arguments of F. I shall write

$$R_{im+j} = \frac{\partial R_i}{\partial K_j} + n \frac{\partial R_i}{\partial Y_j} \text{ and } R_{ij} = \frac{\partial R_i}{\partial Y_j}.$$

We also chose units in which to measure goods such that, in steady state,

$$F_0 = F_2 = \ldots = F_m = -1.$$

I define Z to be the value of capital per man at steady-state prices, i.e., in view of the convention just adopted:

$$Z = \sum_{i=1} K_i.$$

Lastly, I shall use lower-case letters to denote deviations from steady-state values thus:

$$z = Z - Z^* = \Sigma k_i; \quad y_0 = Y_0 - Y_0^*, \quad i = 1, \ldots, m.$$

I start the story with a special case the significance of which is discussed below (section III). That is, I consider all paths starting from $[K_1(0), \ldots, K_m(0)]$, such that there exists a function $g(Y_o)$ such that

$$\frac{\dot{w}}{w} + g(Y_0)(\dot{Y}_0/Y_0) = 0. \tag{14.6}$$

The question of the existence of such paths is also postponed for later consideration. At the moment I am interested in the linear part of the Taylor expansion of (14.1), (14.3) and (14.5) subject to (14.6).

The expansion of (14.1) yields[7]

$$y_o + \dot{z} = 0 \tag{14.1*}$$

[7] From (14.1),

$$\dot{k}_1 + nk_1 = F_o y_o + \sum_{i=2} (nF_i + F_{m+i}) k_i + F_{m+i} k_1 + \sum_{i=2} F_i \dot{k}_i.$$

In steady state all terms in brackets under the summation sign are zero. Also, $F_{m+1} = n$. We use the normalization of goods giving $F_i = -1$ to obtain (14.1*).

The expansion of $R_i - \dot{F}_i = 0$, making use of (14.1*), gives[8]

$$R_{im+1}z - (F_{im+1} + R_{i0})\dot{z} + F_{i0}\ddot{z} + \sum_{j=2} a_{ij}k_j + \sum_{j=2} b_{ij}\dot{k}_j$$

$$- \sum_{j=2} F_{ij}\ddot{k}_j = 0 \qquad (14.3^*)$$

where

$$a_{ij} = R_{im+j} - R_{im+1}, \; b_{ij} = R_{ij} - R_{ji}$$

From this we easily verify[9]

$$a_{ij} = a_{ji}, \; b_{ij} = -b_{ji}, \quad i,j = 2, \ldots, m \qquad (14.7)$$

Next, consider the expansion of (14.5) in the form

$$- \frac{1}{F_0}[-F_0(F_{m+1} - n) + \dot{F}_0)] + g(Y_0)\frac{Y_0}{Y_0} = 0, \qquad (14.8)$$

---

[8] Expansion of $R_i - \dot{F}_i = 0$ gives

$$R_{im+1}k_1 + \sum_{j=2} R_{im+j}\dot{k}_j + R_{i0}y_0 + \sum_{j=2} R_{ij}\dot{k}_j - \sum_{j=2} (nF_{ij} + F_{im+j})\,\dot{k}_j$$

$$- F_{im+1}\dot{k}_1 - F_{i0}\dot{y}_0 - \sum_{j=2} F_{ij}\dot{k}_j.$$

Let

$$k_1 = z - \sum_{j=2} k_j, \dot{k}_1 = z - \sum_{j=2} \dot{k}_j$$

and note from (14.1*) that $y_0 = -\dot{z}, \dot{y}_0 = -\ddot{z}$. Substituting gives (14.3*) since

$$(nF_{ij} + F_{im+j} - F_{im+1}) = R_{ji}.$$

[9] $R_{im+j} = n(nF_{ij} + F_{im+j}) + (nF_{m+ij} + F_{m+im+j}) - (nF_{+1j} + F_{m+1m+j})$
$R_{im+1} = nF_{im+1} + F_{m+im+1} - F_{m+1m+1}$,

whence

$$R_{im+j} - R_{im+1} = n^2 F_{ij} + n(F_{im+j} + F_{m+ij}) + F_{m+im+j} - n(F_{m+1j} + F_{im+1})$$

$$- (F_{m+im+1} + F_{m+1m+j}) + F_{m+1m+1}$$

$$= R_{jm+i} - R_{jm+1}.$$

which gives[10]

$$F_{m+1m+1}z - [F_{00} + g(Y_0^*)]\ddot{z} + \sum_{j=2} R_{jm+1}k_j$$

$$+ \sum_{j=2} (R_{j0} + F_{m+1j})\, \dot{k}_j + \sum_{j=2} F_{0j}\ddot{k}_j = 0. \qquad (14.5^*)$$

$(\hat{g}(Y_0^*) = g(Y_0)/Y_0$ for steady-state Y_0). Let

$$a_{11} = F_{m+1m+1}, \, a_{i1} = R_{im+1} \text{ for } i > 1; \, b_{i1} = -(F_{im+1} + R_{i0}),$$
$$(i > 1),$$

and let $a_{i1} = a_{1i}$, $b_{i1} = -b_{1i}$. Then if A and B are the $m \times m$ matrices with elements a_{ij}, b_{ij} ($i, j = 1, \ldots, m$), respectively, certainly, from (14.7): $A = A'$, $B = -B'$. Lastly, let C be the $m \times m$ matrix defined as

$$C = \begin{bmatrix} F_{00} + g(Y_0^*) - \{F_{20}, \ldots, F_{m0}\} \\ -\left\{\begin{matrix} F_{20} \\ \vdots \\ F_{m0} \end{matrix}\right\} \qquad F_{ij} \end{bmatrix}$$

so that $C = C'$. Then we may write (14.3^*) and (14.5^*) compactly as

$$A\begin{pmatrix} z \\ k \end{pmatrix} + B\begin{pmatrix} \dot{z} \\ \dot{k} \end{pmatrix} - C\begin{pmatrix} \ddot{z} \\ \ddot{k} \end{pmatrix} = 0,$$

[10] The expansion of $-F_0(F_{m+1} - n)$ is given by

$$\sum_{j=2} (nF_{m+1j} + F_{m+1m+j})\, k_j + F_{m+1m+1}k_1 + \sum_{j=2} F_{m+1j}\dot{k}_j + F_{m+10}y_0.$$

Substituting z for k, as before, and $-\dot{z}$ for y_0 then gives

$$\sum_{j=2} R_{jm+1}k_j + F_{m+1m+1}z - F_{m+10}\dot{z} + \sum_{j=2} F_{m+1j}\dot{k}_j. \qquad (1)$$

The expansion of $\dot{F}_0$ is

$$\sum_{j=2} (nF_{0j} + F_{0m+j})\, \dot{k}_j + F_{0m+1}\dot{k}_1 + F_{00}\dot{y}_0 + \sum_{k=2} F_{0j}\ddot{k}_j,$$

which, on the usual substitution, becomes

$$\sum R_{j0}\dot{k}_j + F_{0m+1}\dot{z} - F_{00}\ddot{z} + \sum_{j=2} F_{0j}\ddot{k}_j. \qquad (2)$$

where (z, k) is the m-vector: $\{z, k_2, \ldots, k_m\}$. We thus seek the roots of

$$|A + \lambda B - \lambda^2 C| = 0.$$

But these are the same as those of $|A' + \lambda B' - \lambda^2 C'| = 0$, that is, of

$$|A - \lambda B - \lambda^2 C| = 0.$$

We thus conclude that, for this special case, if λ is a root then so is $-\lambda$. The motions are thus what Samuelson calls catenary. Indeed, the argument here is quite close to that found in the 'Turnpike' discussions (Samuelson, 1959). Since in the local expansion $g'(Y_0)$ does not appear, we obtain the same result if for all neighbouring paths (14.6) holds with $g(Y_0)$ replaced by a constant. However, the economic interpretation of this condition is obscure while that of (14.6) is not (see below).

For the general case, when (14.6) does not hold, the answer is not quite so definite. We know that (14.4) is equal to $\partial(LY_1)/\partial L + F_0 Y_0$, which expression I shall now write as X_0, and this is evidently the value of the excess demand for consumption goods per man (zero throughout the story). I again write

$$X_{0m+j} = \frac{\partial X_0}{\partial K_j} + n \frac{\partial X_0}{\partial Y_j}; \ X_{0j} = \frac{\partial X_0}{\partial Y_j}.$$

The expansion of (14.4) is now given by

$$X_{0m+1}z - X_{00}\dot{z} + \sum_{j=2} (X_{0m+j} - X_{0m+1}) k_j + \sum_{j=2} X_{0j}\dot{k}_k = 0,$$

$$(14.4^*)$$

and one is now interested in the differential equation system (14.3*) and (14.4*).

Let $\hat{A}$, $\hat{B}$ and $\hat{C}$ be the matrices A, B and C with their first rows and columns deleted. Let $\alpha(\lambda)$ be an $(m-1)$-row vector with components $(X_{0m+j} - X_{0m+1}) + \lambda X_{0j}$ $(j = 2, \ldots, m)$ and let $\beta(\lambda)$ be an $(m-1)$-column vector with components $R_{im+1} - \lambda(F_{im+1} + R_{i0}) + \lambda^2 F_{i0}$ $(i = 2, \ldots, m)$. Then we are looking for the roots of $\Delta(\lambda) = 0$, where

$$\Delta(\lambda) = \begin{vmatrix} X_{0m+1} - \lambda X_{00} & \alpha(\lambda) \\ \beta(\lambda) & \hat{A} + \lambda\hat{B} - \lambda^2\hat{C} \end{vmatrix}.$$

Let $\Delta(\lambda, \theta)$ be the determinant $\Delta(\lambda)$ when $\alpha(\lambda)$ is multiplied by $0 \leqslant \theta \leqslant 1$. Then

$$\Delta(\lambda, 0) = (X_{0m+1} - \lambda X_{00})|\hat{A} + \lambda\hat{B} - \lambda^2\hat{C}|.$$

Since A and C are symmetric and $B = -B'$, we conclude that, for 'almost all' roots, if $\lambda(0)$ is a root of $\Delta(\lambda, 0)$, then so is $-\lambda(0)$. (The exception is the root $\lambda^*(0) = X_{0m+1}/X_{00}$.)

Let us generally write $\lambda(\theta)$ as a root of $\Delta(\lambda, \theta) = 0$. Assume that (i) for all θ, $\Delta(0, \theta) \neq 0$, so that there are no zero real roots for any value of θ in the range; (ii) for all (θ) there are no pure imaginary roots; and (iii) for all θ all roots are distinct. Then, since $\lambda(\theta)$ is certainly continuous in θ, we may conclude that the real part of no root can change sign as θ goes from zero to unity. For if it did we would have either some θ^* for which some $\lambda(\theta^*)$ were pure imaginary, or some real root vanished. Also, since no multiple roots are possible, it cannot be that a real root for some value of θ became complex for some other value. For in order for this to happen there would have to be some θ^* for which there are two roots which can be written $a(\theta^*) \pm ib(\theta^*)$ with $b(\theta^*) = 0$, contradicting the supposition that there are no multiple roots.

Hence if these assumptions are made, then $\Delta(\lambda, 1) \equiv \Delta(\lambda)$ has as many roots with positive real parts as does $\Delta(\lambda, 0)$; but we know that there must be roots of $\Delta(\lambda, 0)$ which have positive real parts. Therefore the steady state does not satisfy the necessary conditions for local stability.[11] But for the special cases (i.e., assumptions (14.6)), where the roots were in pairs $(+\lambda, -\lambda)$, there will, for any $[K_1(0), \ldots, K_m(0)]$, be in general only one possible value of $[\dot{K}_2(0), \ldots, \dot{K}_m(0)]$ for which the system would approach the steady state. This need now no longer be the case, and it may be that there are a number of accumulation paths which converge. However, not all such paths, staying in the small neighbourhood of the steady state, can converge to it.

---

[11] It will be obvious that the assumptions just made in the text are a good deal stronger than is required to show that the necessary conditions for local stability do not hold. For the postulates ensure that $\Delta(\lambda, 1) = 0$ has as many roots with positive real parts as does $\Delta(\lambda, 0) = 0$. Even so, they allow the construction of a wide class of examples since the one parameter variation of θ leaves parts of every coefficient in the polynomial unchanged and we have, in the context of the postulate of strict concavity of F, a wide choice of possible values to assign to these. This consideration is *a fortiori* stronger if we only seek to establish the existence of one unstable root in $\Delta(\lambda, 1)$.

I conclude from this that in the general case no completely general propositions can be deduced. Certainly examples can be given, as I did in Hahn (1966), for which, for a wide class of initial conditions, the accumulation paths diverged, and the demonstration of this possibility is really all that is required to make the point that the single-capital-good results are very special. But it does not seem possible, for the very general production assumptions here made, to deduce more than that the steady state will not, in general, satisfy the necessary conditions of local stability. This is *a fortiori* even more the case when one considers constructions with several consumption goods.

IV   THE INVERSE OPTIMUM

We are now in a position to consider the view that the descriptive model (14.1), (14.3) and (14.4)) can be 'mimicked' by a suitable model of optimum accumulation.

Consider a valuation function $u[Y_0(t)]$ and the Ramsey integral,

$$V = \int_0^\infty u[Y_0(t)]\, dt. \tag{14.9}$$

We are given the problem of maximizing V subject to (14.1). Routine calculations give the Euler equations, which here are the equations in (14.3) and

$$F_{m+1} - n - (\dot{F}_0/F_0) + \left(\frac{u''}{u'} Y_0\right)(\dot{Y}_0/Y_0) = 0. \tag{14.10}$$

If we put $g(Y_0) = (u''/u') Y_0$, then we see that (14.10) is condition (14.8), so that this restriction will be satisfied for any accumulation path which behaves according to the Euler equations of the present maximization problem, and we know that these paths in the vicinity of the steady state will have the 'catenary' property. If it could be shown that my descriptive model is such that, for a proper choice of $u(\cdot)$, it behaves like a maximizing one,[12] then (14.8) would cease to be a restriction of this model but instead would be an implication.

---

[12] Note that since in steady state $F_{m+1} = n$, we cannot 'mimic' the descriptive model by a Ramsey model with discounting.

Now it seems pretty plain that this view must, in general, be false: it will not be possible to transform the descriptive into the normative case.

Consider the model at $t = 0$ and write,

$$K(0) = \{K_1(0), \ldots, K_m(0)\} \quad Y(0) = \{Y_2(0), \ldots, Y_m(0)\},$$

$$\mu(0) = \frac{d \log w}{dt} \bigg/ \frac{d \log Y_0}{dt}.$$

With $K(0)$ given, we have, as we know, $(m-1)$ degrees of freedom, and we therefore consider various choices of the vector $Y(0)$. All unknowns at $t = 0$ may be written as functions of $[K(0), Y(0)]$. In particular, $Y_0(0)$ depends on these $2m-1$ 'initial conditions'. Let $H[K(0), \bar{Y}_0(0)] = \{Y(0)|Y_0(0) = \text{constant}, K(0) \text{ given}\}$. In general, $H[K(0), \bar{Y}_0(0)]$ will have many members. Then (14.8) demands that, if $L[K(0), \dot{\mu}(0)] = \{Y(0)|\dot{\mu}(0) = \text{constant}, K(0) \text{ given}\}$, then $L[K(0), \dot{\mu}(0)] = H[K(0), \bar{Y}_0(0)]$.

Now suppose that $H[K(0), Y_0(0)]$ has two components, $Y(0)$, $Y'(0)$, and that (14.8) is indeed satisfied so that $L[K(0), \dot{\mu}(0)]$ has the same two components. Certainly the set $L(\cdot)$ depends on the second-order properties[13] of F, while the set $H(\cdot)$, derived from (14.1) and (14.4),[14] does not, at $Y(0)$ or $Y'(0)$, depend on those second-order properties. But then we are at liberty to distort F slightly say at $Y'(0)$ without in any way affecting $H[K(0)]$ at $Y(0)$ or $Y'(0)$. But then we have a way of constructing any number of counter-examples to the claim that the two sets must coincide.

Although this seems, as I say, quite plain, a simple example may help to make it plainer.

Consider F given by

$$Y_1 = \alpha_0 Y_0 + \sum_{i=2} \left(\alpha_i Y_i - \frac{\beta_i}{2} Y_i^2 \right) + \sum_{i=1} \left(a_i K_i - \frac{b_i}{2} K_i^2 \right)$$

---

[13] Given $Y_0(0)$, we may regard $\mu(0)$ on $K(0)$ and $\dot{Y}(0)$. For any $K(0)$, $Y(0)$, we may use expansions like (14.3*), at this point, to find $\dot{Y}(0)$ in terms of $K(0)$ and $Y(0)$. Doing this involves the inverse Jacobian $(F_{ij})^{-1}$ evaluated at $Y(0), K(0)$.

[14] Equation (14.4) may be written

$$Y_1 = \sum_{i=2} (\alpha_i - \beta_i Y_i) Y_i + \sum_{i=1} (a_i - b_i K_i) K_i.$$

Subtract this from the equation in the text for the production surface.

where we take $\alpha_i < 0$, $i = 0, \ldots, m$, $\beta_i > 0$, $i = 2, \ldots, m$, $a_i > 0$, $b_i > 0$, $i = 1, \ldots, m$, and confine our attention to that part of the frontier where all goods are produced and all marginal products positive.

From (14.1) and (14.4), we now have

$$-\alpha_0 Y_0 = \tfrac{1}{2}\left(\sum_{i=2} \beta_i Y_i^2 + \sum_{i=1} b_i K_i^2 \right)$$

(where time notation is omitted). Fix $\bar{Y}_0 = -1/\alpha_0$ so that

$$H(K, 1) = \{ Y(0) | \Sigma \beta_i Y_i^2 + \Sigma b_i K_i^2 = 1 \}.$$

Equations (14.3) are now

$$(\alpha_i - \beta_i Y_i)(a_1 - b_1 K_1) + a_i - b_i K_i = -\beta_i Y_i, \quad i = 2, \ldots, m.$$
$$(14.3')$$

We note that $\dot{F}_0/F_0 = 0$ in this example so that, since $F_{m+1} - n = a_1 - b_1 K_1 - n$, we may write

$$a_1 - b_1 K_1 - n = \frac{\dot{w}}{w} = g(Y_0)(\dot{Y}_0/Y_0) \tag{14.8'}$$

for condition (14.8).

If we evaluate $\dot{Y}_0/Y_0$, using (14.3'), we find that

$$\dot{Y}_0/Y_0 = -\frac{1}{\alpha_0}\left[\sum_{i=2} \beta_i Y_i^2(a_1 - b_1 K_1) - (a_1 - b_1 K_1) \sum_{i=2} \alpha_i Y_i \right.$$
$$\left. + \sum_{i=1}(a_i + b_i K_i) + \sum_{i=1} b_i K_i Y_i - n \sum_{i=1} b_i K_i^2 \right]. \quad (14.11)$$

Now consider Y and $Y' \in H(K, 1)$. Evidently $\dot{w}/w$ is the same for both these choices. If $\dot{Y}_0/Y_0$ is to be the same (so that Y and $Y' \in L(\dot{K}, 1)$), we must have

$$\frac{1}{\alpha_0}\left[(a_1 - b_1 K_1) \sum_{i=2} a_i(Y_i - Y_i') - \sum_{i=1} b_i K_i(Y_i - Y_i') \right] = 0. \quad (14.12)$$

By an appropriate choice of a_1 and $(\alpha_2, \ldots, \alpha_m)$, we can always falsify (14.12) without in any way affecting $H(K, 1)$.

One may look at the matter in yet another way. If the inverse optimum exists, then knowledge of Y_0 and of $\dot{Y}_0/Y_0$ suffices to determine the common value, in terms of consumption good, of all the own rates of return. But, as the example shows, this cannot generally be done. For using all the information we have, i.e., the production relation, the consumption function and the condition that all rates should be the same, does not allow us to infer, from knowledge of Y_0 and $\dot{Y}_0/Y_0$, what $K_1, \ldots, K_m$ and $Y_2, \ldots, Y_m$ must be uniquely, and so does not allow us to determine what the own rate will be.

This becomes perhaps even clearer if we consider the special case considered by Kurz (1968) when only one single good is produced and there is only one kind of capital. From the production relation $Y_1 = F(Y_0, K_1)$ and the consumption function, it is clear that Y_0 is uniquely determined by K_1, or (since everything is 'well behaved') that K_1 is uniquely determined by Y_0. But then, since the consumption good is identical with the investment good, knowledge of Y_0 uniquely determines $\dot{K}_1$, and so $\dot{Y}_0/Y_0$, and one is home.

V CONCLUDING REMARKS

In an atemporal world of a certain class, it is easy to show that every equilibrium is efficient. In situations where the future extends indefinitely, this is not always the case (see 'Symposium', 1967). In particular, it is important to distinguish between two views of competitive equilibrium. There is the situation where producers are in equilibrium from moment to moment – this is the case of the present paper. However, if we trace the economy forward far enough, this equilibrium may cease to be possible or efficient, although there may be no way of discovering this in finite time. On the other hand, we could think of producers as being in equilibrium also in the sense that at each t the present value of their assets is maximized (if such a maximum exists). The economy then behaves as one which had infinitely many future markets. In such a world the actual path chosen by the economy will be Pareto-efficient, and it will be quite different from the economy investigated here.

Now it is certainly possible for the paths generated by the present construction to be Pareto-inefficient for a long enough horizon (Shell and Stiglitz, 1967). I conclude from this that, if the world behaves in this manner, the way for the economy to be made to behave efficiently is for someone to 'aim' it at a target. Thus there may be, given $K(0)$, a unique choice of $Y(0)$, which, if now made, will lead the economy along its expectation-fulfilling path to the steady state. [If indeed the motion were always 'catenary', we could assert that there will be one such choice of $Y(0)$ – as it is, there may be several.] In that case, if a planning board announced the appropriate rate of change in relative capital goods prices, producers ought to expect that at $t = 0$ the economy thereafter will seek the steady state. In any case, what our idealization shows is that, even if we assume all the frictions which stop, say, the equalization of own rates, at all t away, the Invisible Hand will generally need a visible one to guide it. To say that this is due to the absence of an infinity of futures markets is correct, but not consoling.

The paradoxical fact is that, if we do not make such very strong demands on the Invisible Hand at all moments of time, it may perform in some sense 'better' in the long run. Thus, for instance, if we suppose producers to expect current prices to persist for ever even when the steady state has been perturbed, but retain all our other assumptions, then Morishima (1964) has shown that the economy will seek the steady state. Thus, while at all moments the economy is making mistakes, they are never the big ones it is capable of in the 'correct expectation' case. This suggests that it may well be that, by idealizing as much as we have done, we have not only created some artificial problems, but we are prevented from analysing the role of one of the most important features of a decentralized and unguided economy, namely that at most times economic agents find that their decisions, with consequences for the future, were not the appropriate ones. There is also the plain fact that not all agents have the same expectations as to the future values of the same variable, and of course that these expectations are uncertain. It may well be that it is precisely such 'frictional aspects' of the world we live in which prevent it going disastrously 'off the rails'; but no one really knows.

REFERENCES

Goldman, S. (1968), 'Optimal Growth and Continual Planning Revision', *Review of Economic Studies*, **35**.
Hahn, F. H. (1966), 'Equilibrium Dynamics with Heterogeneous Capital Goods', *Quarterly Journal of Economics*, **80**.

Kurz, M. (1968), 'The General Instability of a Class of Competitive Growth Processes', *Review of Economic Studies*, 35.

McKenzie, L. (1963), 'The Dorfman-Samuelson-Solow Turnpike Theorem', *International Economic Review*, 4.

Morishima, M. (1964), *Equilibrium Stability and Growth*, Oxford.

Samuelson, P. A. (1959), 'Efficient Paths of Capital Accumulation in Terms of the Calculus of Variations', *Mathematical Methods in the Social Sciences*, Stanford, California.

Shell, K. (ed.) (1967), *Essays on the Theory of Optimum Growth*, Cambridge, Mass.

Shell, K. and Stiglitz, J. (1967), 'The Allocation of Investment in a Dynamic Economy', *Quarterly Journal of Economics*, 81.

'Symposium on Optimal Infinite Programmes' (1967), *Review of Economic Studies*, 34.

15

The Stability of Growth Equilibrium

Some years ago, it was a widely held belief that 'full-employment' growth equilibrium might be impossible and, if possible, was bound to be unstable. Recently there has occurred a major revision of this view.[1] It is now maintained that, if due attention is paid to the price mechanism in general and to factor substitution in particular, then full-employment growth equilibrium exists and is likely to be stable. So far, however, no analysis of the behaviour of the system when out of equilibrium has been proposed. Indeed, the rejection of the Harrod–Domar 'Knife Edge' has been based on models in which it is assumed that full-employment savings are at all times equal to full-employment investment.

In this paper, it will be accepted that a full-employment growth equilibrium exists. The main focus of attention will be the stability of this equilibrium. In examining this problem, we will proceed on the more traditional view that prices adjust to market 'errors' and that neither these adjustments nor the correction of errors is instantaneous. It is clear that some such investigation is required if one is to form some view of the actual stability of the system. In what follows, two main models will be examined. In both of these it will be assumed that the production function is of the Cobb–Douglas variety with neutral technical progress. This is convenient but by no means essential to our result.

In the first model (model A), which I call Wicksellian, it is postulated that money wages behave in such a way as to preserve, at every moment of time, equality between the real wage of labour and its full-employment marginal product. In equilibrium, output is growing at a rate determined by the rate of growth in the labour supply and in the productivity of labour. When equilibrium is disturbed, the following chain of events is assumed. Commodity prices rise or fall according as there is an excess demand or excess

---

[1] The most important paper is undoubtedly Solow (1956). See also Kaldor (1957).

supply for goods. Because of our assumption regarding the behaviour of money wages and the form of the production function, changing prices do not affect the distribution of income between wage-earners and capitalists. However, the rise or fall in commodity prices gives rise to expectations as to the future rate of change in prices. This, assuming for the moment money interest rates to be given, changes the real rental of capital, which in turn induces substitution between capital and labour. This substitution in its turn affects the excess demand for goods. The question we ask is whether the process will restore equilibrium. The answer, for any given expectation-formation assumption, is found to depend on a comparison of the rate at which factor substitution changes the marginal product of capital and the rate at which the real rental of capital is changing. Our formulation enables us not only to make this precise but also to form some judgement as to the likelihood of the various outcomes in practice.

Why is this model interesting? In the first place, it is interesting because it isolates the stabilizing effect of factor substitution from other possible stabilizers such as changes in income distribution and money interest rate changes. In the second place, it is interesting because we reach the conclusion that, if money interest rates *are* allowed to vary, equilibrium is almost certain to be stable. It might be objected (as Mr Smithies has objected to me) that this result is only true because of the unrealistic nature of our assumptions. This is not so. For any increase in realism, such as introducing a money wage lag and allowing factor substitution to be slow relative to the speed of price changes, will reinforce our conclusions, provided we assume continued full employment of labour. Thus the model does give some realistic insights into inflationary processes in a growth economy.

In the second model (model B), we drop the assumption of 'perfect wage adjustments'. In particular, we allow real wages to rise above their equilibrium value at any moment of time, if prices are falling. This means that factor substitution occurs not only because of divergences between the real rental of capital and its marginal product, but also because of divergences between the real wage of labour and labour's marginal product. It also means that in times of falling prices the distribution of income moves in favour of labour. This – making Kaldorian assumptions – is supposed to raise the propensity to consume.

When discussing the stability of this system, full account is taken of the fact that a rise in real wages above their equilibrium value will not only induce factor substitution at any given level of output but will also tend to reduce output below what it would otherwise have been. Thus, at the same time as the redistribution of income may increase demand from the consumption side, it also reduces it from the investment side. For if output falls below its equilibrium level, the capital–labour ratio rises so that, even if no factor substitution were induced, investment may fall. All this will be fully discussed below. Here I simply wish to state one of the important conclusions of this model.

If we suppose no 'Kaldor effect' on the propensity to consume, the system may still be stable provided investment responds 'slowly' to 'errors'. For if it does, the marginal product of labour may rise more rapidly (owing to larger capital intensity) than the real wage is rising. But, and this is the important point, if the system were to be unstable without the 'Kaldor effect', it is almost certain to be unstable also when the effect is taken into account. The reason for this is quite simple: if the effect is to stabilize an otherwise unstable situation, it must outweigh the reduction in demand which would have taken place because both investment and income (and hence consumption at the old propensity to consume) are lower than they would have been in equilibrium. This means that the proportionate change in the propensity to save induced by the effect would have to be quite unrealistically large. Mr Kaldor reaches a different conclusion, in an as yet unpublished paper, because he does not allow investment or output to be influenced by a fall in real wages below their equilibrium value. But then, the system is stable in any case since the marginal product of labour will be rising as real wages are rising. It should be added that Kaldor's model is basically different from the 'neoclassical' one investigated here. Hence, the above conclusion need not be valid in the context of his own construction.

I have written this brief outline of the models to be examined in order to make it easier to see what they are about. But such 'intuitive' explanations are extremely limited. We cannot have our cake and eat it: if we use only the simplest models, then they can readily be translated into English but they are correspondingly unrealistic. If we wish to take account of a greater slice of reality, the models are more complicated and translation becomes increasingly difficult. What the economist must do is to make sure that his assumptions make economic sense, and these assumptions should always be translated. It is, however, too much to hope that conclusions deduced will always have a readily understood and intuitively obvious economic meaning. After all, to give but one example, the conclusions of the Cobweb theorem are obvious geometrically and mathematically, but not easily explained otherwise. In what follows I have done as much 'translating' as seemed possible.

The plan of the paper is as follows. We first establish a model of growth equilibrium. We then examine its stability under various assumptions concerning the behaviour of prices, interest rates and money wages.

Since the literature on growth is both large and well-known, the exposition has been made as terse as possible. The details of mathematical manipulations have been confined to those which are easily followed, and will be found in the notes.

The following notational and literary simplifications are made. If a variable x is a function of time, so that $x = x(t)$, the t will be omitted if this fact is clear from the context. We shall use the operators $E = d \log/dt$ and $D = d/dt$. We shall call both Ex and Dx the rate of change (or growth) of x when it is clear from the context which operation is implied.

I

Let y = output per head and k = capital–labour ratio. Assume that some satisfactory method of aggregation has been found and that the production function is of the form

$$\log y = at + b \log k \quad a > 0, 1 > b > 0. \tag{15.1}$$

This production function is of the Cobb–Douglas variety with a trend term added to allow for secular growth in productivity.[2] Innovations are 'factor-neutral'.

From (15.1) we have

$$Ey = a + bEk. \tag{15.2}$$

Let n, the natural rate of growth in productivity (y), be that rate of growth for which $\alpha = y/k$ is constant. (α is the inverse of the

---

[2] If Y is income, K = capital, L = labour employed, the production function from which (15.1) is derived is

$$Y = e^{at} K^b L^{1-b}.$$

capital–output ratio.) Then from (15.2)[3]

$$n = \frac{a}{1-b}. \tag{15.3}$$

Let r = money rate of interest in terms of money and ρ = the money rate of interest in terms of goods. Let P = level of prices. Then it is well-known that[4]

$$\rho = r - EP. \tag{15.4}$$

From (15.1) we easily find the marginal product of capital[5] $= b\alpha$. Choosing suitable units so that the price of a unit of capital is the same as that of a unit of output, we have, in equilibrium under perfect competition,

$$\rho = b\alpha. \tag{15.5}$$

From (15.1), it is clear that α is a function of both k and t.

Equation (15.5) neglects risk, etc. We shall therefore sometimes wish to modify it to read

$$\phi(\rho) = b\alpha, \quad \phi' > 0 \tag{15.5a}$$

where in general $\phi(\rho) > \rho$.

The marginal product of labour[6] is $(1-b)y$. If w = money wages, we shall, for the purposes of this model, make the following assumption.

Assumption I $Ew - EP = Ey.$ $\qquad\qquad\qquad\qquad$ (15.6)

That is, if $w/P = (1-b)y$, then money wages always change in such a way as to preserve this equality.

---

[3] Since $y/k = \alpha$, then $\log y - \log k = \log \alpha$ and $Ey - Ek = 0$. But $Ey = n$, and by using (15.2) we get (15.3).

[4] This is true if the expected and actual rate of change in money prices coincide.

[5] Using the alternative version of the production function of n. 2 above, we have $\partial Y/\partial K = b e^{at} K^{b-1} L^{1-b} = b e^{at} k^{b-1} = b\alpha$.

[6] We have $\partial Y/\partial L = (1-b) e^{at} K^b L^{1-b} = (1-b) e^{at} k^b = (1-b)y$.

Assumption II　If $L(t)$ is the labour supplied at time t, then[7]

$$EL(t) = \lambda \qquad (15.7)$$

and all labour offering itself is employed.

It follows that if N, the natural rate of income, is that rate of growth at which α is constant through time; then[8]

$$N = n + \lambda. \qquad (15.8)$$

It should be noted that, if incomes are growing at the rate N, then k, the capital–labour ratio, will be growing at the rate n. If money prices are constant, money wages will also grow at the rate n.

In equilibrium, savings must equal investment at every moment of time. Various well-known assumptions concerning the behaviour of the propensity to save are possible. Here we shall use only one of these.[9]

Assumption III　If l is the share of wages in the national income, then

$$s = s(l), \quad s' < 0. \qquad (15.9)$$

Because of assumption I, the share of wages is constant throughout so $l = (1 - b)$ and we can treat the propensity to save as constant.

The equality between savings and investment may be stated as[10]

$$Ek + \lambda = s\alpha. \qquad (15.10)$$

---

[7] The supply function of labour is thus $L(t) = L_0 e^{\lambda t}$.

[8] We have that $\dot{y}/y = n$. So $y = e^{nt}$ and $Y = e^{nt}L$. Since $L(t) = L_0 e^{\lambda t}$, we get $Y = e^{(n+\lambda)t}L_0$. Hence $N = \dot{Y}/Y = n + \lambda$, which is (15.8) in the text.

[9] This is the assumption recently expounded by Kaldor (1957).

[10] Using the notation of n. 2, we have $\dot{k} = (\dot{K}/L)\lambda k$. So in equilibrium

$$\frac{\dot{K}}{L} = \dot{k} + \lambda k = sy,$$

and dividing both sides in the last equality by k we obtain equation (15.10).

If incomes are growing at the 'natural' rate N, then $Ek = n$ and so $N = s\alpha$. If we make use of this and substitute from (15.5) into (15.10) we have

$$N = \frac{s}{b}\rho. \tag{15.11}$$

Now b is the share of capital in output.[11] Thus, if capitalists save all their income and workers never save, $N = \rho$ and the rate of growth in output is equal to the money rate of interest in terms of goods. This proposition is familiar from von Neumann and has recently been again discussed by Kaldor (1957).

Recalling the definition of ρ (in equation (15.4)), we see that equilibrium is consistent with a constant price level only if

$$\frac{b}{s}N = r = r^* \text{ (say).} \tag{15.12}$$

We shall, following Wicksell, call r^* the *natural rate of interest*. If, because of liquidity preference considerations, there is some $\bar{r} > 0$ below which the money rate of interest cannot fall, and if $r^* < \bar{r}$, then no equilibrium with constant prices is possible. This difficulty can be overcome by making use of the probably true proposition that there always exists some *level* of prices low enough to make s small enough, and thus r^* high enough, for equilibrium. But we shall not worry about this and shall assume that an equilibrium with constant prices exists.

We are interested in the stability of this equilibrium. Let us first state an answer to this question which has been widely expounded (Solow, 1956).

(i) It is assumed that full-employment investment is always equal to full-employment savings. Hence, writing $Ek = (Ek - n) + n$, we have, from equation (15.10),

$$Ek - n = s\alpha - N. \tag{15.13}$$

In equilibrium, of course, $Ek = n$ and $s\alpha = N$. Expanding the right-hand side of (15.13) about its equilibrium value (equal to zero), we have

$$Ek - n = s(\alpha - \alpha^*) \tag{15.14}$$

---

[11] If $b\alpha = by/k$ is the marginal product of capital $(by/k)(k/y) = b$ is the share of capital in output.

where α^* is the equilibrium value of α. By equation (15.1),

$$(b-1)(Ek-n) = E\alpha.^{12}$$

Making use of this, and writing $\hat{\alpha} = (\alpha - \alpha^*)/\alpha^*$, we easily find

$$D\hat{\alpha} = \alpha^* s(b-1)[\hat{\alpha} + (\hat{\alpha})^2]. \tag{15.15}$$

This equation has the solution

$$\hat{\alpha}(t) = \frac{-1}{1 + Re^{s(1-b)\alpha^* t}} \tag{15.16}$$

where $|R| > 1$, and is a constant depending on initial conditions. Since $(1-b)s > 0$, it is seen that $\hat{\alpha}(t) \to 0$ as $t \to \infty$, and so $\alpha(t) \to \alpha^*$.

(ii) It is assumed that the marginal product of capital is always equal to its real rental and that money prices are constant. Hence $r(t)$ must be changing in exactly the same way as $\alpha(t)$ is changing and so $r(t) \to r^*$ as $\alpha(t) \to \alpha^*$.

(iii) Assumption I is made and so, just as in (ii), $w(t) \to w^*(t)$ as $\alpha(t) \to \alpha^*$. This model may be rationalized as follows. Suppose $r(o) > r^*$ and hence $\alpha(o) > \alpha^*$. Since real wages are perfectly adjusted to labour's marginal product at full employment, $w(o) < w^*(o)$. When $\alpha = \alpha(o)$, savings would exceed investment at full employment unless producers can be induced to increase their capital–output ratio (reduce α), and so interest rates will fall to induce the necessary amount of 'deepening'. Deepening will increase the marginal product of labour faster than it would be increasing due to innovations, and hence money wages will rise

---

[12] From equation (15.1), we get

$$\log y - \log k = at + (b-1)\log k.$$

Hence

$$\log \alpha = at + (b-1)\log k;$$

consequently

$$E\alpha = a + (b-1)Ek.$$

By using (15.3), we get

$$E\alpha = (b-1)(Ek-n).$$

faster than the natural rate. This process continues until the capital–output ratio is such as to make savings equal to investment without deepening. It is seen that it is making the possibility of factor substitution, but above all the flawless working of the price mechanism, which ensures stability.

It is worth noting that stability depends on $(1-b) > 0$. If we had used a rather more general form of production function, this condition would be equivalent to the requirement that there should be diminishing returns to factor substitution.

I do not myself believe that the model we have just examined is very helpful in settling the stability question. We do not usually assume that price movements instantaneously correct an error between supply and demand (keep investment equal to savings). In any case, it will be interesting to see how the model stands up to the relaxation of some of its rather stringent assumptions.

II

Model A

We shall first consider a case, which I shall call 'Wicksellian', in which money interest rates do not change (because of appropriate action on the part of the monetary authorities), but where differences between investment and savings at full employment cause money prices of goods to change. A consideration of this case is useful since it will help us to form some judgement of the burden which must be thrown on interest rate variations to preserve stability.

Assumption AI

$$EP = u\left(\frac{Ek + \lambda}{\alpha} - s\right) \quad u > 0. \tag{15.17}$$

This assumption states that the rate of change in goods prices is a linear and positive function of the difference between the ratio of investment to full employment income and the propensity to save.[13] As assumptions go, it is not too bad, especially when it is recalled that we have also made assumption I.

---

[13] From n. 10, investment per head is $\dot{k} + \lambda k$ and so $(\dot{k} + \lambda k)/y$ is the ratio of investment to income. Dividing top and bottom by k we obtain the first term in equation (15.17).

Assumption AII

$$D\hat{k} = v(b\alpha - \rho), \; v > 0; \; \hat{k} = \frac{k - k^*}{k^*}. \tag{15.18}$$

This assumption has been chosen for its simplicity and because more complicated ones do not seem to affect our results. It requires some explanation. Let a circumflex over a symbol denote the operation, d log. Then $\hat{k} = \hat{K} - \hat{L}$ where K = stock of capital at time t. It is reasonable to suppose that the deviation of the stock of capital from its equilibrium value at time t depends on there being a variation between its real rental (ρ) and its marginal product. Similarly, variations of employment from its equilibrium value will depend on differences between the marginal product of labour and its real wage. But such deviations have been excluded by assumption I, and so $\hat{L} = 0$ and $\hat{k} = \hat{K}$.

This is the first stage in the explanation of equation (15.18). Next, note that $D\hat{k} = (Dk - nk)/k^*$.[14] Now Dk is the actual rate at which the capital–labour ratio is changing and nk is the rate at which it would change if incomes were growing at the natural rate, i.e., if there were no attempt to change α. Thus, equation (15.18) states that the difference between the actual and natural rate of factor substitution is a positive (linear) function of the difference between the marginal product of capital and its real rental. The assumption, however, asserts that the higher the equilibrium ratio of capital to labour ($k^*(t)$), the more 'sensitive' will producers be to divergences between the marginal product of capital and its real rental. This postulate is by no means necessary to what follows, but it simplifies matters quite a bit and is not repugnant to common sense.[15]

---

[14] $\hat{k} = (k - k^*)/k^*$. So

$$D\hat{k} = \frac{\dot{k} - \dot{k}^*}{k^*} - \frac{\dot{k}^*}{k^*}\left(\frac{k - k^*}{k^*}\right) = \frac{\dot{k}}{k^*} - n\left(1 + \frac{k - k^*}{k^*}\right) = \frac{\dot{k} - nk}{k^*}$$

since $\dot{k}^*/k^* = n$. Here a dot over the symbol denotes the operation D.

[15] The reader might prefer to postulate the following: $D\alpha = F[b\alpha - \rho]$; $F' < 0$. This yields identical results in our models as does (15.18). It is because one prefers to think in terms of substitution of capital for labour as caused by the 'error' under review, rather than of the implied changes in the capital–output ratio, that we are using equation (15.18). If we had written (15.18) as $(Ek - n) = v(b\alpha - \rho)$, $v > 0$, we would have finished up with a series of nonlinear differential equations which are rather tiresome to handle. But the results are qualitatively the same as those in our model. For a further explanation of the present assumption, see n. 10 above.

If we use the capital–equilibrium condition, equation (15a), then equation (15.18) becomes

$$D\hat{k} = v[b\alpha - \phi(\rho)].$$ (15.18a)

Before examining this model, let us note that the 'speeds of adjustment' u and v are not independent of the way in which we measure time, commodities and prices. We shall normalize these adjustment speeds by setting $u = 1$, and we shall postulate that $v < 1$, i.e., that prices adjust 'more rapidly' than the capital–labour ratios.

Recalling the definition of ρ (equation (15.4)), and substituting in equation (15.18) and expanding about the equilibrium values $\alpha = \alpha^*, r = r^*$, we soon find[16]

$$D\hat{k} = v'(b-1)\left(b\alpha^* - \frac{N}{\alpha^*}\right)\hat{k}$$ (15.19)

(where $v' = v\alpha^*/(\alpha^* - v) > 0$). From equation (15.1), we have

$$(b-1)\,\hat{k} = \frac{\alpha - \alpha^*}{\alpha^*} = \hat{\alpha},$$

and making use of this (15.18) may be written as

$$D\hat{\alpha} = v'(b-1)\left(b\alpha^* - \frac{N}{\alpha^*}\right)\hat{\alpha}.$$ (15.20)

---

[16] Expand (15.17); i.e., find $D(\dot{k}/k + \lambda)\,1/\alpha$. Using n. 5, this becomes

$$\frac{D\hat{k}}{\alpha^*} - \frac{N}{\alpha^*}\hat{\alpha}.$$

But $(b-1)\hat{k} = \hat{y} - \hat{k} = \hat{\alpha}$ by equation (15.1), and so

$$EP = \left[\frac{D\hat{k}}{\alpha^*} - \frac{N}{\alpha^*}(b-1)\hat{k}\right].$$

Hence substituting in equation (15.18), recalling that $\rho = r - EP$ and expanding and rearranging, we obtain equation (15.19). Now v' must be positive if the postulated relationship is to make any sense. We are here assuming that the normalization of u and v adopted permit this. If not, we would have had to normalize by putting $v > \alpha^*$, and u would then have had to be greater than 1.

Since $(b-1)<0$, the condition for $\hat{\alpha}(t) \to 0$ as $t \to \infty$ is $b\alpha^* > N/\alpha^*$. But in equilibrium, $N = s\alpha^*$, and so the condition for stability is

$$r^* = \frac{b}{s} N > s. \tag{15.21}$$

This condition certainly will not hold for any reasonable value of N if capitalists save the whole of their income. On the other hand, that is rather a silly assumption to make. If b (the share of capitalists) is 0.3 and $N = 0.03$, then $s < 0.09$ will ensure that (15.21) holds. These, on the face of it, are not 'unreasonable' values. But there are other, quite reasonable, values of the parameters – for example, $s = 0.15$ in the above example – for which the condition will not hold.

At this stage, a diagram will be helpful. In figure 15.1, we have plotted the two functions $N/\alpha - s$ and $r^* - b\alpha$. The first function measures the difference between the investment and savings ratio when the stock of capital is growing at the natural rate. The second gives us the difference between the money rate of interest and the marginal product of capital. These two curves intersect at α^*, where $N/\alpha^* = s$ and $r^* = b\alpha^*$. Figure 15.1(a) shows a stable intersection. If there we take a small deviation of α from α^*, say a fall in α, then, if α were constant at that point, the marginal product of capital would be less than its real rental, for then $EP = (N/\alpha) - s > 0$ and $b\alpha - \rho = b\alpha - r + (N/\alpha) - s < 0$, as can

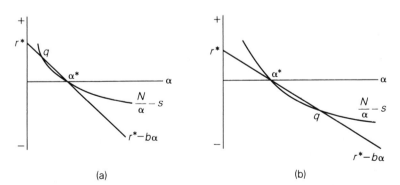

(a)   (b)

FIGURE 15.1

be seen from the two curves. Hence the capital–output ratio will be reduced (α will rise) and we return to α^*. What this really comes down to is this. If the capital–output ratio rises, α falls below α^*, investment will exceed savings, prices will be rising and the real rental of capital will fall. But the marginal product of capital falls faster than the real rental is falling and we return to equilibrium. In figure 15.1(b) this is not true, and hence the system is unstable at α^*.

It should now be noted that, if figure 15.1(a) is relevant and $r < r^*$, then a stable equilibrium with rising prices exists (as can be seen by shifting the curve $r^* - b\alpha$ to the left). By the same token, the monetary authorities could always ensure a stable equilibrium with constant prices by raising r to r^*. This is not true in figure 15.1(b).

It is, I think, fairly obvious that, even if the present model is unstable, this is in no small measure due to the implied assumption that producers expect the current rate of change in prices to continue. In general, this need not be so. If P^e is the expected level of prices, we might, perhaps reasonably, stipulate that $EP^e = \mu EP$, $1 > \mu > 0$. Since it is expected price changes which are relevant to investment decisions, the stability condition now becomes $(b/s) N > \mu s$, and for μ small enough this will always be true. It is not easy to form a judgement in this matter, since expectations are the outcome of experiences over a more or less distant past. In any case, we note that things may not look quite as black as we have so far painted them. There is a further consoling thought. If we had used equation (15.18a), instead of equation (15.18), the stability condition would have been

$$r^* = \frac{b}{s} N > \phi' s \qquad (15.21a)$$

and for ϕ' small enough this will always be true.

It is, I think, however, of considerable interest that, when we drop the assumption of constant money interest rates, the system is almost certain to be stable *even if $EP^e = EP$ and $\phi(\rho) = \rho$*. This we shall now show.

Various assumptions are possible concerning the behaviour of money interest rates. Here we shall investigate only the simplest one since, once again, more complicated, and perhaps more acceptable, hypotheses do not seem to affect the conclusions.

Assumption AIII

$$Dr = z\left(\frac{EK + \lambda}{\alpha} - s\right) \quad z > 0. \tag{15.22a}$$

This assumption states that the rate at which interest rates change is a positive and linear function of the difference between the ratio of investment to full-employment income and the propensity to save. This is a fairly 'classical' assumption, but, as already noted, more 'Keynesian' hypotheses leave our conclusions fairly intact.[17]

Since interest rates are no longer fixed, we must add to equation (15.20) the term $(1-b)v'(r-r^*)$. If, having done this, we differentiate equation (15.20) (with respect to t) and substitute from equation (15.22) for Dr, we easily find[18]

$$D^2\hat\alpha = v'(b-1)\left[b\alpha^* + \frac{z}{\alpha^*(1-b)} - \frac{N}{\alpha^*}\right]D\hat\alpha - \frac{z(1-b)v'}{\alpha^*}N\hat\alpha. \tag{15.22}$$

[17] Assumption AIII may be interpreted as a policy equation. That is, the monetary authorities allow interest rates to rise when investment exceeds savings and to fall in the reverse eventuality.

[18] We may use the expansion of equation (15.18) to gain further insight into assumption AII.

$$D\hat k = \frac{Dk - nk}{k^*} = b(\alpha - \alpha^*) = vb\left(\frac{y - y^*}{k^*} - \frac{k - k^*}{k^*}\alpha^*\right).$$

Hence,

$$Dk - nk = v\alpha^* b\left[\frac{(y - y^*)}{\alpha^*} - (k - k^*)\right].$$

Now we know that under our present assumptions $Dk = DK$ and $k - k^* = K - K^*$ (see p. 286). Hence we have

$$DK - NK = v\alpha^* b\left[\frac{Y - Y^*}{\alpha^*} - (K - K^*)\right].$$

Now the first term in the square bracket is the increase in the 'desired' stock of capital when interest rates are constant, while the second term is the actual increase in the stock of capital. Hence our assumption states that the divergence of investment from its natural rate is a function of the difference between the desired and actual stock of capital, and that seems sensible.

For stability, we require the term in square brackets to be positive.[19] If we substitute for $\alpha^* = N/s$ in this expression, it is found that $z > N$ is a sufficient condition for stability. On our normalization u, the speed of adjustment of prices, is equal to unity and so interest rate changes would have to be very 'slow' indeed relative to price changes if this condition were not to hold.

The economic explanation of this result is very straightforward. Suppose that $\alpha < \alpha^*$ and prices are rising since investment exceeds savings. If now interest rates rise, they have, as it were, a two-fold effect on investment. There is the direct effect of higher interest rates in discouraging investment; and there is the secondary effect due to the fact that the primary effect will have reduced the rate at which prices are rising and thus raised the real rental of capital even further. The reverse case of falling prices is explained in a similar way.

It is seen that moderate flexibility of interest rates ensures stability in the model so far considered. It should be noted that this conclusion would not be upset by the usual postulate that investment demand is relatively interest-inelastic because of uncertainty, etc. For the relevant interest rate is ρ, so if producers do not respond much to changes in r, they will also not respond much to a change in the rate at which prices are expected to change (remember that, so far, money wages are behaving 'perfectly' by assumption I), and so the system would in any case be stable.

We therefore conclude that the present model would have a stable full-employment equilibrium with constant prices if (a) interest rates are constant but expectations are sufficiently inelastic (see p. 290), or (b) the demand for investment is relatively unresponsive to changes in the real interest rate (ϕ' small), or (c) interest rates are moderately flexible.

---

[19] Write equation (15.22) as $D^2\alpha = AD\alpha + B\alpha$, where $B < 0$. Then the roots of this equation are

$$\lambda = \frac{A \neq \sqrt{(A^2 + 4B)}}{2}.$$

Hence if λ is to have real negative parts, we require $A < 0$. Since $(b - 1) < 0$, it follows that the term in square brackets in equation (15.22) must be positive. This necessary condition for stability is also sufficient; for if λ is real, since $|A| > \sqrt{(A^2 + 4B)}$, both roots are negative.

III

Model B

It does not take a great deal of insight to realize that the conclusions we have just reached depend, possibly crucially, on assumption I, which ensured that there were never any lapses from full-employment income. This assumption will be dropped in the present model.

Before doing so, we must note an obvious difficulty. If, when prices are falling, wages are not falling 'rapidly enough' (or increasing 'slowly enough'), employment will fall. In the reverse case, that is when prices are rising and wages are not rising rapidly enough, employment may not increase simply because there is no one left to employ. This 'nonlinearity' is well known. We shall here make a probably unrealistic assumption which none the less will do for our present purposes.

Assumption BI

(a) $Ew - EP = Ey$ when $EP \geqslant 0$

(b) $Ew \qquad = n$ when $EP < 0$

$$(15.23)$$

This assumption states that, when prices are rising or constant, money wages will always rise at such a rate as to preserve the equality between the full-employment marginal product of labour and its real wage. But when prices are falling, money wages will continue to rise at their natural rate. This is quite a drastic hypothesis, and we shall relax it presently. In what follows, we shall concern ourselves only with eventuality (15.23b), i.e., with situations in which employment is less than 'full'.

We shall now state the remaining assumptions of the model.

Assumption BII

$$D\hat{L} = m[(1-b) - l] \quad m > 0 \tag{15.24}$$

Since $D\hat{L} = (DL - \lambda L)/L^*$, this assumption states that the difference between the actual and natural rate of increase in employment is a positive (linear) function of the difference between the equilibrium share of labour in output and its actual share. It further asserts that, the higher the equilibrium level of employment $(L^*(t))$, the more 'sensitive' will employment be to divergences between the actual and equilibrium share. This assumption is highly convenient and not outright silly. If we had made employment adjustments depend on the difference between the marginal product of labour and its real wage, our conclusions would have remained intact.

If equation (15.24) is expanded about its equilibrium value

$$(1-b) = l,$$

we find

$$D\hat{L} = m(1-b)(b\hat{k} + \hat{P}).$$ (15.24a)

We shall retain assumption AII, but now it is no longer true that $DK = Dk$ and so we have

Assumption BIII

$$D\hat{K} = v(b\alpha - \rho)$$ (15.25)

This assumption has already been discussed under assumption AII. If we use equation (15.5a), then equation (15.25) becomes

$$D\hat{K} = v[b\alpha - \phi(\rho)].$$ (15.25a)

Assumption BIV   Money interest rates are kept constant by the actions of the monetary authorities. Prices are never expected to be rising or falling.

This assumption is made in order to allow us to isolate the effect of imperfect wage adjustments. We will discuss the consequence of doing it presently.

Using the assumption just stated, we may expand (15.25) about it equilibrium value $b\alpha^* = \rho^*$ to find[20]

$$D\hat{K} = v(b-1)b\alpha^*\hat{k}.$$ (15.25b)

So using (15.24a),

$$D\hat{k} = D\hat{K} - D\hat{L} = (b-1)b(v\alpha^* + m)\,\hat{k} + m(b-1)\hat{P}.$$ (15.26)

Lastly, we modify assumption AIV to read

[20] Since $\rho = $ constant, $Db\alpha^* = b\alpha^*\hat{\alpha} = (b-1)b\alpha^*\hat{k}$ since $(b-1)\hat{k} = \hat{\alpha}$.

Assumption BV

$$D\hat{P} = \left(\frac{Ek + \lambda}{\alpha} - s\right). \tag{15.27}$$

The modification is rather slight. Since P^* is constant, $D\hat{P} = DP/P^*$, so the assumption states that the rate at which prices are changing is a positive (linear) function of the difference between the ratio of investment to income and the propensity to save. It is asserted that the higher the equilibrium price (P^*), the greater the rate of change in prices induced by a given divergence between investment and savings. This assumption is mathematically more convenient than assumption AIV, while the relation of the latter complicates the calculations without affecting the results.

In expanding (15.27) about its equilibrium value, due care must be taken to take into account any redistributive effects on the propensity to save (see assumption AIII). Such effects will occur when l deviates from its equilibrium value. After various simple manipulations, we find, assuming that employment is less than full,

$$D\hat{P} = (b-1)[b(v-s') - s]\hat{k} + (1-b)s'\hat{P}. \tag{15.28}$$

(Recall that $s' = \partial s/\partial l \leqslant 0$.)

We are now ready to examine the stability of the system given by the two differential equations (15.26) and (15.28). We shall do this in two stages.

(i) If $s' = 0$, then if we imagine (15.26) and (15.28) written in matrix form, the right-hand bottom diagonal term is zero. The remaining diagonal term is negative, as it should be if we are to have a stable system. However, if the system is stable, the determinant of the matrix must be positive.[21] This will be so if $bv - s < 0$.

---

[21] The matrix we are considering is

$$M = \begin{bmatrix} (b-1)\,b(v\alpha^* + m) & m(b-1) \\ (b-1)\,(bv-s) & 0 \end{bmatrix}.$$

If $_1\lambda$ and $_2\lambda$ are the two latent roots of M, then $_1\lambda + _2\lambda$ = sum of the diagonal elements in M and $_1\lambda_2\lambda = |M|$, the determinant of M. Since $(b-1) < 0$ and

$$|M| = -(b-1)^2[bv-s],$$

we find $|M| > 0$ if $bv - s < 0$. Since stability requires that both roots shall have negative real parts, $(bv - s) < 0$ is a necessary condition for this.

It is clear that this condition will be more likely to be fulfilled the more slowly investment responds to a divergence between the marginal product of capital and its real wage. If investment were to respond as rapidly to 'errors' as prices do, i.e., if $v = 1$, then the condition for stability is very unlikely to be fulfilled. Some people might argue that investment in fact responds more quickly than prices. Thus, even though producers are at liberty to vary their factor proportions, stability is problematical. It should also be noted that if the system is unstable it will, starting from $y < y^*$ and $P < P^*$, diverge ever more from its equilibrium value.[22]

(ii) If $s' < 0$, then both the diagonal terms in the matrix described in (i) are negative.[23] For the determinant to be positive we require $bv(m + s'\alpha^*) - sm < 0$. Matters now seem a little more hopeful since, even if $bv - s > 0$, stability may yet be possible. It is difficult to form a judgement as to the probable absolute value of s'/s. But suppose it to be as high as 10 per cent in absolute value. If we put $v = 1$, $\alpha^* = \frac{1}{3}$, $s = 0.15$ and $b = 0.3$ (recall that b is the equilibrium share of capitalists), then stability would require $m = 0.009$, which seems rather drastically small. In general, I think it is fair to say that, taking any reasonable values for α^*, b and s, if the system is unstable for $s' = 0$, it is likely to be unstable for $s' < 0$. The conclusion seems to be that it is not the possibility of factor substitution or of the connection which may exist between the marginal propensity to save and the distribution of income, but rather the relative 'speeds of adjustment' to errors which are important for stability.

---

[22] Using the notation of n. 2, and writing T for the trace of M, the characteristic equation is $\lambda^2 - \lambda T + |M| = 0$. If the system is unstable, $|M| < 0$, then both roots will be real. Hence if the initial conditions are those specified in the text with $\dot{y}(o) = 0$, $\dot{P}(o) = 0$, the system will diverge steadily from its equilibrium value.

[23] The matrix now is

$$\bar{M} = \begin{bmatrix} (b-1) & b(v\alpha^* + m) & m(b-1) \\ (b-1) & [b(v-s')-s] & (1-b)s' \end{bmatrix}$$

The quickest way of finding $|\bar{M}|$ is to multiply the first row by s' and the bottom by m and to add the bottom to the top row. Then

$$s'm|\bar{M}| = ms'(1-b) \quad (b-1)\{m[b(v-s')-s] + b(v\alpha^* + m)s'\}.$$

Since $s' < 0$, the expression on the right-hand side must be negative if $|\bar{M}| > 0$. This, since $(b-1) < 0$, means that the term in braces must be negative and this gives us the stability condition of the text.

So far we have assumed $Ew = n$ throughout, and this assumption is clearly not tenable. It is likely that the rate at which money wages rise will slow down in times of unemployment (and may become negative). It is not difficult to show, however, that, as long as money wages are not adjusting 'perfectly', i.e., as long as real wages are rising in times of unemployment, all our conclusions will remain intact. This seems intuitively ·clear and will not be demonstrated.

Let us now, briefly, relax the assumption that interest rates are constant. A suitable assumption concerning the behaviour of the rate of interest is

Assumption BVI

$$Dr = e\hat{P} + fD\hat{P} \quad e > 0, f > 0. \tag{15.29}$$

This assumption is somewhat more elaborate than assumption AIII in that it also takes account of the effect of the level of prices on the rate of interest. If we set $e = 0$, we have in effect the statement that the rate of change in the rate of interest depends on the difference between the investment and savings ratio, since $D\hat{P}$ depends on that ratio.

It would be too wearisome for the reader to follow the solution of the system (15.26), (15.28) and (15.29) in the text. Here we will simply state the conclusion that, once again, 'moderate' values for e or f will do the trick and ensure stability, provided $\phi(\rho) \equiv \rho$. If this is not so, and ϕ' is small, then, as we would expect, correspondingly 'large variations in interest rates are necessary. Since there are limits below which the rate of interest cannot fall, a pessimistic conclusion is quite open to the 'reasonable' man.

It is time that we attempted an intuitive explanation of model B.

We first note that the model has a good deal of 'optimism' built into it. For we have throughout assumed that, in the absence of 'errors', producers will be investing and expanding their demand for labour at the natural rate, and this in itself implies a considerable faith on their part in continued growth.

Next, suppose that we start from a position of some unemployment, an excess supply of goods and a capital–output ratio, $(1/\alpha)$, which is too high. Money prices fall and, wages not being 'sufficiently' flexible, real wages rise. This leads to a reduction in the demand for labour and a rise in the capital–labour ratio. The marginal product of labour will tend to rise and that of capital to

L

fall. Now, even if interest rates are constant, if producers' investment plans change but slowly, the ratio of investment to income will tend to rise (since income is lower), and the marginal product of labour will also rise more rapidly than it would have done had producers reacted more quickly and reduced their investment. Hence the fall in money prices is slowed down at the same time as the marginal product of labour is rising, and this may be sufficient to return the system to equilibrium. This explains the desirability of a small v and it also makes clear why a small m is useful.

If the reactions of producers are not sufficiently sluggish, there remain two possible stabilizers: changes in the propensity to save due to redistribution in favour of labour, and changes in the rate of interest. Judgements may differ, but in our model, and at a guess in most models, it is very unlikely that changes in the propensity to save will do the trick. Changes in interest rates at first sight may be more important, since they will make a higher capital-labour ratio desirable and hence investment will be reduced by less than it would otherwise have been. Moreover, small changes in the desired capital–output ratio have quite large effects on the investment–income ratio and hence interest rate variations may be of considerable consequence.

But there are two matters which give one some qualms here. First, there is the effect of uncertainty and falling prices to be taken into account. This may well mean that, to get a given reduction in $\phi(\rho)$, we need a large reduction in interest rates. Second, even if this is *not* the case, changes in the capital intensity of production may require changes in 'technique' so that the present capital stock is not suitable for more labour-intensive methods. This 'irreversibility' factor is probably quite important when large deviations from equilibrium are being examined. Here we are justified in ignoring it.

The model just described brings out quite nicely the role of factor substitution in stability. Factor substitution is important to stability because it greatly increases the responsiveness of the system to the price mechanism. If there were no possibility of factor substitution, the chances of interest rate or wage changes stabilizing the system would be much more slender, since producers would have to contend with the deadweight of excess capital. But when that has been granted, it remains true that the speed with which producers react to 'errors' remains of the greatest importance to stability, and since this 'reaction speed' depends, among other things, on the degree of confidence in the continuance of equilibrium, some rather old-fashioned propositions in business cycle theory regain some of their respectability.

IV

Model C

There is one more model which is worthy of a brief examination. We shall now make some rather more 'Keynesian' assumptions than hitherto.

Assumption CI

$$D\hat{Y} = \left(\frac{Ek + \lambda}{\alpha} - s \right). \tag{15.30}$$

This assumption states that the difference between the actual rate of change in output (DY) and its natural rate of change (nY), depends on the difference between the ratio of investment to income and the propensity to save. It is also asserted that, the higher the equilibrium level of output, the more sensitive are producers to the observed 'error'. The justification of (15.30) is obvious. We retain assumptions BIII and BIV of the previous model. Assumption BII is now otiose since, once the change in output and the change in the stock of capital is given, then so is the change in employment. We also note that $D\hat{Y} - D\hat{K} = D\hat{\alpha}$. Thus, expanding (15.30) as usual and combining with equation (15.25b), we have

$$D\hat{\alpha} = D\hat{Y} - D\hat{K} = [vb(1 - \alpha^*) - s]\,\hat{\alpha}. \tag{15.31}$$

Stability requires that the term in square brackets be negative and the chances of that are higher the smaller is v, just as before. But we now note that, since $\alpha^* < 1$, the chances of stability for any given v are greater than we found them to be in the comparable case of model B (see p. 295 above). The reason for this may be understood in the following way.

    In the present model, an excess of savings reduces output. This raises the capital–output ratio and reduces investment by lowering the marginal product of capital. The change in employment is given residually. If, broadly speaking, investment falls less rapidly than incomes, the system will be stable. In model B exactly the same forces were in operation, only there the change in income could be residually inferred from the change in employment and investment. But now there was added to the possible disequilibrating factors the rise in real wages. Thus, in both models the rising capital–output ratio raises the marginal product of labour, but in model B this had to be offset against rising real wages.

Thus it would seem that, if one price (money wages) is relatively rigid, stability may be best served by some other price (the price of goods) also being relatively rigid.

On the other hand, we should note that, if in the present model investment reacts as rapidly to 'errors' as does output – an assumption almost always made in current business cycle models – then $v = 1$, and the stability condition is unlikely to be fulfilled. (Take $b = 0.3, \alpha^* = 0.3, s = 0.1$ or any similar values to check this.)

It is not worthwhile analysing model C any further, since the conclusions we have already reached in section III apply here as well. Thus, if we introduce variability in interest rates, making these also depend on the excess of the investment over the savings ratio or on the level and rate of change of incomes, nothing is found to modify the conclusions we have already reached.

REFERENCES

Kaldor, N. (1957), 'A Model of Economic Growth', *Economic Journal*, **67**.
Solow, R. M. (1956), 'A Contribution to the Theory of Economic Growth', *Quarterly Journal of Economics*, **70**.

16

On the Disequilibrium Behaviour of a Multi-sectoral Growth Model

I INTRODUCTION

Consider an economy capable of balanced growth at a given rate of profit.[1] Two quite distinct interpretations of the disequilibrium of such an economy can be found in the recent literature. On interpretation (a) it is supposed that, at every moment of time, all markets are cleared, actual and desired stocks coincide, price expectations are fulfilled, and the ruling price of each good just covers its cost of production at the given rate of profit. However, initial conditions are such that these requirements cannot all be fulfilled at a balanced growth rate and/or with constant prices. Models of this kind have been investigated by Leontief (1953), Solow (1956), Morishima (1959), Jorgenson (1961) and Uzawa (1961). On interpretation (b) it is recognized that markets may not be cleared, that actual and desired stocks may not coincide, and that expectations may not be fulfilled. In the multi-sectoral growth context such models have been investigated only by Jorgenson (1961). His analysis, however, is open to several objections.

In this paper it is proposed to investigate the behaviour of a model of type (b). The models of the other type have run into several difficulties (Jorgenson, 1960; Solow, 1959), and in any case are not suited to an analysis of what 'actually' happens – they are essentially tâtonnement constructions. On the other hand, (b)-type models are extremely hard to handle, and what follows should be regarded as no more than a first step.

---

[1] I am indebted to my colleagues at Cambridge University and to R. Solow for many useful comments.

II THE PRICE SYSTEM

Notation

Let all prices be expressed in terms of labour, the price of which is set equal to unity. We shall write:

$Q_i =$ the *normal* price of the ith good expected by all *non-i* producers $(i = 1, \ldots, n)$;

$Q(i) = \{Q_1, \ldots, Q_{i-1}, Q_{i+1}, \ldots, Q_n\}$;

$\bar{Q}_i =$ the long-run normal price expected by the ith *producer* $(i = 1, \ldots, n)$;

$\bar{Q} = \{\bar{Q}_1, \ldots, \bar{Q}_n\}$;

$P_i =$ the actual price of the ith good $(P = \{P_1, \ldots, P_n\})$;

$R =$ the expected normal rate of profit.

Time subscripts are omitted, and all the above are to be taken 'at t'. A lower-case letter denotes the log of the corresponding capital one; e.g., $q_i = \log Q_i$. A dot over a symbol gives the operation d/dt. Further notation will be introduced as needed. (The log notation does not apply to t and T.)

The Assumptions

The main feature of this part of the model is to allow the process of price adjustment to proceed independently of supply and demand considerations. This is accomplished as follows. As in all growth models, we assume constant returns to scale in the production of all goods. The typical producer in any sector is assumed to have certain expectations as to the 'normal long-run price' of each of his inputs. These expectations are the outcome of past experience and are modified by experience. The producer also expects to be able to earn a certain normal rate of profit. This expectation we take as unchanged by current events. Since there are constant returns to scale, the two kinds of expectation determine the normal long-run price of the producer independently of the demand for his product. The producer is now supposed to adjust his actual price in the direction of his normal price. As this process proceeds, expectations will have to be reformulated and new normal long-run prices emerge. Our problem is to discover whether this process converges on an equilibrium. We shall now make these assumptions precise.

Suppose that there is no joint production anywhere. Let C_i be the *minimum* unit cost of production in terms of labour of producer i when all inputs are freely and costlessly variable. We introduce the following.

Assumption (A1)
   (a) $C_i = C_i(P, R)$, $C_i > 0$ all $P \geqslant 0$.
   (b) C_i is single-valued and differentiable where required.
   (c) The matrix of differential coefficients $C_{ij} = \partial C_i / \partial P_j$ is indecomposable for all $P \geqslant 0$.
   (d) $\bar{Q}_i = C_i[Q(i), \bar{Q}_i, R]$.

(A1(a)) states that minimum unit costs are independent of the scale of production. No production is possible without the use of labour.

(A1(c)) states that there exists no subgroup of goods which use the other goods in their own production but are not used in the production of these other goods. In Sraffa's (1960) terminology, all goods are 'basics'.

(A1(d)) states that the long-run normal price for his own good expected by the ith producer is such that, at that price and the expected normal prices of inputs, he can, when his technology is fully adjusted, just earn the normal rate of profit R. This may be regarded as a kind of 'full cost' assumption.

In all of this, it is supposed that the ith producer is the typical or 'representative' producer of the ith good, so that what holds for him also holds for the ith sector as a whole.

Assumption (A2)   There exists $P^* > 0$ such that

$$C_i(P^*, R) = P_i^* \qquad (i = 1, \ldots, n).$$

(A2) states that there exists a set of strictly positive prices which if they ruled would ensure $\bar{Q}_i = P_i^*$ all i. It is known (Morishima, 1959; Samuelson, 1961) that, given (A2), such a set of prices exists provided R lies within a certain range. Moreover, labour being the only non-produced input, P^* can be shown to be unique (Samuelson, 1953–4, 1961).

Lastly, we introduce hypotheses on the formation of price expectations and the process of adjustment of actual prices.

Assumption (A3) Let M be a large positive real number. Write $\hat{p}_i = \min(p, m)$ and let $S = \{i \,|\, \hat{p}_i = m\}$.

(a) $\dot{q}_i = \epsilon_i(\hat{p}_i - q_i)$ $(i = 1, \ldots, n,\ \epsilon_i > 0,\ q_i(0) \leqslant m)$.
(b) $\bar{q}_j \leqslant m$ for at least one $j \in S$.
(c) $\dot{p}_i = h_i(\bar{q}_i - p_i)$ $(i = 1, \ldots, n,\ h_i > 0)$.

(A3(a)) is explained as follows. There is an upper bound to the price in terms of labour expected for any *non-own* input. If the actual price should exceed this value it will be regarded as an aberration. This may be justified by the consideration that no one will ever expect any good to be produced at zero labour cost (infinite price in terms of labour).

When the actual price is less than the maximum, then the expected price adjusts itself in a way similar to the familiar 'extrapolation formula'. Essentially, this supposes that expected prices change at such a rate that, if the actual price current today persisted, expected and actual price would approach each other.

(A3(b)) is somewhat artificial. It states that, if the expected prices of some inputs are at their maximum, then at least one of them exceeds the normal expected price of its producer. This assumption is introduced for rather technical reasons (see appendix), and I do not believe it does much harm.

(A3(c)) states that the proportional rate of change in the ith price is a positive linear function of the difference between the log of the normal long-run price and that of the actual price. If the long-run normal price were to remain unchanged, the actual price would approach it indefinitely closely as $t \to \infty$.

This assumption may be rationalized in a number of ways. Producers do not set actual price equal to long-run normal price instantaneously, partly because actual and long-run normal costs differ, partly because they are not certain of their expectations. However, fear of entry or simply rule of thumb will ensure that, if particular expectations persist, the actual price charged approaches the long-run normal price. Each representative producer regards his long-run cost curve as horizontal and follows a pricing rule which just assures him the normal rate of profit in the long run. Such behaviour has been reported by a number of investigations into business behaviour – whether the idealization here presented is adequate or not remains to be seen.

It is worthwhile recalling that all prices are in terms of labour. We are therefore supposing that the desired and actual change in this price always coincide. If money wages are constant, or if their change is perfectly foreseen or if such changes are instantaneously compensated for, this will be so. One or the other of these assumptions is implied by (A3(c)). It would be possible to do without it and to introduce an explicit money-wage equation. This, however, will not be done on this occasion, but this further limitation on the realism of the model should be borne in mind.

This concludes the specification of the price model. Let me recapitulate. On the basis of past prices producers formulate expectations of what they regard as the normal long-run price of their 'non-own' inputs. These prices have an upper bound. Given these expected prices, the expected normal rate of profit and technology, they calculate the normal long-run price they expect to be able to charge. They then adjust their actual price in the direction of the long-run normal price. However, the actual price for inputs ruling may be different from that expected to rule. This causes a certain revision of price expectations. However, in this world – and this is one of its shortcomings – their view of what constitutes the long-run normal rate of profit is as firm as a rock.

The Behaviour of the Model

The basic mathematical manipulations have been confined to the appendix. What follows is a more or less intuitive account of the mode of operation of our construction.

If the model is to be viable we must ensure $P(t) > 0$, $Q(t) > 0$ all $t > 0$. To do this we assume $P(0) > 0$, $Q(0) > 0$ and prove the following.

Proposition (P1) If $P(0) > 0$, $Q(0) > 0$ and (A1)–(A3), then $P(t) > 0$, $Q(t) > 0$ all $t \geqslant 0$.

Proof (i) Suppose not. Let $T > 0$ be the earliest $t = T$ for which $P_i(T) =$ some i. Then by (A1(a)) and (A1(d)), $\bar{Q}_i(T) > P_i(T)$, whence by continuity the same inequality holds for some $T - \theta$, $\theta > 0$ and small. But then, by (A3(b)) and (A3(c)) we have $\dot{p}_i(T - \theta) > 0$, which contradicts $P_i(T) = 0$.

(ii) By the assumption of (P1), (A3(a)) and (i) above, $Q_i(t) > 0$ all $t \geqslant 0$. We have now seen that, if we start with an initial set of strictly positive prices, they will remain so throughout the process – they are bounded from below. By (A3(a)), $Q(i)$ is bounded from above, and so by (A1(c)) is $\bar{Q}$. But then by (A3(c)) so is P. We conclude that for $P(0) > 0$, $Q(0) > 0$ all prices remain inside some positive cube.

We may now state the main conclusion of this part of the model.

Proposition (P2) Given (A1)–(A3), $P(0)$, $Q(0) > 0$, then $P(t) \to P^*$ and $Q(t) \to Q^*$ as $t \to \infty$. P^* here is the price vector defined in (A2).

The detailed proof of (P2) will be found in the appendix. Here I confine myself to an outline of a somewhat simplified case.

There are two kinds of 'errors' producers can make. They may be wrong in their estimate of the long-run normal price of inputs ($Q_i \neq P_i$), or they may find that the price they are currently charging for their output is different from their normal long-run price ($\bar{Q}_i \neq P_i$). These errors may be related, but neither implies the other. We notice, however, that, if there are no 'errors' at all, then $Q_i = P_i = \bar{Q}_i$ all i, and so by (A2) $P_i = P_i^*$ all i.

Now for the purpose of this account only, let us neglect the possibility that some price may exceed the maximum it is ever expected to assume and let us suppose that all adjustment speeds are the same, i.e., $h_1 = h_2 = \ldots = h_n = e_1 = e_n = 1$. Consider the largest, in absolute value, of all the errors. This may be done by squaring all errors and taking the largest. Suppose, again for this account only, that there is a single largest error for each t unless they are all zero. If we can show that the largest of these errors as defined declines as a function of time as long as the error is different from zero, but is constant when it is zero, then we shall have proved (P2).

Suppose, then, that $(P_k - Q_k)^2$ is the largest error at t and that it is not zero. (If it were zero we would be in equilibrium.) Its rate of change with respect to t is found to be $2(p_k - q_k)(\dot{p}_k - \dot{q}_k)$. Using (A3) to substitute for $\dot{p}_k$ and $\dot{q}_k$, we have

$$2(p_k - q_k)[(\bar{q}_k - p_k) - (p_k - q_k)].$$

Evidently since, by assumption, $|p_k - q_k| > |\bar{q}_k - p_k|$, the expression is negative, as it should be.

If $(\bar{q}_k - p_k)^2$ is the largest error at t, the story is somewhat more complex and I give only the roughest outline. To make things simple, suppose $\bar{q}_k > p_k$. Then if this error is to diminish, the rate at which the actual price charged increases (as it will do by (A3(c))) must be greater than the rate of increase in normal cost ($\bar{q}_k$) increases. Now it can be shown that the rate of increase in normal cost must be less than the greatest rate of increase in the price of any one input. This follows from our definition of, and assumption concerning, the function C_i. But by assumption, $(\bar{q}_k - p_k)^2$ is the greatest error, and so no input price can increase faster than p_k itself is increasing. Hence the error will become smaller. An analogous result holds for $\bar{q}_k < p_k$.

It is hard to give a more persuasive account without carrying out the actual manipulations. The outline of the proof, however, makes it clear that the approach to equilibrium may be accompanied by fluctuations in individual prices. For all we can show is the uniform decline in the absolute value of the maximum error, which, of course, does not exclude the possibility that individual errors may be fluctuating in sign during the process.

Conclusion

It is evident that the price model just discussed stands at one extreme of possible approaches to this problem. For it has been supposed that prices are not directly influenced by market events. On the other hand, models which suppose prices to be entirely governed by current market conditions, and which do not distinguish between long-run normal and actual current costs, stand at the other extreme. No doubt, a marriage will be arranged in due course. Yet, considering the common experience in some important sectors of the economy, where considerable current excess demand (positive or negative) seems to have had no, or indeed sometimes a perverse, effect on prices may suggest that the present procedure is not entirely without interest. Moreover, while I have assumed competition to operate (or to be believed to operate) in a manner which ensures a uniform rate of profit, I did not have to suppose competition to be perfect in the technical sense.

Two warnings will conclude this part of the paper. The supposition that R is fixed throughout really implies that the 'disturbance' is in the vicinity of an equilibrium which has persisted for a good time in the past. Hence the 'stability in the large' of (P2) is somewhat misleading, since to suppose R constant for large disturbances would be silly. Second, we recall once again that all prices have been defined in terms of labour. Hence our equilibrium does *not* imply constant money prices – they may be rising or falling as fast as money wages are.

III   THE OUTPUT SYSTEM

This part of the model is at once somewhat more complex than
the previous one and also less satisfactory. I give it partly for the
sake of completeness and partly because it seems possible that it
contains here and there certain features which may be found useful in further work on this difficult topic.

I propose to examine a system of output adjustment in which
expectations do, but prices do not, play a part. The 'signals' which
cause producers to step up their production, or the reverse, are
unexpected changes in the stocks of their own outputs. It will be
supposed that prices have reached their equilibrium, so that the
techniques operated are the equilibrium techniques. Labour is
always in 'abundant' supply. The model which emerges has points
of similarity with many other models of output adjustment from
which price variations are excluded. Such models have largely been
found to be unstable. Here the matter of stability is not quite so
straightforward.

The Expectation Assumptions

It will be supposed that each producer holds a theory of 'normal
demand'. Write $N_i(t)$ as the demand for his product the ith producer regards as normal for t and $D_i(t)$ as the actual demand for
his product. Let λ be the expected rate of growth of normal
demand. We now propose

Assumption (B1)

   (a) $N_i(t) = e^{\lambda t} B_i(t)$.

   (b) $B_i(t) = e^{-\alpha t} \int^t \alpha e^{(\alpha - \lambda) t} D_i(t)\, dt \qquad \alpha > 0$

   (c) $\lambda = F(R) > 0$.

(B1(a)): The producer expects normal demand to grow at the rate
λ. To arrive at the demand expected to be normal for any t he
must choose a certain 'base' (initial value of normal demand). The
'base' chosen at t we write as $B_i(t)$. What this implies is the following: if at $t = 0$ he had chosen $N_i(0) = B_i(t)$ and never varied his
expectations, then his normal demand would be what it is today.
Put somewhat artificially, while producers regard the time deriva-

tive of the log of normal demand as constant, the position of the graph of normal demand will be affected by day-to-day experience.

(B1(b)): If the actual demand ruling at t were always regarded as normal, then by the assumption under discussion we would have $B_i(t) = e^{-\lambda t}D_i(t)$, since in that case $\alpha = \infty$. Substituting in (B1(a)) then gives $N_i(t) = D_i(t)$. However, if past (and current) experience does exert some influence on current expectations ($\alpha \neq \infty$), then the 'base' chosen today is an (exponentially) weighted average of past possible 'bases'.

The formal presentation of (B1(a)) and (B1(b)) may appear somewhat artificial. But producers are reported by many to formulate hypotheses of growth of normal demand. If so, then they will surely also have to decide what it is they expect to grow normally. The above presentation simply formalizes this notion. It is, of course, incomplete, since it takes λ as given, but that is another story.

Using (B1(a)) and (B1(b)), we easily find

$$\dot{n}_i(t) = \lambda + \dot{b}_i(t) \Big\} \tag{16.1}$$
$$\left. \right\} i = 1, \ldots, n$$
$$\dot{b}_i(t) = \alpha_i \mu_i(t) \Big\} \tag{16.2}$$

where

$$\mu_i(t) = \frac{D_i(t) - N_i(t)}{N_i(t)}.$$

(B1(c)) is explained as follows. We write $F(R)$ as the equilibrium rate of growth associated with the equilibrium rate of profit R. By our earlier assumption, (A2), this exists and is positive. We now suppose that the expected rate of growth of normal demand is equal to the equilibrium rate of growth. This is a strong assumption.

The Demand and Output Assumptions

We shall suppose that there are two kinds of goods: capital goods and others. If i is the subscript given to a good, then $i \in K$ means that it is a capital good and $i \in \bar{K}$, that it is not. We also suppose that capital goods are infinitely long-lived; this assumption is of no importance here, and is made only to simplify the exposition.

We write K_{ij}^* as the amount of the stock of the ith good that the jth representative producer would regard as optimal for time t, K_{ij}

as the actual stock of that good held by him. Put $\zeta_{ij} = (K_{ij}^* - K_{ij})/K_{ij}$ and let D_{ij} be the flow demand (at t) of the jth producer for the ith good. Lastly, write X_j as the output of the jth good.

Assumption (B2)

(a) $K_{ij}^* = b_{ij}N_j$ all $i \in K$ and all $i = j$.

(b) $D_{ij} = 2\lambda K_{ij} \dfrac{e^{\zeta ij}}{1 + e^{\zeta ij}}$ all $i \in K$ and all $i = j$, $\infty > K_{ij} > 0$.

(c) $D_{ij} = a_{ji}X_j$ all $i \in \bar{K}, i \neq j$.

(d) $X_j = N_j + D_{jj}$ all j.

(B2(a)): Recalling that we are supposing prices to have reached their equilibrium value, so that the technique of production is the equilibrium technique, this assumption states that the desired amount of any capital good is proportional to normal output. It further asserts that producers hold stocks of their own output – not for 'productive' but for 'market purposes', and that the optimal amount of such stocks is proportional to normal output.

(B2(b)): This is best explained by dividing both sides by K_{ij} and recalling that $D_{ij}/K_{ij} = \dot{k}_{ij}$ the desired rate of increase in the stock of the ith good by the jth sector. Figure 16.1 plots $\dot{k}_{ij}$ as a function of ζ_{ij}. The assumption is thus one of the 'flexible accelerator' type. If $\zeta_{ij} = 0$, i.e., if the desired and actual capital stocks coincide, capital is accumulated at the rate λ. If $\zeta_{ij} > 0$, the rate of accumulation increases, but it never exceeds twice the equilibrium rate. 'Twice' is obviously an arbitrary number, but the point made is simply that there is a limit to the rate at which a representative producer can increase his capital stock. I have supposed infinitely long-lived capital goods, and hence disinvestment is not possible,

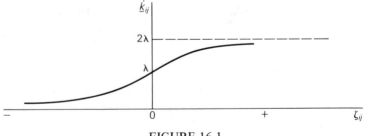

FIGURE 16.1

and $k_{ij} \to 0$ as $\zeta_{ij} \to -\infty$. This, of course, could easily be altered in a more 'realistic' direction.

(B2(c)): This states that the demand for non-capital inputs is proportional to output. This is not a good assumption, since if, say, the jth producer is short of the ith capital good, he may either not be able to produce the desired output (fixed coefficients) or he may have to use more than the 'normal' amount of variable input. Since, however, a model which takes account of this (the variable coefficient case) behaves essentially like the present one, I have thought it best to sacrifice realism to comprehensibility.

(B3(d)) states that the representative producer will produce an output equal to what he considers to be the normal demand for his good plus what he wishes to add to his stocks in the (short) time interval, dt.

So far we have taken no account of labour. Let us denote the latter by the subscript '0' and introduce

Assumption (B3)

(a) $D_{0j} = a_{0j} X_j$.

(b) $D_{i0} = c_i \sum_j a_{0j} X_j \quad (i \in \bar{K})$.

(B3(a)) is similar to'(B2(c)) and requires no further comment.

(B3(b)) assumes that, at the given prices, labour's demand for a given, non-capital good is a constant fraction of its income. Once again, no comment is required.

The Market Assumption

To accomplish the transition from planned to actual events, we must have a mechanism by which any inconsistency in plans can be resolved. The method proposed here is to suppose that all demands for any good i are met by current production plus accumulation (decumulation) of the stocks of the ith good in the hands of its producers. This assumption has two consequences: we cannot investigate a model in which initial stocks of goods in the hands of their producers are zero, and we must ensure that during any adjustment process such stocks never become zero. It is the neglect of these matters which is one of the weaknesses of Jorgenson's paper, to which reference has already been made. These two problems will be discussed more fully below. Here we state the assumption formally.

Assumption (B4)   Let S_{ij} be the amount of the *i*th good *actually* supplied to *j*. Then $D_{ij} = S_{ij}$ all $i \neq j$.

As a consequence of (B4) it follows that, if $\dot{K}_{ii}$ is the *actual* change in the stock of the *i*th good held by the representative producer of *i*, then

$$\dot{K}_{ii} \equiv X_i - \sum_{j \neq i} D_{ij} \quad \text{(all } i \neq 0\text{)}.$$

As already noted at an earlier occasion, it is supposed that there is no labour shortage. If there were, we should have to resolve the problem of the allocation of the available labour supply out of equilibrium, and that is a problem I have not cared to face here.

The Working of the Model

Once again, I propose to give an intuitive account only. Let us again concentrate attention on the possible errors of the system. These are of two kinds: a producer may have less (or more) of a good than he desires ($\zeta_{ij} \neq 0$), and/or he may incorrectly forecast what at a given date he will regard as normal demand ($\mu_i \neq 0$).

Let us first suppose that there are no forecasting errors and consider $(\zeta_{rr})^2$, which we suppose to be the largest of the stock errors. If it can be shown that this is always declining as a function of time as long as it is not zero, then the system will evidently approach an equilibrium. Now differentiating $(\zeta_{rr})^2$ with respect to *t* yields $2\zeta_{rr}\dot{\zeta}_{rr}$. But, by the definition of ζ_{rr},[2]

---

[2] By definition, $\zeta_{rr} = (K_{rr}^* - K_{rr})/K_{rr}$. So

$$\dot{\zeta}_{rr} = \frac{(\dot{K}_{rr}^* - \dot{K}_{rr}) K_{rr} - (K_{rr}^* - K_{rr}) \dot{K}_{rr}}{(K_{rr})^2}$$

$$= \frac{\dot{K}_{rr}^* K_{rr} - K_{rr}^* \dot{K}_{rr}}{(K_{rr})^2}$$

from which the expression in the text is derived.
    Also note that

$$\frac{\dot{K}_{rr}^*}{K_{rr}^*} = \frac{\dot{b}_{rr} N_r + b_{rr} \dot{N}_r}{K_{rr}^*}$$

$$= \frac{\dot{b}_{rr}}{b_{rr}} + \frac{\dot{N}_r}{N} = \lambda, \text{ for } \mu_r = 0.$$

$$\dot{\zeta}_{rr} = \frac{K_{rr}^*}{K_{rr}} \left(\frac{\dot{K}_{rr}^*}{K_{rr}^*} - \frac{\dot{K}_{rr}}{K_{rr}} \right).$$

By (B2(a)), $\dot{K}_{rr}^*/K_{rr}^* = \lambda$ (when $\mu_r = 0$ as here assumed), and

$$\frac{\dot{K}_{rr}}{K_{rr}} = 2\lambda \frac{e^{\zeta_{rr}}}{1 + e^{\zeta_{rr}}}.$$

Substituting in the expression for $\dot{\zeta}_{rr}$ and simplifying, we obtain

$$\zeta_{rr}\dot{\zeta}_{rr} = \zeta_{rr} \left[\frac{K_{rr}^*}{K_{rr}} \frac{\lambda(1 - e^{\zeta_{rr}})}{1 + e^{\zeta_{rr}}} \right].$$

This expression is evidently negative for $\zeta_{rr} \neq 0$, and so the maximum error will surely decline. It is on the basis of this kind of argument that Rose (1959) proposed to refute the Harrodian 'knife edge'.

Let us now take the forecasting error into account ($\mu_r \neq 0$). Two main possibilities arise; either the largest of the squared forecasting errors ($\max_i(\mu_i)^2$) is no larger than the largest of the squared 'stock errors' ($\max_{i,j}(\zeta_{ij})^2$), or this is the other way round. Let us consider the two possibilities in turn.

(a) $\max_{i,j}(\zeta_{ij})^2 = (\zeta_{rr})^2 \geqslant \max_i(\mu_i)^2$. We can now no longer assume that the desired rate of increase in K_{rr} will be the same as the actual rate of increase. Thus, if $\mu_r > 0$ the actual stock of the rth good will increase by less than expected, since the difference between actual and expected demand will be made up by loss of stock. (If $\mu_r < 0$ there will be an unforeseen gain in stock.) Now the actual rate of increase in K_{rr} is $(X_r - D_r)/K_{rr}$, by assumption (B4). By (B2(d)), the desired rate of increase in K_{rr} is $(X_r - N_r)/K_{rr}$. But

$$\frac{X_r - D_r}{K_{rr}} \equiv \frac{X_r - N_r}{K_{rr}} + \frac{N_r - D_r}{K_{rr}} \equiv \frac{X_r - N_r}{K_{rr}} - \mu_r \frac{N_r}{K_{rr}}$$

and so we may express the actual rate of increase in K_{rr} in terms of the desired rate of increase (by (B2(b)) $= 2\lambda[e^{\zeta_{rr}}/(1 + e^{\zeta_{rr}})])$ and the forecasting error.

But not only will the actual stock of the rth good turn out to be different than expected, but so will be the desired stock; for the forecasting error affects the producers' view of normal demand.

Hence the actual rate of increase in the desired capital stock is given by

$$\frac{\dot{K}_{rr}^*}{K_{rr}^*} = \alpha_r \mu_r + \lambda.$$

Now to see whether $(\zeta_{rr})^2$ declines, we differentiate as before with respect to t. Taking the foregoing into account, we find

$$\zeta_{rr}\dot{\zeta}_{rr} = \zeta_{rr}\left[\frac{\lambda(1 - e^{\zeta rr})}{1 + e^{\zeta rr}} + \left(\alpha_r + \frac{N_r}{K_{rr}}\right)\mu_r\right]\frac{K_{rr}^*}{K_{rr}}.$$

Evidently the sign of $\zeta_{rr}\dot{\zeta}_{rr}$ is now in doubt. It is the expectational errors which lie behind the 'knife edge', and in ignoring them Mr Rose may have missed the main point. It should also be noted that, even if $\alpha_r \simeq 0$ (inelastic expectations), the unexpected loss (gain) in stocks may cause trouble.

(b) $\max(\mu_i)^2 = (\mu_r)^2 \geqslant \max(\zeta_{ij})^2$. Once again we wish to show that the maximum error is diminishing in t. Let us for convenience write $W = (\mu_r)^2$ so that $\dot{W} = 2\mu_r\dot{\mu}_r$. From the definition of μ_r we thus have

$$\dot{W} = 2\mu_r \frac{D_r}{N_r}(\dot{d}_r - \lambda - \mu_r)$$

where $d_r = \log D_r$, $D_r = \Sigma_j D_{rj}$. To ensure that this expression is negative we require $|\dot{d}_r - \lambda| < |\mu_r|$. It is not hard to show that

$$|\dot{d}_r - \lambda| \leqslant \max_j |\dot{d}_{rj} - \lambda|.$$

Suppose then that for $j = s$, $|\dot{d}_{rj} - \lambda|$ reaches its maximum. If $r \in K$, then we find

$$|\dot{d}_{rs} - \lambda| = \left|\frac{-e^{\zeta rs}}{1 + e^{\zeta rs}}\frac{\lambda(1 - e^{\zeta rs})}{1 + e^{\zeta rs}} + \frac{\alpha_s}{1 + e^{\zeta rs}}\mu_s\right|.$$

Evidently if we can show that this expression is less than $|\mu_s|$, then, since $|\mu_s| \leqslant |\mu_r|$ by assumption, we will have shown $\dot{W} < 0$ for all $\mu_r \neq 0$. Let us now consider the common sense of this expression. If $\zeta_{rs} = 0$, then the rate of increase of demand for the

rth good by the sth sector can exceed (fall short of) λ only if that sector has made a mistake in forecasting the demand for its own output. For by assumption (B4), the sth sector always gets as much of the rth good as it demands. Hence, provided this mistake does not cause a drastic revision of expectations (α_s 'small enough'), the rate of growth in its demand for the rth good will not exceed (fall short of) λ by more than μ_s, and thus $\dot{W}$ will be negative.

But if $\zeta_{rs} \neq 0$, then the rate of change in demand will differ from λ also, because the sth sector has managed to reduce its 'stock error', and therefore will change its desired rate of accumulation of the rth good. We now see that, the more 'rapidly' a sector attempts to adjust its 'stock error', the more likely it is that $\dot{V} < 0$ and the less likely that $\dot{W} < 0$. The common sense of this is clear: rapid stock adjustment will mean 'large' changes in the demands facing other sectors, and may therefore increase the 'errors' of their forecasts. If $r \in \bar{K}$ the story is a little different – but not much. It will be found in the appendix.

Now it can be shown that in the present model all errors go to zero, provided (a) that at $t = 0$ no error exceeds a critical maximum in absolute value; (b) the expectation coefficients (α_i) are 'suitably' small; and (c) the ratio of own-stock to normal output at $t = 0$ is suitably large! All this is simply the outcome of mathematical manipulations which are indicated in the appendix. The conditions are sufficient, but not necessary, for all errors to go to zero. It should be noted that, even so, the approach to equilibrium may be oscillatory. Lastly, since under these conditions every $|\zeta_{ij}|$ is bounded from above, stocks never run out.

Conclusion

In the section just concluded I have attempted to incorporate two features of the world which seem of some importance. They are, first, the observation that investment plans are made on a 'longish' view and that such a view is not only the outcome of current happenings, and, second, the fairly well established fact that, except for vegetable markets and the like, excess demands are not always met by price changes but by inventory changes. But of course this last point holds only for disturbances which are 'suitably small', and this is one of the reasons why the above model is probably unsuited for an analysis of the behaviour of the system for arbitrary initial conditions.

Even so, I have loaded the dice pretty heavily in favour of stability, by, for instance, supposing the expected rate of growth in normal demand to be fixed and given. It has therefore been mildly surprising that, even so, stability is problematical. It seems to me now that the Harrodian 'knife edge' is of greater importance than recent work would have us believe. The main feature of the latter is that it allows no 'mistakes' (see Introduction), and it is therefore of only marginal relevance to the work of an author who distinguishes between a 'warranted' and an 'actual' rate of growth.

Finally, I should like to re-emphasize that the above is *not* regarded as a 'true picture' of the world we live in. Rather, it is hoped to contain some ingredients which might find a place in such a true picture.

APPENDIX

Proof of Proposition (P2)

It is known (Samuelson, 1953–54) that, under constant returns to scale $C_{ij} > 0$, if the jth good is used in the production of the ith. By (A1), which ensures that labour is always an input and that the production system is indecomposable, it is quickly established that

$$0 < C_i[Q(i), \bar{Q}_i] \equiv \sum_{j \neq i} \hat{C}_{ij} \frac{Q_j}{\bar{Q}_j} < 1 \quad \text{all } [Q(i), \bar{Q}_i] \in L \qquad (\text{A}16.1)$$

where $\hat{C}_{ij} = C_{ij}/(1 - C_{ii})$, and we recall that L is the strictly positive and bounded space to which prices are confined. It follows from (A16.1) that the maximum value of Q_i over L is less than unity, and so there exist numbers $1 > \lambda_i > 0$ such that

$$\lambda_i C_i[Q(i), \bar{Q}_i] < 1 \text{ all } [Q(i), \bar{Q}_i] \in L \quad (i = 1, \ldots, n). \qquad (\text{A}16.2)$$

Now consider

$$W = \max \{\lambda_1 |\dot{p}_1| \ldots \lambda_n |\dot{p}_n|, |\dot{q}_1| \ldots |\dot{q}_n|\}. \qquad (\text{A}16.3)$$

Evidently $W \geqslant 0$. It is obvious that in equilibrium ($\bar{Q}_i = P_i = Q_i$) we have $W = 0$ by (A3). We must show the obverse to be true as well; i.e., if $W = 0$, then the system is in equilibrium. By (A3(c)), if $W = 0$, then certainly $p_i = \bar{q}_i$ all i and by (A3(a)), if $W = 0$, then

$$\min(p_i, m_i) = q_i \quad (i = 1, \ldots, n).$$

Hence

$$\min(\bar{q}_i, m_i) = q_i \quad (i = 1, \ldots, n).$$

But then by (A3(b)) $\bar{q}_i = q_i$ all i. For suppose not; i.e., suppose that the set

$$S = \{i \,|\, q_i = m_i\}$$

is not empty. Then by assumption for at least one i, say k, $\bar{q}_k < m_k$; hence $p_k < m_k$, which contradicts $\dot{q}_k = 0$.

We must now show $\dot{W} < 0$ for all $W > 0$.

Suppose that, at t, $\lambda_r |\dot{p}_r| = W = \lambda_r h_r |\bar{q}_r - p_r|$. Let σ stand for 'sign$(\bar{q}_r = p_r)$'. We have

$$\dot{W} = \sigma h_r \lambda_r \left(\sum_{j \neq r} \hat{C}_{rj} \frac{Q_j}{\bar{Q}_r} - \dot{p}_r \right) = \text{by (A3)}$$

$$= \sigma h_r \lambda_r \left[\sum_{j \neq r} \hat{C}_{rj} \frac{Q_j}{\bar{Q}_r} \epsilon_j (\hat{p}_j - q_j) - h_r(\bar{q}_r - p_r) \right]$$

$$\leqslant \lambda_r \sigma h_r^2 (\bar{q}_r - p_r) \{\lambda_r C_r [Q(r), \bar{Q}_r] - 1\} < 0 \text{ by (A16.2)}$$

$$(A16.4)$$

(The inequality arises since $\lambda_r h_r |\bar{q}_r - p_r| \geqslant \epsilon_j |\hat{p}_j - q_j|$ all j and $\hat{C}_{rj} \geqslant 0$.)

Suppose that, at t, $W = |\dot{q}_r| = \epsilon_r |\hat{p}_r - q_r|$. Let s stand for 'sign$(\hat{p}_r - q_r)$'. We have

$$\dot{W} = s\epsilon_r(\dot{p}_r - \dot{q}_r) = \begin{cases} s\epsilon_r[-\epsilon_r(\hat{p}_r - q_r)] < 0 \text{ for } \hat{p}_r = 0 \quad p \geqslant m \\ s\epsilon_r[h_r(\bar{q}_r - p_r) - \epsilon_r(\hat{p}_r - q_r)] < 0 \quad \text{otherwise.} \end{cases}$$

The second inequality (for $\hat{p}_r \neq 0$) follows from the assumption

$$\epsilon_r |\hat{p}_r - q_r| > \lambda_r h_r |\bar{q}_r - p_r| > h_r |\bar{q}_r - p_r| \text{ since } \lambda > 1.$$

Comment It is seen that (A3(b)) plays a fairly important role in this proof. If it did not hold, the system might get stuck in a quasi-equilibrium with $\bar{Q}_i = P_i$ everywhere, but $\bar{Q}_i < P_i$ for some i. It would then have to be argued that this cannot persist, since if a price continues to rule higher than the highest ever contemplated, the latter will be revised. If, after the revision, (A3(b)) holds, then we shall be all right; otherwise the same problem might again arise. If it turned out that (A3(b)), cannot be sensibly imposed, then the danger exists that the 'errors' will be eliminated only at infinitely high prices, in which case the whole model would cease to be of interest.

Notes on the Output System

In these notes I shall do no more than indicate the lines of a stability analysis. The model is not convincing enough to make detailed manipulations worth-while.

Using the notation of the text, let h be any number such that

$$h < \frac{\lambda}{2}.$$

Let

$$2V = \max \{h\zeta_{11}^2, \ldots, h\zeta_{n1}^2, \ldots, h\zeta_{1n}^2, \ldots, h\zeta_{nn}^2, \mu_1^2, \ldots, \mu_n^2\}.$$

Evidently $V \geqslant 0$ and $V = 0$ if, and only if, all 'errors' are zero. In the latter case it is easily verified that the system is in balanced growth equilibrium. If we could show that $\dot{V} < 0$ for all $V > 0$, then we could conclude that the system approaches its equilibrium path.

Let us introduce the following, where H is some positive number.

(A) $\alpha_j + \dfrac{1+H}{b_{jj}} < 1$ all j

(B) $|\zeta_{ij}(0)| \leqslant H$ all i, j

(C) $|\mu_j(0)| \leqslant hH$ all j.

Suppose that $h\zeta_{rs}^2(0) \neq 0$ belongs to the set of maximal squared errors at $t = 0$. Then $2V(0) = h\zeta_{rs}^2$ and

$$\dot{V}(0) = h\zeta_{rs} \frac{K_{rs}^*}{K_{rs}} \left[\lambda + (\alpha_s + m_{rs}\delta_{rs}) \mu_s - \frac{2\lambda e^{\zeta_{rs}}}{1 + e^{\zeta_{rs}}} \right] \tag{A16.5}$$

where δ_{rs} is the Kronecker delta. Now by (B), the definition of ζ_{rs}, and (B2(a)) of the text, we have

$$m_{rs} \equiv \frac{N_s}{K_{rs}} \leqslant \frac{1+H}{b_{rs}}$$

(since $(b_{rs}N_s/K_{rs}) - 1 \equiv \zeta_{rs} \leqslant H$). Write this upper bound of m_{rs} at $t = 0$ as $\bar{m}_{rs}$ and let $q_s \equiv (\alpha_s + \bar{m}_{rs}\delta_{rs})$. We may then rewrite (A16.5) more compactly as

$$\dot{V}(0) = h\zeta_{rs}\frac{K_{rs}^*}{K_{rs}}\left[\lambda\frac{(1 - e^{\zeta_{rs}})}{1 + e^{\zeta_{rs}}} + q_s\mu_s\right]. \tag{A16.5'}$$

It is not hard to verify by using (A) and recalling that, by definition, $\mu_s \leqslant (\lambda/2)|\zeta_{rs}|$, this expression is negative for $\zeta_{rs} \neq 0$, *provided* that $|\zeta_{rs}|$ is 'small enough'. If H is of the order of magnitude of λ, this will be so.

Next, suppose that $\mu_s^2 \neq 0$ belongs to the set of maximal squared errors at $t = 0$, so that $2V(0) = \mu_s^2$.

We find, using the assumptions of the text, that

$$\dot{V}(0) = \mu_s\frac{D_s}{N_s}(\dot{d}_s - \lambda - \mu_s). \tag{A16.6}$$

If $\dot{V}(0)$ is to be unambiguously negative for $\mu_s \neq 0$, we require

$$|\dot{d}_s - \lambda| < |\mu_s|.$$

But

$$|\dot{d}_s - \lambda| = \left|\frac{1}{D_s}\sum_j \dot{D}_{sj} - \lambda\right| = \left|\sum_j (\dot{d}_{sj} - \lambda)\frac{D_{sj}}{D_s}\right| \leqslant \max|\dot{d}_{sj} - \lambda|.$$

Let $\max|\dot{d}_{sj} - \lambda| = |\dot{d}_{sr} - \lambda|$, say. If this is less than $|\mu_s|$, then (A16.6) is certainly negative.

Suppose $s \in K$. Using the assumptions of the text, we find

$$|\dot{d}_{sr} - \lambda| = \left|\frac{e^{\zeta_{sr}}(e^{\zeta_{sr}} - 1)}{(1 + e^{\zeta_{sr}})^2} + \frac{\alpha_r\mu_r}{1 + e^{\zeta_{sr}}}\right|. \tag{A16.7}$$

It is again not hard to verify that, provided $|\zeta_{sr}|$ is 'small enough' (of the order of λ), the $|\dot{d}_{sr} - \lambda| < |\mu_r|$. But by assumption $|\mu_r| \leqslant |\mu_s|$, and so by the above argument (A16.6) is negative for $\mu_s \neq 0$.

Suppose $s \in \bar{K}, r \neq 0$. Then by (B2) of the text we easily find

$$|\dot{d}_{sr} - \lambda| = \left| \frac{\dot{N}_r + \ddot{K}_{rr}}{N_r + \dot{K}_{rr}} - \lambda \right| \equiv \frac{\dot{n}_r N_r + (\ddot{K}_{rr}/\dot{K}_{rr})\,\dot{K}_{rr}}{N_r + \dot{K}_{rr}} - \lambda. \quad \text{(A16.8)}$$

Now $\dot{K}_{rr} > 0$, $N_r > 0$, and so, if $\dot{n}_r \leqslant \ddot{K}_{rr}/\dot{K}_{rr}$, we have

$$|\dot{d}_{sr} - \lambda| \leqslant |\dot{n}_r - \lambda| = |\lambda + \alpha_r \mu_r - \lambda| = \alpha_r |\mu_r| < |\mu_s|$$

and so (A16.6) is again negative.

If $\ddot{K}_{rr}/\dot{K}_{rr} < \dot{n}_r$, we have

$$|\dot{d}_{sr} - \lambda| \leqslant \left| \frac{\ddot{K}_{rr}}{\dot{K}_{rr}} - \lambda \right| = \left| 2\lambda \left(\frac{e^{\zeta rr}}{1 + e^{\zeta rr}} \right)^2 \right.$$

$$\left. + \frac{\lambda + (\alpha_r - \bar{m}_{rr} e^{\zeta rr})\,\mu_r}{1 + e^{\zeta rr}} - \lambda \right|. \quad \text{(A16.9)}$$

Once again, for $|\zeta_{rr}|$ small enough (of the order of λ), this expression can be shown to be less than $|\mu_s|$.

The last possibility is $s \in \bar{K}$, $r = 0$. But since the proportionate change in workers' income must in absolute value be less than the highest, in absolute value, proportionate change in output, and since the proportion of income spent on any one good is constant, we may again use the above argument.

We have thus shown that, given (A), (B), (C), and provided H is 'small enough', the maximum error at $t = 0$ diminishes. But then evidently it will diminish, as long as it is positive for all $t \geqslant 0$. For clearly $\zeta_{ij}(t) \leqslant H$ all $t \geqslant 0$, and so $m_{rs}(t) \leqslant \bar{m}_{rs}$ all $t \geqslant 0$. Therefore under the conditions specified the system is stable within a small neighbourhood of equilibrium.

It should now be noted that: (1) the above conclusion does not exclude the possibility that individual errors may oscillate in sign during the process of adjustment; (2) that stocks can never run out;[3] (3) the neighbourhood for which our result holds *is* small;

---

[3] Mr Jorgenson neglects the problem of 'running out of speculative stocks', and I have not been able to understand the behavioural content of his model.

and (iv) the result requires either rather insensitive expectations (α small) and/or high optimum stocks in relation to normal output ($\bar{m}_{rs}$ small).

REFERENCES

Jorgenson, D. (1960), 'On a Dual Stability Theorem', *Econometrica*, **28**.

Jorgenson, D. (1961), 'Stability of a Dynamic Input-Output System', *Review of Economic Studies*, **28**.

Leontief, W. (1953), 'Dynamic Analysis', in *Studies in the Structure of the American Economy*, ed. W. Leontief, New York and Oxford.

Morishima, M. (1959), 'Some Properties of a Dynamic Leontief System with a Spectrum of Techniques', *Econometrica*, **27** (4).

Rose, H. (1959), 'The Possibility of Warranted Growth', *Economic Journal*, **69**.

Samuelson, P. A. (1953-4), 'Prices of Factors and Goods in General Equilibrium', *Review of Economic Studies*, **21**.

Samuelson, P. A. (1961), 'A New Theorem on Nonsubstitution', in *Money, Growth and Methodology and Other Essays in Economics in Honor of Johan Akerman*, ed. H. Hegeland, Lund, Sweden.

Solow, R. (1956), 'A Contribution to the Theory of Growth', *Quarterly Journal of Economics*, **70**.

Solow, R. (1959), 'Competitive Valuation in a Dynamic Input-Output System', *Econometrica*, **27**.

Sraffa, P. (1960), *Production of Commodities by Means of Commodities*, Cambridge.

Uzawa, H. (1961), 'On a Two-sector Model of Economic Growth', *Review of Economic Studies*, **29**.

17

On Some Equilibrium Paths

I INTRODUCTION

I was asked to discuss the special problems which arise in the analysis of a sequence of equilibria in a neoclassical model of economic growth when there are many capital goods. Some of the results of this kind of investigation are by now well known, but it is the case that it is possible to make considerable simplifications of analysis, and that is one of my tasks.

The constructions which have been most discussed consider cases in which necessary conditions of intertemporal efficiency are satisfied. It is certainly hard to see why they should be. In a world of malleable and freely transferable capital goods, myopia can be justified, but 'correct myopia' has little to recommend it. Accordingly, I shall also be interested in situations where foresight is not correct. This, in part, extends and simplifies an earlier analysis of my own (Hahn, 1970). I shall also take the opportunity to comment on my predecessors in this field.

Everything which follows must be regarded as tentative in one important respect. The conditions for a momentary equilibrium to be uniquely determined, once the resources are known, are in some respects still not properly understood, and at best are only sufficient and never very appealing. But I am not now clear how important this question of uniqueness really is. Certainly, traditional differential equations analysis requires it, and there are some suggestive examples for a simple case, due to Inada, where lack of uniqueness causes serious problems. But I suspect that there may be results on 'differential correspondences' which would have considerable bearing on the problem at hand, but of which, if they yet exist, I am ignorant.

Lastly, I should like to enter the further disclaimer to the effect that I do not believe that these models capture at all accurately the accumulation process of a capitalist economy.

II BASIC CONSTRUCTION

Let the economy have one consumption good labelled 'O' and m capital goods ($i = 1, \ldots, m$). Write y_i and k_j as the output of the ith good, and the amount of the jth capital good, both per man in the economy. Also, $y = (y_1, \ldots, y_m)$, $k = (k_1, \ldots, k_m)$. All prices are taken in unit of account. P_0 is the price of consumption good, and $P = (P_1, \ldots, P_m)$ is the price vector of capital goods.

There are constant returns to scale, and, throughout the analysis, the efficiency frontier of the economy can be represented by a strictly concave, twice differentiable, function:

$$F(y_0, y, k) = 0. \tag{17.1}$$

It will also be assumed that

$$\partial F / \partial k_i > 0 \quad \text{for } k_i < +\infty$$

$$\partial F / \partial k_i < +\infty \quad \text{for } k_i > 0.$$

It is convenient to define a set $A(k)$ by

$$A(k) = \{(y_0, y) | F(y_0, y, k) \geq 0\}.$$

Throughout, I shall want to examine situations in which the economy is 'momentarily efficient', by which I mean that, with all resources fully used, it is not possible, at that moment, to have more of one good without having less of another. I shall therefore be interested in a function $R(P_0, P, k)$ defined by

$$R = \max_{A(k)} (Py + P_0 y_0). \tag{17.2}$$

It is clear that R is convex in its price arguments and concave in k. On my assumptions, R will be differentiable everywhere.

Let $R_i = \partial R / \partial P_i$. Then

$$R_i(P_0, P, k) = y_i \quad (i = 0, \ldots, m). \tag{17.3}$$

If one is examining an economy where population is growing at the geometric rate n and capital lives for ever, then

$$R_i(P_0, P, k) - nk_i = \dot{k}_i \quad (i = 1, \ldots, m) \tag{17.4}$$

will be the differential equations one will have to analyse.

Let $R_{m+1} = \partial R / \partial k_i$. The R_{m+i} is the shadow price of the service of capital for the moment under consideration. There are a number of possibilities, two of which I take note of now.

Static Price Expectations

All agents take it for granted that current prices will persist into the future. In this case I shall be interested in the question whether there exists a scalar $r > 0$, such that

$$R_{m+j}(P_0, P, k) = rP_j \quad (j = 1, \dots, m). \tag{17.5}$$

The argument behind (17.5) is this. When the economy is in equilibrium, a unit of account invested in any one of the capital goods must have the same rate of return as it has in any other. In the present case this is given by r, since by assumption there are no capital gains or losses. But then, the rental of a unit of capital of type j is rP_j and classic duality theory then tells us that this rental should measure the increase in the maximal receipts of the economy which would result from a little more of capital good j.

Correct Myopic Expectations

In this case, here at $t = 0$ agents have predetermined expectation $\dot{P}_i(0)$, $i = 1, \dots, m$. The system evolves so as to justify this. So in this case, by an argument already given, we shall be interested in the solution of

$$R_{m+j}(P_0, P, k) - rP_j = -\dot{P}_j, \quad \dot{P}_j(0) \quad \text{given } (j = 1, \dots, m). \tag{17.6}$$

Next, there are two kinds of savings assumptions we can make:

1 *Classical savings*, i.e.,

$$R^0(P_0, P, k) - P_0 R_0(P_0, P, k) = 0 \tag{17.7}$$

where

$$R^0 = R - \Sigma R_{m+j} k_j. \tag{17.8}$$

Note that, by constant returns to scale, R^0 is the shadow price of labour, so that (17.7) demands equality between the wage per man and the value of consumption goods per man.

2 *Proportional savings*, i.e.,

$$(1-S)R(P_0, P, k) = P_0 R_0(P_0, P, k), \quad 0 < S < 1. \tag{17.9}$$

Equation (17.9) is self-explanatory.

III THE EXISTENCE OF MOMENTARY EQUILIBRIUM

I shall here consider only the case of classical savings and static price expectations. The situation with myopically correct expectations has already been discussed fairly generally in Hahn (1966).

I shall confine myself to the case $k \gg 0$. I want to show that one can solve:

$$R_{m+j}(P_0, P, k) - rP_j = 0, \quad (j = 1, \ldots, m)$$
$$R^0(P_0, P, k) - P_0 R_0(P_0, P, k) = 0.$$

Since all equations are homogeneous of degree zero in the prices, I normalize prices by requiring them to belong to a set $S(k)$:

$$S(k) = \{(P_0, P) | Pk + P_0 = 1, (P_0, P) \geq 0\}.$$

I shall also make the following assumption.

Assumption (AI) For all $(P_0, P) \in S(k)$, $\sum_{j \neq 0} R_{m+j}(P_0, P) k_j > 0$.

This postulate serves to exclude 'capital satiation' at some prices. I shall also want the following.

Lemma 1 There is a scalar $\lambda > 0$ such that

$$Pk + \lambda(P_0 R_0 - R^0) \geq 0, \quad \text{all } (P_0, P) \in S(k).$$

Proof (a) If $Pk = 0$, $R = P_0 R_0$. By (A1), $R - R^0 > 0$ and so certainly $P_0 R_0 - R^0 > 0$.

.

(b) Let $g(P_0, P) = R^0 - P_0 R_0$. If $g(\cdot) \leqslant 0$ all $(P_0 P) \in S(k)$ there is nothing left to prove. So take it that the set

$$V = \{Pk \,|\, g(\cdot) > 0, \quad (P_0 P) \in S(k) \,|\}$$

is not empty. Let

$$h = \inf_v (Pk).$$

By the argument of (a), $h > 0$. Also, since R^0 is bounded, $R_0 \geqslant 0$, we may define

$$\hat{g} = \sup_{S(k)} g(P_0, P).$$

By hypothesis, $\hat{g} > 0$. Then let

$$\lambda = h/\hat{g}$$

and verify the correctness of the lemma for this λ.

Lemma 2   (a) $R(P_0, P, k)$ is differentiable on $S(k)$ and on

$$0 \ll k \ll +\infty.$$

(b) The partial differential coefficients are continuous on $S(k)$.

Proof   (a) (i) Let $z = y_0$, y, $\tilde{P} = (P_0, P)$, and let $z(\tilde{P}, k)$ be the value of z which maximizes R on $A(k)$. By assumption, $A(k)$ is strictly convex and so $z(\tilde{P}, k)$ is a vector valued function.

(ii) $R(\tilde{P} + h, k) \geqslant (\tilde{P} + h) z(\tilde{P}, k) = R(\tilde{P}, k) + hz(\tilde{P}, k)$

$\qquad R(\tilde{P}, k) \geqslant \tilde{P} z(\tilde{P} + h, k) = R(\tilde{P} + h, k) - hz(\tilde{P} + h, k)$

so

$$\frac{h(z(P + h, k) - z(P, k))}{|h|} \geqslant \frac{R(\tilde{P} + h, k) - R(\tilde{P}, k) - hz(\tilde{P}, k)}{|h|} \geqslant 0.$$

Since $h/|h|$ is bounded, the argument of (i) ensures that the left-hand side converges to zero.

(iii) Since $z(\tilde{P}, k)$ maximizes $\tilde{P}z + \mu^*F(z) + \lambda^*z$ where μ^* is a positive scalar, λ^* a non-negative vector, $\lambda^*z(\tilde{P}, k) = 0$, the differentiability of $F(\cdot)$ establishes that of $R(\tilde{P}, k)$ with respect to k.

(b) (iv) The continuity of $z(\tilde{P}, k)$ over $S(k)$ is a well-established proposition for our assumptions. But $R_i(\tilde{P}, k) = z_i(\tilde{P}, k)$.

(v) $R_{m+i}(\tilde{P}, k)$ is proportional to $\partial F[z(\tilde{P}, k)k]/\partial k_i$. Since F is twice differentiable and $z(\tilde{P}, k)$ continuous on $S(k)$, $R_{m+i}(\tilde{P}, k)$ is continuous on $S(k)$.

One can now prove

Theorem 1   If (A1), then the system

$$R_{m+j}(P_0, P, k) = rP_j \quad (j = 1, \ldots, m)$$

$$R^0 - P_0R_0 = 0$$

$$(P_0, P) \in S(k)$$

has a solution, $Pk > 0, P_0 < 1, r > 0$.

Proof   Consider the mapping

$$T_i(P_0, P) = \min\left[1, Pk + \lambda(P_0R_0 - R^0)\right]\frac{R_{m+i}}{R - R^0} \quad (i = 1, \ldots, m)$$

$$T_0(P_0, P) = \max[0, P_0 + \lambda(R^0 - P_0R_0)]$$

where I have omitted the argument of the functions.

By (A1), $R - R^0 > 0$ everywhere on $S(k)$. By lemma 1, $T_i \geqslant 0$ on $S(k)$. Also $\Sigma R_{m+i}k_i = R - R^0$ everywhere. If on $S(k)$, $Pk + \lambda(P_0R_0 - R^0) \geqslant 1$, then $P_0 + \lambda(R^0 - P_0R_0) \leqslant 0$. Hence the mapping takes $S(k)$ into itself. By lemma 2 it is continuous and so has a fixed point.

Let (P_0^*, P^*) be a fixed point. If $P_0^* = 1$, $R_0(P_0^*, P^*, k) = R(P_0^*, P^*, k)$. But by (A1), $R(P_0^*, P^*, k) - R^0(P_0^*, P^*, k) > 0$ and so by the definition of $T_0(\cdot)$, $(1, 0)$ cannot be a fixed point. A similar argument shows $P_0^* = 0$ to be impossible. Therefore $P^*k > 0, p_0^* > 0$, and $R^0 = P_0^*R_0$ at the fixed point. Also,

$$r^* = \frac{R(P_0^*, P^*, k) - R^0(P_0^*, P^*, k)}{P^*k} > 0$$

$$P_i^* = \frac{1}{r^*} R_{m+i}(P_0^*, P^*, k) \quad (i = 1, \ldots, m).$$

The case of proportional savings and static expectations can be treated in a similar fashion. By an argument similar to that of lemma 1, one establishes the existence of a scalar, $\mu > 0$, such that everywhere on $S(k)$,

$$Pk + \mu(P_0 R_0 - cR) \geqslant 0, \quad 0 < c < 1.$$

The mapping used is that of theorem 1, with $\mu(P_0 R_0 - cR)$ replacing $\lambda(P_0 R_0 - R^0)$ and with the analogous replacement in $T_0(\cdot)$.

IV   UNIQUENESS PROBLEMS

Since I have not assumed the absence of joint production, one cannot expect to find very economically appealing conditions which assure that for $k \geqslant 0$ there is only one equilibrium. But even when joint production is excluded, the multiplicity of capital goods makes such meaningful conditions as there are very artificial.

Consider the case of classical savings and static expectations. We know that, in any equilibrium, $P_0 > 0$, and we may accordingly, for the moment, change the price normalization by setting $P_0 = 1$. Under this normalization, since in the present case *the* rate of profit is well defined, we know that P is uniquely determined by r. (Factor price frontier arguments apply here.) If it were further the case that P is decreasing in r, as it would do if the consumption good used every capital good more intensively than does any other industry, then $R^0 - R_0$ would be monotone in r and uniqueness is assumed. But the story is surely very silly indeed.

For many purposes one is really interested in local uniqueness because the behaviour of the systems in the large is too complicated anyway. Let $B(r) = [R_{m+j,i}] - rI$, an $m \times m$ matrix, and let c be an m-vector with elements $R_j^0 - R_{0j}$. (I have here assumed $R(\cdot)$ to be twice differentiable.) Then one wants E to be nonsingular, where

$$E = \begin{bmatrix} B & -P \\ c & 0 \end{bmatrix}.$$

Of course, B and c are evaluated at an equilibrium. Since

$$R_{m+i,j} = R_{j,m+i} \quad \text{and} \quad R_{j,m+i} = \frac{\partial y_j(1, P, k)}{\partial k_i}$$

one has $b = BP$, where b is the vector with elements

$$\frac{\partial y_0(1, P, k)}{\partial k_j}$$

If b is not null, one may reasonably argue that $B = Bx$ has a unique solution $x = P$, so that B is not singular. This would certainly ensure that in a small neighbourhood P is uniquely determined by r. But that is not enough for the non-singularity of E and I can find no good interpretation other than the very special ones already discussed.

As is well known, the proportional savings assumption with static expectations does ensure a unique momentary equilibrium in the 'two-sector case'. This is so because the economy behaves 'as if' it were maximizing a Cobb–Douglas utility function. With many capital goods this argument will no longer do. By the underlying assumptions, this 'as if' utility function would have the sum of investment outlay as an argument, and this is not sufficient for the desired result. In particular, the set of preferred vectors $(y_0(1, P, k), Py(1, P, k))$ will not in general be convex. Once again, in the no-joint-production case an intensity assumption seems to be required. Recall that in the two-sector case the steady state is generally not unique and that this is due to the lack of one-to-oneness of the rate of profit and the value capital–output ratio. Intensity assumptions overcome this difficulty. In the present case, if $Py(1, P, k)/Pk$ (which is the value output–capital ratio) is one-to-one with the rate of profit, as it will be under suitable intensity assumptions, the momentary equilibrium is unique for given k.

I do not pursue these matters simply because I can find no economically interesting conditions for momentary uniqueness.

V STABILITY

I shall begin by a brief re-examination of the case of correct myopic foresight with classical savings.

Certainly the assumptions ensure the existence of a unique steady state. I denote it by an asterisk and I write R_p and R_k as the vectors (R_i) and (R_{m+i}), evaluated at the steady state. R_{pp}, R_{pk}, etc., are the matrices of second derivatives of R. Also H is a

M

$2m \times 2m$ matrix:

$$\begin{pmatrix} R_{pk} - nI & R_{pp} \\ -R_{kk} & -R_{kp} + nI \end{pmatrix}.$$

Since R_{pp} is positive definite, R_{kk} negative semi-definite, $R_{pk} = R_{kp}$, H has the 'saddle-point property'; i.e., if λ is a root, so is $-\lambda$.

I am concerned with linear approximations near the steady state. I may write

$$\dot{r} = c' \begin{pmatrix} k - k^* \\ P - P^* \\ r - n \end{pmatrix}$$

where c' is a $2m + 1$ vector, and of course $r^* = n$. The whole system becomes

$$\begin{pmatrix} \dot{k} \\ \dot{P} \\ \dot{r} \end{pmatrix} = \begin{pmatrix} & 0 \\ H & P^* \\ \hline & c' \end{pmatrix} \begin{pmatrix} k - k^* \\ P - P^* \\ r - n \end{pmatrix}.$$

Let H have distinct roots, and let Λ be the diagonal matrix of these roots. Then there exists a matrix T such that

$$T^{-1}HT = \Lambda.$$

Define z by

$$\begin{pmatrix} T & 0 \\ 0 & 1 \end{pmatrix} z = (k - k^*, P - P^*, r - n).$$

Then one finds

$$\dot{z}_i = \lambda_i z_i \qquad\qquad (i = 1, \ldots, m)$$
$$\dot{z}_{m+i} = \lambda_{m+i} z_{m+i} - P_i^*(r - n) \quad (i = 1, \ldots, m).$$

Suppose that it is asserted that $z_i(t) \to 0$ for all i, $r(t) \to n$. Then certainly $Rl(\lambda_i) < 0$, $i = 1, \ldots, m$, where $Rl(\cdot)$ stands for 'real part of the root'.

But also then $Rl(\lambda_{m+i}) > 0, i = 1, \ldots, m$, and

$$z_{m+i}(t) = e^{(\lambda_{m+i})t} \int_0^t e^{-(\lambda_{m+i})u} [r(u) - n] du + e^{(\lambda_{m+i})t} c_{m+i}.$$

By assumption, the integral is bounded. But then in general it will not be the case that $z_{m+i}(t) \to 0$. Hence the system is not in general stable. I do not pursue this further beyond noting how useful the dual formulation is for this case. It is of course closely connected with the Hamiltonian of an appropriate intertemporal efficiency problem.

Let me now turn to the inefficient paths generated by an economy with stationary expectations and classical savings. I am once again concerned with expansions close to the steady state. From $rPk = Py$ one obtains easily

$$(r - n) = P^* \dot{k}/P^* k^*.$$

If one could show that

$$P^*(k - k^*)(r - n) < 0$$

everywhere, then one would have enough to deduce stability. From

$$R_k = rP$$

one obtains

$$R_{kk}(k - k^*) + R_{kp}(P - P^*) - n(P - P^*) = (r - n)P^*$$

so

$$(k' - k^*)' R_{kk}(k - k^*) + (k - k^*)'(R_{kp} - nI)(P - P^*)$$
$$= (r - n) P^*(k - k^*).$$

Certainly R_{kk} is negative semi-definite, but we have no information on the second term on the left-hand side. In general, therefore, no easy answer is available and one suspects that there certainly may be cases where the system is unstable.

As an example, let me consider the following stable case. I write

$$F(y_0, y, k) = G(y, k) - y_0 = 0$$

with

$$G(y, k) = y'Ay + \Sigma \log k_i \alpha_i$$

where A is a negative definite matrix and $B = -A^{-1}$ is positive. Routine calculations give

$$R_p = BP$$
$$R_k = \{\alpha_i/k_i\}.$$

One notes that R_p is independent of k and R_k independent of P. This is just the sort of situation one would expect to be well-behaved.

It is easy to check that momentary equilibrium is unique. Also, $R_{kp} = R_{pk} = 0$. Also, since $R_k = rP$, one has

$$rP'k = \Sigma \alpha_i$$

whence $Py = rP'k$ is a constant and

$$(P-P^*) y^* + P^*(y - y^*) = (P-P^*)'BP^* + P^*B(P-P^*).$$

But B is symmetric, and so

$$P^*B(P-P^*) = 0.$$

Now

$$k = -In(k-k^*) + B(P-P^*)$$

and

$$P^*k = -P^*n(k-k^*) + P^*B(P-P^*) = -P^*(k-k^*)$$

which is what one wants.

It is plain that this is a very special case indeed. For instance, the relative equilibrium value of capital goods is independent of prices and of endowments. Also, it is easily checked that momentary equilibria are unique. Shell and Stiglitz discuss an even more special situation which in the context of this example would arise if $\Sigma\alpha_i \log k_i$ were replaced by $\alpha\Sigma \log k_i$. Then the relative prices of capital goods would be constant and capital goods could be aggregated.

The special cases suggest that the system may do better than it does under myopic expectations, but it is not the case it *must* do better. Before discussing this, it is instructive to return to the traditional two-sector model with classical savings. Suppose it to be the case that, for a small displacement of the capital–labour ratio from its steady-state value, one can always find a momentary equilibrium such that the rate of profit deviates from n in the same direction as the capital–labour ratio does. Then, because of the Inada (1963) conditions, momentary equilibrium cannot be unique in the vicinity of the steady state. Although Inada has given an example of instability in this case, the use of ordinary differential equation analysis is difficult. In any event, the steady state may be unstable only when momentary equilibrium is not unique.

The question arises whether the same conclusion holds when there are a number of different capital goods. To investigate this, I must first make a small digression.

Suppose there is no joint production anywhere. Suppose $k \neq k'$ (k is again a vector), but let r be the same in both situations. Certainly, from the substitution theorem, P will be the same in both situations. Suppose that it is possible to find a product mix such that all inputs are utilized fully when the endowment is k' or k. Then the rental of each capital good will be the same in both situations and both will be momentarily efficient. By this I mean that, with k (or k'), it is impossible to produce more of one good without producing less of another. Hence revenue will be at a maximum in both situations, and since the snadow and private rental coincide, $R_k(P, k) = R_k(P, k')$. Hence for certain ranges of the domain of R, R is linear in k. In particular, that will be the case in the vicinity of a steady state where all goods are produced in positive quantities. Note that, by the strict concavity of $F(\cdot)$, there is a one-to-one correspondence between P and product mix. Hence if, because of factor reversal, another r, say r', were also to give the same P, it could not find a product mix which utilized all resources.

With this in mind, one may write the linear expansion of $nP^* - R_k(\cdot)$ about the steady state as

$$(nI - R_{kp})(P - P^*) + e(r - n) = 0,$$

where e is the unit vector. One notes that, if R_{kp} were a positive matrix, $(nI - R_{kp})$ would not have a positive inverse. To see this, choose units such that $P^* = e$. Since R_k is homogeneous of degree one in all prices, one has, for the ith row of R_{kp},

$$\sum_{j=0} R_{m+i,j} = n - R_{m+i,0}.$$

But $R_{m+i,j} = R_{j,m+i}$. So if $R_{m+i,j} > 0$ all j, $R_{j,m+i} > 0$ all j. That means that there is an increase in the production of every capital good when there is an increase in the amount of the ith capital good and prices are constant. But then there cannot be an increase in the output of consumption good, and indeed $R_{0,m+i} = R_{m+i,0} < 0$. But then

$$\sum_{j \neq 0} R_{m+i,j} > n$$

and this is true for all j, whence, by a well-known theorem, $(nI - R_{kp})$ does not have a positive inverse when R_{kp} is positive. Of course, if R_{kp} is not positive this is not necessarily true.

If momentary equilibrium in the vicinity of the steady state is not unique, a local expansion may make no sense. I shall accordingly assume that the production of the consumption good is more intensive in every machine than is the production of any other good. Even so strong an assumption does not take us very far in the present case.

From the requirement that in each momentary equilibrium the demand for consumption goods should equal its supply, I find

$$\begin{pmatrix} 0 \\ -\Sigma R_{0,m+j}(k_j - k_j^*) \end{pmatrix} = \begin{pmatrix} A & ne \\ (R_{0j}) & P^*k^*n \end{pmatrix} \begin{pmatrix} P - P^* \\ r - n \\ n \end{pmatrix}$$

where $A = (nI - R_{kp})$ and $\{R_{0j}\}$ is the vector with components R_{0j}. It is clear that, even if, say, A should have a positive inverse, this does not give one very much information. Indeed, suppose that the matrix on the right is a P-matrix. Then it is trivial to show that

$$\text{sign}\,(r - n) = \text{sign} -\Sigma R_{0,m+j}(k_j - k_j^*).$$

But even so, and even taking $R_{0,m+j} > 0$ all j, this is not quite what we require, since $\Sigma P_j^*(k_j - k_j^*)$ need not have the same sign as $\Sigma R_{0,m+j}(k_j - k_j^*)$. Certainly, in this case, if every capital good is increased beyond the steady state, the rate of profit must be lower, but this is a poor result. It would tell us that the system cannot 'explode', but it would not, for instance, exclude the possibility that in the phase space of the capital goods the steady state is a saddle-point. Indeed, elsewhere (Hahn, 1970) I have given an example where this is so.

Let the solution for $(r-n)$ in the above equations be written $y(k - k^*)$. Then the output system becomes

$$\dot{k} = -A(k - k^*) + BA^{-1}ey(k - k^*).$$

There is nothing useful one can say about this even if A has a positive inverse, and of course B is known to be positive definite.

One must conclude that uniqueness of momentary equilibrium with stationary expectations does not, as in the two-sector case, ensure stability. The reasons now seem to me obvious: with many capital goods the uniqueness assumption is not enough to ensure that the rate of profit and the value of the capital–labour ratio are related in any simple way. In the two-sector case one can reduce the system to a miniature general equilibrium one in labour and capital. It is known that a two-goods general equilibrium system has a unique equilibrium if and only if the Weak Axiom of Revealed Preference holds. In this context, the Weak Axiom is simply the 'proper' relationship between the rate of profit and the capital stock. When the Weak Axiom holds, stability also is assured. In a many-goods world the Weak Axiom is sufficient for uniqueness but not necessary.

It may be instructive to see how far one can get. I choose an example in which production functions are everywhere Cobb–Douglas.

I write α_{ij} as the share of the ith capital good in the receipts of the production of the jth, α_{i0} as its share in the receipts of the consumption sector. Also, the suffix '0' refers both to labour and consumption good and

$$\beta_{ij} = \alpha_{ij}\alpha_{00} - \alpha_{i0}\alpha_{0j}, \quad B = (\beta_{ij})\frac{1}{\alpha_{00}}.$$

I suppose the consumption sector to be more intensive in the use of any capital good than is any capital good. (Note the absurdity of this.) This makes B a negative matrix which I assume to be non-singular. One calculates at $P^* - e$ that $R_{kp} = nB^{-1}$ and

$$(P - P^*) = \frac{r - n}{n} eB(I - B)^{-1} \tag{17.10}$$

and verifies that $(P - P^*)$ is inversely related to $(r - n)$.

The basic differential equations are

$$\dot{k} = (B^{-1} - I)(k - k^*) n + R_{pp}(P - P^*)$$

or

$$-B\dot{k} = -(I - B)(k - k^*) n - BR_{pp}(P - P^*).$$

Let $C = (I - B)^{-1}$, then also, after substitution from (17.10),

$$-e'CB\dot{k} = -e'nI(k - k^*) - e'CBR_{pp}C'B'e \frac{r - n}{n}. \tag{17.11}$$

Let $v = e'CBR_{pp}e$. Then, since R_{pp} is positive definite, $v > 0$. Also, we know that the classical savings assumption gives $e'k = (r - n)e'k^*$. Then finally, one has

$$e'(wI - CB)\dot{k} = -ne'(k - k^*) \tag{17.12}$$

where $w = v/ne'k^*$. The left-hand matrix is positive.

From (17.12), one concludes that, in the vicinity of the steady state, if the value, at steady-state prices, of capital per man is higher (lower) than in the steady state, a certain weighted sum of capital per man must be falling (rising).

This seems to be the furthest one can get, and it is not very far, even though the case is a rather favourable one. For instance, (17.12) does not exclude the saddle-point property of the steady state in the phase space of k. Moreover, in the Cobb–Douglas case, certainly, the strong intensity assumption is not required to give a unique momentary equilibrium. When it is not used, all is confusion.

VI SOME CONCLUSIONS

The reason for dwelling so long on the case with static price expectations is this. When I first noted that the case of myopically correct expectations may be ill behaved, I and most others believed that this was simply due to the 'catenary' property of paths that satisfy the necessary condition of intertemporal efficiency. It seemed that the case of static expectations ought to do much better. This belief was reinforced by a misinterpretation of a well-known result due to Morishima: he showed that, if the steady-state rate of profit is always expected to rule, then the price system would be stable and the output system might be so. This of course is a different problem, and in any case does not claim that outputs must converge on the steady state.

It would now seem to me that all these beliefs were mistaken. Even with static expectations, heterogeneous capital means that we are dealing with many goods, and, as students of general equilibrium know, there are no theories which, for instance, ensure a link between uniqueness and stability. The fact that the rate of profit is not simply related to some measure of the capital stock is here the main source of trouble, and this trouble does not arise when there is only one capital good or when the relative prices of capital goods are always constant. The question of whether the economy tends to the steady state has no simple answer at present; I should add again that I doubt that the equilibrium dynamics approach to answering it is the proper one.

REFERENCES

Hahn, F. H. (1966), 'Equilibrium Dynamics with Heterogeneous Capital Goods', *Quarterly Journal of Economics*, **80**.
Hahn, F. H. (1970), 'On Some Adjustment Problems', *Econometrica*, **38**.
Inada, K. (1963), 'On a Two-sector Model of Economic Growth', *Review of Economic Studies*, June, **30**.
Shell, K. and Stiglitz, J. E. (1967), 'The Allocation of Investment in a Dynamic Economy', *Quarterly Journal of Economics*, **81**.

Part V

Miscellaneous

18

Savings and Uncertainty

The question whether increasing uncertainty of future prospects should cause a rational agent to provide more or less generously for the future is one of some practical and theoretical interest.[1] The papers by Phelps (1962), Levhari and Srinivasan (L–S) (1969) and Mirrlees (1965) have taken us a long way in this problem. However, they are, quite properly, much concerned with the logically prior question of 'existence'. My purpose here is more modest: it is to show how, taking it for granted that a solution exists, one may obtain some of the properties of the optimum path rather simply. This has the virtue that it becomes easier to understand the main consideration involved.

I THE SIMPLEST CASE

Let U be a concave function of consumption c, $r \geqslant 0$ a random variable, distributed independently of t. Let $k(t)$ be wealth at t. The (L–S) problem is

$$\max E\left\{ \sum_{t=0}^{\infty} \beta^t U[c(t)] \right\}; \quad \beta > 0 \tag{18.1}$$

subject to

$$k(t) = [k(t-1) - c(t-1)]r; \quad k(0) > 0, k(t) \geqslant 0. \tag{18.2}$$

Assume that the problem can be solved. Let $[c]_t$ be the infinite consumption path starting at t. Certainly, given expectations, the feasible set of these depends only on $k(t)$. But the utility function

[1] I wish to acknowledge valuable comments from Professor J. R. Mirrlees.

is separable and the utility of any period's consumption is independent of t. Hence, the horizon being infinite, the maximand looked at from t is the same for all t. Hence it must be true that the solution to the problem is given by a policy $c(t) = c[k(t)]$.

When will $[c]_0$ be optimal? A necessary condition must be that any substitution between the consumption of adjacent periods, which leaves wealth for any realization of r in any other periods unchanged, must not increase (18.1). Taking $t = 0, 1$, this gives[2]

$$\beta E\langle U'\{c[k(1)]\}\rangle = U'\{c[k(0)]\}. \tag{18.3}$$

Consider an increase in uncertainty – say, in the variance of r. If this increases the left-hand side of (18.3) it will lead to an increased transfer of consumption to period 1. If it reduces the left-hand side, the reverse will be true. But let

$$g\{r, c[k(0)]\} = U\{c[k(1)]\}\, r.$$

Then the behaviour of the left-hand side of (18.3) will depend on whether $g(\cdot)$ is a concave or convex function of r. If $g(\cdot)$ is concave, increased uncertainty will reduce (if it is convex, increase) the provision made for the future. The following familiar diagrams illustrate this.

Figures 18.1(a) and 18.1(b) are almost self-explanatory (α will be defined presently). They show the case when there are only two

---

[2] The maximand of problem (18.1), (18.2) is written as

$$\beta^t U[c(t)] + \beta^{t+1} U[c(t+1)] - \lambda^t \{k(t+1) - [k(t) - c(t)]r\}$$
$$- \lambda^{t+1} \{k(t+2) - [k(t+1) - c(t+1)]r\}.$$

So

$$c(t): \qquad \beta^t U'[c(t)] = \lambda^t r$$
$$c(t+1): \quad \beta^{t+1} U'[c(t+1)] = \lambda^{t+1} r$$
$$k(t+1): \quad -\lambda^t + \lambda^{t+1} r = 0.$$

Therefore the stochastic Euler equation is

$$\beta E U'[c(t+1)]r = U'[c(t)].$$

For $t = 0$ we obtain equation (18.3), given that

$$c(t) = c[k(t)] \ \forall\, t.$$

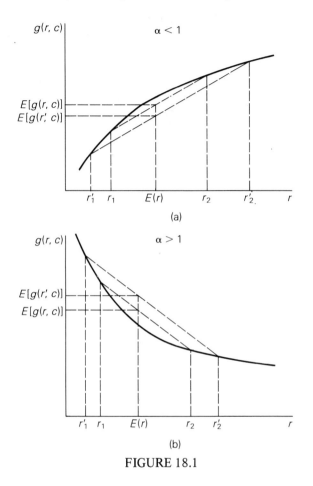

FIGURE 18.1

possible returns (r_1, r_2) which are then changed to (r'_1, r'_2), leaving the mean $E(r)$ unchanged. In the concave case (figure 18.1(a)) the left-hand side of (18.3) is reduced (leading to greater present consumption), while in the convex case (figure 18.1(b)) the reverse is the case.

The question therefore turns on the sign of g_{rr}. In general, this cannot be calculated until we know the optimum policy, $c(k)$. In particular, we need to know $c'(k)$ and $c''(k)$. Now (L–S) assume $U(\cdot)$ to be a homogeneous function of constant degree. But then, in the present model, one shows that $c(k)$ must be homogeneous of degree one in k; i.e., $c/k = \gamma$, a constant.

To see this, consider the following argument due to Mirrlees. Let $k'(0) = \lambda k(0)$, $\lambda > 0$. Let $[c^*]_0$ be the optimum stream at $k(0)$. Then certainly $[\lambda c^*]$ is feasible at $k'(0)$. Let $[c']_0$ be any other stream feasible at $k'(0)$. Consider $U(\lambda c^*) - U(c')$. In view of homogeneity,[3] this is equal to $\lambda^{-\beta}[U(c^*) - U(c'/\lambda)]$. But the stream $[c'/\lambda]_0$ was feasible at $k(0)$ and so, in view of optimality,

$$E\left\{ \sum_{t=0}^{\infty} \beta^t [U(\lambda c^*) - U(c')] \right\} = E\left\{ \sum_{t=0}^{\infty} \beta^t \lambda^{-\beta}[U(c^*) - U(c'/\lambda)] \right\}$$

$$\geqslant 0$$

which shows that indeed $[\lambda c^*]_0$ is the optimum stream at $k'(0)$.

With this information we can now compute $c(k) = \gamma k$ directly from (18.3) (see L–S). I prefer to compute g_r and g_{rr} which are given by

$$g_r = U'\{c[k(1)]\}\,(1 - \alpha)$$

$$g_{rr} = U'\{c[k(1)]\}\,\alpha(1 - \alpha)/r$$

where

$$\alpha = -U''c/U'.$$

Hence it follows that, when $\alpha > 1$, $g(\cdot)$ is a decreasing convex function of r (figure 18.1(b)) and when $\alpha < 1$, $g(\cdot)$ is an increasing concave function of r. Of course, when $\alpha = 1$, g is linear in r.

The 'common sense' of these results is analogous to that of the familiar distinction between 'gamblers' and 'insurers', even though the utility function is strictly concave. For what is relevant to the saving decision is the marginal gain, in any period, from consuming a little less in the preceding period. Thus, for instance, when $\alpha < 1$, this marginal valuation increases by less as a consequence of entertaining the more favourable prospect r'_2 than it falls by entertaining the less favourable one, r'_1, and consequently the expected marginal valuation falls. There is thus a 'marginal preference' for the 'safe' course of action, which is present consumption. When $\alpha > 1$ the reverse is true and the agent is 'marginally' willing to 'gamble' on future consumption. Of course, one can look at the same phenomenon the other way up: when $\alpha > 1$, the agent is 'insuring'

---

[3] I here take $U(c) = -c^{-\beta}/\beta$, so that α defined below is given by $\alpha = \beta + 1$.

his future standard, while if $\alpha < 1$ he is 'gambling' on his future standard. As David Gale has pointed out to me, this becomes more intuitive by noting that, when $\alpha > 1$, U is bounded above but unbounded below (so there may be 'infinite' disasters but only finite gains), while the reverse is the case when $\alpha < 1$.

Lastly, one notes that, whereas in the standard (Friedman and Savage) analysis of insurance and gambling, the answer turns on the second derivative of $U(\cdot)$, here, in so far as we are concerned with a change in the variance of r, it is the third derivative which is important.

II PORTFOLIO SELECTION

The analysis of section I allows us to deal with the example of L–S more simply and completely. One assumes that there are two assets with returns r_1 and r_2, respectively. The latter are independently distributed random variables. Let

$$w(t) = k(t-1) - c(t-1)$$

and

$$k(t) = [\lambda r_1 + (1-\lambda)r_2]w(t), \quad 0 \leqslant \lambda \leqslant 1$$

where λ is the proportion of wealth spent on asset of type 1.

For given λ, the analogue of equation (18.3) is

$$U'\{c[k(0)]\} = \beta E\langle U'\{c[k(1)]\}[\lambda r_1 + (1-\lambda)r_2]\rangle \qquad (18.3')$$

and it is clear that, for fixed λ, the analysis of saving behaviour when the variance of $[\lambda r_1 + (1-\lambda)r_2]$ changes is as before. However, one must now also determine λ.

For any $c(0)$ one has the problem

$$\max E\langle U\{c[k(1)]\}\rangle$$

subject to $\lambda \geqslant 0$, $1 - \lambda \geqslant 0$, $c(0)$ given, since for any optimal policy it must not be possible to increase the expected utility of any period by changing the composition of assets in the previous period. Since U is concave, the problem is solved when

$$E\langle U'\{c[k(1)]\}(r_1 - r_2)\rangle + \mu_1 - \mu_2 = 0$$

where $\mu_i \geqslant 0$ $(i = 1, 2)$ are the Kuhn–Tucker multipliers. One has at once

$$E\langle U'\{c[k(1)]\} (r_1 - r_2)\rangle = 0 \quad \text{implies } 0 \leqslant \lambda \leqslant 1,$$
$$E\langle U'\{c[k(1)]\} (r_1 - r_2)\rangle < 0 \quad \text{implies } \lambda = 0,$$
$$E\langle U'\{c[k(1)]\} (r_1 - r_2)\rangle > 0 \quad \text{implies } \lambda = 1.$$

These are commonplace results and need not detain us. The question I wish to investigate is whether, when uncertainty can be measured by variance, an increase in the uncertainty in the yield of the asset will cause the proportion of wealth invested in it to decline (if that is possible). I only look at the case of an 'interior' solution since the other cases follow quite trivially.

Let $h(r_1) = U'\{c[k(1)]\}_1$. Then taking U to be homogeneous, and using the notation of section I, we find

$$h' = U'\{c[k(1)]\}\left[1 - \alpha \frac{\lambda^* w}{k(1)} r_1\right] \tag{18.5a}$$

$$h'' = \frac{\alpha U' \lambda w}{k(1)} \left\{(1 + \alpha)\left[\frac{\lambda^* w}{k(1)} r_1 - 1\right]\right\} \tag{18.5b}$$

where λ^* is the optimum value of λ. For an interior solution, $h'' < 0$, for then

$$\lambda^* w r_1 / k(1) < 1.$$

Hence, whether $h(r_1)$ is increasing or decreasing in r_1, it is *concave*. But then, from our discussion in section I, we know that an increase in the variance of r_1, leaving $E(r_1)$ unchanged, must cause $E(U' r_1)$ to fall, and this means that in the new situation a marginal transfer to asset of type 1 reduces expected utility in period (1) (whereas previously it left it unchanged). Hence, for given $c(0)$ the proportion of wealth invested in asset 1 will decline. However, (18.4) is clearly independent of w, and so of $c(0)$, when U is homogeneous and $\mu_1 = \mu_2 = 0$. Hence, whatever the effect of the changed variance on $c(0)$, *the conclusion stands: the proportion of wealth invested in the asset will decline*.

It is clear that this (quite expected) result must be kept distinct from an answer to the question of how an increase in the variance will affect the total amount of the asset bought. If $\alpha < 1$, there is no problem, since we already know that less will be saved. When

$\alpha > 1$, the matter is more problematical. Indeed, the reader can construct examples for which the amount of the now riskier asset bought is increased. This kind of 'Hicksian' result is again quite in accordance with common sense.

III SOME CONCLUDING REMARKS

No one will deny that the economic assumptions of the Mirrlees model are pretty drastic. Yet it is fairly hard work to get any results. (Mirrlees, who found approximate explicit solutions for $c(a, k)$, had a much harder time still.) I conclude that the exercise is not to be taken in a practical spirit but rather as a demonstration that a rational planner may make more provision for the future when the future becomes more uncertain. This sort of qualitative counter-example to what was once the prevailing contrary view is eminently worth having.

REFERENCES

Levhari, D. and Srinivasan, T. N. (1969), 'Optimal Savings under Uncertainty', *Review of Economic Studies*, 36, 27–38.
Mirrlees, J. A. (1965), 'Optimum Accumulation under Uncertainty', unpublished paper.
Phelps, E. S. (1962), 'The Accumulation of Risky Capital: a Sequential Utility Analysis', *Econometrica*, 30, 729–43.

19

Excess Capacity and Imperfect Competition

I

In the *Oxford Economic Papers*, Professor Hicks (1954) has re-examined some orthodox conclusions of Imperfect Competition Theory in the light of Mr Harrod's re-appraisal (1952). In doing so he distinguishes between two periods: the closed period, when the number of competitors remains the same, and the open period, when the number and kind of competitors may change. An entrepreneur entering the industry is assumed to take decisions of (a) how much to produce in each of these periods, and (b) on what 'scale' to produce. Various possible outcomes are classified by the type of expectations and the type of entrepreneur.

In reading Professor Hicks' important contribution, I felt the desire to attempt an extension of his analysis in order to examine some of Mr Harrod's objections to orthodoxy a little further. It soon emerged, however, that the Hicksian model did not lend itself easily to this purpose, first because there is a rather important slip in the analysis, and second because the model does not carry the story far enough into Harrodian territory. In particular, Mr Harrod's 'entrepreneurial ritual' finds no place in the Hicksian cosmos. Since what follows was directly inspired by Professor Hicks' article, we shall first re-examine his model, and then proceed, with what we have learned, to discuss Mr Harrod's proposition. This I define as follows: the fact that the demand curve facing a unit of supply is downward-sloping is not a sufficient condition for the emergence of excess capacity, even if the unit of supply has polypolistic expectations.

II

Since we are concerned with excess capacity, it will be convenient to define this term right at the outset. We shall distinguish between three kinds of excess capacity.

1 *Orthodox excess capacity* is said to exist if long-run average costs are diminishing at that output at which the given equipment (scale) enables that output to be produced at lowest average cost.

2 *Transitional excess capacity* is said to exist if the given equipment (scale) exceeds that at which the contemplated output(s) could be produced at lowest average cost.

3 *Dynamic excess capacity* is said to exist if the given equipment (scale) is larger than it would have been had the future been correctly foreseen.

These definitions are unfortunately a little clumsy. The reason for putting them forward in this way is as follows. Mr Harrod is interested in situations in which the scale of production planned is related not to a single, but to a number of possible, contemplated outputs. In other words, we shall wish to investigate situations where the position of the demand curve is not exactly known. We cannot therefore define excess capacity with reference to a single output. Thus, for instance, instead of defining orthodox excess capacity as existing when, at the given output, the short-run average cost curve is tangential to a downward-sloping long-run average cost curve, we say that this kind of excess capacity exists if, at a hypothetical cost-minimizing output (with given equipment), long-run average costs are declining.

In the definitions we speak of scale, or size of equipment. The exact way of giving some measure to these concepts will be discussed presently.

III

We shall now restate the Hicksian model (HM) with some slight modifications. It is clear that some concept of utility maximization is implicit in HM. For reasons which will become obvious later, we shall make this assumption explicit. No difference whatsoever is thereby made to HM.

The notation is the same as in HM. Capital letters stand for open-period and lower-case letters for closed-period, variables and functions. Thus, x, X are outputs, c, C are costs, r, R are revenues. Professor Hicks defines four functions:

$$c = c(x, X) \tag{19.1}$$

$$C = C(X) \tag{19.2}$$

$$R = R(x, X) \tag{19.3}$$

$$r = r(x). \tag{19.4}$$

The exact meaning of these will be discussed shortly. Let

$$g = r(x) - c(x, X) \tag{19.5}$$

$$G = R(x, X) - C(X) \tag{19.6}$$

and interpret g as closed-period and G as open-period profit. There are two unknowns, x and X. Solve for these by maximizing

$$U = U(g, G), \tag{19.7}$$

the utility function of the entrepreneur. This gives us two equations:

$$U_g(r_x - c_x) + U_G R_x = 0 \tag{19.8}$$

$$U_g(-c_X) + U_G(R_X - c_X) = 0. \tag{19.9}$$

These two equations are in all respects similar to those of HM ($U_g = l$, $U_G = m$, in HM). Subscripts denote partial differentiation.

IV

It will have been noticed that at present, the definition of G is ambiguous. It might be legitimately asked why not, instead of (19.6), write

$$G = R(x, X) - c(x, X). \tag{19.10}$$

The same question might be put slightly differently: are there not three rather than two unknowns to the problem, namely x, X, and the scale of production? Professor Hicks (1954), aware of these difficulties, has resolved them as follows. He writes: 'we are making the usual Marshallian assumption that the size of the plant is determined by long-period output only.'[1] Thus the third unknown is not determined analytically but by an extraneous assumption. This explains (19.1), for X really becomes an index of 'scale' and enters in a unique way into $c(\cdot)$. But this assumption has some rather curious consequences.

V

Consider (19.9). The equilibrium condition described by this equation is quite general. Let us therefore assume $x > X$, $U_g > 0$, $U_G > 0$. By the Marshallian assumptions, short-run and long-run average costs are equal for output X. Since the long-run average cost curve is the envelope of the short-run average cost curves, it follows that, at output x, short-run average cost is greater than long-run average cost. For the same reason (since $x > X$), an increase in scale would reduce the cost of producing x, i.e. $c_X < 0$. From our assumptions and (19.9), it must then be true that $R_X < C_X$. Now C_X is the long-run marginal cost of producing X. Again by the Marshallian assumptions, this long-run marginal cost must equal the short-run marginal cost of producing X.[2] Hence (19.9) tells us that open-period marginal revenue is less than short-run marginal cost in the open period.

---

[1] It should here be noted that Professor Hicks' justifications for this assumption, namely that the life of equipment is long and *hence* will be determined by long-period considerations, cannot be used in his model. For by the same argument the entrepreneur should only be interested in long-period profit, i.e. be a perfect sticker.

[2] If K is long-period and k short-period total cost, then at X, by the Marshallian assumption,

$$\frac{\partial(K/X)}{\partial X} = \frac{\partial(k/X)}{\partial X}; \quad k = K \tag{1}$$

$$\therefore X\frac{\partial K}{\partial X} - K = X\frac{\partial k}{\partial x} - k \tag{2}$$

$$\therefore \frac{\partial K}{\partial X} = \frac{\partial k}{\partial X}. \tag{3}$$

But this cannot be so. For our producer could, without changing scale, i.e. without affecting closed-period profits, find a position in the open period where short-run marginal cost is equal to open-period marginal revenue, and thus increase his open-period profits without reducing closed-period profits. On any definition of the utility function, he will do so.

Thus, Professor Hicks' assumption leads to the conclusion that the producer will prefer a lower profit to a higher one, and I cannot believe that this was his intention. If it was, some sort of explanation is clearly required.

VI

We shall now restate HM without the Marshallian assumptions. That is, we shall explicitly solve for three unknowns: x, X, and scale.

Instead of two cost functions we shall define only one, which we write as

$$K = K(x \text{ or } X, y) \tag{19.11}$$

where y is a variable indicating 'scale'. It is defined in the following way: it measures the output at which, with any given method of production, costs cannot be lowered by substituting one input for another. Thus, instead of saying that the entrepreneur chooses to have so and so much equipment, we say, what comes to the same thing, that he chooses a (hypothetical) minimum cost output. The greater this hypothetical output (y), the greater is the scale of production. The equation in the partial derivative of K,

$$\partial K/\partial y = 0, \tag{19.12}$$

defines the scale at which any actual given output is produced at lowest cost. At this value of y, actual and hypothetical output coincide.

It may help readers to think of y in the following way. Affix a label (the value of y) to each of the short-run average cost curves of which the long-run average cost curve is an envelope. Let the label given to any short-run cost curve be the output at which the latter is tangential to the long-run cost curve.

Our definitions of g and G now are

$$g = r(x) - K(x, y) \tag{19.13}$$

$$G = R(x, X) - K(X, y). \tag{19.14}$$

Proceeding as before, but remembering that we have three unknowns, x, X, and y, we obtain the equilbrium equations:

$$U_g(r_x - K_x) + U_G R_x = 0 \tag{19.15}$$

$$U_G(R_X - K_X) = 0 \tag{19.16}$$

$$\left.\begin{array}{l} U_{gx} K_y + U_{Gx} K_y = 0 \\[2mm] \text{or } \dfrac{U_g}{U_G} = - \dfrac{{}_x K_y}{{}_x K_y} \end{array}\right\} \tag{19.17}$$

where ${}_x K_y$ and ${}_x K_y$ are the partial derivatives of K with respect to y, when x and X are produced respectively.

Equation (19.15) is in all respects similar to (19.8) and requires no comment. (19.16) tells us that $(U_G > 0)$ marginal revenue will equal marginal cost in the open period. The question is, Should K_X be interpreted as long-run or short-run marginal cost? The answer to this is provided by (19.17). As long as $U_g > 0$, $U_G > 0$, $x > X$, it follows from (19.17) that (a) ${}_x K_y$ and ${}_x K_y$ must be of opposite sign, and this implies that y lies between x and X, and hence that (b) ${}_x K_y > 0$ and ${}_x K_y < 0$. But ${}_x K_y > 0$ means that a reduction in scale would lower open-period costs. Hence K_X must be interpreted as short-period marginal cost, and open-period output will be produced with transitional excess capacity. There is no information in the model to tell us whether there will also be orthodox excess capacity.

By similar reasoning, it becomes clear that the perfect sticker $(U_g = 0)$ will produce X at 'optimum' scale $({}_x K_y = 0)$, while the perfect snatcher $(U_G = 0)$ will produce x at 'optimum' scale $({}_x K_y = 0)$. In all other cases there will be transitional excess capacity.

The intuitive reason for this result is fairly clear. Anyone who is not a perfect sticker (derives some pleasure or displeasure from $g \gtreqless 0$) will take account of the fact that, if $x > X$, he can increase g at the expense of G by producing at a slightly larger scale, as long as x is not produced at lowest cost. Hence the marginal rate of substitution between g and G (in the utility sense) must equal the marginal rate of transformation between g and G owing to changes in scale.

VII

It is thus seen that the problem remains perfectly tractable, besides giving us further insights, if we do not utilize the 'Marshallian assumption'. But, while the HM tells us something about the process of competition, it is not adequate for an analysis of final equilibrium and thus orthodox excess capacity. It also ignores uncertainty and the Harrodian ritual.

Before, however, going any further, there is another point in HM to which I wish to draw attention.

I find it difficult to understand why open-period revenue should depend on closed-period output. This is not the traditional interpretation of the interdependence of revenue functions, and is plainly contradictory to Mr Harrod's hypothesis. Surely it is more natural (and traditional) to regard the appearance of competitors in oligopolistic situations as being due to the excess profits earned by existing producers, rather than to their output.

Let us then assume that 'normal' profit, however defined, is included in K. We now rewrite (19.3) as

$$R' = R'(g, X). \tag{19.18}$$

We are only interested in situations for which $\partial R'/\partial g = R'_g < 0$. (19.15) and (19.17) now become

$$(U_g + U_G R'_g)(r_x - K_x) = 0, \tag{19.19}$$

$$(U_g + U_G R'_g)(-_x K_y) + U_G(-_x K_y) = 0. \tag{19.20}$$

From (19.19) we obtain the startling result that, except in the case where the expression in the first bracket is zero, $r_x = K_x$ (marginal revenue equals marginal cost in the closed period). Before explaining this, note that, if the expression in the first bracket is zero, then (19.20), $_x K_y = 0$; i.e., X is produced at optimum scale and there is no transitional excess capacity.

We now come to the explanation. Consider figure 19.1. Or is the total closed-period revenue function and $K(x, y_1)$ is the closed-

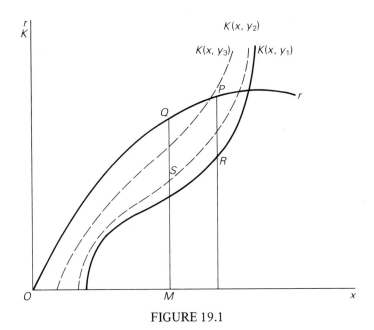

FIGURE 19.1

period cost function when 'scale' $= y_1$. Suppose now that X is not planned to be produced at optimum scale; i.e., $_xK_y > 0$. PR measures closed-period profit. Suppose that the slope of $K(\cdot)$ at $R >$ slope of r at P $(r_x < K_x)$. Then if our producer reduced the scale of his operation he could certainly increase open-period profit $(_xK_y > 0)$. There must exist a closed-period output OM, at which $QS = PR$.[3] Thus, as long as (a) $r_x < K_x$ and (b) $_xK_y > 0$, our producer can always arrange matters such that he keeps closed-period profit the same and thus does not affect R, while increasing his open-period profit.

[3] The definition of g is

$$g = r(x) - K(x, y) \tag{1}$$

and thus

$$dg = r_x\,dx - K_x\,dx - {_xK_y}\,dy. \tag{2}$$

As long as $r_x < K_x$, since $_xK_y < 0$, there must exist some value of $dx < 0$ and $dy < 0$ for which $dg = 0$.

Thus $U_G > 0$ (the entrepreneur is not a perfect snatcher) is not a necessary or sufficient condition for the non-maximization of closed-period profit. Oligopolistic expectations certainly lead to closed-period profits being lower than they would have been in the absence of such expectations. But that may only mean that closed-period output will be produced on a scale less appropriate to it (smaller) than would otherwise have been the case.

On the other hand, the expression in the first bracket of (19.19) will be equal to zero, and closed-period profits need not be maximized on one of two assumptions: (a) if $U_g = 0$ (perfect sticker), then it is easily seen that $R'_g = 0$, and thus in this case Professor Hicks' conclusions apply as before; (b) if the utility and open-period revenue functions are such that closed-period output is determined entirely by reference to the effect of closed-period profit on open-period revenue. This is likely to be the case where potential closed-period profits are rather large relatively to 'normal' profit. For it is mainly a question of which of two functions, the utility function or the closed-period profit function, attains its maximum first, as closed-period profits are increased by changes in either x or y. These results are, however, of limited interest only, since as we shall show (in section X below), HM is not suitable to a discussion of oligopolistic behaviour.

VIII

We are now ready to turn to the Harrodian proposition (HP), defined in section I. Mr Harrod's point, if I understand it correctly, can be summarized as follows. The orthodox conclusion that a downward-sloping demand curve will lead to orthodox excess capacity is based on two basic assumptions: (a) there is free entry in the sense that close substitutes can be and are easily produced in response to abnormal profits in the industry; and (b) producers at all times maximize their profits. But assumption (b) ignores the known preoccupation of many businessmen with the long run, their difficulties of estimating short-run marginal quantities, their uncertainty with regard to the future, and the ritualistic way in which businessmen are forced to deal with a hazy reality. This ritual is two-fold: on the one hand, producers will choose a price such that, on average, normal profits are earned. On the other hand, they will stick to that price, even though actual demand may fluctuate about its mean level, as long as these fluctuations are not large or systematic. Such a price is chosen, there are no abnormal profits (on the average), and hence new competitors will not appear. Thus, whether orthodox excess capacity appears or not is simply a matter of whether or not the mean demand curve intersects the long-run average cost curve including normal profits on its downward-sloping part.

IX

Professor Hicks, in discussing HP, has concentrated on the ritual-istic behaviour described by Mr Harrod. He very properly con-cludes that the Harrodian entrepreneur is a 'perfect sticker', although he also seems to imply that Mr Harrod assumes oligo-polistic expectations, which is not the case. But when Professor Hicks comes to examine the consequences of his model to the excess capacity hypothesis, it is difficult to see whether he has in mind orthodox or transitional excess capacity; nor is it easy to verify his conclusions at all rigorously. This of course does not mean that we do not gain some valuable insights from HM. For instance, the analysis of the role of snatchers in HM is most illuminating.

That Professor Hicks' analysis, however, is inadequate from Mr Harrod's point of view can be seen as follows. Suppose all entrepreneurs are perfect stickers. Then, as long as the long-run demand curve is not tangent to the long-run average cost curve, there will be abnormal profits leading to entry. This will be true if expectations are oligopolistic; for oligopolistic expectations do not affect the maximization of profit in the open period. This suggests that Professor Hicks' period dichotomy is unsatisfactory. For if I have succeeded in keeping out competitors in one period, I cannot then be assumed to be indifferent to the possibility of attracting competitors in another. Indeed, in so far as one suc-ceeds in keeping out competitors, the lapse of time simply brings one into another closed period.

Thus the only way to interpret HM is as follows. The length of the open period is such that abnormal profits during that period attract no competitors in that period. The entrepreneur's horizon is equal to the time span made up of the closed and open period. If that is true, then, whether the entrepreneur is a perfect sticker with oligopolistic expectations or not, orthodox excess capacity must eventually arise. But, from the remarks about the durability of equipment made by Professor Hicks, we conclude that this is not the interpretation he wishes to put on the periods, and hence that HM needs further modification.

X

The modification is fairly obvious and also gives some insight into the plausibility of Mr Harrod's assumption. That assumption may be restated as follows. Entrepreneurs act in such a manner as to ensure constant average profits through time given that the demand conditions remain the same. This is the only way I can interpret the ritual.

The appropriate utility function could now be written as

$$U = U(g_1, g_2, \ldots, g_n, G) \tag{19.21}$$

where $g_1, \ldots, g_n$ are profits earned in each of a number of n periods, the length of each period being such that during it the number of competitors may be taken as given. G is the expected price at which the business could be sold at the end of the nth period. The economic horizon is n periods. It is assumed, without further analysis, that the perfect sticker keeps his capital intact if it is of the appropriate size. The symbols $x_1, \ldots, x_n$ stand for the outputs planned for each period.

Maximizing as before, we obtain a series of n equations in the partial derivatives of the x_j:

$$U_{g_j}(r_x - k_{x_j}) + \sum_{i=j+1}^{n} U_{g_i} \frac{\partial g_i}{\partial x_j} + U_G \frac{\partial G}{\partial x_j} = 0 \quad (j = 1, \ldots, n).$$
$$\tag{19.22}$$

The perfect sticker is now the entrepreneur for whom $U_{g_1} = U_{g_2} = \ldots U_{g_n} = 0$. That is, he is the entrepreneur whose utility depends only on the expected capital value of his business at the end of the economic horizon. Since $\partial g_k / \partial x_j \gtreqless 0$ implies $\partial G / \partial x_j \gtreqless 0$,[4] it follows from (19.22) that, for this entrepreneur,

$$\frac{\partial G}{\partial x_1} = \frac{\partial G}{\partial x_2} = \ldots = \frac{\partial G}{\partial x_n} = \frac{\partial g_2}{\partial x_1} = \frac{\partial g_n}{\partial x_1} = \frac{\partial g_3}{\partial x_2} = \frac{\partial g_n}{\partial x_2} \ldots = 0. \tag{19.23}$$

[4] For if $\partial g_k / \partial x_j < 0$, then that implies new entrants and the demand curve is permanently shifted to the left, and the reverse for $\partial g_k / \partial x_j > 0$. Of course this is an assumption.

This is only another way of stating the common-sense conclusion that the capital value of the business at the end of n periods will be maximized if the entrepreneur succeeds in keeping all competitors out of the intervening stages.[5]

The startling result of section VII has now disappeared. Profits will in general not be maximized in any period. The even more startling result obtained by Professor Hicks also disappears. For in HM, $U_g = 0$ (perfect sticker) implied $R_x = 0$. From this Professor Hicks concluded that, since R and r were now the same, and since in the open period marginal cost equals marginal revenue, and since open and closed-period output were the same, marginal cost would also equal marginal revenue in the closed period. So the oligopolist wasn't an oligopolist after all! (19.22) rids us of this rather odd result. It should, however, be noted that, even in the context of section VII, Professor Hicks' results do not follow. For $R'_g = 0$, and $R'_X = K_X$ do not imply $x = X$.

---

[5] To determine the 'scale' of production we partially differentiate (19.21) with respect to y and set equal to zero. Remembering that $U_{g_i} = 0$ $(i = 1, \ldots, n)$, we have

$$U_G \frac{\partial G}{\partial y} = 0 \qquad (U_G > 0). \tag{1}$$

Now from (19.22) and our assumptions, we have

$$\frac{\partial g_k}{\partial x_j} = \frac{\partial g_k}{\partial g_j} \frac{\partial g_j}{\partial x_j} = 0 \tag{2}$$

and thus, unless in the special case of $\partial g_j / \partial x_j = 0$,

$$\frac{\partial g_k}{\partial g_j} = 0. \tag{3}$$

But on the assumption that capital is kept intact, $dg_k / dy \gtrless 0$ implies $\partial G / \partial y \gtrless 0$. Thus

$$\frac{dg_k}{dy} = \frac{\partial g_k}{\partial g_j} \frac{\partial g_j}{\partial y} + \frac{\partial g_k}{\partial y} = 0 \tag{4}$$

and hence, by (3),

$$\frac{dg_k}{dy} = -x_k K_y = 0. \tag{5}$$

Since $x_1 = x_2 = \ldots = x_n$, it follows that the scale will be such as to minimize the cost of producing the steady output. This also is Mr Harrod's contention.

This, rather than HM, seems to me the proper rationalization of the behaviour of the Harrodian entrepreneur with oligopolistic expectations. Whether this sort of behaviour, and these sort of assumptions, are justified by the empirical evidence I cannot say. The behaviour of the Harrodian entrepreneur with polypolistic expectations cannot be rationalized by any maximization procedure, and must be interpreted as a behaviouristic principle. The best way of doing this is to say that the entrepreneur acts *as if* he were an oligopolistic sticker.[6]

XI

We can now at last turn to what I regard as the major difficulty of Mr Harrod's analysis, assuming throughout that entrepreneurial behaviour is adequately described by the postulates of section X. Mr Harrod defines normal profit as 'the rate of profit which the entrepreneur would himself deem just sufficient in considering whether or not to undertake an extension of his plant'. This is the rate of profit which will be employed at arriving at the 'full-cost' price, which Mr Harrod assumes will be charged. We are not now concerned with the rationalization of this procedure, but accept it as a correct description of the real world of which Mr Harrod has evidence.

Now suppose that the existing entrepreneurs have found their equilibrium price and output, and that this position can be described by the intersection of the long-run demand curve with the long-run average cost curve including normal profit. If we now say that at this price no new entrants will appear, we are in some difficulty in explaining why anyone should ever enter an industry. For, by assumption, every potential entrant, when making his calculations, assumes that he will earn only normal profit, but normal profit does not attract him into the industry! The full-cost principle, coupled with the assumption that only abnormal profits induce entrants, leaves us with the problem of why anyone is producing what he is producing at all. Not only has Mr Harrod abolished price competition (because of the double ritual), he has also abolished the competition of newcomers. If a potential entrant must charge a price which gives a profit which keeps

---

[6] Since Mr Harrod believes that the ritual keeps out competitors, the entrepreneur acts as if he were an oligopolist even if he is not one!

others out, then by the same argument it should have kept him out.

There are only two ways out of this dilemma. Either we drop the full-cost principle, or we drop the assumption that only the ability to charge a full-cost price keeps out entrants. My personal predilections are for the former procedure. But this is not the place to launch an attack on this principle. We shall therefore investigate the consequences of the second procedure.

The sensible way out here is to assume that entrants continue to arrive as long as they believe that they can charge a full-cost price, that is, as long as it is 'just worth-while'. The full-cost price can thus be regarded as the supply price of entrants. This then explains why a producer entered an industry fully knowing that he would charge a full-cost price.

That this assumption leads to the following two conclusions is clear: (a) existing producers cannot keep out entrants by charging a full-cost price unless their 'normal profit' is much lower than the average of normal profits; and (b) unless (a), orthodox excess capacity will again appear.

The proviso in (b), 'unless (a)', is similar to the proviso of orthodox theory. We thus conclude that, if our analysis of entrants is accepted, a downward-sloping demand curve is a sufficient condition for the appearance of excess capacity.

XII

I would like to put the conclusions of section XI into the language of the modified HM of section X, since that may clarify the position. If producers are very much alike (i.e. have similar utility functions), then the requirements for an oligopolistic sticker are that all the 'cross-terms' such as $\partial g_i / \partial x_j$, $\partial G / \partial x_j$, etc., be zero; and that in turn must mean that, at the values of $g_1, \ldots, g_n$ and G thus defined, the utility of all competitors when contemplating these values must be zero. But this, on the assumption of similarity of utility functions, means that the utility of our producer of this profit stream is also zero! This, to repeat our earlier statement, means that to keep others out you must keep yourself out! This suggests that perfect stickers must be very rare indeed!

It may now be argued that potential entrants will take account not of the actual profits of existing producers but of the profits they themselves could earn if they entered. If that is so, the oligo-

N

polistic behaviour will find expression not in the profits charged but in the ability to engage in price wars, etc. This seems in fact to be the case.

XIII

We may now sum up the conclusions reached in the paper.

1   The expectation that long-run demand is less than short-run demand, that the long-run demand schedule is to the left of the short-run demand curve, will lead to production with transitional excess capacity in the long run, unless no importance is attached to short-run profit at all.

2   If we follow Professor Hicks and assume an oligopolistic entrepreneur to be only concerned with keeping out entrants in the closed period, being indifferent as to whether they enter as a result of his action in the open period, and if we make the reasonable hypothesis that open-period revenue is a function of closed-period profit (rather than output), then the prcducer may maximize short-run profit even if he is not a 'perfect snatcher'.

3   The proper rationalization of the Harrodian entrepreneur's behaviour seems to be the following. The entrepreneur acts *as if* he were maximizing the capital value of his enterprise at the end of the economic horizon, and on the assumption that he is in an oligopolistic situation. Profits in any period are then maximized only in exceptional circumstances.

4   As far as the emergence of orthodox excess capacity is concerned (under the assumptions contained in conclusion 3), the real question turns on whether the Harrodian ritual keeps out entrants. If, as in orthodox theory, we assume the entrepreneurs similar, then an entrepreneur entering an industry can stop others from following him by a number of devices. He cannot, however, do so by manipulating his own profit margin without making it not worth-while for himself to enter the industry.

5   In a world where businessmen act as high priests of the full-cost principle, it is necessary to assume that they will enter every industry as long as they are able to perform their ritual there, i.e. cover full costs. Hence, charging full cost will not prevent the emergence of orthodox excess capacity.

6   Lastly, we may draw a general conclusion. There can be few economists who would regard a downward-sloping demand curve as sufficient for the emergence of excess capacity when there is

free entry. The possible lumpiness of investment (to which Mr Kaldor drew attention), the wide disparity in the abilities of potential entrants, the diversity of their utility functions (aversion to risk, trade of a particular kind, etc.), and the variations of the availability of finance must all operate to modify the orthodox proposition. In any case, 'free entry' is difficult to define in a non-circular fashion.

The full-cost principle, however, as such does not modify the orthodox conclusion. This seems to me to lend weight to the belief that the full-cost principle describes the actions of people who are members of an industry which has already reached equilibrium. As a tool of analysis of how this equilibrium is established, it seems of doubtful use and validity.

REFERENCES

Harrod, R. F. (1952), 'Theory of Imperfect Competition Revisited', *Economic Essays*, Macmillan and Co., London.

Hicks, J. R. (1954), 'The Process of Imperfect Competition', *Oxford Economic Papers*, **6**

20

On Optimum Taxation

I INTRODUCTION

In this paper I reformulate and somewhat extend the qualitative theorems concerned with production efficiency which are found in the splendid work of Diamond and Mirrlees (D–M) (1971) and Mirrlees (M) (1972).[1] My object here is to bring out more clearly the connection between this work and the theory of the second-best and also to set the stage for my contention that, while these studies have increased our understanding of what is involved, the tax formulae which they contain cannot be taken very seriously. This will lead me then to some rather general remarks on the formulation of second-best methods.

II A SIMPLE PROPOSITION

Let $x \in R^n$ and c^i, $i = 1, 2$ be two closed subsets of R^n; also $V(x)$ a continuous real valued function from R^n.

Assumption (A1)   Local non-satiation on c^2: For every $x \in c^2$ and $\epsilon > 0$ there is $x' \in c^2$, $\|x - x'\| \leqslant \epsilon$ such that $V(x') > V(x)$.
  Call

$$\max_{c^1 \cap c^2} V(x)$$

the second-best problem. Then

Proposition 1   If (A1), then if the second-best problem has a solution it must be on the frontier of c^1.

---

[1] Some of the preliminary work on this was done while the author was Visiting Professor at the Massachusetts Institute of Technology.

Proof If x^* is the solution and interior to c^1, then by (A1) there is $x \in c^2$, $V(x) > V(x^*)$, $\|x - x^*\| \leqslant \epsilon$, i.e., $x \in c^1$, a contradiction.

Obvious as this result is, it is plainly a source of counter-examples to the Lancaster–Lipsey 'theorem' of the second-best. It is also the foundation of the qualitative results of (D–M) and (M).

III   THE APPLICATION

There is a Debreu economy with H households which have strictly quasi-concave utility functions $u_h = u_h(x_h)$ where $x_h \in X_h \subset R^{n+}$. Each household is endowed with $\bar{x}_h \in R^{n+}$. (Leisure is consumed and is also an endowment.) Note that, at present, no household owns claims to the profits of production. I use

$$z_h = x_h - \bar{x}_h, \quad z = \Sigma z_h, \quad x = \Sigma x_h, \quad \hat{x} = (x_1, \ldots, x_H),$$

$$\hat{u} = (u, \ldots, u_H).$$

The government has a continuous social welfare function $W(\hat{u})$ which is monotone increasing in each argument. We may also write this welfare function as $V(\hat{x})$.

The production set of the economy is Y with elements y, whose negative components denote inputs. The 'first-best' problem is

$$\max_{c^1} V(\hat{x}) \quad \text{where} \quad c^1 = \{x \mid z \in Y, x_h \in X_h \text{ all } h\}.$$

Here it is supposed that any production feasible allocation can be achieved.

A second-best problem arises when the government must take $\bar{x}_h$ as given for each h and must decentralize consumption decisions. Let $x_h(q)$ be the solution to

$$\max_{q z_h \leqslant 0} u_h(x_h)$$

where q is a price vector. By our assumptions, $x_h(q)$ is single-valued. The problem now is

$$\max_{c^1 \cap c^2} V(\hat{x}) \quad \text{where} \quad c^2 = \{x \mid x_h = x_h(q) \text{ all } h \text{ some } q > 0\}.$$

$$(20.1)$$

The following assumption is now made.

Assumption (A2) (i) $x(q)$ is continuous where it is defined and $\|x(q)\| = \infty$ when $x(q)$ is not defined.

(ii) (D–M): For all $x \in c^2$ either

$$z_i > 0, \quad z_i z_{hi} \geqslant 0, \quad \text{all } h \text{ some } i \text{ with } q_i > 0$$

or $z_i < 0, z_i z_{hi} \geqslant 0$ all h some i.

(A2(ii)) implies that either reducing the price of good i ($z_i > 0$) or raising it ($z_i < 0$) will induce a Pareto-superior consumption. I shall refer to such price changes as Pareto-improving.

Proposition 2 For all finite x, (A2) implies (A1).

Proof Let $\hat{x} = \hat{x}(q) \in c^2$. Let $q' - q$ be Pareto-improving with $\|q' - q\|$ as small as we like. By (A2(i)) and x finite, $\|x(q') - x(q)\| \leqslant \epsilon$ for $\|q' - q\| \leqslant \delta$, some δ. By constructive $V[x(q')] > V[x(q)]$.

Corollary 2 If (20.1) has a finite solution, it is on the boundary of c^1.

Proof Propositions 2 and 1.

Corollary 2' If c^1 is bounded and closed, the second-best problem has a solution on the frontier of c^1.

Proof By (A2(i)), c^2 is closed, whence $c^1 \cap c^2$ is bounded and closed while $V(\hat{x})$ is continuous. Hence a solution exists. Since c^1 is bounded the solution is finite when by corollary 2 it is a frontier point of c^1.

A frontier point $\hat{x}$ of c^1 is associated with a frontier point z of Y. Not every frontier point of Y need be production-efficient, but the exceptions are well-known and I shall simply refer to such points as production-efficient.

Corollaries 2 and 2' show the second-best solution to be production-efficient without any restrictions having been placed on the kind of returns which operate in production. For a tax interpretation, however, one takes Y to be convex. We have also implicitly assumed that households have no entitlements to any profits which may arise in production (their wealth depends only on their endowments $\bar{x}_h$ and on q). Then if r^* is the vector of support prices (in the unit simplex) at the solution $\hat{x} = \hat{x}(q^*)$ where q^* is in the unit simplex, one defines the optimum commodity tax vector t^* by $q^* = r^* + t^*$, and the normalization $\Sigma t_i^* = 0$. Here r^* is the price vector appropriate to government production managers and q^* the price vector appropriate to households. All the necessary conditions in production required by the first-best problem also hold in the second-best one.

If part of production is controlled by firms with production sets Y_f (with members y_f) and these firms are owned by households in a given way, problems arise unless all Y_f are cones. In the latter case profits are zero and one can continue to use the model in which household wealth depends only on $\bar{x}_h$ and consumer prices. The price vector r^* is the proper decentralizing production price vector for this economy.

If there is always some private production which is not carried out under constant returns to scale, the analysis becomes a little harder and more interesting.

Let $Y_F = \Sigma Y_f$ with members y_F and let G be the production set of the government with members g. One has

$$Y = Y_F + G.$$

I assume, for each f, Y_f closed convex and containing the origin and allows free disposal. $P(y_F)$ is a subset of the unit simplex of support prices p of y_F and $\pi(p)$ is the vector of the profits of firms given p.

One is first interested in the set of profit vectors which can be generated by some allocation between private and public production which makes a given x, (z), feasible. Let

$$Y_F(x) = \{y_F \mid y_F + g \geqslant z, y_F \in Y_F, g \in G\}$$

the set of private production vectors which for some choice of g allows z to be produced. Then

$$\Pi(x) = \{\pi \mid \pi = \pi(p) \text{ some } p \in P(y_F), y_F \in Y_F(x)\}$$

is the set of profit vectors we want. This set is empty if and only if $z \notin Y$.

It is now assumed that profits can be taxed. The profits of different firms can be taxed differently but (a) no firm can be made to have negative net profits and (b) no firm can be given positive net profits if its profits are zero. I return to these somewhat arbitrary restrictions later. If n is the vector of net profits, the set of such vectors made possible by x is

$$N(x) = \{n \mid n \geq 0, n_f = 0 \text{ if } \pi_f = 0, \pi \in \pi(x)\}.$$

Firms are owned by households in a given way which cannot be changed and one may therefore write the demand functions as

$$x_h = x_h(q, n).$$

The planners' problem is now

$$\max_{c^{-2} \cap c^2} V(\hat{x}) \begin{cases} \bar{c}^2 = \{\hat{x}, n \mid x_h = x_h(q, n) \text{ all } h, q > 0, n \geq 0\} \\ c^2 = \{\hat{x}, n \mid n \in N(x)\}. \end{cases} \tag{20.2}$$

Let $\hat{x}^*, n^*$ solve the problem. Then $\hat{x}^*$ must solve

$$\max_{c^{-2}(n^*) \cap c^3(n^*)} V(\hat{x}) \begin{cases} \bar{c}^2(n^*) = \{\hat{x} \mid x_h = x_h(q, n^*) \text{ all } h, q > 0\} \\ c^3(n^*) = \{x \mid n^* \in N(x)\}. \end{cases}$$

$$\tag{20.3}$$

Since (A2) continues to apply, we use proposition 2 and its corollaries to establish that the solution of (20.3) must be a frontier point of $c^3(n^*)$. The question to be studied is the conditions under which this implies that the solution is also a frontier point of Y.

Proposition 3 If a solution exists and $\Pi(x)$ is lower semi-continuous, then the solution is production-efficient.

Proof Let $x^* = x(q^*, n^*)$, $\pi^* \in \Pi(x^*)$ where asterisks denote solution values. Suppose z^* is the interior of Y. Let $q^\nu \to q^*$ be a price sequence in the unit simplex such that, when $x^\nu = x(q^\nu, n^*)$, $x^{\nu-1}$ is Pareto-superior to x^ν. By (A2) such a price sequence exists. By the lower semi-continuity of $\Pi(x)$ and the continuity of $x(q, n^*)$, for every $\delta > 0$ there will be ϵ such that, for all $\|x^\nu - x^*\| \leq \epsilon$, there is $\pi^\nu \in \Pi(x^\nu)$ with $\|\pi^\nu - \pi^*\| \leq \delta$. Hence for δ small enough $\pi_f^* > 0$ implies $\pi_f^\nu > 0$, since $\pi_f^\nu \geq 0$ all ν. Since z^* is in the interior of Y, $z^\nu \in Y$ for ν large enough, whence for all such ν, $n^* \in N(x^\nu)$, i.e. $x^\nu \in c^3(n^*)$. But x^ν is Pareto-superior to x^*, which is a contradiction.

One sees at once that when Y_F is a cone one has a special instance of proposition 3 since then $\pi = 0$ identically in x. Are there any other interesting special cases? There are really two problems. One looks for instances for which a small variation in total demand can be accompanied by small changes in private production and small changes in private production go with small changes in profits before tax.

Here is an example which does not meet the first requirement. Suppose that the private sector uses inputs in fixed supply which cannot be used by the government and vice versa. Here the private sector and government are like two countries in the simple theory of international trade. Suppose Y_F convex but not G. In figure 20.1 the tilde denotes projection into the output space given inputs. It illustrates the case where a small change in aggregate production, which is not production-efficient, may require a large change in private production. The example suggests that we shall have to take G convex if we cannot suppose that private profits are always zero. Since private production is to be decentralizable under perfect competition, Y_F will certainly have to be convex.

Corollary 3 Let Y_F be convex and have a differentiable frontier and G convex. Then if a solution to (20.2) exists, it is on the frontier of Y.

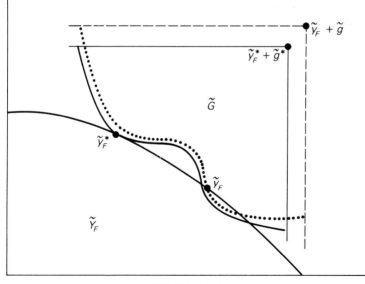

FIGURE 20.1

Proof   (a) Suppose z^* is not production-efficient. I first show that all $z \in Y$, z in a small neighbourhood of z^* are producible with y_F in a small neighbourhood of y_F^*. Let

$$K(\epsilon) = \{z \mid z \in Y, \, \|y_F - y_F^*\| \leqslant \epsilon\}.$$

By our assumptions this set is convex and closed. Suppose there were a sequence z^ν in Y, $z^\nu \to z^*$ with $z^\nu \notin K(\epsilon)$ for any finite ν. Then there is a vector a^ν such that $a^\nu z^\nu \geqslant a^\nu z$ all $z \in K(\epsilon)$, and normalizing the vector a^ν and taking limits, $a^* z^* \geqslant a^* z$ all $z \in K(\epsilon)$. Since all Y_f contain the origin and Y_F convex, a^* is non-negative.

Now consider any $z' \in Y$, $z' \notin K(\epsilon)$ and let

$$z(\lambda) = y_F^* + g^* + \lambda(y_F' - y_F^*) + \lambda(g' - g^*),$$

$$0 \leqslant \lambda \leqslant 1, \quad z' = y_F' + g'$$

Certainly $z(\lambda) \in Y$. But for λ small enough $z(\lambda) \in K(\epsilon)$. But then $a^* z' > a^* z^*$ is impossible, since then $a^* z(\lambda) > a^* z^*$, $z(\lambda) \in K(\epsilon)$. Hence $a^* z' \leqslant a^* z^*$. But then $a^* z \leqslant a^* z^*$ for all $z \in Y$, whence z^* is production-efficient contrary to assumption. So for ν large enough, $z^\nu \in K(\epsilon)$.

(b) By (a), $Y_F(x^*)$ is lower semi-continuous at x^*. Since the frontier points of Y_F are differentiable, $P(y_F)$ is a continuous function and $\pi(p)$ is continuous in p. Hence $\Pi(x^*)$ is lower semi-continuous at x^*, and so by proposition 3 no interior point (of Y) can be a solution. But a solution exists.

This result seems similar to that given by Mirrlees. Yet he gives an example which seems to go counter to corollary 3. This example is instructive since it shows the care that must be taken in the formulation of second-best problems.

In this example there is an f such that $y_f = 0$ for any frontier point of Y_F. Mirrlees supposes that there is an e such that there are frontier points of Y_F/Y_e in which $y_f \neq 0$. Such points are attainable only if firm e can be prohibited from producing. Such a prohibition may be 'beneficial'. The simplest case arises when all of firm f is owned by particularly deserving households who, say, own no other firms, and Y_f is strictly convex. But the problem for which this example is an illustration of a non-production-efficient solution is not the problem (20.2) which we started out with. For it is now supposed that the government can make private producers behave differently than they would wish to do at the prices facing them. It is therefore not a counter-example to corollary 3. Indeed, if we are permitted to use this further instrument it becomes harder, as I shall argue later, than it already is to justify the supposition that there are not quite mild instruments available which ensure production efficiency for a wide class of cases.

On the other hand, corollary 3 is at first sight quite robust. It would appear that corollary 3 will not hold if the problem (20.2) is modified to a new one (say (20.2′)) which arises when $N(x)$ is replaced by

$$N'(x) = \{n \,|\, n_f \geqslant k\pi_f \text{ some } k > 0, \, \pi \in \pi(x)\}.$$

Thus the government is now prevented from levying 100 per cent profit tax. The argument of proposition 3 will certainly not now work. For a small Pareto-improving change from q^*, while still permitting $\pi_f > 0$ if $\pi_f^* > 0$, may not allow n_f^*. For instance, this will be so if $n_f^* = k\pi_f^*$ and $\pi_f > \pi_f^*$, i.e., if the profits of f are already taxed at the maximum rate and a Pareto-improving change in q^* increases these profits. However, I shall now show that, none the less, corollary 3 continues to hold for the problem (20.2′), so that we do not have to be able to levy 100 per cent profit taxes to obtain the Pareto-efficiency result.

I introduce the following notation:

$$P(\epsilon) = \{p \,|\, p \in P(y_F), \, \|y_F - y_F^*\| \leqslant \epsilon\}$$

$$\lambda_f(p) = \max \{0, k[\pi_f(p) - \pi_f^*]\}, \quad f = 1, \ldots, F$$

$$\lambda_f = \max_{p \in P(\epsilon)} \lambda_f(p), \quad f = 1, \ldots, F, \quad \lambda = (\lambda_1, \ldots, \lambda_F)$$

$$\tilde{n}_f = n_f^* + \lambda_f, \quad f = 1, \ldots, F, \quad \tilde{n} = (\tilde{n}_1, \ldots, \tilde{n}_F).$$

Lemma If (20.2′) has a solution in the interior of Y and the conditions of corollary 3 hold, then $\lambda \neq 0$.

Proof Let (q^*, n^*) be the solution of (20.2′) which gives an allocation interior to Y, and suppose $\lambda = 0$. Let there be a small enough Pareto-improving change in q^* such that it is made feasible with y_F; $\|y_F - y_F^*\| \leqslant \epsilon$. Let π be the new vector of profits. Then by the definition of λ and $\lambda = 0$ one has

$$\pi_f = \pi_f^* \text{ all } f$$

and the usual argument is used to show $\pi_f^* > 0 \rightarrow \pi_f > 0$. But $n_f^* \geqslant k\pi_f^*$ all f, so

$$n_f^* \geqslant k\pi_f \text{ all } f.$$

But then $n^* \in N'[x(q, n^*)]$, which then implies that (q^*, n^*) cannot be the solution to (20.2').

Proposition 4   Let $x(q, n)$ be continuous in n (as well as q). Then under the conditions of corollary 3, if (20.2') has a solution it must be production-efficient.

Proof   By the lemma and the definition of λ we may take $\lambda > 0$ if the solution of (20.2') is interior to Y as we now suppose it to be. Hence $\tilde{n} > n^*$, and $(q^*, \tilde{n})$ evidently allows household choices which are Pareto-superior to those under (q^*, n^*). By the definitions,

$$\lambda_f \geqslant k[\pi_f(p) - \pi_f^*] \quad \text{all } p \in P(\epsilon)$$

whence

$$\tilde{n}_f = n_f^* + \lambda_f = k\pi_f^* + \lambda_f = k\pi_f(p) \quad \text{all } p \in P(\epsilon).$$

By the assumptions, taking k small enough allows $x(q^*, \tilde{n})$ to be produced. But then

$$\tilde{n} \in N'[x(q^*, \tilde{n})]$$

and (q^*, n^*) is feasible and Pareto-superior.

Therefore as long as profits are the pure surplus of the Arrow–Debreu theory, it is by no means always the case that a 100 per cent profit tax must be permissible if the second-best is to be production-efficient.

It has, however, been suggested (M) that profits may be the payments required to cause owner–managers of firms to provide their services. This of course is not in the spirit of the model. In a world such as we live in, where real uncertainties arise and the Arrow–Debreu paradigm is far from being a description, no doubt profits are related to actions. In such a world the concept of production efficiency is itself ambiguous. It is very doubtful that one is justified in continuing to use the Arrow–Debreu model when one is concerned to allow profits of production to be other than pure rents.

But even so, consider the suggested treatment. Let m be the vector $(m_1, \ldots, m_H)$ of managerial services supplied by household, $u_h = u_h(x_h, m_h)$ all h, and assume that every firm corresponds to some household which is entitled to all of its profits. Mirrlees assumes that $Y_h = Y_h(m_h)$, so that the production set of household h depends on the managerial services supplied and we must write $Y(m)$ as the production set of the economy. We assume that, for any q, $n_h = 0$ implies $m_h = 0$, so that at zero net profits no managerial services are supplied. Also, for every h and m_h, $Y_h(m_h)$ is strictly convex.

One is now concerned with what one may call m production efficiency. That is, $y(m)$ is m-production-efficient if it is not in the interior of $Y(m)$. (The usual exceptions are ignored.) It should be noted that we have been told nothing about managerial services used in G and, silly though it is, we suppose that the government has managerial services which are totally specific to G, just as m_h is specific to Y_h.

Introduce the mild assumption that owner–managers supply no labour services and consider an optimum in the interior of $Y(m^*)$. A Pareto-improving change in q^* can be accomplished by changing the price of some or all labour services which we take no household as demanding. By the usual argument, when $Y(m^*)$ has the properties of corollary 3, a small enough change in q^*, keeping m^* constant, leads to a change in x^* which can be accommodated by small changes in private production in $Y(m^*)$. Since profits before tax are positive, we can associate with the new profits the old net profits n^*. But, by assumption, m does not depend on the consumer prices of labour services. Hence, since for all other goods q_i^* is unchanged and net profits are the same as before the Pareto-improving move, owner–managers will continue to be willing to supply m^*. But then the allocation in the interior of $Y(m^*)$ could not have been optimal.

This sketch suggests that the production efficiency result survives the mild modification which must be made in the model when an extremely simple role is assigned to profits. But I wish to re-emphasize that I consider this treatment of the role of profits as quite unsatisfactory and that an acceptable procedure would almost certainly require a drastic departure from Arrow and Debreu.

There is one further technical point which belongs to this section. The results stated are of the form: if a solution exists, etc. Now the only general sufficient condition for a solution in fact to exist is that the constraint set be closed and bounded. Now consider (20.3) and take q^0 such that $x(q^0, n^*)$ is in the interior of Y. Let q^ν with $\nu = 0$, 1, ... be a Pareto-improving sequence converging on $\bar{q}$ and $x(\bar{q}, n^*) \in Y$. We know that if, for all such sequences, $n^* \in N[x(\bar{q}, n^*)]$, we shall be able to prove the solution, if it exists, to (20.2) to be production-efficient. But in the problem (20.2), $n^* \in N[x(q, n^*)]$ as long as $\pi_f^0 > 0$ implies $\pi_f^\nu > 0$. But there may be a Pareto-improving sequence with $\pi_f^\nu > 0$ all finite ν, $\lim \pi_f^\nu = 0$ and $n_f^* > 0$. In that case, $N(x)$ will not be closed. A solution may not exist.

Suppose that it is in fact claimed that (20.2) has a solution in the interior of Y and that $N(x)$ is closed. Then it must be that n^* is a frontier point of $N(x^*)$. But also, it must be the case that any small Pareto-improving change makes $\pi_f = 0$ when $\pi_f^* > 0$ some f. In that case one is ill-advised in using calculus to characterize the solution. Quite similar remarks apply when problem (20.2') is considered.

IV THE FORMULATION OF THE PROBLEM

The notable feature of the foregoing is the incongruity between the theoretical construction and the problems it is designed to study. I do not now mean that the Arrow–Debreu economy is not a suitable starting point for Treasury advisers, although I suspect that this is the case. What I mean is that the restrictions on the available instruments make no sense in the context of the model.

Consider the difficulties which profits raise for the analysis. Let it be proposed that a licensing fee a_f of any sign be levied on each firm f so that profit taxes are levied on $\pi_f - a_f$. It is immediate that the set of possible vectors n is now independent of y_F, and it can be left to the reader to show that optima will be production-efficient. This will continue to be the case if net profits are constrained to be non-zero if profits are non-zero or when a managerial supply problem exists. The proposal at once permits the qualitative result of (D–M) to be of wide application.

Why should the proposal be rejected? One cannot argue that the government lacks the information, since it knows what firms there are and how they are owned. The collection costs cannot be greater and indeed are almost certainly much smaller. Are there 'political' objections? No, because this is a world of rational individuals; should the (D–M)–(M) procedure lead to an interior solution, there is a licensing policy which would not receive a single adverse vote. The government would also prefer this policy. It might be argued that some agents fear that, once this has been agreed to, the government will charge licensing fees so as to make them worse off. But not so: in this economy any announced set of prices, etc., is taken as given once and for all.

It may be that some case could be made for the present procedure on the grounds that political constraints arise from considerations which may be difficult to reconcile with the model but do not necessarily contradict it. But I do not think so. The reasons which the Treasury will advance against a Pareto-improving instrument will be mostly reasons which make the model inappropriate. They will turn on lack of information, collection costs and lack of rationality. They will also of course turn on the difficulties there may be in the actual economy of recognizing a Pareto-improving change.

Somehow, the belief has grown up among economists that lump-sum taxes and fees, etc., are simply impractical for unexplained reasons. But this is both unsatisfactory and hasty. The Poll Tax Act of 1660 taxed dukes at £100, earls at £60, baronets at £30, squires at £10 and everyone over the age of 16 at 1s. It levied a fee of £100 on archbishops and £40 on dons. It taxed every £100 worth of land, money or stock at £2 (Ogg, 1963). In the world of section III above the government has no less information than the seventeenth-century legislators; indeed, it has a good deal more. What is stopping them from using appropriate instruments?

My point, then, is that it is a mistake to import unexplained second-best constraints into a model which leaves no room for their justification. If lack of information inhibits the use of an instrument, then lack of information should be a feature of the construction. If there is no agreement about objectives and this makes certain actions impossible, then this disagreement should be central to the analysis. To do otherwise when the object of the study is practical policy is dangerous to the reputation of the subject. Optimum tax formulae are either guides to actions or nothing at all.

With this in mind, let us return to the issue of the previous section. Suppose that the government does not have the information required for poll taxes. It cannot now solve for an optimum of the sort which we have considered. To have supposed that it could is in any case a disagreeable assumption. But, given any allocation known to be interior to Y, it knows that it can be improved upon provided it is permitted to compensate net profit loss and stop gains in net profits. It is hard to see why it should not be able to do this by suitable compensation. After all, there are balance sheets used for tax purposes all over the world. But whether this is true or not, the contribution of D–M to the subject is greater than they claim. Welfare economics is the grammar of arguments about policy, not the policy. We need not be able to calculate optima – indeed, I myself believe such calculations to be of dubious meaning. What D–M have done is to make it much harder than it was to sustain an argument in favour of a tax system which causes production inefficiency.

REFERENCES

Diamond, P. A. and Mirrlees, J. A. (1971), 'Optimal Taxation and Public Production', *American Economic Review*, **61**.
Mirrlees, J. (1972), 'On Producer Taxation', *Review of Economic Studies*, **39**.
Ogg, D. (1963), *England Under the Reign of Charles II*, Oxford University Press, Oxford.

21

On Equilibrium with Market-dependent Information

I INTRODUCTION

Radner (1968) taught us how to formulate general equilibrium models relatively to a given information structure. In recent years we have begun to consider the problems which arise when the partition of, say, the Arrow–Debreu commodity space available to agents depends on the market events which they observe.

In this short paper I discuss one such problem in the context of an interesting example due to Rothschild and Stiglitz (1976).[1] In part, I repeat their arguments in a slightly different way, but I hope to have also provided some clarification of what is involved. In particular, it is not the imperfection of information which appears in the title of their paper which is of interest, but its market dependence.

I reach the view that the equilibrium notion which they propose is not suitable for their example or for any case where an agent can calculate the informational externality which his action provides. A very short and tentative section proposes an alternative. In the last section I note why the problems of market-dependent information cannot in general be got rid of as simply.

II THE EXAMPLE

There are N households (N large), of which $\lambda_H N$ have the 'high' probability of an accident (α_H) and $\lambda_L N = (1 - \lambda_H) N$ have the 'low' accident probability (α_L), i.e., $\alpha_H > \alpha_L$. Ket S_{i1} be the set of

---

[1] Much of this paper was written in 1974 after hearing an early version of the Rothschild–Stiglitz (1976) paper delivered by Stiglitz in Cambridge.

states of the world in which a household of type i (i.e. $i = H$ or $i = L$) has an accident, and S_{i0} the set of states of the world in which a household of type i does not have an accident. An insurance company is a firm trading units of one pound contingent on an accident to the buyer. If the insurance company is able to partition the states of the world into the four sets S_{i1}, S_{i0}, $i = H$, L, then we say that it has the *fine* partition, and if it can only partition the states into the two sets $S_{H1} \cup S_{L1}$ and $S_{H0} \cup S_{L0}$, we say it has the *coarse* partition. The interest of this example, as we shall see, derives from the fact that we cannot specify in advance whether insurance companies have the fine or the coarse partition.

Let $c_i = (y_{i1}, y_{i0})$ where $y_{i1} < 0$ is net payment to agent type i if he has an accident and $y_{i0} > 0$ is the payment by agent type i if he does not have an accident. We write $W(c_i, \alpha_i)$ as the expected utility of agent i from the 'contract' c_i. Notice that this assumes that all agents have the same utility function and endowment. (The utility functions are taken as strictly concave.) Every insurance company knows the common utility function and endowment.

Insurance companies, because they have many customers, are risk-neutral and seek to maximize expected profit. Let $a_i = (\alpha_i, 1 - \alpha_i)$. Then an insurance company having the fine partition maximizes $a_i c_i$. If insurance companies have the coarse partition they maximize $\Sigma \lambda_i a_i c_i$. The following important assumption is made by Rothschild and Stiglitz (R–S).

Assumption (Free Entry)   (1) If the expected profit on any contract is positive, a large number of companies will enter the market for that contract.

(2) If $\hat{c} = (c_H, c_L)$ is any given contract pair on offer, then, if there exists an offer $\hat{c}'$ which will have positive expected profit *given that the contracts $\hat{c}$ continue on offer*, some insurance company will offer $\hat{c}'$.

We will now show that each of the two most natural concepts of equilibrium run into difficulties with this example.

III   COMPETITIVE EQUILIBRIUM

Let $p_i = (p_{i1}, p_{i0})$ ($i = H, L$) a price vector, where p_{i1} is the price per pound contingent on an accident to an agent of type i etc.

Suppose (p_H^0, p_L^0) is a competitive equilibrium at which agents of each type transact. Then part (1) of the Free Entry assumption requires $p_i^0 c_i^0 = 0$, $i = H, L$ or, on a suitable normalization,

$$p_i^0 = a_i \qquad i = H, L. \tag{21.1}$$

But in a competitive economy all households will wish to transact at prices p_L^0, since they give more favourable terms. That is, no household will demand c_h^0 if it can get insurance at p_L^0. But an insurance company trading at p_L^0 can only recognize type h after it has observed its demand (it demands more than does type l). Since by definition the company stands ready to supply whatever is demanded at the given price, the observation does it no good. Hence there cannot be a competitive equilibrium where both types trade and insurance companies have the fine partition.

Let $p = (p_1, p_0)$ where p_1 is the price of a pound contingent on an accident to a household (regardless of type), and p_0 is the price of a pound contingent on no accident to a household. If p^0 is a competitive equilibrium relatively to the coarse partition, it must be consistent with zero expected profits of the insurance company. If $p = a_L$ then, since both types buy at p, expected profit is negative. If $p = a_H$ it is positive. Since one easily shows expected profit to be continuous in p, there will be p^0 such that

$$\frac{\alpha_L}{1 - \alpha_L} < p_1^0 / p_0^0 < \frac{\alpha_H}{1 - \alpha_H}$$

and expected profits are zero. One therefore concludes that a competitive equilibrium relatively to the coarse partition exists.

Suppose now that $\hat{c}^0 = (c_H^0, c_L^0)$ are the contracts of the typical agents of each type in such an equilibrium. By definition,

$$\sum \lambda_i a_i c_i^0 = 0.$$

Since every component of c_H^0 exceeds in absolute value the corresponding component of c_L^0, there is a set of contracts c such that, if $c_i = c$, $i = H, L$,

$$\left(\sum \lambda_i a_i \right) c \geqslant 0. \tag{21.2}$$

Let $\bar{c}$ satisfy (21.2) with equality and write $\bar{p}_1 = \sum \lambda_i \alpha_i$, $\bar{p}_0 = \sum \lambda_i (1 - \alpha_i)$. But $p_1^0 = \sum \alpha_i \lambda_i y_{i1}^0 / y_1^0$, $p_0^0 = \sum (1 - \alpha_i) \lambda_i y_{i0}^0 / y_0^0$ where

$y_1^0 = \Sigma \lambda_i y_{i1}^0$, $y_0^0 = \Sigma \lambda_i y_{i0}^0$. Then easily from $\alpha_H > \alpha_L$ one has

$$p_1^0/p_0^0 > \tilde{p}_1/\tilde{p}_0. \tag{21.3}$$

So certainly for some $k > 0$ there is a contract $k\tilde{c}$ which, if offered to every household, would be accepted since it makes them better' off irrespective of type and would leave the insurance company with zero expected profit. By continuity, then, there is a contract c which will be accepted by every household at present buying c_i^0 and will yield positive expected profit to the company. Hence

Proposition (P1) The Competitive Competition Equilibrium Allocation is unstable under part (2) of the Free Entry assumption.

If one thinks of all households entering a coalition with an insurance company and trading c with it, we may say that this coalition blocks the Competitive Allocation. So if the Core is any allocation of contracts which cannot be blocked, we see that the competitive equilibrium is not in the Core. This will be so however large the economy. Hence competitive equilibrium is not robust in this example. Figure 21.1 repeats the argument leading to (P1).

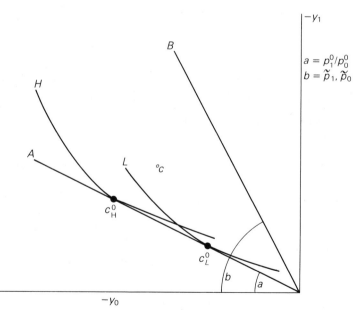

FIGURE 21.1

In figure 21.1, H and L are indifference curves for typical households of these types. One verifies that any contract which is bought by both types and is south-west of the line B yields positive expected profits.

What is the 'explanation' of (P1)? If insurance companies with a coarse partition quote a price and supply whatever is demanded, then the probability of, say, paying a pound depends not only on the given type frequencies λ_H and λ_L but also on the differences in the amount of insurance bought by each type. But the latter is not independent of price, and hence the possibility of paying a pound is not independent of price. The blocking probability arises from the fact that insurance companies acting as perfect competitors do not use this dependence of probabilities on prices. All this in turn, of course, is a consequence of only the coarse partition being possible in a competitive equilibrium.

IV   AN R-S EQUILIBRIUM

I do not know whether (P1) or something like it led R–S to consider an alternative equilibrium concept or rather an alternative institutional arrangement. Certainly (P1) justifies such an attempt.

It is now assumed that companies do not quote prices at which they are willing to transact whatever is desired, but rather that they offer particular contracts. Once again let $\hat{c}^0 = (c_H^0, c_L^0)$. If in an equilibrium of this new economy $c_H^0 \neq c_L^0$, R–S say that the equilibrium is *separating* (companies have the fine partition), and if $c_H^0 = c_L^0 \equiv c^0$, say it is *pooling* (i.e., the partition is coarse). An equilibrium is an offer $\hat{c}^0$ which yields zero expected profit, is accepted by households and cannot be blocked in the sense of part (2) of the Free Entry assumption.

One now proves

Proposition (P2)   There are economies for which no R–S equilibrium exists.

Proof   (1) Let $a = \Sigma a_i \lambda_i$ and suppose a pooling R–S equilibrium $\hat{c}^0 = (c^0, c^0)$ exists. Then certainly $ac^0 = 0$ whence $a_L c^0 > 0$ (since $\alpha_L < \alpha_H$). But at c^0 the indifference curve of agent type H cuts that of agent type L from below (once again, since $\alpha_L < \alpha_H$ and both types have the same utility function). Hence there is c' such that

$$c' > c^0 \quad \text{and} \quad c' \leqslant c^0 \quad \text{and} \quad c'$$
$$\,_L \qquad\qquad\qquad\quad \,_H$$

in a small neighbourhood of c^0. But then $a_L c' > 0$, and since the company offering c', given c^0, has now the fine partition (no agent type H accepts the offer), it follows for part (2) of the Free Entry assumption that c' will 'block' c^0. Hence no R–S equilibrium relatively to the coarse partition exists.

(2) Let us write $c_i(p_i)$ as the choice of agent type i, in the competitive economy of the previous section, if that agent faces the budget line $p_i c_i = 0$. Suppose

$$W[c_L(a), \alpha_L] > W(c_L^0, \alpha_L) \qquad (21.4)$$

when $\hat{c}^0 = (c_H^0, c_L^0)$ is an R–S separating equilibrium. Then for every c' in a small neighbourhood of $c_L(a)$, agent type L prefers c' to c_L^0 and will accept the former. Since $ac_i(a) = 0$, there will thus be c in the neighbourhood of $c_L(a)$ which L accepts and for which

$$ac > 0. \qquad (21.5)$$

But c will also be accepted by type H. For if not, there would have been a separating contract (c, c_H^0) at which positive expected profits can be earned. So if (21.4), there exists a pooling contract which breaks the R–S separating equilibrium. But by part (1) of this proof no pooling contract can be an R–S equilibrium. So then no R–S equilibrium exists.

(3) It remains to show that (21.4) is possible. Certainly if $\hat{c}^0$ is a separating equilibrium one has

$$W[c_H(a_H), \alpha_H] = W(c_H^0, \alpha_H) \geqslant W(c_L^0, \alpha_H). \qquad (21.6)$$

If the first equality did not hold, then $W[c_H(a_H), \alpha_H] > W(c_H^0, \alpha_H)$ (since $a_H c_H^0 = 0$). But then, every c_H' in a small neighbourhood of $c_H(a_H)$ would, by H, be preferred to c_H^0. Also, there is c_H in that neighbourhood with $a_H c_H > 0$ and c_H acceptable to H which contradicts the definition of c_H^0 as an equilibrium contract. The last inequality of (21.6) is required if the insurance companies are to have the fine partition.

Now let

$$R(\alpha_H) = \{c_L \mid W[c_H(a_H), \alpha_H] \geqslant W(c_L, \alpha_H), a_L c_L = 0\}$$

and

$$R(\alpha_L) = \{c_L \mid W[c_L(a_L), \alpha_L] > W(c_L, \alpha_L), a_L c_L = 0\}.$$

Then it is easy to see that there is $\bar{\alpha}_h$ such that

$$R(\alpha_H) \cap R(\alpha_L) \neq \emptyset \qquad \text{for } \alpha_H \geqslant \bar{\alpha}_H. \tag{21.7}$$

For as $\alpha_H \to 1$, $R(\alpha_H)$ converges to the singleton $c_L = 0$. But now one also has

$$W[c_H(a_H), \alpha_H] = W(c_L^0, \alpha_H) \qquad \text{for } \alpha_H \geqslant \bar{\alpha}_H. \tag{21.8}$$

For, by the usual argument, if not, there would be c_L close to c_L^0 which is preferred by L and for which $a_L c_L > 0$ while c_L is inferior to c_H^0 for H. But then (c_H^0, c_L^0) is not an equilibrium.

So for $\alpha_H \geqslant \bar{\alpha}_H$, (21.8) defines c_L^0 as a function of α_H so the right-hand side of (21.4) is given once α_H is given. Now let $\lambda_H \to 0$ so that $a \to a_L$, so

$$W_L[c_L(a), a_L] \to W_L[c_L(a_L), \alpha_L] > W_L(c_L, \alpha_L).$$

Hence there is some $\bar{\lambda}_H$ such that (21.4) holds for all $\lambda_H \leqslant \bar{\lambda}_H$.

The 'explanation' of this melancholy result at a technical level is to be found in an essential discontinuity in the 'reaction functions' of insurance companies, and the economic reason for that is an essential informational externality.

Let $\hat{c}$ be a given contract pair which is accepted by households. Let

$$F(\hat{c}) = \{\hat{c}' \,|\, W(c_H', \alpha_H) \geqslant W(c_H, \alpha_H), \, W(c_L', \alpha_L) \geqslant W(c_L, \alpha_L)\}$$

$$I = \{\hat{c}' \,|\, W(c_H', \alpha_H) \geqslant W(c_L', \alpha_L) \geqslant W(c_H', \alpha_L)\}$$

and consider the action of a potential company. We interpret it as choosing in $F(\hat{c}) \cap I$ a pair of contracts which will be accepted by households. In particular, if it chooses $c_i' = c_i$ this is interpreted as the potential firm making no new offer to agent of type i. The potential firm then chooses new offers in $F(\hat{c}) \cap I$ which maximize its expected profits. Let $\Psi(\hat{c})$ be the firm's choice correspondence. Then $\hat{c} \in \Psi(\hat{c})$ if and only if (a) the expected profits of $\hat{c}$ are zero and (b) there is no offer in $F(\hat{c})I$ with positive expected profits. Hence $\hat{c} \in \Psi(\hat{c})$ is an R–S equilibrium.

Now $\Psi(\hat{c})$ is a correspondence of the space of contracts into itself. The space of contracts may be taken as a compact convex subspace of R^4. However, the correspondence may lack the fixed-point property, i.e., it may not be convex-valued.

Suppose $\hat{c}$ is separating where c_H satisfies

$$W[c_H(a_H), \alpha_H] = W(c_H, \alpha_H)$$

and c_L satisfies

$$W(c_H, \alpha_H) > W(c_L, \alpha_H), \quad a_L c_L = 0.$$

Then certainly there will be a separating contract $\hat{c}'$ yielding positive expected profits, so $\hat{c} \notin \Psi(\hat{c})$. Assume that $\Psi(\hat{c})$ yields the single element $\hat{c}'$.

Now take the R–S case already discussed. That is, let $\bar{c}_L$ satisfy

$$W(c_H, \alpha_H) = W(\bar{c}_L, \alpha_H), \quad \alpha_L \bar{c}_L = 0$$
$$W[c_L(a), \alpha_L] > W(\bar{c}_L, \alpha_L).$$

Consider a sequence $\hat{c}^r$ with $\hat{c}^0 = \hat{c}$, $c_H^r = c_H$ all r and $c_L^r \to \bar{c}_L$, $a_L c_L^r = 0$ all r. Then there will be $\bar{r}$ such that

$\Psi(\hat{c}^r)$ is separating $r < \bar{r}$

$\Psi(\hat{c}^r)$ is pooling $r > \bar{r}$.

Also, $\Psi(\hat{c}^{\bar{r}})$ will be a two-element set consisting of a pooling and a separating contract pair. Hence $\Psi(\cdot)$ is not convex-valued at $\hat{c}^{\bar{r}}$.

These technicalities are simple, but one wants to understand the difficulties in a less formal manner.

If everyone in the economy were always fully informed, then the economy would have four contingent goods; if all agents have the coarse partition, then there would be only two. Now the Cournot-like assumption (part (2) of the Free Entry assumption) has the consequence that the dimension of the relevant commodity space depends on $\hat{c}$, i.e., on the set of contracts a given group of firms is actually selling and which potential competitors assume will continue to be offered. In particular, if everyone is fully informed and earning zero-expected profit, then in the economy of (P2) the information is worthless, since agents can do as well (strictly, better) with a coarse partition. On the other hand, when all agents have the coarse partition, the value of the information induced by observing actual contract is positive. Thus the value of information depends discontinuously on the observed contracts $\hat{c}$.

The reason why this example is of such interest is because it has illuminated a kind of externality which had previously not been noticed. This consists of the actions of some agents affecting the number of goods other agents can distinguish, i.e., the dimension of the commodity space. As R–S notice, there are a good number of other examples of this kind of externality. The fact that in this sort of situation an R–S equilibrium may not exist (P2) is of interest. But even when an equilibrium exists it has some new features. In particular, as the above discussion makes clear, the cost of sustaining the fine partition will be borne entirely by those households that have something to gain from a fine partition. That is, the high-risk households would do as well in an R–S equilibrium as they could in a perfectly competitive equilibrium relatively to the fine partition (i.e., $c_H(a_H) = c_H^0$). It is the low-risk households who bear the utility cost

$$W[c_L(a_L) \, \alpha_L] - W(c_L^0, \alpha_L).$$

R–S call this a dissipative externality. If one thinks about it, one sees that one has informally known of this phenomenon for a long time: for instance, the honest bear the cost distinguishing between them and the dishonest.

V   AN ALTERNATIVE EQUILIBRIUM

The R–S equilibrium may be understood in the context of the following game. A firm proposes an offer $\hat{c}$ and announces this to other firms. An objection to this proposal by another firm is a proposal $\hat{c}'$ such that, if $\hat{c}$ is persisted in, it will either attract no customers or bankrupt the proposer. A solution $\hat{c}^0$ is an offer which has no objection. If every offer in a compact set of offers has an objection, no solution exists. In a sense, one may think of an R–S equilibrium as the stationary point in a tâtonnement of offers.

The game has the following curious feature. An objection to $\hat{c}$ makes $\hat{c}$ unviable for its proposer. Yet the objector bases this objection on information which is contingent on $\hat{c}$ being offered. This certainly does not make the story very convincing. When a somewhat dubious assumption leads to an unsatisfactory theory, the possible non-existence of equilibrium here, one is encouraged to look again.

One idea which I briefly explore in this section is the following. If a firm observes that some households have entered into a binding contract with another firm, then it treats the resulting information as non-contingent. For instance, if all high-risk households have entered into a binding contract, then the firm treats the information that all its customers will be low-risk as certain. However, the firm knows that its own offer will destroy any information it might receive from another offer which has not been the subject of binding contracts.

So let us think of coalitions of more than one firm. A coalition is a binding agreement between household members and the firm on a contract $\hat{c}$. A firm will join such a coalition only if it yields non-negative profits. A household will join such a coalition only if there is no other which it prefers. An equilibium is $\hat{c}^0$ such that all households are members of a coalition.

Now if $\hat{c}^0$ is an R–S equilibrium, it is also an equilibrium in the above sense. But consider $\hat{c}^x$ a pooling equilibrium with

$$W'[c(a), \alpha_L] = W(c^*, \alpha_L).$$

Then $\hat{c}^*$ will also be an equilibrium for the present proposal. For consider a household type l. If it is not prepared to join the coalition with c^*, then no preferred contract will be available to it in another coalition.[2] For by its refusal to join a c^* coalition it destroys the latter, and so with it the information which allows it to be distinguished as a low-risk household. Hence there will be no firm with which it can form a preferred coalition. But if $\hat{c}^*$ is an equilibrium, it now follows that there always exists an equilibrium in the sense here proposed.

There are almost certainly other equilibrium concepts, and they may be more appealing than the present suggestion. The latter was made to illustrate the advantage there might be in not following R–S in throwing away half of their story. This they do when they consider only the informational externality of a given offer and not the possible destruction of this benefit when someone tries to take advantage of it. A pooling offer, for instance, can remain viable and so persist only if it yields information which is of no value. The moment the externality is valuable (i.e., gives rise to an offer to the low-risk households), it must be destroyed by the act

---

[2] The reader will notice the fudge: all households of a given type suppose that they will act in the same manner. This may be a serious objection.

of appropriating the value, This is an essential and interesting feature of the situation, and in the present context it seems quite unconvincing to suppose that agents are not aware of it.

VI CONCLUDING REMARKS

The discussion of the previous section leads one to a related but different class of problems.

Suppose there are two states of nature which can only be distinguished directly by a subset of agents, say $M \subset N$, there being N agents altogether. However, when that is the case, the equilibrium prices of the economy are different for each of the two states, whence we can assume that the remaining agents become informed, i.e., can distinguish between states by virtue of the information carried by prices. On the other hand, it may be that, in an economy in which all agents can distinguish between states, there is one where equilibrium prices are identical for the two states. But then there cannot exist an equilibrium in which actions based on expected prices yield these as equilibria.[3]

This problem also arises from informational externalities. However, it will be harder to resolve than is the R–S problem. It is an essential feature of the latter that an agent can calculate the information externality of this action. This is not the case in the above situation.

REFERENCES

Radner, R. (1968), 'General Equilibrium with Uncertainty', *Econometrica*, **36**.

Rothschild, M. and Stiglitz, J. (1976), 'Equilibrium in Competitive Insurance Markets: An Essay on the Economics of Imperfect Information', *Quarterly Journal of Economics*, **90**.

[3] These ideas will be formed in recent short mimeo notes of Roy Radner.

Index